Tall Ships Down

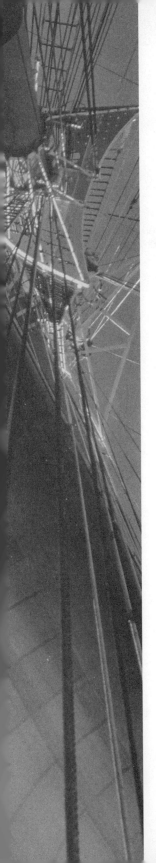

Tall Ships Down

THE LAST VOYAGES OF THE
Pamir, Albatross,
Marques, Pride of Baltimore,
AND *Maria Asumpta*

DANIEL S. PARROTT

CAPTAIN OF THE *Pride of Baltimore II*

INTERNATIONAL MARINE / McGRAW-HILL
Camden, Maine • New York • Chicago • San Francisco
Lisbon • London • Madrid • Mexico City • Milan • New Delhi
San Juan • Seoul • Singapore • Sydney • Toronto

The **McGraw·Hill** Companies

Visit us at: www.internationalmarine.com

1 2 3 4 5 6 7 8 9 0 DOC DOC 0 10 9 8 7 6 5 4 3 2

Library of Congress Cataloging-in-Publication Data

Parrott, Daniel S. (Daniel Sargent)
  Tall ships down : the last voyages of the Pamir, Albatross, Marques,
Pride of Baltimore, and Maria Asumpta / Daniel S. Parrott.
        p.   cm.
  Includes bibliographical references and index.
  ISBN 0-07-139092-8 (pbk. : alk. paper)
  1. Shipwrecks. 2. Sailing ships. I. Title.
  G525 .P3719 2002
  910.4´52—dc21   2002014991

Photo on page ii by Corbis. Map on pages xiv–xv by Equator Graphics. Maps on pages 237
and 238 reproduced from Admiralty Charts 1123 and 1168 by permission of the Controller
of Her Majesty's Stationery Office and the UK Hydrographic Office (www.ukho.gov.uk). All
other credits are noted in the captions.

To those lost at sea
keeping the traditions of sail alive.

CONTENTS

PREFACE

IT MIGHT STRIKE some as odd that a person whose life has been so enriched by the rebirth of interest in "tall ships" should write about five of the worst incidents within living memory involving these vessels. The purpose of addressing these casualties is not to suggest that they are representative of sailing ship activities of recent decades, for this is not the case. Tragedy marks every human endeavor in some measure. If we choose to focus on the potential for things to go wrong, we will quickly discover that disaster stalks our every waking hour, nor is it idle while we sleep. That is no way to live. The fact that a handful of sailing ships was lost in a process of maritime rediscovery should not cast a blight on the larger proposition of going to sea in sailing ships as our forebears once did. Those who have been there know that the "tall-ship experience" is overwhelmingly positive. But all wise mariners attempt to learn from the mistakes of the past. Three of the five incidents explored here occurred during the course of my career, and in various ways they have shaped it. More than that, they have shaped the entire resurgence of traditional sail. This project arose out of a conviction that I, and any sailing ship captain, would be better off with a deeper understanding of what went so utterly wrong for our recent predecessors. I conducted the original research for this book for a project at the University of Rhode Island's Marine Affairs Department between 1995 and 1998. It has grown into much more than that.

Many books have been written documenting the dying days of commercial sail and life at sea in the age of sail. Some of these were inspired by the experience itself: the awesome ferocity and majesty of the sea, and the power and grace of a sailing ship in its element. Other accounts were inspired by recognition that commercial sail—that extraordinary partnership between humanity's ingenuity and nature's might—was about to depart the world forever. But this book is not for posterity. This is a book about sailing ships in our times. It takes a close look at five shipwrecks that have placed, or should place, an indelible stamp on the conduct of tall-ship and traditional sailing activities in the modern era. The ground rules by which these ships now flourish or fail have changed. Tall ships continue to exist because they exert a force on our emotions, like art or nature. This is well. This is as it should be. But at the end of the day this activity cannot afford many accidents. Though I have aimed to write a coolly analytical, objective book, the roots of the project are intensely personal.

I made my first voyage in a schooner in the spring of 1981. The vessel was the *Harvey Gamage* and I was a student, or a trainee, if you will. We sailed that schooner from the Caribbean to Mystic, Connecticut, stopping at all manner of exotic and fascinating places. At age nineteen, my eyes were opened fast. Our schooner was a thrilling new world that I hadn't known existed. In a sense it hadn't, until recently. After nearly vanishing, traditional sailing ships were then experiencing a renaissance of sorts that had been percolating for a couple of decades in many parts of the world. An old wooden schooner was restored here, a new steel sail training barque was launched there, a historic replica was being constructed somewhere else. It was slow, but it was steady. It seems unlikely that anyone could have guessed the degree to which these unconnected dots of activity could link up and develop into the chain reaction that has launched whole fleets of sailing ships around the world.

A year after that first voyage I landed a summer job as a deckhand on that same schooner and, upon my release from college, I began to pursue this line of work exclusively. I found that I was far from alone in my attraction to the sea and sailing ships. It was a culture and a way of life. It might be said that, growing up in New England, surrounded by icons of a maritime past, I was especially vulnerable to this form of enticement. Yet my shipmates were men and women from different places and different backgrounds, each satisfying some personal passion that was not always readily articulated. Therefore, it would seem that for many, the sea and these ships speak to something primitive embedded deep within, regardless of where one's hometown is. To others the whole unlikely spectacle may look like some indefensible infatuation, an outrageous form of theater taken too far. To each his own.

In June 1984, while the *Harvey Gamage* was being overhauled in Gloucester, Massachusetts, word was passed that a sailing ship called the *Marques* had sunk in a tall-ship race from Bermuda to Halifax. She had been knocked down by a big wind and quite a few people died. Several of these people were well-known in the sailing circles I had recently entered. A good explanation never made it down to the deckhand level or perhaps any other level at the time. Our captain said something about the hatches. Tragic as it was, the incident did not daunt my desire to sail in the slightest. This tragedy was no more real to me than the nightly news. This is a common response to the world's misfortunes and it is probably just as well, else we would all be paralyzed with the horror of daily life. It was also, no doubt, a reflection of youth, and the world needs a certain amount of fearlessness in it, too.

A year later I became one of the luckiest people alive, landing a berth on the topsail schooner *Pride of Baltimore* for her first transatlantic crossing and a ten-country tour of Europe. This was a dream come true. This was the big time. My picture was in my hometown paper. I would cross the Atlantic Ocean in a sailing ship! The names of the ports awaiting on the other side rang in my ears like the incantations of a sorcerer.

The voyage was a great success, and at the end of 1985 I paid off in Spain as scheduled. The experience had been everything I'd hoped for and more. As one thing leads to another, a few months later the mate from the *Pride of Baltimore* and I found ourselves aboard the British brigantine, the *Eye of the Wind*, in the western Pacific. The *Eye* was a stout ship, built of iron and riveted together in Germany in 1911. We were being chased around Micronesia by cyclones when we got word over the single-sideband radio from a friend in the Marshall Islands, who relayed it from another friend in Hawaii, who got it off the nightly news, that the *Pride* had been lost on her way home from Europe.

How bizarre to sit beside the transceiver, braced against the rolling of the ship, hearing the warbled and distorted sounds come over thousands of miles of airwaves that said our lovely topsail schooner was gone, and some of our shipmates with her. So this is how it felt to know someone on the *Marques*. When mail had occasion to find us, bits of newspaper clippings sent by friends and family gradually illuminated the tragedy. Arriving in Australia four months later, we learned the rest. Some concerned people had even telephoned my parents: "Yes, he's fine. He's in the middle of the Pacific."

In April 1987 the *Marques* returned to haunt me. I was still aboard the *Eye of the Wind*, but by now we were down in the Roaring Forties, sailing around the wild capes of Tasmania. The skipper learned that the investigation into the sinking of the *Marques* almost three years earlier had finally been wrapped up. Among its official conclusions was a finding that the *Eye of the Wind* possessed the same basic stability deficiency that doomed the *Marques*. A six-month winter cruise out into the Pacific had already been booked. The only sensible thing to do was to run away. We sailed the ship up to Sydney quick-time in hopes we wouldn't be detained before leaving for the Pacific. If we were detained, Sydney was the best place for it to happen. We hadn't been there long when the Australian authorities, acting on behalf of the British authorities, trooped down the dock. They stayed for lunch, and the ship was forbidden to sail until a complete stability assessment had been carried out.

I well recall the outrage, the indignation, and the remonstrations directed toward those pencil-pushing bureaucrats in the forecastle that night. What did they know of the sea? What did they know of sailing, or how strong our ship was, or how skilled our skipper? They were out to ruin a good thing because they just didn't get it. *We* would tell them where that pencil belonged!

A few mornings later we were shifting weights back and forth across the deck of the ship for the stability test while the naval architects jotted on their clipboards and a representative of the British Department of Transport looked on. After the stability test, the ship was ordered to haul out at the nearest dry dock to have her lines lifted. This was necessary because the records for this old ship were incomplete regarding the actual displacement of the hull. Knowing her displacement was critical to understanding her stability. Our Pacific cruise was now in serious jeopardy. The morning it was announced that the ship would have to be reballasted, the crew got drunk. The next six months were spent dockside in Sydney chipping and painting bilges, shifting ballast, chipping and painting the ballast, shifting it back, and so forth. Other mandated work involved watertight hatches, subdivision, and some plate renewal. It seemed incomprehensible that our ship could be penalized for some other ship sinking, but the authorities were unwavering, and so the work was done. Years later the skipper freely admitted that the *Eye of the Wind* was better off as a result of the reballasting, but it hurt at the time, and he was financially blindsided by it. Much later I came to understand why the authorities had been so draconian. They had dropped the ball with *Marques* and were in a panic to make amends on the *Eye of the Wind*.

Several years later, in 1991, I sailed into East London aboard the *Pride of Baltimore II*, the vessel that was built to replace the lost *Pride*. I had signed on as chief mate this time. The derelict old docklands that still bore the scars of the Blitz were being transformed into shimmering new office buildings served by a gleaming Light Rail link that whooshed the tenants in from the London Underground. Yuppies hovered in their lofty catacombs of steel and glass, and at lunch hour they ventured out to smoke and view our ship where she lay moored to the freshly painted bollards. *Pride II* had come to London to host a cocktail party. Just as the riverfront docks and quays were given over to a new purpose, so too were the sailing ships that once frequented them. Astern of us lay a stunning wooden brig called the *Maria Asumpta*. She looked to be the real thing, very shippy, very salty, and traditional. She had been built in 1858 and was the oldest operational sailing ship afloat, eleven years older than the *Cutty Sark*. She could have called at London when Lincoln was president. Over the next few days the two crews spent much of their free time together. We admired the cut of each other's jib, you might say. It was a pleasant exchange. They were operating coastwise, attending festivals and doing the occasional reception or promotional event. We, on the other hand were "blue water," having lately crossed the Atlantic.

One day down in the hold of the *Maria Asumpta* I noticed on the bulkhead a photograph of a sailing ship I did not know. She was a black-hulled barque. Upon inquiring I was told that it was the *Marques*, and that she used to belong to the same man who now owned the *Maria Asumpta*. I mentioned that I remembered her loss, something about the hatches and her stability. I was told in no uncertain terms that there was nothing wrong with that ship. She was caught in a freak squall that no ship could have survived. My host contended that the owner had been unfairly maligned by the press and that people had formed false impressions about the safety of the *Marques*. Though I remembered well my experience with the *Eye of the Wind*, my host seemed knowledgeable on the subject and obviously felt strongly about it. In the interest of fellowship I let the matter lie.

Four years later, I was back in New England when I saw the newspaper photos of the *Maria Asumpta* being smashed into an unrecognizable slurry of tide and timber at the foot of a Cornwall cliff. Her bright orange life rafts bobbed cheerfully amid the white foam and wreckage, still tethered to the dead and disintegrating mother ship. At the fringes of the foam, the dull green waters of the Celtic Sea heaved. Along the cliff tops figures could be discerned looking down on the sorry end of this beautiful ship. It was upon seeing those images that the seed of this book was planted. The question was, and is, what has been learned from all of this so that the loss will not have been in vain?

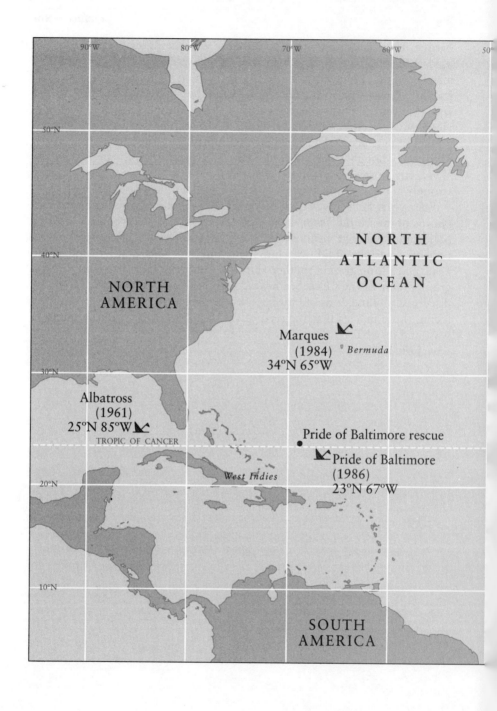

90°W   80°W   70°W   60°W   50°

50°N

40°N

NORTH
ATLANTIC
OCEAN

NORTH
AMERICA

Marques
(1984)   *Bermuda*
34°N 65°W

30°N

Albatross
(1961)
25°N 85°W
TROPIC OF CANCER

Pride of Baltimore rescue

Pride of Baltimore
(1986)
23°N 67°W

West Indies

20°N

10°N

SOUTH
AMERICA

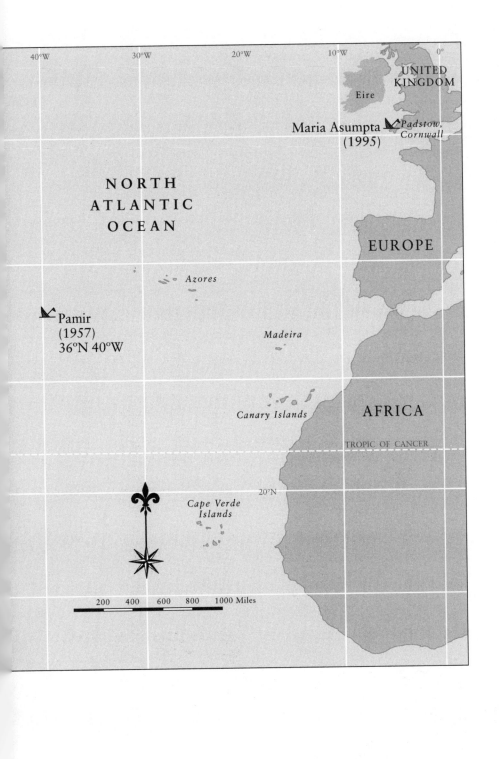

40°W 　　30°W 　　20°W 　　10°W 　　0°

UNITED
KINGDOM

Eire

Maria Asumpta — Padstow,
(1995) 　　　　　　　Cornwall

NORTH
ATLANTIC
OCEAN

EUROPE

Azores

Pamir
(1957)
36°N 40°W

Madeira

Canary Islands

AFRICA

TROPIC OF CANCER

20°N

Cape Verde
Islands

200 　400 　600 　800 　1000 Miles

INTRODUCTION
Signing On

IN THE FINAL WEEK of September 1957, hurricane season loomed large over the North Atlantic. Soviet technicians worked feverishly to complete preparations for the first man-made satellite, and on 4 October *Sputnik 1* was launched into orbit around the earth, leading the world into the Space Age. The United States had begun production of the first class of nuclear submarines and the Atoms for Peace project was drafting plans for a nuclear-powered merchant ship, the *Savannah*. Elvis was in his prime, and in Liverpool, John Lennon and Paul McCartney were penning songs after school. Indeed, the technology of transportation and concepts of distance were being transformed beyond all recognition, and an ascendant new pop culture appeared to have little use for the past. It must have been with extreme bewilderment, then, that on 21 September the world learned that the *Pamir*, a fifty-two-year-old four-masted barque loaded down with grain, was fighting for her life in the North Atlantic. Successive radio transmissions reported that the ship was rapidly listing. And then there was silence.

Ships from all over that quadrant of the Atlantic altered course toward the scene. United States naval and air forces stationed in the Azores and the U.S. Coast Guard cutter *Absecon* battled through heavy weather toward the stricken vessel's last known position. The search went on for a week as the seas gradually abated. In the end, after finding several empty lifeboats, the would-be rescuers plucked only six survivors from the North Atlantic. Eighty crew and cadets were missing.

The line of questioning in the aftermath of the catastrophe was predictable: in a wonderfully modern era, with all the technological advancements that two World Wars and a Cold War can buy, what justification was there for delivering grain under sail and exposing naïve teenagers to the hazards of the sea aboard an anachronistic square-rigged sailing ship? Not only was it uneconomical, but was there any practical purpose for the skills learned aboard such a vessel? The newspapers broadcast a bitter commentary: "Sailing ships, even training ships, exact too high a price in lives for this epoch." Defenders quietly said what they had always said: sailing ships are a priceless part of our collective maritime heritage, and the experience obtained from sailing them has lifelong value transferable to other disciplines. Nevertheless, those defenders had to face the judgment that tradition and character-building, however desirable, were of dubious value when weighed against the eighty lives lost with the *Pamir*.

A century earlier, the *Pamir*'s loss would have elicited no outcry. In the Great Age of Sail, such catastrophes were commonplace and were deemed an acceptable cost in the drive for commerce and profit. But by 1957 this had changed. The loss of the *Pamir* seemed to signal that a crossroads had been reached with respect to what risks the public would tolerate. Traditional sailing would have to change, and above all become safer, if it were to survive.

THOUGH THE ROLE played by sail in shaping modern world history cannot be overstated, that role is long since over. Yet, remarkably, sailing ships have not disappeared from the face of the earth. Instead, after sinking to their nadir in the 1950s and '60s, traditional sailing vessels of all shapes and sizes now ply the oceans of the world in increasing numbers. Sailing ships have defied obsolescence by offering an extraordinary experience in a sometimes ordinary world. People line up by the thousands to go aboard these ships at festivals and to view the parades of sail that celebrate the traditions and history of the sea. This renewal has not been achieved without mishap, however. Presented here are five stories within living memory in which traditional sailing ships engaged in modern missions met with tragedy. In chronological order they are the *Pamir* (1905–1957), the *Albatross* (1921–1961), the *Marques* (1917–1984), the *Pride of Baltimore* (1977–1986), and the *Maria Asumpta* (1858–1995).

The modern conduct of traditional sail has much to be proud of. Despite its near-total severance from an ancient culture of sailing ship wisdom and practice, the tall-ship movement survived a process of rediscovery and has earned an excellent overall safety record. Nevertheless, whether we use the clinical term *casualty* or the more emotionally charged *tragedy*, the events explored in this book constitute significant chapters in that rebirth. The men and women who go to sea in sailing ships, especially those newly in command, as well as the organizations that run the ships have much to learn from these cases. These five incidents not only hold specific practical lessons, they illuminate larger issues concerning the philosophical approach that captains, crew, and organizations take toward their ships and the sea. In looking at what went wrong, we trace the course of this renaissance, and by inference we can discern the future direction traditional sail must take if it is to thrive.

No matter how the marine environment may be desecrated by industry, shipping, or commercial fishing practices, as long as people need oil, food, and other products, business on great waters will go on. Sailing ships are no longer essential to that business, however. They may be desirable for many reasons, but their original purpose has been superseded. They exist by choice, not necessity, and therefore must be deemed safe if they are to survive. One way or another, each of the five cases in this book raised questions about the wisdom of continuing to sail such ships. To one degree or another, each of these cases attracted the attention of marine safety agencies around the world. And in each case, at one level or another, the "industry" was forced to come to terms with failure and reassess concepts regarding the bounds of good practice and the appropriate limits of authenticity. Yet the bounds of good practice are not static. Either through technology or changes in society itself, the threshold of acceptable risk has a tendency to shift in ways that become evident only in the wake of a disaster.

HOMAGE TO THE PAST is achieved at great expense and often through exhaustive research and debate. The question of what qualifies as a traditional sailing vessel therefore invites many rarefied distinctions. A look at something as basic as a block-and-tackle system provides an interesting example. In the 1960s, when the revival of traditional sail was gaining momentum, the use of synthetic line was often vociferously shunned. Within a decade very few active traditional sailing vessels used natural fiber running rigging. Those that still use hemp, manila, or sisal are typically associated with maritime museums and sail at most only on a limited basis. For these vessels, durability is less of an issue because the gear never sees heavy use. Although the benefits of synthetic laid line are now widely accepted, this departure from tradition has not generally extended to braided line, which remains more or less taboo aboard traditional sailing ships. While conferring superior strength and durability, braided line costs more. Perhaps more significantly, splicing it involves a procedure that even many professionals, let alone trainees, find daunting. Most of all, though, it just doesn't look right. Another example of aesthetic preference relates to the blocks themselves. Wooden blocks have remained the standard on most traditional sailing ships. Their continued use generates little debate despite their expense and major maintenance burden, which stainless steel and plastic yacht blocks avoid. Issues of cost and safety notwithstanding, a consensus of taste plays an important if not wholly rational role in defining the bounds of tradition.

There are also delineations of tradition based on the antiquity of the vessel itself, or the period it represents. The sailing school vessel *Ernestina* of New Bedford is a surviving Grand Banks fishing schooner built in 1894 and operated continuously in commerce until 1974. She made regular Atlantic crossings under sail with immigrants from the Cape Verde Islands to Rhode Island until 1965. After having undergone many permutations in her long life, the *Ernestina* was credibly restored to her fishing rig in the 1980s and is now a reasonably authentic traditional sailing vessel. A very different example is the *Half Moon* of New York. This vessel was built in 1989 to replicate Henry Hudson's 1609 vessel of exploration. Although incorporating features that had been obsolete for centuries at the time the *Ernestina*'s keel was laid, the *Half Moon* was built with power tools and many other benefits of technology that have come about since the *Ernestina*'s builders practiced their craft, not to mention since 1609. In an extraordinary gesture to historical accuracy, the *Half Moon* steers by a whipstaff operated from below. Although impractical from the perspective of a later generation, this is how it was done at one time, and it works. On one hand, the *Half Moon* is an interpretation involving considerable guesswork, whereas our knowledge of the *Ernestina* is quite complete. The *Half Moon* represents a greater measure of antiquity, but the *Ernestina* may in some respects be more faithful to her original appearance. On the other hand, the *Ernestina* is certified by the U.S. Coast Guard for taking trainees to sea, and this entails sacrificing numerous authentic features in order to meet the applicable regulations, though those sacrifices are not always readily apparent from the dock. As an uninspected "attraction vessel," the *Half Moon* has been able to avoid jumping through many of these regulatory hoops and thus keep a freer hand to pursue historical accuracy. The bounds of tradition are elusive.

Other lines of debate center on construction materials. The building of the *Providence* of Rhode Island, a square-rigged sloop-of-war replicating John Paul Jones's first naval command circa 1776, committed a major departure from tradition with a fiberglass hull. From the deck up, though, a sailor of the period would probably be very much at home. The interest in traditional sail has spawned a number of schooners that appear at a distance to be plausible approximations of nineteenth-century coasting schooners. However, the gaff rig, the wooden spars, the masthoops and decks in many cases conceal ferro-cement, steel, or cold-molded hulls beneath. Both the *Pride of Baltimore* and the *Pride of Baltimore II* are considered traditional sailing vessels of some importance, yet there is little argument that the first was more authentic than the second. Both were constructed from tropical hardwoods imported from Central America, whereas the original Baltimore clippers used less durable local timbers. The three-masted topsail schooner *Tole Mour*, built in 1988, has a sail plan that handles and is proportioned very much like a cargo schooner of a century ago, but closer inspection reveals stainless steel standing rigging, aluminum topmasts, composite spars, a hydraulic steering system, a bow-thruster, and the expansive topsides characteristic of ocean-certified sail-training vessels. If these innovations represent advantages that a sailor from a century ago would have welcomed with open arms, who are we to define tradition?

The fact is, most purpose-built sail training vessels around the world sport traditional-looking sail plans that utilize all manner of latter-day technology and materials. Nearly all of today's tall ships use synthetic sailcloth and running rigging and are fitted with engines. Since the emotional value of today's sailing ships now transcends the commercial value that would have been assigned to them in days of yore, we are also willing to try anything in the way of new products that will preserve these ships better and at less cost. In the past, many a Down East schooner captain would have chucked the old girl on a mudbank and built a new one because it was cheaper than taking care of her. Nowadays we view our tall ships as heirlooms to be passed down in perpetuity.

Virtually all of the vessels in today's traditional sailing fleet incorporate modern concessions to safety and practicality. Those few vessels that claim to be purely authentic seldom leave the dock, and there is nothing traditional about that. Whereas some vessels in today's tall-ship fleet convey a palpable sense of history, others are caricatures best suited to amusement parks. Yet without the resurgence of interest in traditional sail, none of them might exist.

Even in nautical circles, tradition finds varied emphasis. The naval architect is concerned primarily with the design, proportions, and performance of the hull as well as its ability to meet relevant regulations. The builder is interested in these, too, but is also focused on solving problems related to construction, materials, layout, functionality, and the details of appearance. The sailmaker and the rigger must consider separate matters of performance, as well as the tools and techniques pertinent to practicing their trades in the traditional manner. To the maritime historian, all of the above are important, as well as the original purpose a vessel may have served, if it is of a historical nature. For the sailor, both in the past and now, it is the rig that is of paramount importance, for that is the interface through which the vessel is experienced most intensely. The rig is also what sets traditional sailing vessels apart from any other watercraft. In terms of training, it is through the rig that the demands of a sailing ship, particularly a square-rigger, are most vividly transmitted. Opportunities for interaction and teamwork arise as a matter of routine in a way that simply does not occur on a modern sailing yacht or power vessel. Climbing aloft to handle sail is a powerful experience for the simple reason that it appears to be much more difficult and dangerous than it actually is. Bracing yards from one tack to the next is a relatively basic maneuver, but it requires a common language and cooperation among people who may not ordinarily be able to communicate with one another. Under proper leadership, the uninitiated learn quickly how to contribute to the venture, and the veterans learn to trust them.

In reality, *traditional* is an imperfect term of art, but like another generic

Five days out of San Diego and two hundred miles off the tip of Baja, the crew of the U.S. Coast Guard barque *Eagle* furls sails. (U.S. Coast Guard)

term, *tall ship*, it refuses to go away. For our purposes, the term *traditional* applies to a vessel whose sailing rig approximates a type that was used as primary propulsion for some sort of maritime enterprise prior to World War II. In general, a traditional sailing vessel incorporates a gaff, a sprit, or a yard for the purpose of setting sail, and relies upon block and tackle for mechanical advantage in handling sail and for general shipboard labor. All five vessels considered here substantially meet this definition.

THE DEATH OF commercial sail was a gradual process spanning roughly a century, though it accelerated noticeably with the arrival of the twentieth century. The inexorable transition to steam was briefly forestalled by a spike in the demand for tonnage of any description during World War I. Commercial sail hung on between the wars but was facing extinction, and new sailing ship construction waned precipitously. World War II interrupted the Australian grain trade, the only deep-sea trade still regularly handled by sailing ships, and slammed shut the door on the age of sail in global commerce. Coastal trading under sail persisted where local conditions allowed, and a few deep-sea voyages were made even after the war, but the world had changed fundamentally by this time and there would be no going back. Even as commercial sail was in its death throes, however, there was a broad recognition, both inside and outside the maritime community, that something of extraordinary beauty and value would be lost forever if a new purpose could not be found for such ships.

The renewal of traditional sail has proceeded in a decentralized fashion, largely at the fringes of maritime endeavor and not readily traced to any single event or person. As much as any other year, though, 1956 marks the point at which traditional sail took a big step back from the brink of extinction, though it was not appreciated at the time. In that year a group of large square-rigged training vessels held a race from Torbay, England, to Lisbon as a sort of novelty event undertaken while it was still possible. What was conceived as a swan song for the age of sail instead proved to be the seminal tall-ship event of the modern era. The following year the *Pamir* was lost and all but one of the remaining Cape Horners were tied up, never to sail again. But the 1956 gathering had made its mark, and a model was established for future tall-ship and sail training activities. In 1957, the same year the *Pamir* sank, a replica of the immigrant ship *Mayflower* crossed the Atlantic from England to America. In Maine and in the Chesapeake Bay a few well-hogged old cargo schooners offered "dude" cruises to those seeking a taste of the sea and a rustic holiday. Irving and Exy Johnson continued to draw attention to the virtues of traditional sail with their global circumnavigations aboard the *Yankee*. Less-celebrated endeavors far and wide added to the momentum. Longstanding adherents of sail training—navy and merchant marine services—were increasingly joined by advocates of sail training for nonvocational purposes. As interest grew, traditional sail eventually came to embrace "a multiplicity of traditions and visions."

The motivations that sustain sailing ships in the modern era defy easy definition. Kurt Hahn, the founder of Outward Bound, described the value of going to sea under sail as "less a training for the sea, than through the sea, and so benefit all walks of life." Whether aboard a 300-foot full-rigged training ship or a 30-foot Outward Bound pulling boat, traditional sailing pursuits in modern times are something of an act of faith. There is a consensus that the experience works a kind of magic on the human spirit that is both humbling and ennobling. I believe that to be true.

One striking feature of traditional sail in the modern era is that it reaches out to populations that would otherwise have no connection to the sea. The goals of the programs carried out by today's traditional sailing fleet are remarkably diverse. They include historic preservation and reenactment; environmental awareness; scientific research; rehabilitation for adjudicated youth; and the fulfillment of academic credit for studies in literature, history, marine sciences, and, of course, navigation and seamanship. Underlying all these is an assumption that universal lessons in leadership, responsibility, teamwork, and community inevitably emerge from the physical and mental rigors imposed by a ship at sea. Such vessels may range from enormous square-riggers of several thousand tons undertaking intercontinental voyages to small, local vessels operating from minor seaports for only a few hours at a time. Traditional sail has retained a strong international flavor, best exemplified by the tall-ship races, rallies, crew exchanges, and conferences that take place each year around the world. Enthusiasm for these ships is very much a local phenomenon, as well. In some cases governments actively support traditional sailing vessels, but elsewhere projects owe their existence to a handful of determined individuals, a donation bucket, a cadre of volunteers, and a volume of sweat. Although the focus may vary from program to program, what they all have in common is framing a positive human experience by taking a sailing vessel to sea. This is the stock in trade that has conveyed the traditional sailing ship from the trash heap of man's discarded inventions to an honored—if honorary—place in the firmament of maritime affairs.

THE RETURN TO traditional sail has been visited by all the usual perils of the sea. There have been groundings, knockdowns, fires, explosions, injuries, and every conceivable type of close call. A number of vessels have been lost, though generally not with loss of life, and there have been fatalities associated with crew overboard, falling from aloft, and so forth. For the most part none of this has happened with alarming frequency. Most sectors of commercial maritime activity experience such difficulties with far greater regularity. What makes the five stories in this book stand out is that the ships themselves were lost, with multiple loss of life. Thus, it is the extraordinary dimensions of these incidents that recommend them to our attention. If such tragedies do not hold lessons or have the power to shape future practices, nothing does. Indeed, each of these cases has had repercussions, though not of equal weight. In some instances research was conducted in the aftermath that significantly added to knowledge. In other cases people learned the hard way what was already known or should have been known, and there are lessons in that, too. Each tragedy unfolded under unique circumstances, yet there are compelling themes that bind them to one another like the yarns of a coarsely laid line. Though we are dealing with ships seemingly from another era, it is not the distant past that makes them of interest but rather the present and the future. These five stories, however distinct from one another, together illuminate and define the world of traditional sail today.

Changes in the maritime world, like changes anywhere, too often come in response to spectacular failure. A loss of lives, especially young people who cannot truly understand the dangers of the sea, focuses attention as few things can. Disaster has the potential to fling open a window for reform, either through public policy or through voluntary industry initiatives. Reform can be measured, constructive, and logical if it is not conceived in an atmosphere of hysteria. On the other hand, a prevailing sense of outrage may induce a panicky knee-jerk response that creates the impression of decisiveness and accountability when in fact it is hollow, propagandistic, and not connected to an actual problem.

Investigations played an important role in understanding the incidents in this book. Four of the five were followed by an official inquiry of some sort. One advantage of official investigations is that they are able to marshal resources, call upon experts, amass information, and conduct studies and tests far beyond the capabilities of any individual. An investigation may reveal flawed practices that were imperfectly understood, thus enhancing the future safety of all. For example, it was an investigation of a pattern of fishing-vessel disappearances that underscored the negative effect on stability of loose fish sliding back and forth across a rolling deck. The dangers of this "free-surface effect" became more widely understood by the fishing industry, and casualties from that particular cause declined.

The investigative process may also point the way toward new regulations when existing safeguards insufficiently reflect new technology or a new threshold of acceptable risk. The advent of double-hulled tankers is an example of this. Although regulations already addressed the issue of oil pollution, in the aftermath of the *Exxon Valdez* spill in Prince William Sound in 1989, single-hulled tankers no longer provided the margin of security that public interest demanded. Double-hulled tankers and barges were built to reduce the risk of oil spill to a more acceptable level.

An investigation may also result in a charge of negligence, thus creating an imperative that justice be served. Captain Hazelwood of the *Exxon Valdez* became America's best-known maritime culprit of recent years for his perceived role in the worst oil spill in U.S. history. Hazelwood was sentenced, and Exxon paid out billions of dollars in damages.

Inquiries and investigations are not without their flaws, however. An inquiry, after all, is a human process and a very delicate one at that. At the most basic level, an inquiry exists to establish facts and present findings, yet this seemingly straightforward task is nearly impossible to insulate from bias; thus, it may be that no outcome can truly be regarded as neutral, though every effort be made. Perhaps most important, an inquiry cannot help but consider the ramifications of its findings, and this in turn can influence the findings themselves. In any event, the integrity of an inquiry is not only morally desirable, it is essential to the guidance of rational consequences.

Among the repercussions of a maritime disaster, another possible outcome is that nothing happens. There may be no investigation, no hearings,

A hermaphrodite brig and barque maneuver for advantage in July 1999 off Paimpol, Brittany, at the start of the Cutty Sark sailing race to Scotland. (Corbis)

no response. Or an investigation may conclude that events were caused by an act of God, thus obscuring the path to better preparation in the future. For any number of reasons an incident may simply fade or be buried away, leaving no footprint on official policy or accepted practice. Valid lessons may be learned but not widely disseminated. This is a tragedy of a different sort, because the door is left ajar for a repetition of that particular failure. The potential of a casualty to effect change is no guarantee that change will occur, or, if it does occur, that it will reflect the true nature of what transpired. In this book all of these scenarios play out: the constructive policy response, the knee-jerk reaction, the full-blown regulatory overhaul, the disputed findings, the criminal conviction, and the missed opportunity.

THE MODERN INCARNATION of traditional sail has had to work hard to establish its professional credentials amid the heady potion of its romantic appeal. The very term *tall ship* would have been scorned by the jack-tars of old, who knew enough to call a vessel by its proper name: a schooner, a barque, a brigantine, and so forth. The term *tall ship* was lifted from John Masefield's poem "Sea Fever" (1902), whose threadbare but evocative lines have been reproduced in countless brochures designed to lure new converts to traditional sail:

> I must go down to the seas again, to the lonely sea and the sky,
> And all I ask is a tall ship and a star to steer her by,
> And the wheel's kick and the wind's song and the white sail's shaking,
> And a gray mist on the sea's face and a gray dawn breaking.

The need for a simple, generic term for today's public underscores the truth that something has been lost in carving a modern role for traditional sailing ships.

This romantic appeal has been both godsend and curse for the renaissance of traditional sail. The ability of these vessels to transfix and inspire simply by existing has guaranteed them a patronage that, in turn, has made it possible to perpetuate the ships and the knowledge needed to sail them. However, the revival of tall ships has historically been open to all comers. In consequence, the process of rediscovery has at times advanced on the strength of inspiration rather than a thorough grounding in maritime fundamentals. Even when there appears to be sufficient mastery of the old methods, the context in which they are practiced has now changed, and this is just as important to understand as knowing how to set and strike a stunsail. Romance is the lifeblood of the revival, but it can also be an impediment to attaining a full professional status among maritime industries, which have sometimes tended to view the tall-ship business as something akin to yachting. Taking a hard look at five of the worst incidents to plague

The headrig—bowsprit, jibboom, and associated rigging—is the key to supporting the masts. (Corbis)

the renaissance of traditional sail may help advance the process of professionalization. Grim though these stories may be, they hold abiding lessons. This is not to say that a lack of professionalism is a common denominator in these casualties. It is not. Quite simply, these tales hold too much of relevance to be understood only through waterfront tavern chatter.

Another reason for collecting and analyzing these incidents is that the modern-day tall-ship industry has been dogged by a short institutional memory. There are several causes of this. Being a professional tall-ship sailor is hard work requiring total immersion for months at a time far from home and for low pay. In consequence, people have tended to move on after a few years, seeking what has sometimes been described as a "real job"—though going to sea in these ships is about as real as life gets. Thus it is possible for a whole generation of captains, mates, executive directors, and others to take up their responsibilities having little insight or perspective on the worst debacles their profession has had to bear.

Bad luck had a part in each of these five casualties, but bad luck seldom acts alone. Close examination reveals instead a range of factors revolving around the ship itself and the actions of various people, which we are free to emphasize according to our individual beliefs. Four issues recur regarding the seaworthiness of the ships: structural integrity, watertight subdivision, resistance to downflooding, and stability. We must always consider the human factor in a casualty, as well. Seamanship comes down to instinct rooted in experience. At its best, seamanship can do much to even the odds with the sea; at its worst, it doesn't. But the human factor in these cases is not limited to the actions of those aboard. Shoreside management, regulatory authorities, and naval architects all make appearances. Additionally, weather is a crucial external factor in several of the incidents, and shipboard equipment also warrants consideration.

It may seem uncharitable to analyze these tragedies with hindsight's refined perspective. Yet it is often through hindsight that we comprehend what tragedy lays bare. What seemed reasonable before an incident may prove unworthy in its aftermath. This recurrent theme transcends the particulars of any one casualty. Courts of inquiry may proceed with calm deliberation, but the sailor's real judge, the sea, is far less deliberative. Whereas the benefit of doubt may be appropriate to the first forum, a different standard is demanded of those who go to sea daily in these ships. Sailors need to prepare in their mind's eye how they will handle or avoid situations such as those that thrust these five ships into this book. The lure of the sea and fear of the sea have always existed side by side, and, in part, these stories show why.

Pamir

1905–1957

The *Pamir* around 1947 off Sydney Heads under nearly full sail. The power of the ship can be seen in the churning wake astern. (Alexander Turnbull Library, Wellington, New Zealand)

BUILDER: Blohm and Voss, Hamburg

RIG: Four-masted barque

HULL: Steel

SAIL AREA: 40,000 square feet

LOA: 316 feet

DRAFT: 27 feet

BEAM: 46 feet

TONNAGE: 3,103 gross registered tons; 2,777 net tons

DISPLACEMENT: 4,591 tons

POWER: After 1952, 900-horsepower single-screw diesel

FLAG HISTORY: Germany, Britain, Italy, Germany, Finland, New Zealand, Finland, Germany

WHEN THE *Pamir* slid down the ways on 29 July 1905, she represented a commitment to the future of commercial shipping under sail. Named for a landlocked region in the central Caucasus, the ship was built by the House of Laeisz, a mercantile family in Hamburg, Germany. The *Pamir* joined a fleet of sailing ships operating between Chile and Europe in the nitrate trade, a lucrative business that, to a great extent, had been pioneered by the Laeisz family. She was a strongly built vessel, designed to make the punishing passage the "wrong way" (east to west) around Cape Horn and back again on a routine basis. Although the maritime world's conversion from sail to steam was well advanced by 1905, the *Pamir* was not built as some quaint reminder of yesteryear to thrill the hearts of armchair sailors and nautical enthusiasts. Rather, the barque was a carefully calculated profit-motivated investment and a state-of-the-art sailing machine intended to make swift, efficient passages with a reliability that her owners, investors, and customers could bank on. The first sentence of Carl Laeisz's standing orders to the company's sailing ship masters read, "My ships can and shall make *fast* passages."

Though the *Pamir* was not especially renowned for her speed, in the larger scheme of maritime commerce she delivered admirably on her owner's expectations. But the *Pamir* was more than a cargo ship. Her story is unique among the cases in this book in that, when she met her fatal hurricane in 1957, she was literally attempting to span the gap between the age-old enterprise of transporting the world's goods under sail and a more modern mission of delivering the intangible benefits of sail training to a new generation. That gap proved too wide for her, and the result was a tragedy. The loss of the *Pamir* finally convinced those most dedicated to preserving the traditions of the sea that moving cargo under sail, an undertaking so integral to the history of the world, was a thing of the past.

Sail training was not new aboard the *Pamir* at the time of her loss: trainees, cadets, or some such version of maritime apprentices had been on virtually every voyage she made. Carrying midshipmen and aspiring officers, either for instruction or fulfillment of a sea-time requirement, was an established part of merchant marine training in many nations at the time of *Pamir*'s commissioning. In the latter decades of deep-sea commercial sail, trainees formed an increasingly important part of the ship's company aboard Cape Horners and significantly defrayed operating expenses for the owners. But even as advances in maritime technology were drawing the curtain on commercial sail, the *Pamir* was giving life to more humanistic notions regarding the purpose of such ships. Of her time under the New Zealand flag during World War II, the following was written:

> In terms of cold economics it would have been better if she had been laid up throughout the conflict, [but] in terms of the human spirit one can say infinitely more was gained by sailing this lovely vessel, however uneconomic her voyages, than would have been accomplished by laying her up.
>
> The *Pamir*'s ultimate benefit was to be more meaningful than cargo-carrying alone and was to extend far beyond the few years she flew our ensign. How can a price be put on the untold pleasure she gave to the many thousands who saw and visited her in every port she graced, especially war-ravaged London and Antwerp. She spelled romance and adventure particularly for the scores of youth fortunate to sail in her. Many were embarking on their careers and no matter what their fields of endeavour in various parts of the world, their early experience in the *Pamir* remains a high point that enriched their lives as well as adding to their seamanship.

Even now, over half a century beyond the shadow of that conflagration, the notion of a sailing ship conferring benefits of a higher order that defy a neatly calculated sum is alive and well in every quadrant of modern sail training and in every project dedicated to building or restoring a traditional sailing vessel.

But at the time of her construction, the *Pamir* was a utilitarian tool in the contest between sail and steam, the outcome of which some felt was not necessarily a foregone conclusion. It was her fate, through the vagaries of two world wars and numerous reflaggings and economic dislocations, to outlast her original purpose so entirely that she ended up a flagship for the emergence of modern sail training. This role was never envisioned by those who built her. Perhaps more than that of any other ship, the tale of the *Pamir* tells us how traditional sail was sustained long enough for a new generation of participants—one that never knew the world of commercial sail—to recognize the value of what went before them and breathe new life into an ancient and dying heritage while some vestige of it remained.

THE HISTORY

The House of Laeisz was founded by a mercantile family in the former Hanseatic port city of Hamburg in the late eighteenth century. After an apprenticeship as a haberdasher, the entrepreneurial Ferdinand Laeisz chartered a ship to carry a cargo of hats to Rio de Janeiro. Upon the success of this voyage, he expanded operations in South America, which eventually came to be dominated by the Chilean nitrate trade. Laeisz had his family's first sailing ship built in 1839. The trade prospered, and the resultant maritime dynasty operated merchant sailing ships continuously until World War II, a century later.

The Laeisz fleet was known as the Flying P-Line because the name of every ship started with the letter *P*. The fleet eventually came to embody the largest and most powerful breed of sailing ship ever built. Despite the obvious trend toward steamships, Ferdinand, followed by Carl, and later Erich Laeisz all believed that the world would continue to have a place for well-built and properly run deep-sea sailing ships as long as economies of scale could be achieved and costs contained. The strength of that faith is evident in the enormous sailing ships built by Laeisz as late as 1926, when the four-masted barque *Padua* was launched. It is truly astounding that an endeavor of such magnitude could be undertaken by hard-nosed merchants so deep into the mechanized world of the twentieth century. The *Padua*, and the four-masted barque *Priwall* of a few years earlier, are the last known sailing ships to compete against steamships for investment capital on such a scale. The competitive inroads of steamships propelled sailing ships to their pinnacle in the period that produced the *Pamir*. The vessels of this period were perhaps the embodiment of deepwater sail. It has often been postulated that commercial sail might have been viably sustained but for the interruptions of the world wars. Though this can never be proven, there is little question that the wars fundamentally altered shipping practices and disrupted the system by which sailing ship knowledge was perpetuated just when commercial sail had reached a critical watershed.

The Nitrate Trade

By 1870 the House of Laeisz was heavily involved in the transport of sodium nitrate from the west coast of South America. Sailing ships at that time still dominated world trade and had access to the most profitable cargoes and routes. Politically unified only since 1871, Germany was a latecomer in the race for empire and the global spoils maritime power could garner. Partly in consequence, German merchants sought markets in places not already dominated by more established commercial interests. Rounding Cape Horn against the prevailing westerlies was a harrowing test that had bested many a strong ship. One Laeisz captain summed it up: "Cape Horn is the place where the devil made the biggest mess he could. It is no place for any sort of handicapped ship, or men, and most certainly not in winter." Not only was the voyage difficult, but upon arrival in Chile mariners had to deal with primitive ports and exposed roadsteads that were prone to earthquakes and tsunamis and were utterly lacking in port services or infrastructure. Irving Johnson's film *Around Cape Horn*, featuring the Laeisz ship *Peking*, shows that as late as 1930 there was no tug in Talcahuano capable of assisting the *Peking* into port. To Johnson's disgust, "the captain had to beat the ship up the harbor as if it were a private yacht." But by systematically studying and investing in the nitrate trade, Laeisz learned to cope with the hazards and exploit the opportunities.

Sodium nitrate came from Chile's Atacama Desert and was an essential ingredient in both fertilizer and munitions. Demand for "Chilean saltpeter" in Europe during the nineteenth century was strong. Laeisz vessels carried general cargo and manufactured goods outbound and brought nitrate home, making Hamburg the depot for the supply of nitrates deep into the river systems of Europe and to Scandinavia. Nitrate was a good cargo for a sailing ship—relatively clean and, when properly bagged, not prone to shifting.

The Flying P-Line

A major blow to worldwide commercial sail came with the opening of the Suez Canal in 1869. Not only were steamers capital intensive to build, they also required fuel, which introduced additional costs, and they needed a reliable system of coaling stations at strategic points along their routes. For all these reasons, the long trip around the Cape of Good Hope was not cost-effective in a steamer, but it could be in a sailing ship. Conversely, the confined waters and inconsistent winds of the Mediterranean and the Red Seas, through which the Suez route passed, brought no advantage to a sailing ship. Though the impact of the Suez Canal was not felt immediately, in due course it ushered in a new era of steamship dominance in the high-value Eastern trades with India, China, and elsewhere. This development helped spur the flow of shipping capital from sail to steam, and sailing vessels were dispersed toward more remote, less-profitable trades. Although sailing ships continued to pay their way, they were increasingly relegated to lower-value, less-time-sensitive cargoes. But as steamships became increasingly efficient, so did the Flying P-Line. The House of Laeisz continued to build successful, state-of-the art sailing ships even as others were retiring their windjammers. Laeisz did not view the business as one of last resort for a dying form of transport. On the contrary, it was a long-term proposition that justified continued investment.

As the end of the nineteenth century approached, the Laeisz fleet, along with that of A. D. Bordes of France and a few others, had become an ongoing research and development project for the movement of cargo by sailing ship. As economies of scale required ever larger hulls, rigs and mast heights increased apace. By the 1870s the three-masted ship, for centuries the rig of choice in the world's largest ships, came up against its natural physical limitations. The spars necessary to drive a 3,000-ton vessel of only three masts required yards so massive that sailors could not reach around them to handle sail when aloft on the footropes. Similarly, the lower yards were so heavy as to be cumbersome to manage on deck, and still the space between the masts was not fully utilized by sail area. This is obvious in sail plans from the period. The failure to maximize sail area translated into noticeably slower passages, as the ships were insufficiently canvased to sail well in all weather. In response, by 1874 four-masted ships and eventually barques came into vogue. Whereas a ship is square-rigged on all masts, a barque is square-rigged on all but the last mast, which is fore-and-aft rigged and therefore less labor-intensive and less costly to rig and maintain. The Laeisz fleet was very much a part of this process of experimentation, which culminated in two monstrous sailing ships: the 4,029-ton, five-masted barque *Postosi*, launched in 1895, and the 5,081-ton, five-masted, full-rigged ship *Preussen* in 1902. Regardless of the sailing cruise liners of recent times, these two Laeisz ships remain the last word on square rig. Operational lessons learned by the company and its shipmasters through routine roundings of the Horn benefited the new vessels and led to

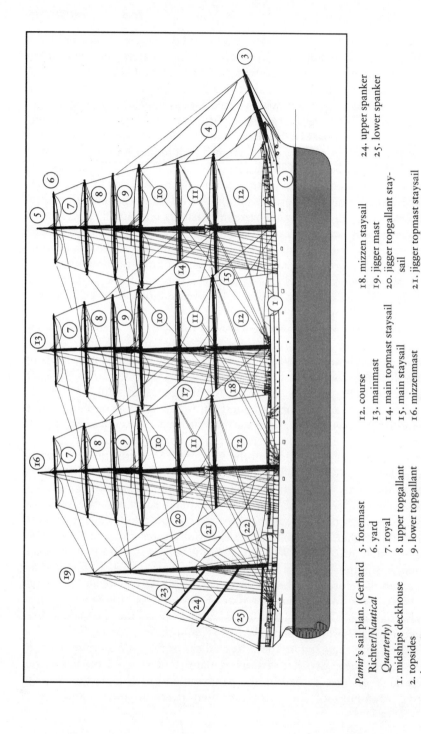

Pamir's sail plan. (Gerhard Richter/*Nautical Quarterly*)

1. midships deckhouse
2. topsides
3. bowsprit
4. headsails
5. foremast
6. yard
7. royal
8. upper topgallant
9. lower topgallant
10. upper topsail
11. lower topsail
12. course
13. mainmast
14. main topmast staysail
15. main staysail
16. mizzenmast
17. mizzen topmast staysail
18. mizzen staysail
19. jigger mast
20. jigger topgallant staysail
21. jigger topmast staysail
22. jigger staysail
23. jigger topsail
24. upper spanker
25. lower spanker

increasingly efficient voyages. By the early 1900s, Laeisz had come to favor the four-masted barque of around *Pamir*'s size.

The P-Liners employed a number of innovations to make them stronger, safer, and more efficient than other ships of their type. Steel hulls and spars and wire standing rigging enabled the vessels to be driven hard. None of the four- or five-masted Laeisz ships ever foundered or was dismasted in a Cape Horn storm in the course of countless voyages. Safety nets helped prevent crew from falling overboard. A midships bridge deck provided an elevated working platform to break the force of boarding seas and diminish the volume of water on deck at any given time. Laborsaving devices such as the Jarvis brace winch made it possible to brace the yards with only one watch. Such improvements increased efficiency while reducing injury and crew size.

The effectiveness of the Flying P-Line lay not only in the construction of the vessels but also in their management. By the early twentieth century, most sailing ships were winding down their careers and therefore received lower priority from their owners and from the shipping world in general. Maintenance often suffered, and weeks passed while a ship waited to load or discharge cargo—if there was any to be had at all. In contrast, the House of Laeisz not only maintained its vessels to a high standard but also kept a pool of dependable masters, mates, and seamen. Laeisz's lightering and transshipment systems in primitive Chilean ports enabled the rapid turnarounds more commonly associated with capital-intensive steamers. By such means Laeisz delivered quality service and profitable passages and kept building new ships.

The Pamir *at Work*

Upon her commissioning, *Pamir* immediately entered the nitrate trade. If not a star performer with respect to speed, she was nevertheless effective and managed some superb passages even late in her career. On her maiden voyage she ran from the Lizard, in Cornwall, to Valparaíso, on the central Chilean coast, in seventy days; on her second outbound voyage she was sixty-four days over the same route, and more than forty years later, in 1947, she logged seventy-eight days from New Zealand to the Lizard. The shipyard of Blohm and Voss built ships more heavily than other yards, which compromised speed and responsiveness under light conditions. The *Pamir* has been described as having "much clumsier lines" than other P-Liners, and this may explain the fact that no sister ships were ever built to that design. At the age of ninety-three, Captain Robert Miethe, a former master of *Pamir*, described her in an interview with Alan Villiers:

She was a sort of dog with a bad name . . . heavy, sluggish in anything short of half a gale, fat in the buttocks and full of drag but powerful as a 3,000 ton elephant. Liable to turn bitchy at dangerous moments, or stand still in light winds when other ships would be sailing.

After twenty-two years rounding the Horn in square-riggers, almost all in P-Liners, Miethe must have known what he was talking about. Similar descriptions fault the vessel primarily for being slow, heavy, and wet. One former Cape Horn officer, however, remarked that *Pamir* was a favorite among some captains for the very reason that she was heavier. He said, "You could really drive her hard." All ships have their idiosyncrasies, but nothing on record marks *Pamir* as having a flaw that would have made her especially susceptible to foundering, and her long history of Cape Horn passages attests to her qualities.

   Pamir sailed continuously for Laeisz in the Chilean run until 1914. Upon the outbreak of World War I she took refuge in the Canary Islands, which belonged to neutral Spain, and at the close of hostilities she was taken by

The *Pamir* ghosting along under high canvas only. (John Pascoe Collection, Alexander Turnbull Library, Wellington, New Zealand)

The crew of the barque *Garthsnaid* scrambles to bring in sail as it rounds Cape Horn in 1924. One hand for yourself; one hand for the ship. As Irving Johnson might have said, they're not up there playing tiddlywinks. (Photo attributed to H. Ibbetson, courtesy Peabody Essex Museum, Salem, Massachusetts)

the British as a war prize. Under the Treaty of Versailles, she and all the largest P-Liners were redistributed among the victors as reparations. *Pamir* went to the Italian flag, where she languished for four years.

In what has been described as a "considerable investment and quite an act of faith," a remarkable thing happened in 1921: Carl Laeisz began to buy back his confiscated ships and to restore his fleet of four-masted barques. In 1923 the *Pamir* was bought back and rejoined the *Peking, Passat, Parma, Pinnas,* and *Peiho* in the Chilean nitrate trade. Reassembling the proud Laeisz fleet, however, could not undo the effects of the Great War or reverse a changing world. The opening of the Panama Canal in 1914 created another shortcut (along with the Suez Canal) for fuel-dependent steamships bound for the Pacific Ocean. The war had stimulated a boom in shipbuilding and brought work to vessels of all kinds, including many a rundown old sailing hull, but then a postwar glut of tonnage led to falling freight rates, and older vessels depreciated even further. Moreover, fundamental changes in the nitrate trade gradually robbed the P-Liners of their competitive edge. A procedure for deriving nitrogen from the atmosphere was developed by Haber and Bosch in Germany during World War I, and this further depressed the demand for Chilean saltpeter.

But commercial sail still had a role to play. In the period after World War I, merchant marine cadets continued to ship out in sail because Germany and much of Scandinavia continued to require that officers have sea time in sail to qualify for a license. These paying cadets helped subsidize the cost of voyaging, not only by providing revenue but by augmenting the professional crew so that payrolls could be kept to a minimum. There was nothing new about cadets paying to acquire sea time and training, but as profit margins from cargo continued to narrow, this source of labor and revenue acquired increased significance.

Though Laeisz built the four-masted barque *Padua* in 1926—the last really sizable, pure sailing cargo ship ever built—by the end of the 1920s it was clear that the *Pamir* and the Flying P-Line would not remain viable under the German flag. In 1931 the *Pamir* was sold to Gustaf Erikson of Finland, and within a few years all but two of the big barques were sold abroad, mainly to Erikson. Nevertheless, Laeisz continued to operate its two newest vessels, *Priwall* and *Padua*, right up to 1939, when war again decimated their fleet. These vessels accommodated upward of forty cadets.

Gustaf Erikson and the Grain Race Years

Like the Laeisz dynasty before him, Gustaf Erikson was a figure of huge moment in the last years of commercial sail. Under Erikson, the last significant fleet of square-rigged merchantmen in the world operated in deep-sea trade. The primary cargo that sustained the fleet was Australian grain, which remained viable for sailing ships through World War II. Unlike Laeisz, however, Erikson did not build Cape Horners. He bought them up where he found them, lying around the ports of the world, paying little more than scrap value for them. When the cost of keeping a vessel in survey exceeded its anticipated revenue, it was scrapped and another one found. In this manner Erikson assembled a fleet that averaged fifteen to twenty sailing vessels through the 1920s and 1930s.

Erikson's fleet operated out of Mariehamn in the Åland Islands at the mouth of the Gulf of Bothnia between Sweden and Finland. An autonomous province of Finland, Åland is culturally and linguistically linked to Sweden. Erikson and other Åland-based sailing ship owners enjoyed a significant comparative advantage in crew costs while also having access to virtually the last pool of seamen in Europe for whom the traditions of commercial sail were unbroken. Like Laeisz before him, Erikson made wide use of his vessels to carry paying trainees. Most of these were Germans, Finns, Swedes, and Ålanders, many of whom needed the sea time in sail for officer licenses. By the 1930s these aspiring officers had little choice but to sail for Erikson, though after the Nazis came to power German candidates generally served out their time in the German fleet of purpose-built sail training ships and the two remaining P-Liners, *Priwall* and *Padua*. Norwegians, Australians, New Zealanders, Britons, and the occasional American also berthed in the forecastles of Erikson's ships. During this period a variation on the square-rigger sailor profile began to emerge.

For some time Erikson had manned his ships with what he spoke of as "boys," as the professional adult sailor was a rapidly disappearing breed after World War I. Backed up by a cadre of seasoned professionals, these lads in their late teens and early twenties evidently could get the job done. But by the 1930s individuals were increasingly signing onto "windjammers" for a taste of adventure and the rare opportunity to experience a real blue-water sailing ship voyage. Many of these trainees were aware of the precarious future of commercial sail, and several made their voyages as documentarians. Irving Johnson, who ultimately had a distinguished career as a pioneer of modern sail training, made his famous voyage in 1929–30 aboard the *Peking* as a paying member of the ship's company. Like others, his objective was the experience itself, as well as the opportunity to record a world about to vanish. He accomplished the latter admirably in his film *Sailing Adventures: Around Cape Horn* and its companion book. In the same period, German journalist Heinrich Hauser made a film and a book, *Die letzten Segelschiffe* (The last sailing ships), documenting his voyage in the *Pamir* under Laeisz. Eric Newby, an aspiring writer, made a round-trip voyage to Australia for grain in the four-masted barque *Moshulu* in 1938–39 and documented his experience in two excellent books, *The Last Grain Race* and *Windjammer*. Also in 1939, the American marine artist Thomas Wells made *Odyssey at Sea*, a color film of a voyage in the *Passat*. In 1947 Briton Duncan Carse made a voyage in *Passat* to South Africa, resulting in the film *Proud Canvas*.

Obviously, those who left a record of their experiences are best known to us now, but they were not the only ones who in the declining days of sail sought out and were willing to pay for the chance to make the voyage of a lifetime. Quite possibly this voyeuristic fascination was scorned by hard-case shellbacks, but it is in the paying trainee motivated by curiosity and adventure rather than a career path that one perceives the forerunner of the modern sail trainee. As the opportunity to sail in such ships became rarer in an increasingly mechanized world, the mystique of traditional sail was enhanced by its contrast to the very forces that were obliterating it. This same contrast continues to be part of the appeal of sail training today.

Although Erikson's vessels were scrupulously maintained, they operated on frugal budgets and without hull insurance. Their crews were small, twenty-five to thirty-one, including the trainees. Unlike the celebrated P-Liners with their rapid turnarounds, under Erikson vessels like *Pamir* eked out a living by making one long eastward circumnavigation a year out to Australia in ballast by way of Good Hope and then home to Europe by way of the Horn with grain. Like the Chilean ports of years earlier, the remote outports of the Spencer Gulf in South Australia were sufficiently crude that only sailing ships, with their low overheads and amortization, could afford to lay at anchor for weeks while the lengthy and laborious process of sacking, lightering, and stowing the grain was carried out. The investment represented by a steamship of comparable tonnage made such a proposition prohibitive. Erikson's ships, along with the last two Laeisz ships and a handful of others, continued to take part in other trades, including lumber to South Africa, guano from the Seychelles, and timber from Canada to various destinations. Australian grain, however, was the mainstay.

The annual return voyages from Australia in the 1920s and 1930s gave rise to what became known as the Grain Race. Grain being a seasonal cargo, the ships loaded and sailed within a fairly narrow window of time. Homeward-bound grain ships would run east from Australia through Bass Straits, across the Southern Ocean, around the Horn and up the length of the Atlantic to the English Channel. Because few of the spartanly equipped Cape Horners carried a wireless radio, it was customary to put in either

Loading grain at Tumby Bay, Australia, 1905. The wheat was stacked in sacks shoreside, then run out on the long pier by light railway for loading into small ketches that would lighter it out to the anchored Cape Horners. (Courtesy the State Library of South Australia/B54055)

Grain loading into ketches at Port Broughton, Australia, 1928. When the bags were later transferred to the waiting Cape Horners, the ships would disgorge their ballast over the side at a counterbalancing rate so there was always enough weight in the ship to keep her upright and trimmed. (Courtesy the State Library of South Australia/B48930)

at Falmouth, England, or Cóbh (then Queenstown), Ireland, for orders regarding the final destination and port of discharge. Though the grain races were not as glamorous as their illustrious forebears, the Tea Races or the Wool Races, for the masters and the crews of the grain ships it was still a chance to break a record on a long ocean haul and bring a little color to a fading profession. In 1928 the International Paint Company in Britain went so far as to put up an exquisite silver globe as a prize, which was won by the four-masted barque *Herzogin Cecilie*. The Grain Races ran until 1939, when war broke out.

The New Zealand Ensign and the End of Commercial Sail

There is no saying what might have come of the *Pamir* had she not fallen victim to a curious bit of wartime intrigue in the early years of World War II. She sailed from Mariehamn in the spring of 1941 bound for the Seychelles and then on to New Zealand. Earlier, with the outbreak of war, the various dominions of the British Empire, including New Zealand, had quickly joined the British cause. Meanwhile, Finland, with a close proximity to both Germany and the Soviet Union, declared itself neutral. Capitalizing on the international disarray arising from Hitler's aggression, as well as an agreement with Nazi Germany, Soviet Russia moved against Finland, her former imperial possession, in what became known as the Winter War of 1940. Though Finland received much sympathy from the West for her spirited defense against her gargantuan neighbor, she was caught without allies. When the uneasy peace between Germany and the Soviet Union abruptly ended, beleaguered Britain allied with the Soviet Union, and Finland's best defense against the Soviets appeared to lie in cooperating with Germany. By the time the *Pamir* sailed into Wellington with a load of guano in July 1941, Germany had invaded Russia, and Finland was technically at war with Britain despite the fact there was no bilateral basis for hostilities between the two nations. Britain declared Finland to be "constructive enemy territory," and the *Pamir* was seized and placed under the New Zealand flag, despite the neutrality insignia emblazoned on her topsides.

Under the New Zealand ensign, the *Pamir* became a sort of national maritime mascot during the war. Several of her Åland and Finnish crew stayed with her, and her transom continued to bear the name Mariehamn as her home port. The government of New Zealand maintained and operated the vessel to a high standard and at great expense for the next seven years. *Pamir* sailed right through the war, making eight voyages to North America, one to Australia, and one to Europe after the war. She carried cargo, cadets, and a core of professional sailors and officers. On most of these voyages between a third to half of the ship's company were cadets in their midteens.

On one trip near the end of the war, a Japanese A-12 submarine under command of a certain Commander Kudo surfaced close by the *Pamir* off the west coast of North America. Being at the mercy of a belligerent, those aboard the *Pamir* prepared to abandon ship. However, despite orders to sink Allied shipping, the submarine commander allowed the ship to sail on. It was learned after the war that the commander of the Japanese submarine had been a cadet in a Japanese sail training ship before the war, and it would appear that he chose not to sink the *Pamir*. We are left to wonder if Commander Kudo's hand was stayed by an affinity for his training experience; Kudo and his A-12 submarine did not return from their final mission to tell us.

In 1948 the *Pamir* returned to Europe and became the object of a tremendous outpouring of public fascination. No lesser dignitaries than Princess Elizabeth and Philip, Duke of Edinburgh, went aboard the vessel when she called at London. The attention lavished on this old steel workhorse can only be explained by a sort of inarticulate mass refusal to see the last sailing ship go to the scrapyard. The mood of the day was described by maritime historian Alex Hurst, who knew these ships well and wrote extensively about them:

> If popular interest, as evinced in the *Pamir*, could have kept sailing ships afloat and trading, there would have been whole fleets of them at this time. Before the war, when the grain ships were in port, one might meet the odd enthusiast aboard, if he was noticed at all. Now, the *Pamir* stood for . . . a breath of another sort of life to a people drugged by war, by rationing and by the sheer weight of bureaucracy. They queued in their thousands to go aboard, few of them knowing or understanding what they saw.

The power of the romantic element, both then and now, cannot be underestimated when attempting to understand the renaissance of traditional sail and sail training in the decades since the war. But whatever the effect on morale in port, the *Pamir*'s voyages after World War II lost money for New Zealand at a time when subsidies required solid justification. The *Pamir* had many advocates who proposed a total conversion into a sail training vessel, but such a substantial investment in a vessel that was already in her fifth decade of service was as much an object of criticism as support. After threats of legal action by Erikson to reacquire the vessel, the *Pamir* was handed back to her Finnish owners at Wellington in November 1948. So great was the impact of the *Pamir* on the people of New Zealand that decades later her name remained something of a household word.

Pamir's former Finnish master, Captain Björkfeldt, rejoined the ship where he had left her in 1941 and sailed immediately to South Australia to load grain. While *Pamir* was loading, the former P-Liner *Passat* also sailed into the anchorage to take on a cargo of wheat. Though the *Passat* and the *Pamir* were not sister ships in the conventional sense, from this point onward until *Pamir*'s loss, the fates of the two ships remain curiously intertwined. On 28 May 1949, *Pamir* sailed for Europe with a hold full of barley, followed three days later by *Passat*. This was truly the last grain race, and the last carriage of commercial cargoes around Cape Horn in sailing ships. The *Passat* made port first, leaving *Pamir* the honor of being the last pure square-rigged sailing vessel to make a deep-sea voyage in commercial service around the Horn.

Pamir *and Sail Training*

These final voyages under the Finnish flag failed to turn a profit, and upon arrival in England no profitable cargoes could be found for either vessel. Both ships were chartered out as stationary granaries in Wales until 1951, at which point they were sold to shipbreakers in Belgium. It seemed that the long voyage had finally run its course, but just as the two ships were about to be cut up at Antwerp, a German shipowner by the name of Heinz Schliewen purchased them back, proposing to operate them under the German flag once more as cargo-carrying training ships. The return of the former Flying P-Liners to Germany generated intense public excitement. This enthusiasm was reflected in the German government's decision to subsidize the project, despite misgivings within the shipping world. Although the idea of using sailing ships for a beneficent purpose had supporters, its practicality was questioned. As early as 1949, Erich Laeisz wrote:

> I doubt very much that a sailing ship can ever again pay her way, barring wartimes. So the only way left would be to do it internationally, i.e., to run cargo-carrying school ships and train all-comers from western Europe to the U.S.A. It would surely be a grand thing on the road to international understanding. But can such an idea grow roots strong enough to sprout branches that carry the necessary funds?

Erich Laeisz's affinity for sailing ships was second only to his practical knowledge of the business.

What distinguished Schliewen's proposition from past training activities aboard the *Pamir* and *Passat* was that cargo would defray the cost of sail training, rather than the other way around. The reordering of these priorities marks the point at which the *Pamir* can truly be said to have become a sail training ship, or *Segelschulschiff*. The concept was not revolutionary, but because of the scale of the project and the lateness of the day for sailing ships in general, the undertaking was hugely significant. Schliewen had big plans. While the *Passat* and *Pamir* were being overhauled for the new project, he acquired another Cape Horner, *Moshulu*, and was negotiating for the old P-Liner *Pommern*, still laying at Mariehamn. The scope of this venture gives some indication of the extraordinary enthusiasm and financial commitment that these ships inspired, despite the fact that they had outlived the purpose for which they were originally conceived. Had Schliewen succeeded in his effort to assemble and operate a fleet of four cargo-carrying square-riggers, the face of sail training might look very different today.

The *Pamir* and the *Passat* underwent a major refit at Kiel between September 1951 and January 1952. Both vessels were drilled to test plate thickness, and between thirty and forty plates were renewed on each ship. Whether the new plates were riveted in keeping with the original construction or welded using later technology is not entirely clear. Though there are many examples of riveted ships being successfully restored with welded plate, the possibility of structural failure would later arise in connection with *Pamir*'s loss.

The vessels were significantly modified for the new venture, including the installation of transverse watertight bulkheads and guides for fitting longitudinal dividers called *shifting boards* to prevent cargo from moving at sea. Ballast tanks, cargo gear, extra lifeboats, radios, and a 900-horsepower auxiliary diesel engine were also installed. After the refit, both vessels received the "highest classification at Lloyd's Register of Shipping and Germanischer Lloyd." Chancellor Konrad Adenauer of the Federal German Republic (West Germany) sailed aboard the *Pamir* for sea trials. In 1952 and 1953 two voyages were made between Hamburg and the Río de la Plata in Argentina. Despite the fact that the propellers on both vessels "obligingly dropped off" and the *Pamir* lost an anchor, the first voyage was actually profitable, in part due to the inflationary effect of the Korean War on freight rates. The second voyage, however, was ruinous. Freight rates slumped while fixed operating costs remained high, and the expensive conversion bankrupted Schliewen's short-lived enterprise. The ships were auctioned off in April 1954 to the Schleswig-Holstein Landesbank, thus confirming the early concerns expressed by Erich Laeisz regarding the financial burden of operating the two barques.

Despite this setback, in 1955 a public-private venture formed by some forty shipowners and the government of the German state of Schleswig-Holstein set up a nonprofit foundation to operate the vessels as training ships under the professional management of Zerssen and Co. of Lübeck. Under the new organization and the experienced oversight of Captain Hermann Eggers, the *Pamir* underwent another thorough refit. Erich Laiesz, who was still in shipping, was approached by the organizers but opted not to participate in the project. The project went ahead, however, and the ships continued to make the run to the east coast of South America, generally with cement or ballast outbound and bulk grain homeward.

Thus far, the record shows that considerable investment had been made in maintenance and retrofitting since the two barques were converted to sail training. In 1956 the *Pamir* was again overhauled at Bremen and underwent an "extensive refit for reclassification" at Hamburg. In May 1957 the *Pamir* again received "routine repairs and overhaul" at the Blohm and Voss shipyard, where she had been built. The frequency of maintenance and repair undoubtedly reflects the vessel's advanced age, but also the increasing complexity of her systems. Without examining the actual shipyard invoices, we can still presume that there was a bona fide effort to upgrade and maintain the vessel to prevailing standards.

Though the ultimate failure of the *Pamir-Passat* projects of the 1950s was not inevitable, there is evidence of a strain between the expectations of a modern shipping world and the reality of operating a turn-of-the-century Cape Horner as it was intended to be operated. Alan Villiers, who had considerable firsthand experience in the field, wrote, "the scheme was ill-conceived and poorly executed, splendid as the principle was." The method of lading grain under the Schliewen project represented a significant departure from the traditional method. Niels Jannasch, who sailed in Cape Horners under both the Finnish flag in the late 1940s and the German flag in the 1950s, described the method of lading the *Passat* in 1952 in Argentina under Schliewen's ownership: "The grain arrived in bags, which we split open and dumped into the hold. Then bags were stacked over the entire hold several layers deep. Under Erikson's flag the entire cargo of grain was always carried in bags."

An incident aboard the *Pamir* in early 1956 boded the problems of cargo handling and stowage during the period in which Zerssen managed the ships. At Antwerp, 2,500 tons of methyl alcohol (methanol) in barrels were taken aboard for transport. Due to stability concerns, the royal yards were sent down at the anchorage. Once at sea the vessel adopted an abnormal list, compelling the master to put into the nearest port under auxiliary power. Upon her arrival at Falmouth, the vessel's stability was assessed through an inclining experiment (see Stability, in appendix) and was found to be severely impaired: "the disposition of the comparatively light cargo and the failure to fill the ballast tank with 750 tons of water instead of cargo was the cause of the lack of sufficient metacentric height."

An agreement to lade a particular cargo is normally the responsibility of the shipping company that makes space on its ship available to a shipper, or customer. The chief mate is traditionally responsible for stowing the cargo and preparing the ship for sea, though obviously the master and others carry responsibility in this matter, as well. The master has a duty to reject an unsafe stowage plan or cargo, but that duty is accompanied by an expectation on the part of the company that the job will get done. When there is a precedent for a particular activity, human nature is such that people are inclined to perpetuate that activity rather than analyze it afresh: "If it ain't broke, don't fix it." But sometimes things are broken and we just don't know it yet.

It is evident that in the instance described above the vessel was badly laden. This was due to the stowage, the inherent nature of the cargo itself, or a combination of the two. Eggers, however, knew enough to enter port and correct the situation, despite the negative effect on the economics of the voyage. The interruption of a voyage in the face of a schedule takes a certain amount of courage, even when justified. If the company is not persuaded of the reasoning, it can be detrimental to a captain's career. In this case it appears that Eggers was vindicated, but he had the benefit of an established reputation as a Cape Horn skipper. He also had the benefit of a safe harbor of refuge nearby. A less-seasoned skipper might have acted differently, not only due to inexperience but out of concern for the professional consequences.

FINAL VOYAGE

On 1 June 1957, the *Pamir* sailed in ballast to Buenos Aires. There were fifty-one cadets and thirty-five crew aboard, making a total ship's company of eighty-six. Due to illness, *Pamir*'s usual master, Captain Eggers, was relieved for the voyage by Captain Johannes Diebitsch. Diebitsch had served aboard *Pamir* early in his career as an able-bodied seaman, though most of that time was spent laid up in the Canary Islands during World War I. The chief mate had joined two trips earlier and was new to sail at that time. By 1957, finding seasoned square-rigger masters, mates, and seamen was increasingly difficult, while at the same time opportunities for younger sailors to gain experience were becoming severely curtailed by a lack of ships.

In Buenos Aires the *Pamir* loaded 3,525 tons of loose barley and 255 tons of barley in sacks. The sacks were stowed atop the loose barley in the area under the hatches, and the ballast tanks were filled with loose barley to maximize the payload. There was a dock strike in Buenos Aires at the time, about which maritime historian Alex Hurst wrote: "Loading had been carried out by soldiers, which is seldom a good thing." On 10 August the *Pamir* sailed for Hamburg.

About two-thirds of the way home and forty days out from Buenos Aires, the barque encountered deteriorating weather. Hurricane Carrie had recurved north of Bermuda and was tracking eastward back across the Atlantic toward North Africa. According to one eyewitness, Hans Wirth, the trouble started at around 0800. The vessel was sailing along at about 12 knots "when the winds suddenly changed direction and became shrill." An order was given to furl sails, but before it could be executed in a seamanlike fashion, the sails began to blow out. According to Wirth, in a desperate attempt to reduce windage, an order was given to cut the sails away. He described the situation: "With our sails cut away the gale forced us on our side until one rail was continuously under water. Now 40-foot-high waves were smashing across the deck."

At about midday (ship's time) on 21 September, at approximately 36 degrees north, 40 degrees west, about 600 nautical miles southwest of the Azores, the *Pamir* issued three radio distress calls. Roughly an hour elapsed between the first and last calls. The radio calls were received as far east as the coast of Tunisia in the Mediterranean Sea and as far west as the United States, so time zone differences are reflected in the reports from various sources. After adjusting for zone, however, nearly all sources corroborate the timing of events described by Wirth. An exception is the account of survivor Gunter Hasselbach, which is starkly at odds with Wirth's on both the timing and sequence of events: "It was Saturday night and the cadets were at supper. The ship's big sails had been furled and the spanker set. Then the storm struck."

Despite this version, radio transmissions received elsewhere confirm Wirth's account that the ship had lost her sails. Another point of confusion centers on different interpretations of a radio transmission that in some places is transcribed as "foremast broken" and in others as "four-masted barque broken." Some accounts speak of masts carrying away but others do not. Historically speaking, deliberate dismasting was a known course of action for righting a vessel *in extremis*, but the advent of wire rigging and rigging screws by the late nineteenth century made it more difficult to execute this option. In this case, the removal of the foremast would have reduced wind resistance at the forward part of the ship and helped keep the ship bow to the seas, which was the captain's strategy when he decided to heave-to and execute a controlled drift. However, there is no report or evidence that the ship was deliberately dismasted. Also, we do not know whether the loss of the foremast, such as it was, occurred aloft or at deck level, or what sort of damage the ship may have sustained in the process. A

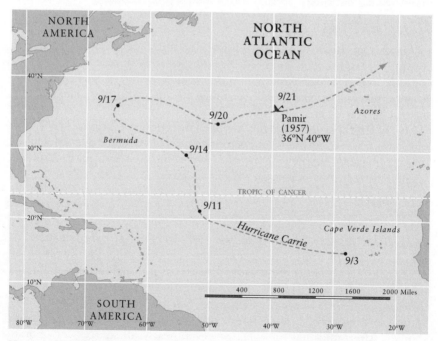

Hurricane Carrie's path relative to the *Pamir*'s final position. (Equator Graphics)

mast breaking at deck level can peel back the deck, allowing torrents of sea-water to enter the hull. The following excerpt is from Hasselbach's account:

> Eighty-foot waves tossed us about like a shuttlecock. Our cargo shifted and we took on a 45 degree list. We fought to right her, and at the same time calm the cadets. It was impossible to calm them. The captain went to the well of the ship to lead them in prayer. Cigarettes and liquor were issued and the cadets ordered away in three boats. But as the boats were launched they were caught by the mountainous waves and sent hurtling hundreds of feet from the ship. It seemed to me that our boat was the only one successfully launched. The pounding of the seas . . . heeled the ship over further and further. It was impossible to keep the bow head-on to those tremendous waves. She was lying broadside on. The masts snapped and her sails blew away. The end only took thirty seconds. In the trough of a giant wave she rolled right over and we last saw her bottom up and going down by the bow like a submarine slowly diving.

Would-be rescuers came across several empty lifeboats in various states of seaworthiness. Survivor Karl Dummer, who had been in a boat for fifty-four hours, described the ship rolling and hurling men into the water: "We saw twenty-five men climb into a damaged lifeboat almost awash. In our boat five men died from exposure or jumped out despite the efforts of others to hold them. We saw the Cutter *Absecon* but it passed us by." Although the *Absecon* missed Dummer's boat, they found Hasselbach "half-crazed" and sobbing in his lifeboat, alone except for the body of a dead man. Of twenty-two men in his boat, seventeen were washed overboard and three jumped "screaming like demons." Hasselbach said that he was prepared to do the same when he was found. A number of other lost souls were last seen atop the overturned hull, riding it down.

Hasselbach's account of how the ship sank actually matches closely with Wirth's, but a striking exception is the assessment of wave height (80 versus 40 feet) and the conduct of personnel under pressure. Whereas Hasselbach described hysteria, Wirth described stiff-upper-lip decorum: "There was no panic. The cook continued making coffee until the pot overturned."

None of the officers or career seamen survived the ordeal, therefore truly expert firsthand accounts of what took place have never been available. Conjecture regarding what occurred and when it occurred is perhaps inevitable. Most of the survivors were cadets. The most seasoned mariner of the lot was Dummer, a ship's baker who had been going to sea for about six years. The following from the official inquiry gives what is perhaps a more measured picture of what took place:

> The *Pamir* carried all topsails (six), the foresail, and several staysails and sailed close-hauled on the starboard tack, when the wind in a short time

increased severely after having blown Force 9, Beaufort. With those sails set, the yards close hauled, her state of loading and her ballast tanks not flooded, the stability was not sufficient, so that the vessel got a heavy list to port. Because the angle of slope was exceeded, the barley which for the greatest part had been loaded loose, and had settled during the voyage, began to move in spite of the erected shifting boards and was going over to port in an increasing degree. Furthermore, water poured into the superstructures which were not closed everywhere and which were already immersed on the port side so that their buoyancy was lost. In this way the vessel capsized.

It is evident that the ship was already sailing under fairly fresh conditions when the wind abruptly increased. Being close-hauled, the ship already had a greater angle of heel than she would have had at any other point of sail. The increase in wind heeled the ship farther still, which almost immediately precipitated problems from shifting cargo and flooding through deckhouse openings before sail area could be effectively reduced.

A massive and highly publicized international search effort ensued and was twice extended at the request of the West German government. The *New York Times* covered the story for eight days straight, a level of interest seldom accorded maritime matters. At its peak the search involved fourteen merchant ships as well as military vessels and aircraft, but this

Survivors from the loss of *Pamir* on the rescue ship *Geiger*. (Howard Sochurek/TimePix)

concentration of assets produced only meager results. Many of the sailors never got away from the ship, and those who did had difficulty staying in the damaged boats. Severe weather hampered the response time, and exposure took its toll. Of the eighty-six people aboard, only six survived. Five of these, including Dummer and Wirth, were found in one boat, and, as we know, Hasselbach was found alone in another.

POSTMORTEM

Several factors distinguish the *Pamir* from other severe casualty cases of the postcommercial era. Of the five cases examined in this book, the loss of the *Pamir* took by far the greatest toll in human life, incurring a casualty figure more typically associated with a maritime disaster from an earlier era or the developing world than one from a modern maritime nation. The *Pamir* is the only case involving a major storm system and the only disaster in this book that did not develop more or less instantaneously. The *Pamir* was caught up in a bad situation that progressively deteriorated, and for various reasons those aboard were unable to bring the situation back under control.

The list of possible causes of the sinking is long, and the diversity of opinion is wide. Hurst wrote: "Of course, there were all sorts of contributory factors, for the reasons for any disaster are seldom cut and dried." In examining the loss of the *Pamir*, structural failure, weather, and human error all warrant consideration. The *Pamir* is also unique among the five casualties in that she was carrying cargo at the time, and many sources agree that the cargo shifted to the detriment of the ship's stability. Despite a lengthy inquiry conducted by German maritime authorities through the Seeamt (maritime court) at Lübeck, Germany, a lack of consensus persists regarding the causes of the casualty. The "secret questioning" of the survivors by authorities in the immediate aftermath of the casualty, and the closed-door nature of the inquiry, did little to inspire confidence in the integrity of the inquiry. The knowledge that major shipping interests and government officials behind the *Pamir-Passat* project may have wished to avoid embarrassment led to criticism of the process before the inquiry was even finished.

A large number of retired square-rigger sailors were living at the time of the *Pamir's* loss, many of whom had wide experience in Cape Horners under Laeisz, Erikson, or the handful of other operators only a decade or two earlier. The resurrection of the *Pamir* and *Passat* in the 1950s was of great interest to these individuals, many of whom followed the events surrounding the loss of the *Pamir* closely. Their firsthand knowledge of sailing ship operations must be regarded as expert. Though this expertise is unfortunately much harder to find in the world today, several "old-timers" contributed their views on the loss of the *Pamir* to my investigation of this story.

Structural Integrity

Given that the *Pamir* was fifty-two years old at the time of her loss, the possibility of hull fatigue is a natural starting point for any discussion of causes. There is a divergence of opinion in this matter. Many of those personally familiar with the vessel dismiss the prospect of hull failure outright. The view most commonly expressed is that the ship was exceedingly strong and well maintained and should not have failed under those conditions. Likewise, most of the literature dealing with the incident does not emphasize this particular possibility. Nevertheless, some question remains.

The issue of structural integrity is important for several reasons. If, indeed, the hull was weak and prone to failure, then the role of shipboard experience and the lading of the cargo is much diminished. If the ship itself did not give out, then we need to look elsewhere to gain insight into what brought about the calamity.

The *Pamir* was designed and built for Cape Horn, the most demanding sailing waters in the world. She had a long, successful career battling heavy weather in every ocean of the world. She went into service at what was probably the pinnacle of knowledge and technology for that particular undertaking. The shipyard that built her had a reputation for using larger scantlings (structural members of greater dimension), and a variety of sources agree that the *Pamir* was heavily built. This fact may have contributed to her ability to meet survey standards long after other ships of her vintage were scrapped. The history of the *Pamir* also shows that each of her successive owners considered the vessel worth the expense of maintaining her, and did so. Her late history included costly upgrades, renewal of hull plating, and thorough surveys resulting in the "highest classification." Judging from the money spent, *neglect* is not a word that comes to mind.

Nevertheless, the question of hull integrity was foreshadowed when Villiers wrote the following in 1953 in respect to the Schliewen project:

> I was the more dubious because I had been thoroughly over the *Pamir* when she was in London [1948] under the New Zealand flag. . . . She had over a thousand tons of wet sand in her for years and there was no telling what condition some of her plates might be in. After all, she was an oldish ship in 1950.

Concern for the condition of the plates was absolutely appropriate, yet it is precisely the sort of thing that surveys are intended to discover and have corrected at a shipyard. Furthermore, high-quality steel is not necessarily compromised by age alone.

It might be said that those same voyages in which the *Pamir* proved her mettle in countless engagements with the worst weather imaginable had taken a cumulative toll on the hull. The year and a half in the early 1950s during which she was laid up as a granary would not have done her any good, either. Though one could speculate that seasoned sailors declined to participate in the projects of the 1950s because of doubts about the amount of life remaining in the ships, this sentiment does not resonate in the statements and writings of those who knew such ships intimately. As already noted, the view most widely articulated was that the ships were fine—it was the people who were wearing out.

There is some consensus that the *Pamir* was taking on water prior to her capsizing. The source of this conviction is a radio transmission that accompanied the Mayday call. But even if true, an accumulation of water in the hold can be explained in ways other than structural failure. For instance, the inquiry indicated that there were openings in the deck structure that were not secured. If the ship adopted a pronounced list early in the ordeal, as it appears to have done, then the engine room ventilators and other apertures at deck level could have provided an inlet for water while the hull remained intact. An account by an American college student who sailed in the *Pamir* from Australia in 1949, on her last rounding of the Horn, is relevant in this regard. The *Pamir* had been loaded in the Spencer Gulf with barley in sacks in the traditional fashion:

> One of the starboard watch had discovered salt water in the storeroom and fear that one of the ship's plates had been sprung led to an immediate investigation. One sprung plate meant that the entire ship was in danger of filling with water and cargo such as barley expands when dampened with such tremendous pressure that the sides of the ship would be forced out. . . . Ten hours and several split barley bags later, the leak proved to be nothing but a goose necked ventilator on deck that had been facing windward and taking in heavy spray all night.

The notion of wet barley expanding and damaging the *Pamir* from the inside has not been explored in connection with her foundering, but the anecdote illustrates how water can find its way into a hold by means other than structural failure, particularly in rough weather. The modifications made to the *Pamir* upon her conversion to an engined sail training ship can only have increased the number of vents and apertures from when she was a straight sailer.

Most persistent on the point of structural failure is Horst Willner's book, *Pamir, ihr Untergang und die Irrtümer des Seeamtes* (*Pamir*, her loss, and the errors of the maritime court). Willner's work was not published until 1991 but found a ready audience in Germany. Willner was a former seaman who became a lawyer and acted as legal counsel for Captain Diebitsch's widow during the hearings of the court of inquiry. Willner took issue with many findings of the court, but in particular he argued that structural failure was the principal cause of the loss. Naturally, a finding of structural failure would help exonerate those aboard and deflect blame to some other quarter. Willner advanced the idea that modifications to the hull during the refits of the 1950s ultimately had a destabilizing effect. In riveted ships, it was normal for sections of hull plating to work and grind under stress at sea. A possibility exists that the hull plating, structural reinforcement, and transverse watertight bulkheads added in the 1950s may have had flex moments that were incompatible with the original construction, thus causing the hull to breach under severe conditions. If welding was combined with riveting during the later refits, problems could have developed in a hull of *Pamir*'s size. There is, of course, no hard evidence for this, and many a riveted ship has been repaired by welding without ill effect. In support of his ideas Willner cited the testimony of Karl Dummer, the ship's baker, who survived the ordeal. Dummer described geysers of water shooting up from the plate margins at the turn of the bilge, shrieking like steam from a kettle when the ship rolled on her side. The suggestion is that pockets of trapped air found their way through the hull plating, displacing seawater as they went. Dummer also described seeing water below decks shortly before capsizing, thus confirming what was heard over the radio. In a statement to the inquiry, Captain Grubbe, master of the *Passat*, also emphasized the possibility that water below initiated the loss of stability.

Willner cited the speed with which the vessel sank as further evidence of structural failure. Survivors agreed that the vessel took about twenty minutes to sink after capsizing. According to Willner, this is a time frame that some experts, relying upon models and calculations, believe to be too short for a vessel of *Pamir*'s size and design, provided its structural integrity is still intact. But under the dynamic conditions of a capsize in a hurricane, with the rigging carrying away and doing untold damage to the hull, a cargo of loose grain, and the ship known to be partially flooded already, it is impossible to say precisely how much time a ship should take to go about the business of sinking. Willner's theory of structural failure also does not address whether the forces exerted on the hull during the capsizing could have ruptured the plating at some point even if the loss of stability was initiated by the cargo. The full-rigger *Bengairn* experienced such difficulties in 1907 while carrying coal from Newcastle, Australia, to Valparaíso, Chile. The cargo shifted and the ship was thrown on her beam. Captain James S.

Learmont wrote, "Unknown to us, the bulwark stanchions under the strain of the ship lying on her side had been sheared off in the scuppers and water was pouring in there as well as through the No. 2 hatch." Through extreme measures the *Bengairn* was saved, but she was the only ship known to survive a shifted cargo in that particular trade. Learmont remarked that the carriage of coal, which was also a bulk (loose) cargo, from Australia to South America was responsible for the loss of more ships than any other trade he had known. Neither does Willner address the possibility that damage to the hull from the act of dismasting or from expansion of the grain may have resulted in water entering the ship.

Willner's argument for structural failure in the loss of the *Pamir* is not without merit, particularly given an eyewitness account of air escaping from the hull, but the countervailing arguments have equal merit. Without the ship as evidence, no verdict is possible. Willner does, however, raise two important questions that recur in other cases. The first is the appropriateness of converting older vessels that were designed with something different in mind to new purposes. In particular, what are the consequences of converting ships to sail training, which by its nature involves taking large numbers of young, inexperienced people into a potentially hostile environment? Vessel conversions may be carried out with the best of intentions, yet it would be grimly ironic if modifications intended to make the *Pamir* safer instead contributed to a catastrophe. If so, it would not be the first time that modern and traditional methods were mixed with disastrous results (see Modern Materials on Traditional Ships in the appendix).

A second important contribution by Willner concerns the nature of official postmortem inquiries and the consequences when they fail to inquire. Willner's theories are based largely on facts and testimonies that emerged at the *Pamir* inquiry but were ignored in the conclusions or simply not pursued by the maritime court. Willner's dissatisfaction with the court's handling of the evidence merely articulates a view that has been widely held in the maritime world for over four decades. This is a serious indictment of a procedure utterly predicated on public faith and perception.

Weather

Although the possibility of hull fatigue and structural failure cannot be dismissed, it is clear that other factors deserve consideration if we are to form a more complete picture of the demise of the venerable barque. First among these is the weather she was experiencing. Every voyage of any duration contains the potential for adverse weather, and for a voyage made in the North Atlantic in autumn that probability is somewhat higher. Although there was an element of chance that the paths of the *Pamir* and Hurricane

Carrie intersected, the presence of such a weather system out there at that time was not simply bad luck. It was hurricane season.

The firsthand accounts of the weather experienced by the *Pamir* during Hurricane Carrie describe conditions that were dreadful but no worse than in earlier accounts involving *Pamir* in which heavy weather was portrayed as a relatively prosaic affair. Further complicating matters is the question of accuracy, as vividly illustrated by the discrepancy between two survivors' accounts regarding wave height, but the *Pamir* was no stranger to heavy weather. Every stage of her diverse career involved exposure to fierce weather: the nitrate run to Chile around Cape Horn, the Australian grain run through the westerlies of the Southern Ocean, and the transpacific routes during World War II all entailed heavy-weather sailing. Villiers commented: "Those ships were built and rigged to *use* storms." Some entries from the *Pamir*'s log during her New Zealand years convey the vessel's ability to handle weather:

> By midnight the glass started to fall rapidly. At 0130 high sea and wind over Force 12. What sails I had were blowing out. At 0200, the glass being 28.86, the wind blew steadily over Force 12. Although a tremendous sea was running, the ship behaved wonderfully, although she unfortunately flooded all the accommodation. *(Mid-Pacific, 1945)*

> Tropical hurricane blowing well in excess of 100 knots by 0600 hours. Blinding rain, visibility nil. Inner jib and main topmast staysail blew to ribbons. Huge confused seas. Whole side of ship submerged. *(Near the Cape Verdes, 1947)*

> Glass dropping quickly. Snow falling. Reducing sail. 1515 hours: ship laid on beam ends by hurricane force squall. Midships accommodation flooded by terrific seas. *(Southern Ocean, 1949)*

A trainee described his travails aboard the *Pamir* in the Southern Ocean on the run from South Australia to Cape Horn:

> We had large seas coming aboard the week before, but now the amount of green water pouring onto the decks was phenomenal. Just before dark a terrific squall hit. An immense sea accompanied it, which crashed over the entire ship, stoving in the mess room skylight and flooding our quarters. . . . Immense seas kept both the after and foredecks completely immersed.

The narrator's tone is almost humorous when he later describes the experience in the Atlantic Ocean, including an encounter with a tropical hurricane, as "enjoyable when compared to the run from Australia to Cape Horn."

If hurricane forces alone were sufficient to doom the *Pamir*, she should have sunk, on average, once every two years in the late 1940s. It is safe to say that most present-day adherents of tall-ship sailing would not be interested in facing such conditions even once, let alone over and over again. Yet the record shows that severe weather was a routine experience that *Pamir* was well suited to endure, whatever the discomfort to those aboard. Villiers shared his view of the casualty:

> Taking a dispassionate look at the record, knowing the ship, one may think that if the *Pamir* had not been badly laden, if she had not a vulnerable engine room for her unnecessary power, if she were officered and manned from that reservoir of the bred and trained Cape Horn men which used to exist in Germany, then she never would have been overwhelmed by a hurricane in the North Atlantic no matter how vicious or oddly behaved.

While even the weakest hurricane is no trifling affair, Hurricane Carrie is not described as particularly deep or powerful. Though it is not out of the question, the idea that weather alone was responsible for the vessel's demise is not well supported by what we know. Therefore, what was different about the *Pamir* in 1957 that might have changed her ability to withstand the same sort of weather that she had stood up to so magnificently in the past?

The Human Factor at Sea

Any discussion of the choices, decisions, and actions of people in a casualty is a delicate business. But the choices and actions of others are precisely what seamen need to think about while asking themselves what they would do under similar circumstances.

The precise licenses and endorsements held by the officers aboard *Pamir* are buried deep in the investigation file and do not concern us especially. As an officially supported, high-profile maritime-training project, there is little doubt that those aboard were duly certified to operate the ship in their respective capacities; there was no evidence of any sort of license deficiency. But while there is no discrepancy regarding the paper credentials, hands-on experience is a different matter.

Neither Captain Diebitsch nor the chief mate, Rolf Koehler, was a novice mariner, but when measured against the career officers of a generation earlier, it is apparent that they and others aboard lacked equivalent exposure to the operation in which they were engaged—namely, deep-sea cargo carrying in square-rig. This is not surprising, nor does it necessarily mean that they were improperly equipped for the job.

Years earlier—under Laeisz, Erikson, and in other fleets—everyone started at the bottom, and each promotion followed extensive experience in the position beneath it. The position of master was usually attained only after a long tenure as chief mate, frequently in the very same ship. Only the most senior skippers in a fleet were less constrained. This situation was in contrast to that aboard the *Pamir* at the time of her loss.

The chief mate on the *Pamir* in 1957 was exceptional in his lack of experience. He had no previous sea time in sail prior to joining the ship as second mate two trips earlier. Though Captain Diebitsch had showed a persistent interest in sail throughout his career, he was not immersed in it with the consistency of earlier generations of Cape Horn skippers. He started out as a ship's boy on the *Reigel* in 1911 and then was an able-bodied seaman (A.B.) aboard *Pamir* during World War I while the ship was laid up in the Canary Islands. He served as third mate in a four-masted barque for a period between 1920 and 1922, but this was the limit of his experience in sail with cargo, and it had come twenty-five years before commanding the *Pamir*. At another point he was chief mate in the school ship *Deutschland*, but this gave him no cargo experience. During World War II he served in the cruiser *Kormoran* and then spent time in Australia as a prisoner of war. After the war he made a deep-sea diving voyage in the three-masted auxiliary schooner *Xarifa*. Despite these significant episodes in sail, Diebitsch's career had nowhere near the depth that earlier masters of cargo-carrying four-masted barques typically possessed. Indeed, the inquiry did not shy from raising this point:

> Difficulties, which have existed for many years have influenced the manning of the vessel with master, officers and a nucleus crew. It is possible that an unfavorable effect was caused by the master's lack of thorough knowledge of *Pamir*'s special sailing qualities and her stability as well as by the Chief Mate's limited experience in sailing vessels.

Although diplomatically phrased, the meaning is unequivocal: lack of experience was a problem.

For a number of years reservations had been expressed, sometimes murkily, sometimes outspokenly, that the requisite level of skill and experience for operating such ships was rapidly waning. When Erich Laeisz declined involvement with the project, Captain Hermann Piening, his marine superintendent, explained why:

> Mr. Erich Laeisz, whose heart, of course, was still in sailing ships, was approached and we put our heads together. As I had asked already all of our skippers who had been masters in sail and made sure that none of them had a notion of taking on the job in either of the two barques on account of the lack of sufficient real sailors, and due to the proposed cargo operation of the ships, I thought it my duty to advise against it. Perhaps it was a pity that Laeisz did not join: they were in a better position to advise than any other

German owners, and the weight of their authority might have prevented what occurred.

Piening was not alone in his opinions. As early as 1953 Villiers wrote:

When I heard that the *Pamir* and *Passat* had been bought back from the breakers I was astonished. If those ships were worth sailing, then the House of Laeisz would sail them. If Laeisz were not interested, then I was very dubious about the whole thing. . . . So we watched the experiment with interest. But who would sail them? It is futile to find one man who will handle such a ship. There has to be a living tradition . . . a sufficient reservoir of competent seamen able and eager to serve. Those things have gone.

Years after the *Pamir* was lost, Villiers revisited the subject:

Pamir sailed for years in the Cape Horn trades, but with masters, watchkeepers, tradesmen and the essential nucleus of able seamen, dyed-in-the-wool, cargo-carrying, square-rigger men. On that last voyage, the *Pamir* had the best officers that could be found for her. There was some reluctance on the part of many experienced, former Cape Horn masters to join the ship. They had their reasons. Poor Captain Diebitsch had been in as much sail as he could find.

Although not unkind to Diebitsch, Villiers left no doubt that in his opinion the level of available experience no longer measured up to that which had gone before. The lack of interest on the part of more seasoned masters may well have reflected an appreciation that, indeed, even the very best captain cannot run a vessel properly alone. A sufficiently broad range of competence is required at every level. In Germany, retirement and casualties of war had greatly reduced the pool of old-school sailors by the 1950s. Those who remained were unmoved by romance; they knew better. While men of considerable expertise still resided on the Åland Islands from the not-yet-distant days of the Erikson fleet, the revival of the two P-Liners was an object of excitement and national pride in Germany. Their purpose, after all, was to serve the German merchant marine and Germany.

What happens when continuity is lost in a profession that is not quite yet extinct? Among other things, people improvise. Half-remembered and half-understood techniques are combined with available materials and whatever common sense is at hand. If a second chance is granted, people can learn from their mistakes. Let us consider an example of how the loss of continuity aboard the *Passat* and *Pamir* may have resulted in new approaches to an old problem: the securing of hatches for sea. Because Niels Jannasch sailed in the *Passat* under the Finnish flag in 1948–49 on the last voyage from Australia, and then again to South America under the German flag in 1952 after the conversion to sail training, he had a basis for comparing the respective methods of securing hatches.

1948: *Finnish Flag*	1952: *German Flag*
1. Wooden hatch covers were caulked.	1. Wooden hatch covers were not caulked.
2. Three tarpaulins were laid over the hatch, each carefully folded and the corners hand stitched in place, and then sewn to each cleat.	2. Two tarpaulins were used, not stitched in corners, nor to cleats.
3. The third and last tarpaulin coated with a warm mixture of tallow, fish oil, and pine tar.	3. Third tarpaulin was omitted.
4. After battens were placed, each wedge was nailed.	4. Battens placed and wedged, but wedges were not nailed.
5. Two-inch planks were placed fore and aft over the whole hatch.	5. Three wires were stretched fore and aft over hatch and tightened with bottle screws.
6. Three heavy wooden beams were placed across the hatch and bolted down to rings in the coaming.	6. Three flat steel straps were placed across the hatch, over the wire, and fastened to the coaming.
7. Buntline wire was stretched, with the help of the capstan, over the wooden beams.	7. The buntline wire was omitted.

The departure from traditional methods is evident, and one cannot help but surmise that a contributing factor in this change was a failure to appreciate what had already been learned through long experience. At the time of the inquiry into *Pamir*'s loss, Jannasch twice wrote the Court of Inquiry with his observations regarding the hatches and other concerns, but did not receive a reply. Although there were no specific allegations regarding the hatches, the comparison provides a good example of how traditional methods can come to be blended with newer ideas in a manner that does not necessarily bring better results. Upon returning from South America in the *Passat* in 1952, Jannasch wrote in a letter, "the red line of tradition has been broken."

So what actually went wrong aboard the *Pamir* that warrants this examination of shipboard experience? Our knowledge of the decision making and strategies employed is actually quite limited by the lack of survivors, but being caught close-hauled certainly put the ship at a disadvantage. An intensifying wind induced the greatest angle of heel, thus creating an opportunity for the loose grain to begin flowing. As a matter of interest, the very notion of being close-hauled in force 9 conveys something of the *Pamir*'s power and her ability to stand into strong weather. As the hurricane began to take control of the *Pamir*'s environment, the captain had two basic options. One was to run with the wind and the other was to heave-to. Each had advantages and disadvantages.

According to the inquiry, the fiercest winds came from the north-north-east. This means that the *Pamir* was in the *navigable semicircle* of the hurricane, with the eye to the south and perhaps already somewhat east and past the ship. The *navigable semicircle* is so named because when a hurricane is encountered at sea, it is usually the best position to be in. There are two reasons for this. One, the direction of the winds in the navigable side of the system are roughly opposite the direction in which the storm is traveling. This means the wind and seas will tend to carry a vessel away from and behind the path of the eye. The other benefit is that, unlike the *dangerous semicircle*, the wind strength in the navigable semicircle is not augmented by the forward motion of the storm system itself. While still ferocious, the winds are not as strong, nor do they carry a vessel along with the hurricane and toward its path. The prescribed avoidance tactic for a sailing vessel in the navigable semicircle (Northern Hemisphere) is to put the wind on the starboard quarter and get out of there. No matter how the hurricane behaves, this maneuver results in the ship and the eye of the storm moving in nearly opposite directions, opening the distance between them as rapidly as possible. The prescribed tactic for a ship in the dangerous semicircle is to heave-to and take all measures to avoid being carried into the path of the hurricane and so buy time for the threat to move on. That the *Pamir* was in the navigable semicircle is important because it means that, all things being equal, the option existed to leave the area. She was already on the starboard tack and had plenty of sea room in which to run, so long as she was still maneuverable. Once she was running, the heeling effect of the wind on the cargo would have been minimized, thus giving the crew a fighting chance at restowing. Running with the weather under such conditions would have made for a wild ride to be sure, but it was what the *Pamir* was built to do. Instead, the captain chose to heave-to. In retrospect this may not have been the best course of action unless, of course, it was for some reason the only choice available.

Heaving-to in the navigable semicircle not only contradicted standard practice, but it deprived the ship of maneuverability and exposed the hull and rig to the effects of pounding as she pitched forward into the head seas. This certainly could have contributed to an unintentional dismasting. In not

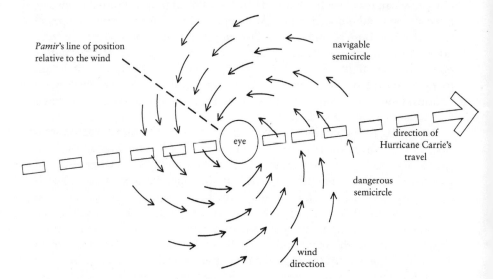

Pamir's line of position relative to the wind

navigable semicircle

eye

direction of Hurricane Carrie's travel

dangerous semicircle

wind direction

While we cannot know *Pamir*'s exact position relative to the eye of Hurricane Carrie, we do know she was experiencing north-northeast winds and was therefore in the navigable semicircle as the hurricane moved past her. (Source: G. Andy Chase, *Auxiliary Sail Vessel Operations for the Aspiring Professional Sailor*)

running before the storm, the captain did not open the distance between the ship and the eye as quickly as possible and instead risked a longer and closer encounter with the hurricane. But hurricane avoidance tactics are the stuff of midshipman's manuals and were surely no mystery to any blue-water captain, including Diebitsch. The matter of inexperience as it applies to this stage does not bear scrutiny.

Two reasons come to mind to explain a captain's decision to heave-to in the navigable semicircle of a hurricane. Running on the starboard tack may have taken the ship away from the worst of Hurricane Carrie, but it also would have amounted to sailing west, toward North America and away from the route to Europe. Had the *Pamir* run for twenty-four hours or so it easily could have taken her 250 miles to the west, miles she would then have to recover. Heaving-to may have amounted to as little as a 40-mile loss. A captain has a duty to try his or her best to make efficient passages, and there is a certain amount of pride that goes into accomplishing this. While one cannot blame a captain for weighing the consequences of running with the weather, if this was a consideration aboard the *Pamir*, it proved to be either arrogant with respect to the hurricane, or overly solicitous with respect to the company's schedule.

A second possibility is that the ship was unable to run away due to an extenuating circumstance. Such a circumstance might include a loss of stability almost immediately with the onset of the hurricane. The loss of sails or a portion of the rig would not have helped matters at this point, though it is possible to run under bare poles under most circumstances. For these reasons and maybe others the option of running may have been eliminated as quickly as it became necessary. While better seamanship might have preserved the sails, if the ship's stability was compromised abruptly and catastrophically, then heaving-to and broadcasting a Mayday may have seemed the only sane thing to do. Captain Diebitsch cannot then be faulted if it didn't work. We should also keep in mind that the earlier accounts of the *Pamir* in heavy weather predated her conversion to sail training. As a straight cargo ship the hull could be virtually submerged without water finding its way in. Modifications related to a large number of people living aboard for sail training, and the installation of an engine room, resulted in openings in the deck that had not previously existed. Although they presumably had closures, any type of hole represents a weak point in terms of watertight integrity.

What can be said in the matter of experience is this: mundane as the transport of grain by sailing ship may seem, there were right ways and wrong ways to do it, and those methods were long established. The carriage of bulk (not bagged) grain by sailing ship was a relatively novel departure from those methods. A command structure that understood this and the consequent vulnerability might have acted differently to effect a different outcome. A command structure that did not understand these things would have been at a disadvantage, and foul weather is just the sort of bad luck that finds these things out. So, while it is appropriate to consider the role of shipboard experience, no firm conclusions can be drawn.

The Human Factor Ashore

The inquiry agreed that by 1957 it had become difficult for mariners to accumulate the appropriate experience in cargo-carrying square-riggers, resulting in "an unfavorable effect." Of the incident, Villiers wrote: "No committee, no matter how splendidly led or widely based, can substitute for competent professional management."

Though we know little about the individuals and daily decisions behind the administration of the *Pamir*, the prospect of a diminished knowledge base within her shoreside management is entirely believable. Given the difference between sailing ship operations and modern freighter management, the atrophying of experience within the *Pamir*'s shoreside management is at least as credible as suggesting the same of her shipboard manning.

It is long established under admiralty law that the legal duty of a shipowner or shipowning organization is to provide a vessel reasonably fit for the intended voyage. Could it be that carrying grain in bulk affected the *Pamir*'s fitness for the intended voyage? The last voyage of the *Passat* may give a clue. Before hastily attributing the *Pamir*'s loss to structural failure, weather, shipboard inexperience, or some freak convergence of circumstances, we must first contemplate that two weeks after the *Pamir* was lost, the *Passat* nearly met the same fate. She had been modified in essentially the same ways as the *Pamir* and was conducting the same type of cargo operation. She was making the same homeward run from Buenos Aires laden with bulk barley and under the command of Captain Grubbe, an experienced Cape Horn master. The vessel encountered heavy weather, her cargo shifted, and she heeled over to angles up to 60 degrees. Knowing what befell the *Pamir*, Grubbe flooded his starboard ballast tanks to counteract the weight of the barley that had slipped to port, and by doing so averted disaster. The vessel was towed into Lisbon, where the cargo was restowed before continuing on to Germany. The *Passat* discharged her cargo and has not sailed since. This incident, taken in conjunction with the stability problem Captain Eggers experienced a year earlier aboard *Pamir* with a cargo of methyl alcohol, advances the issue of stability in respect to cargo operations under the management of Zerssen and Co. As Hurst pointed out, "*Pamir* and vessels like her—the *Passat*, *Moshulu*, *Herzogin Cecilie*, and so on had also been on their beam ends in past years without fear of capsize." We also know from the ship's log the type of conditions the *Pamir* had handled on other occasions. But that was years earlier, when the grain was carried in sacks. The movement away from sacks and toward bulk was a shoreside management decision that is well supported by economics but not so well supported by experience. Although other factors may have contributed to problems aboard the *Pamir*, the fact that the same fate nearly befell the *Passat* while commanded by a seasoned master under similar circumstances, and with no speculation of structural failure, loudly suggests that we consider the cargo and the manner of its lading.

Cargo: The Achilles Heel

The longshoreman's strike at Buenos Aires made for an inauspicious start to the voyage. But the decision to load bulk grain was made by prior arrangement, and the mate and master were powerless to alter it without creating considerable turmoil for what was for them an unfamiliar organization. Shoreside management scheduled the voyages, designated the ports of lading and discharge, and procured the cargoes, all on the assumption that the grain was to be loaded in bulk. At great expense the ship had been reconfigured for this type of operation, and several voyages had already been completed. But not everyone was convinced it was a good idea.

Captain Piening had advised Laeisz against involvement in the project not only because of concerns about available skill, but also due to the "proposed cargo operation." Piening, who is described as an "unimpeachable authority on the subject of square-rigged ships," had served as a mate in P-Liners before World War I and as master in the *Peking* and the *Padua* between the wars before becoming marine superintendent for Laeisz. Memos between Erich Laeisz and Piening confirm that the method of loading the P-Liners had always called for bagging the entire cargo and carrying 250 to 300 tons of ballast (usually sand) as well. Though variations certainly occurred, this approach remained the standard all through the Erikson years in the Australian grain run. The transition into bulk grain began in 1952 under Schliewen. Jannasch, who had served under Erikson, described loading loose grain in 1952 and then covering the entire hold in sacks as much as twenty layers deep to form a sort of lid over the loose stuff. By 1957 this method had given way to an even smaller proportion of the cargo being loaded in sacks. Leaving Buenos Aires in 1957, a mere 255 out of 3,780 tons of grain were loaded in sacks. Instead of covering the entire hold in sacked grain "several layers deep," the sacks were laid only in the area beneath the hatches and for several yards around "in a sort of a big hollow." By no method of reasoning can this technique be regarded as an effective countermeasure to shifting of loose grain on an oceangoing sailing ship, especially one heading out into hurricane season. Looking into the hold from on deck, however, even an experienced mariner would be given the impression that the contents of the hold were bagged.

Loose cargo is a concern because it can move and cause changes to a vessel's center of gravity. When a vessel is heeled by a wind, the contents of a hold will behave like a solid mass as long as they cannot move. Likewise, the liquid contents of a tank will act like a solid weight as long as the tank is completely full. If the cargo's center of gravity remains constant then so will the ship's. However, when the contents of a hold or tank are free to move, as with bulk cargoes, the center of gravity of the ship will move with the shifting weight, thus changing the stability characteristics of the entire ship. A ship may start a voyage with a bulk cargo such as grain evenly distributed, but if the roll of the ship exceeds the *angle of repose* of the cargo, it will slide under the influence of gravity, like sand down the face of a dune, resulting in a change to the vessel's stability. In the case of grain, the change may be gradual as the cargo exceeds its angle of repose a little at a time, but where liquids are involved, stability can change with every roll. This is *free-surface effect*. When a ship rolls and the cargo flows to the low side of the ship, it will act against the ship's desire to right itself, like adding weight to the low side of a seesaw. This free-surface effect applies to all manner of tanks, cargo holds, bilges, and even rainwater moving across the deck of a supertanker. The traditional practice of sacking grain was laborious, but it had the effect of compartmentalizing the cargo and arresting its tendency to flow. All ships experience some degree of free-surface effect in the course of a voyage as the contents of water and fuel tanks are consumed. If conditions and circumstances are extreme enough, a ship can most certainly be capsized this way.

An additional characteristic of grain is that it settles over the duration of a voyage. What starts out as a full compartment and therefore a solid mass will eventually settle and consolidate, leaving voids into which the cargo can begin to flow.

Basil Lubbock, another renowned authority on sailing ships, described his experience attempting to heave-to off Cape Horn in 1899 with a cargo of bagged barley in the full-rigger *Royalshire*. The *Royalshire* had not undergone the type of modifications the *Pamir* had with respect to engine room ventilation and alterations relating to accommodation.

> Over and over went the poor old *Royalshire*, until the lower yardarms were dipping into the whirl of broken water to leeward. The main lower topsail yard was almost straight up and down, and we hung on like so many frightened flies. . . . Was she going? After some terrible moments of suspense, we all felt that she had stopped going over and lay steady almost on her beam ends. . . . The hatches were half submerged and the lee side of the poop was under water.

But the *Royalshire* did not go. She rode it out and came into port safely.

In the aftermath of the *Pamir*'s loss, there was a legitimate concern that efforts to sustain or resurrect sailing ships would suffer unfairly from a flawed public understanding of the casualty. Alex Hurst wrote extensively on the subject and corresponded with many sailing ship captains, including Piening, in an effort to offset negative public perceptions. At one point he wrote in frustration:

> A great deal was written about this disaster, including a great deal of nonsense in the press, which held that sailing vessels were unsafe! There was a court of inquiry . . . at which a great deal was said, but . . . the root of the matter was hardly discussed at all. It is true that she had a relief captain who had not been in square-rig for years, but there was no evidence that he was at fault in his handling of the ship. The first officer was certainly limited in his experience and the question of whether the cargo was stowed properly was discussed. . . .
>
> The hard fact was that grain in bulk was known to be an unsafe cargo for a sailing ship and, for this reason, had never been carried. It was true that bulkheads had been fitted in the ships [but] they were not sufficient to prevent

shifting. If the [ballast] tanks had been filled with water, instead of barley (which is light anyway) it certainly would have mitigated . . . the disaster.

Responding to Hurst's articles on the subject, Piening wrote: "You have said it and there can be no doubt at all—the barley in bulk did it!" This view was affirmed by Ingemar Palmer, a former officer in the barque *Viking* on the Australian grain run under Erikson, and later a marine underwriter. On the issue of carrying bulk barley aboard the *Pamir* he simply said, "It was suicide. Complete suicide. You always put the grain in sacks." Carrying cargo under sail was not inherently dangerous, nor was carrying grain under sail, as centuries of practice show. What *was* dangerous was the manner in which it was carried on the *Pamir* during her last voyages, despite all that was known.

Decisions and Consequences

Acrimony is one of the first and most hysterical responses to any disaster, and the *Pamir* was no exception. The loss of the ship was a bad business that left no one involved better off. Even a cooler and more distant analysis does not paint a flattering picture of the decision making prior to the casualty.

Pamir had been retrofitted in 1951–52 with a 750-ton ballast tank to improve stability and therefore safety, particularly when no cargo was aboard and the ship was light. When the tank was not needed for ballast, it could be filled with cargo, as it was on her last voyage. Like the grain in the holds, the contents of the tank were subject to settling and shifting. The option to flood the ballast tank in an emergency always exists in theory, but this process is not instantaneous and may take hours to complete. We don't know the extent to which the ballast tank played a role in the handling of the *Pamir*, but with a loaded ship obviating the need for ballast in the usual way, a master would not be inclined to flood a cargo-filled ballast tank as a mere precaution. Of course, by the time a clear threat reveals itself, it may be too late. Using the ballast tank for grain complicated the master's decision as to when or whether to flood it, all of which was completely foreseeable from the moment the decision was made to use the tank for cargo. Thus it is possible that a feature installed to enhance the vessel's stability actually ended up blurring the line between unequal priorities, safety, and profitability. The master of *Passat*, as we know, did use the ballast tank to stabilize his ship when the cargo began to move, but that was with the knowledge of what had already befallen the *Pamir*.

Throughout the history of commercial sail, a wide variety of cargoes were carried by sailing ships as trades rose and fell with the fortunes of civilization. Each cargo had its own characteristics and specialized techniques for handling and stowage so as to minimize the risk to the ship and the venture. While casualty always was and remains an inherent part of seafaring, adherence to hard-earned rules of thumb could generally be relied upon to bring success, whereas ignoring them would likely have the opposite result. The fluidity of grain and its tendency to settle were characteristics understood long before 1957, even if the concept of free-surface effect was less widely appreciated. Unlike a sailing ship, motorized bulk carriers do not heel in their normal mode of operation. Although modern bulk carriers are not immune to cargo-related disaster, they get around the particular problem of free-surface effect and cargo shift by using specialized feeders to top off the holds as the voyage progresses. Careful management of partially filled tanks is also normal procedure. This was not necessarily the case in the *Pamir-Passat* venture. According to one critic, "That they survived as long as they did was by luck." Though several voyages had been successfully completed with bulk grain, this cannot really be considered a track record. Compartmentalizing grain in sacks was the track record. In the case of *Passat* on her last voyage, literally tons of barley were found to have seeped through the slits where structural members intersected.

Barley is less dense than wheat. A ship laden with barley is lighter and potentially less stable than a ship loaded with an equal amount of wheat, which is a denser cargo. Wheat was the predominant cargo coming out of Australia in the years when the method of lading was perfected in Cape Horners. Barley was not inherently dangerous, and *Pamir* did carry barley—in sacks—on her last voyage from Australia. Problems attendant to a light cargo had already been experienced by the *Pamir* in 1956, when the cargo of methyl alcohol sent the ship into port. All of this goes to say that a tremendous amount of knowledge existed, most of it learned the hard way at one time or another, about sailing ship cargoes prior to the loss of the *Pamir*. Though shipping was an increasingly technological enterprise, in 1957 there were mariners, shipowners, cargo brokers, and others walking the face of the earth who appreciated the nuances and fundamentals of transporting grain under sail. Knowing this, the inevitable question arises, how did this knowledge become disconnected from the operation of the *Pamir* and the *Passat*? This question was not pursued by the investigation.

It is a sad fact that the information needed to avoid disaster is often available but doesn't get where it is needed, and history unfolds accordingly. Given that the latest *Pamir-Passat* project had been going on for nearly two years at the time of the casualty, one can be skeptical that the problems of bulk grain in a sailing ship were not better appreciated.

However, grain in bulk is more economical. As a rule of thumb, a vessel can carry between 8 and 10 percent more grain in bulk than in sacks, not to mention avoiding the additional time and expense of bagging and handling. By whatever path the traditional method of loading grain was abandoned in this case—whether from arrogance, miscalculation, or wishful thinking—an inquiry that finds a lack of seamanship to be the heart of the matter misses the mark.

Whatever the quality of leadership aboard the *Pamir* and the *Passat* on those final voyages, the masters and officers participated in perpetuating a practice that was known to be unsafe in sailing ships by long international practice. Those aboard the *Pamir* paid a high price for the chance they took, if they even knew they were taking one. The fact that a precedent had already been set by earlier voyages may go some way toward explaining their actions, but Hurst offered up another angle: "If anyone argues that the master is responsible for his ship, then that person must answer what the master was to do, in direct defiance of his owners—in this case a powerful confederation of leading shipping companies in Germany."

Indeed, the decision to engage in bulk grain operations was made at higher levels—perhaps too high and too far from the sea itself. The enterprise received enthusiastic government sanction, and the vessels were approved for bulk grain operations by the German national maritime regulatory agency, *Seeberufsgenossenschaft*, and Germanischer Lloyd, Germany's preeminent and internationally recognized classification society. A finding that the ships were engaged in a practice known to be dangerous and that stability problems had already been experienced would have been awkward for the maritime establishment in Germany. The insinuation of operator error was less objectionable.

Captain Piening, who served as an assessor at the inquiry into the loss of the *Pamir*, took a dim view of the proceedings and described it at one point as "nothing but a scam." Naturally, he was extremely familiar with shipping practices and the concerns of owners and appreciated the subtleties of the case. He wrote:

> I think his [Diebitsch's] only guilt was leaving port with a ship loaded in that fashion, but he and other skippers had done the same thing before him and the owners (quite a bunch) . . . and the Board of Trade, had found no fault with it. The diverse owners had very likely figured the cost of x thousand bags plus the bagging and emptying [and found it] unbearable.

The most generous interpretation of the organizational decision making is that the operation of *Pamir* and *Passat* suffered from divergent and conflicting priorities. On the one hand there was the desire to keep the ships sailing and give cadets a valuable training experience that would benefit the

German merchant marine. On the other hand, there were the economic considerations of the cargo and the need to have the ships contribute to the cost of operation. A Cape Horner is not cheap to run, and public funding for such an enterprise can be difficult to defend. If the operation could be made more cost-effective through an innovation such as bulk grain, then the future of the ships for training would be more secure. What may have been overlooked is that, although bagging grain was obsolete on a properly equipped modern bulk carrier, the method was still correct for a sailing ship. But 8 or 10 percent additional cargo is no trifling matter. A statement to the press after the *Pamir* had already gone to the bottom of the Atlantic captures the hapless situation at Zerssen and Co. A spokesman for the company gave his assessment of the *Pamir*'s plight: "Capt. Fritz Dominik said that the 45 degree list the *Pamir* reported yesterday was not too grave. He expressed the belief that the crew might even be able to shift the grain cargo and restore the vessel to an even keel."

Even allowing for the lack of on-scene information, most mariners would agree that a 45-degree list bespeaks an alarming situation. Fortunately for the *Passat*, a few weeks later, Captain Grubbe took a less sanguine view of matters.

REPERCUSSIONS

Although seemingly ancient history now, the loss of the *Pamir* profoundly shaped the development of sail training, fundamentally changing its direction in ways that are still felt. Many older ships were retired in favor of purpose-built training ships. Cargo carrying was discontinued. Above all, public opinion had been heard and safety received renewed priority for such activities.

In the immediate aftermath there was significant anger in Germany, and the already tenuous commitment to traditional sail elsewhere suffered from the bad publicity. One article written at the time captured the mood: "End of Sailing Ships Urged: The loss of the *Pamir* has brought forth suggestion that the era of the German sailing ships be brought to an end. Commentators suggested that sailing ships, even in the role of training ships, exact too high a price in lives for this epoch."

This line of argument made no effort to discern between a particular incident and sailing ship activities as a whole. Nevertheless, in the world of public relations, absurd statements often have more impact than accurate ones. In Belgium, plans had already been approved and funding appropriated for a new sail training barque, but in response to the reports coming out of the Seeamt the Belgian administration "simply threw the whole scheme into the waste-paper basket." Nascent plans to restore and sail other large commercial sailing ships such as *Pommern*, *Moshulu*, and *Viking* were discarded, and *Passat* was quickly tied up for good. Though these older ships first would have had to pass a rigorous survey anyway, if only for insurance reasons, the shock of the *Pamir*'s sinking raised concerns among tall-ship advocates and their critics everywhere. Budgetary issues aside, government sponsorship for such activities was no longer a simple matter of goodwill and tradition. More than ever, such projects needed to be justified to a new community of critics on the grounds of safety.

With the other Cape Horners retired, only the *Padua*, the last of the Laeisz Flying P-Liners built, continued to sail after the loss of the *Pamir*. The *Padua* became a Soviet war prize and returned to sail training as the *Kruzenstern*. Now under the Russian flag, she is the last Cape Horner still sailing, though cargo has long since ceased to play a part in her operation.

The End of Cargo-in-Sail

The angst and hysteria generated by the loss of the *Pamir* eventually subsided, and sail training and the renaissance of traditional sail moved ahead, though in a changed world. The single most obvious consequence of the *Pamir* has been what appears to be a permanent unlinking of cargo and sail training. Though cargo-in-sail continues to hold out on a small scale where indigenous conditions allow, and talk of high-tech auxiliary-sail merchant ships accompanies each spike in the price of fuel, the *Pamir-Passat* project was the last gasp of cargo-in-sail as it was known. That it survived as long as it did was solely due to its relationship with sail training. Once cargo was divorced from sail training, it was divorced from sail. This is the practical legacy of the *Pamir*'s loss. In the immediate aftermath of the incident, public opinion discouraged others from trying. Gradually it became codified into law as regulations governing sail training emerged.

In recent years a number of former cargo-carrying square-riggers have been restored to sailing trim as a result of the general renaissance of traditional sail, but primarily as museum ships. None of them has carried cargo. Two barques in the United States, the *Elissa* of Galveston and the *Star of India* of San Diego, sail with volunteer trainees on a limited basis, but neither is certified to carry trainees commercially. Efforts are underway to sail the full-rigger *Wavertree*, in New York, and may yet come to fruition. In 1950, the *Pommern* was in Mariehamn in full readiness for a run to Australia when she was stood down from active service because the economic prospects were not favorable. Soon thereafter she was bequeathed to the city of Mariehamn by the Erikson family as a museum.

Because she transitioned directly from seagoing condition into a museum ship without leaving her home port or being modernized, she is considered to be the most authentic and intact Cape Horner in existence. As part of an initiative documenting the art of sailmaking, *Pommern* received a new suit of twenty-eight sails between 1984 and 1998 built by the hands of retired Cape Horn mariners and their local apprentices. There are, however, no plans to sail the *Pommern*, and no other organization has plans to carry cargo.

An exception is the barque *Picton Castle*, which has carried trainees on two global circumnavigations in 1997–99 and in 2000–2002. In a 50-ton cargo hold the *Picton Castle* carries trade items such as used bicycles, tools, clothing, and tires, along with school supplies and relief supplies for needy communities. Obviously, this is not cargo carrying in the traditional sense, nor does it represent a cargo training opportunity for merchant mariners, but it may prove to be a practical and safe way to reintroduce a cargo element and contribute to the solvency of a modern sail training voyage. Not only were trade goods used to advantage during the voyages of the *Picton Castle*, but a three-day pier-side sale in Lunenburg, Nova Scotia, at the end of the voyage is said to have doubled the original cargo investment.

Trainees and Sail Training

The loss of the *Pamir* is a sort of capstone on the age of commercial sail, an age that had already ended by the time she turned her hand to sail training. A subtle and indirect repercussion of this transition from commercial sail relates to the status and nature of trainees. Until the latter part of the twentieth century, trainees were almost universally regarded as entry-level professionals, and the experience they received was viewed as a necessary foundation upon which professional development depended. Lowly as it was, a trainee's relationship to the vessel was that of a professional seaman. Though not as true for government-operated training ships, in the years since removing the ancient link between cargo and sail, the sail trainee has in many respects evolved into a unique species of seagoing creature for which there is no historical precedent and no equivalent aboard motorized vessels. Unlike the exercises carried out aboard motorized training ships, the technical skills acquired through sail training have little direct connection to modern ships. Without any compelling practical use for sailing knowledge (even lifeboats no longer have sailing rigs), sail training in the postcommercial era is mostly justified in terms of its experiential value and its character building. In consequence, the practical status of the sail trainee has come to resemble that of a client or customer who is neither seaman nor passenger but something in between. This has ramifications for the two-way street of obligations and expectations that define the individual's relationship to his or her ship. Like crew, the modern paying trainee is expected to work, follow orders, and serve the ship. Like a passenger, the trainee is not expected to harbor professional seafaring aspirations or go into harm's way for the safety of the ship. Under such an arrangement, the credo "one hand for yourself, one hand for the ship" no longer applies. At some level the modern trainee expects a challenging but ultimately enjoyable experience, and sailing ships are designed, crewed, and sailed accordingly. Regulations affecting sail training in many countries incorporate legal definitions for sail trainees in an effort to clarify this relationship. In the evolving status of the sail trainee, the loss of the *Pamir* played a part.

LOOSE ENDS

Collisions between steamers and sailing vessels were common a century ago, in part, of course, because there were more sailing ships to run into at the time. But it also seems reasonable to suggest that officers who began their careers in steam had difficulty anticipating the behavior of a sailing ship because it was not part of their experience. Buttoned up inside a cozy wheelhouse, the second mate on a steamer would not feel the gust of wind that caused a barque to accelerate from 6 to 9 knots, or vice versa in a lull. The young steamer captain strutting the bridge might not appreciate that a schooner slogging along at 4½ knots close-hauled would step up to 8 knots upon clearing a shoal and bearing off, or that the opposite might occur when that same schooner ghosted into the lee of a headland. Collision avoidance would be very much hampered in such an environment where two traditions, one ascendant and one in decline but both equally professional and legitimate, were forced to coexist.

Perhaps similar logic can shed light on the case of the *Pamir*. Like the sailing ships of a half century earlier, the *Pamir* was overtaken by more modern approaches to doing business, including the bulk carriage of grain and the business of sail training. In the attempt to make her way in this new world, the *Pamir* was run down by the risks that come with obsolescence: a break in the continuity of experience, the mingling of new methods with old, and possibly plain old age. What was commonsense for one era was not so common for another.

The renaissance of traditional sail is not necessarily condemned to repeat this failure, but it will always have to grapple with the tension between being faithful to what is admired about the past while being open and accountable to what is expected in the advancing present. By definition, traditional sailing ships in the postcommercial age are shadowed by the conundrum of sailing in a fundamentally different epoch from that which they first existed to serve.

Since no remotely comparable incident has occurred since the loss of the *Pamir*, it would appear that the fleet of large square-rigged training ships is riding the tension between past and present successfully. The best that can be hoped for in the aftermath of such a casualty is that lessons are learned, and that the lessons learned are accurate. Unfortunately, this is only partially true for the *Pamir*, and the inquiry had much to do with it.

The Inquiry Revisited

A considerable weight of informed opinion found fault with the official inquiry into the loss of the *Pamir*. As one authority put it: "It was not a satisfactory inquiry, and I doubt if anyone was happy about it, if for differing reasons." Captain Piening, who participated in the process, was more forthright when he described it as "a scam." The inquiry specifically held that shipboard inexperience contributed to the casualty, but the proposal to carry barley in bulk was made by shoreside management with the approval of the owners and regulatory authorities. The inquiry was faulted in many quarters of the maritime community as much for what went unsaid as for what was said:

> There was no formal criticism of the authorities for allowing these vessels to load such unacceptable cargoes, and by implication *Pamir*'s crew came to be blamed for failing to take extreme actions similar to those of *Passat* to counter a situation in which neither ship should have been placed. The court also fails to mention that a hurricane can cause problems for all vessels, not just sailing ships, as shown by the loss with all hands of the modern large bulk carrier *Derbyshire* in 1980.

Although there may not be any reason at the moment for modern sail training to conduct cargo operations, this does not diminish the importance of deriving accurate conclusions from casualty investigations.

After any casualty, the inquiry is the linchpin that couples a problem to a solution. The failure to address adequately the decision to carry bulk grain or the question of structural failure undermined the credibility of this inquiry, even if elements of it were constructive. Whether or not one agrees with all of Willner's views, the appearance of his book disputing the inquiry almost forty years after the fact testifies to the way in which the perception of injustice becomes haunted by unstill ghosts. Policy that flows from a process so tainted lacks legitimacy. If tall ship safety is to evolve constructively and rationally, the link between casualty and policy must be faithful to the facts. Not only does the case of the *Pamir* provide a fascinating window into the evolution of sail from an ancient instrument of commerce to an innovative educational medium, it illustrates the implications for policy when an inquiry is perceived to be flawed.

Regulation

The downstream bureaucratic regulatory process is subject to the same fallibility as the inquiry, a situation not unique to incidents involving traditional sail. The move to separate cargo from sail training was a choice for safety, but that is not the same as saying it cannot be done safely. Nevertheless, eliminating cargo from sail training removes a potential conflict between economics and safety along with a host of variables that are vulnerable to human error: the longshoreman's lading; the bosun's securing of the hatches; the stability calculations of the master, mate, or the cargo superintendent ashore. Yet all marine operations involve variables that are subject to human judgment and choice. History shows nothing uniquely dangerous about carrying cargo in sail, and by extension in sail training ships, as long as proper procedures are followed. Both cargo and sail introduce variables that have to be understood and taken into account like all other variables associated with ships and the sea. If bulk grain was indeed the fatal flaw, then it was the very departure *from* tradition, rather than some quaint, misguided attempt at reenactment, that jeopardized the ship. Even the maritime court of inquiry agreed that in the future, grain aboard square-riggers should be carried in sacks. This conclusion was of dubious utility because, of course, there was no future for grain in square-riggers, and the court wasn't telling the world anything it didn't already know.

The point of focusing on this issue is not to suggest that we turn back the hands of time. The marriage of cargo and sail, which covers a wide range of possibilities, appears to be over for the moment. There are surely many practical reasons for this, but rationally speaking, the loss of the *Pamir* should not have been one of them. Yet it was, and this has important ramifications for the way in which regulations come into being. In a litigious world, marine regulatory bodies are tempted to protect themselves from liability by wielding the broadax of "safety," thus sparing themselves the trouble of understanding the distinctive characteristics of the maritime activities they are charged with regulating. Sail training associations have a crucial role to play in representing the unusual nature of their constituents. In the absence of effective representation, traditional sailing activities can safely assume that every attempt will be made by the authorities to squeeze them into a neat, prefabricated regulatory box that results in an exceedingly poor fit.

Experience and Risk

If inexperience had a role to play in the loss of the *Pamir*, then clearly it was not limited to shipboard leadership. Shoreside management and even the regulatory structure participated in the decision to load bulk grain. The broad assumptions articulated at the time about the *Pamir* representing the end of traditional sail due to a lack of "real sailors" have not been borne out by the passage of time. The traditions of sail may be attenuated at one level, but clearly they have survived and thrived at another. Traditionally rigged sailing vessels of all shapes and sizes have proliferated since that time. It is difficult to establish whether or not the depth of knowledge found in this field today exceeds what was available in 1957. The seamen of the time were closer to the source and certainly less technologically dependent, which cultivated a resourcefulness that was based on skill. They were, indeed, born to it. Yet the traditional sailors of today have greater opportunity, and they work in an environment that accepts the premise of keeping knowledge alive for its own sake. Refinements in equipment, ship design, and more conservative operations may compensate for lost skills so far as safety is concerned, but as instinct is rooted in repetition, other aspects of seafaring simply become lost.

In the matter of experience, the loss of the *Pamir* occupies a sort of crossroads for traditional sail. The tired and faded ranks of men who knew the sea as their heirs never will were reluctant to get involved in the renaissance of traditional sail partly because they didn't feel there were enough people of their own caliber to carry on. In stepping back, it could be said that they abandoned the field to the neophyte romantics of the world, thus dooming them to a painful process of rediscovery rather than facilitating a smooth passing of the torch. The process of rediscovery has involved more than reacquiring technical know-how. It has included the tuning of agendas and aspirations to a fundamentally different world from that the Grain Racers knew. The loss of the *Pamir* shifted the threshold of acceptable risk higher than it had previously been. In order for tall ships to flourish in the modern world, traditionalists have had to relinquish many things authentic and appealing about the bygone world that they have sought to sustain or re-create. One manifestation of this compromise is the need to reevaluate operations continually in light of the experience available to carry them out, and resist the temptation to indulge too much in another era while at the same time celebrating it.

In the pursuit of safety, the elimination of a single variable guarantees nothing. The potential for conflicting priorities always exists. The extent to which any duality of purpose can lead to problems is something tall-ship organizations must always be alert to, whether cargo is involved or not.

Watch Below

The loss of the *Pamir* was a devastating blow to efforts to perpetuate traditional sail beyond the age that first gave rise to it. In the hue and cry of the moment, voices railed against the dangers of old vessels, converted vessels, vessels whose purposes had been changed. It was said, and has been oft repeated since, that sail training could only be conducted safely aboard purpose-built vessels, solely dedicated to training. Right or wrong, each of these points speaks to concerns that are central to the renaissance of traditional sail and have been revisited often in the years since the *Pamir* was lost.

Operating a vessel like the *Pamir* in the old way required a consummate appreciation of capabilities and limitations, not only on the part of the masters, officers, and crew, but also the pilots, harbor tugs, longshoremen, insurers, managers, and owners—in short, the entire shipping industry. Even while the *Pamir* still sailed, Villiers remarked that "those things have gone." At the time, perhaps, that seemed to be the case, for there was no way of anticipating the revival of traditional sail that has unfolded since. Knowing what we know now, it would be more accurate to describe the period in which the *Pamir* was lost as the nadir, rather than the end, of traditional sail. In retrospect, her loss was more a turning point than an endgame.

The *Albatross* under nearly full sail with the Ocean Academy. Two deckhouses are visible, the forward of which contained the galley. Notice two substantial boats stowed amidships well above the deck. The starboard stunsail boom is visible above the course yard; its shadow is on the main staysail. (Courtesy Christopher B. Sheldon)

Albatross
1921–1961

BUILDER: Dutch Royal Navy Shipyard, Amsterdam

RIG: Gaff schooner, topsail schooner, hermaphrodite brig/brigantine

HULL: Riveted iron or "treated steel"

SAIL AREA: 5,000 square feet

LOA: 117 feet

LOD: 92 feet

LWL: 82 feet

DRAFT: 10 feet, 6 inches

BEAM: 21 feet

TONNAGE: 97 gross registered tons; 49 net tons

POWER: Caterpillar 100-horsepower diesel

FLAG HISTORY: Netherlands, Germany, Britain, Netherlands, Panama

*A*T THE TIME of her loss in 1961, the *Albatross* was home to the Ocean Academy, a sailing prep school. Aboard ship a small number of students received high school education and seamanship training while serving as crew on an extended ocean voyage under the supervision of the captain, Christopher Sheldon, and other instructors. Thus, the *Albatross* represents a very different type of vessel from the *Pamir*—and a new approach to sail training. Sail training for merchant marine and naval services was a long tradition that had waned but never ceased. The story of the *Albatross* shows how smaller tall ships began to bring the same valuable experience to people who never intended to make a living at sea. Although fatal for the *Albatross*, this new direction has helped fuel the growth of traditional sailing activities, and in the process gave many old ships a new lease on life.

The *Albatross*'s mission was progressive but not necessarily ground-breaking. Other programs had endeavored to combine educational curricula with an intense shipboard experience. Although much more structured academically, the Ocean Academy was in some respects a descendent of Irving and Exy Johnson's model of sail training as conducted aboard the *Yankee* in a series of circumnavigations in the 1930s, '40s, and '50s. Documented in *National Geographic* magazine as well as in the Johnsons' own books, the voyages generated considerable interest in what we would now call *experiential education* or *adventure learning*. Like the *Yankee*, the *Albatross* was a North Sea pilot schooner, much smaller than ships of *Pamir*'s ilk. The *Yankee* and the *Albatross* were owner operated: the owner also sailed as master. Neither vessel carried cargo in the customary sense. Both vessels carried young people and, though navigation and seamanship were integral to the experience, neither program was dedicated to the vocational training of aspiring professional mariners. Both enterprises were motivated in part by idealism, thus sharing a kinship with the nonprofit foundations that are the organizational backbone of today's sail training fleet. The *Albatross*'s stock in trade was the educational and experiential opportunity of a lifetime.

Although the *Albatross* was registered as a Panamanian yacht at the time she sank, both the ship and the Ocean Academy were closely linked to the United States, making this essentially an American case. Ultimately the sinking had resounding repercussions for the practice of traditional sail, primarily through the development of sailing school vessel regulations in the United States.

There was no formal investigation of the sinking, but the survivors were landed at Tampa, Florida, where U.S. Coast Guard officials gathered the relevant details. The brief report issued included the following: "It is noted that there is no apparent Coast Guard jurisdiction to investigate a casualty for a foreign flag vessel operating in international waters, but in view of the fact that the entire crew and passengers aboard the vessel were American such investigation as was practical was deemed appropriate."

In the absence of a formal investigation, the background for this incident must be drawn from a variety of less conventional resources, both published and unpublished. What emerges, nevertheless, is a clear picture of how the casualty evolved.

The tragedy of the *Albatross* was a sensational story line for journalists at the time, but it quickly dissolved into obscurity. By 1980 few of the young watchstanders on U.S. tall ships were familiar with the event. Then

Hollywood came to the rescue with *White Squall*, a 1996 feature film based on the *Albatross*. The film did not fare well at the box office, but it revived the incident for the tall-ship community and ultimately prompted Captain Sheldon to break his long public silence on the subject. Though Hollywood took predictable liberties with the movie, Sheldon noted that *White Squall* portrayed reasonably accurately how young people responded to the intensity of the sea and the shipboard experience through teamwork, leadership, and maturity. The vessel used in the film was the brigantine *Eye of the Wind*, built in Germany in 1911 and sharing the *Albatross*'s rugged North Sea lines. Chuck Gieg, a student who survived the sinking and was closely involved with the script for *White Squall*, noted that the *Eye of the Wind* was bigger, "but the stern section, right down to the rivets and taffrail, were eerily close to the *Albatross*." Sheldon commented wryly, "At least they got the right ship for the job."

THE HISTORY

The *Albatross* was built in 1921 at the Royal Navy Shipyard in Amsterdam. She went by the Dutch spelling *Albatros* until Sheldon anglicized it when he bought her in 1958. She was one of ten in a class of pilot schooners built between 1914 and the early 1920s. Well conceived for the rigors of North Sea service, the class compiled an excellent record for seaworthiness. According to Irving Johnson, "While one of these ships was on duty, no excuse ever brought her back to port."

Ernest K. Gann owned the *Albatross* from 1954 to 1958. Gann assembled much of what is now known about the vessel's early history at the time he acquired her in the Netherlands, near where she worked for much of her life. Gann compiled his findings in a small booklet for the enjoyment of guests, and it remains one of the only concise sources of information regarding the early years of the vessel. In the booklet he described her pilot schooner appearance:

> Originally she was a straight schooner rig with fore and mainsail loose-footed to the booms. The decks were almost entirely clear except for two boats used by the pilots for boarding their customers, and three hatches for entrance below. There were no deck houses. Air tanks were provided between the twelve bunks and the outer skin, to make her unsinkable in event of collision. These tanks are still an inherent part of her structure. A more than ordinary number of watertight bulkheads and doors were provided for the same reason.

This description confirms the impression that the *Albatross* was well designed to carry out her intended purpose. Gann also addressed the quality of her construction:

It has been fairly well established that no expense was spared in her original building and outfitting. The hull plating and frames are much over-strength for a vessel of this size. Surveyors are of two opinions; one that she is built of iron, the other that she is treated steel. The riveted construction is the best proof that expense was certainly not a primary consideration. At time of commissioning her many belaying pins were of solid brass. These of course, were inevitably stolen, but her solid bronze chocks remain.

Heavy construction combined with a conservative sail plan is not a recipe for speed. However, milling about in the North Sea in the dead of winter waiting for a ship that needs a pilot was no trifling task. It called for a sturdy vessel. Pilot schooners were station-keepers; therefore, speed was secondary to the ability to keep the sea in all manner of weather.

Not much is written about the *Albatross* as a pilot schooner, but Gann's account offers insight into her life and her seaworthiness:

> She was at sea and did survive a famous storm in the early thirties, which devastated the entire Netherlands. Winds of over a hundred knots were reported during this blow. At this time she must have been entirely dependent on her sailing qualities, for her screw was on the port side and her engine was a feeble two cylinder affair which would only have been of dubious reliability.

Clearly, the synthesis of rig, hull, and seamanship served the *Albatross* well under fierce conditions.

In 1937 the Dutch Pilot Service sold the *Albatross* to the German government and she was remaned the *Alk*. In Hamburg she was repowered with a centerline MAN engine. Captain Sheldon once described a chance encounter with Count Felix von Luckner in Lisbon in 1958 shortly after acquiring the *Albatross*. Von Luckner was the illustrious Sea Devil and master of the full-rigger *Seeadler*, a sailing commerce raider in World War I. While visiting aboard the *Albatross* von Luckner recognized the main engine. "Hah!" he declared, "That engine is built to withstand depth charges!" He was correct, for that type of engine had been used in German U-boats. Under the terms of the Treaty of Versailles that ended World War I, Germany was restricted from redeveloping its submarine capability. One response to this restriction was to fit nonmilitary vessels with U-boat engines, including a number of sail training ships. This clever ruse enabled the German navy to continue testing engines and training engineers while abiding by the letter, if not the spirit, of the treaty. It may well be that the *Albatross* (as the *Alk*) was used in this way. Gann's narrative claims she was "ostensibly used as a training ship for U-boat navigators."

During World War II the *Albatross* operated in the South Atlantic and served as a U-boat radio direction-finding (RDF) station in various parts of the Atlantic. She eventually returned to Hamburg and remained there until the end of the war.

At the close of World War II the *Albatross* was seized as a war prize by the British. The same fate befell a sister ship, the *Bestebaer*. The second of the same class to be built, the *Bestebaer* is still sailing as the school ship *Tabor Boy* for Tabor Academy in Massachusetts.

Yet a third North Sea pilot schooner underwent a similar change of hands at the close of the war and was purchased by Irving Johnson to become his second *Yankee*.

No new notable career emerged for the *Albatross* while in British hands, and in 1948 the Royal Rotterdamsche Lloyd Steamship Line purchased her back for sail training. Restored to the Dutch flag and her old name, the *Albatross* was extensively overhauled to serve as a sail training ship for "young officers and prospective seamen" seeking careers with the company. Gann documented the work Rotterdamsche Lloyd did to the ship: "In 1949 they spent over $25,000 reconditioning her for that purpose, and since this was a considerable amount at that time . . . she became a pet of the organization. Two new suits of flax sails were made, a yard was added to her foremast, and once again she put to sea with trainees."

Between 1949 and 1953 the *Albatross* made routine training cruises throughout the waters of western Europe from her hailing port of Rotterdam. However, before long even the most ardent supporters of the concept were hard pressed to justify the expense of operating a sail training vessel while running a modern shipping company:

> Sail training, for young Dutch seamen at least, was doomed to end. Machinery and electronics were considered of more practical benefit to prospective seamen, and even the fabulous ninety year old chief executive of the Rotterdamsche Lloyd, who still attended his office everyday, and who originally sponsored the *Albatros*, could not save her. Her fate was sealed when, much to the old Dutchman's distress, it became nearly impossible to find young candidates who were willing, or even mildly interested, in serving out their apprenticeship aboard a sailing ship.

Rotterdamsche Lloyd abandoned sail training with reluctance, and the *Albatross* was laid up in a Rotterdam canal until Gann found her in 1954. Within a few years a vibrant traditional sailing community began to flourish in the Netherlands, but this resurgence had not made itself felt yet.

A New Life

Ernest Gann was a self-styled adventurer, sailor, actor, barnstormer, commercial aircraft pilot, and a best-selling novelist. He was piloting for Matson Airline when that storied Pacific shipping firm ventured briefly into transpacific air travel. Shortly after acquiring the *Albatross* in 1954, Gann placed her under Panamanian registry and sailed with "a crew of amateurs" across the Atlantic and on to San Francisco through the Panama Canal. Years later he recounted his adventures with the *Albatross* in a book, *Song of the Sirens*, which documents his love affair with the sea through a series of watery autobiographical vignettes.

The following year the *Albatross* underwent an extensive rerig and refit in anticipation of a role in a film based on Gann's best-selling novel, *Twilight for the Gods*. The work was done at Moore Shipyard in Alameda, California. The modifications transformed the vessel from a simple fore-and-aft schooner with a single yard on the foremast for deck-setting square sails into what was described as a brigantine, though in fact it was a hermaphrodite brig. The converted *Albatross* carried a course yard, lower topyard, upper topyard, and topgallant yard on her foremast. She was fore-and-aft rigged on the main mast. As customary, the two uppermost yards were hoisting yards. Unlike the earlier deck-setting sails, which could quickly be dropped to the deck, the new square sails were permanently bent to the yards in traditional trading fashion. These new rig components were, of course, accompanied by the usual running gear and standing rigging necessary to handle the sails and support the spars. As normal with the rig type, the upper topsail and topgallant were generously cut for light-air sailing, thus placing a large proportion of the total square sail area in the upper half of the foremast rig. Between the masts two staysails replaced the gaff foresail. The result was a handsome, well-proportioned rig that would have been familiar to many old-time sailors.

Other modifications made during this period in the San Francisco area also contributed to an upward drift in the *Albatross*'s center of gravity. A galley house was constructed on deck just forward of amidships. Two heavy, clinker-built ship's boats approximately 13 feet long were placed upon a gallows frame about 6 feet above the deck. At the time of the sinking, these boats contained the additional weight of sailing rigs as well as food and water for fourteen days.

Photographs from the period of Gann's ownership show a second deckhouse aft of the mainmast. How and when this was constructed is uncertain, but it seems likely to have been the product of an earlier renovation under the Dutch or German flag. However it came to be there, the original pilot schooner is described as having "no deck houses." The deckhouses, the boats, and the rig expansion together created a legacy of significant changes. These modifications were undoubtedly seen individually as improvements, but in transforming the *Albatross* from an exceptionally conservative schooner with a narrowly defined coastwise mission into a lofty brigantine accompanied by aspirations for ocean voyaging and moviemaking, there were unintended consequences. Left uncompensated,

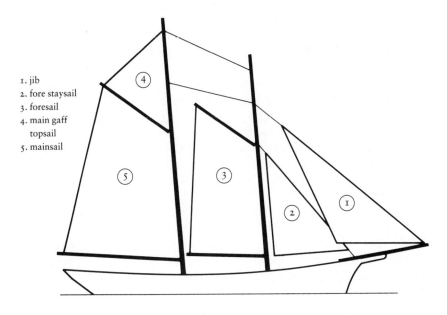

1. jib
2. fore staysail
3. foresail
4. main gaff
   topsail
5. mainsail

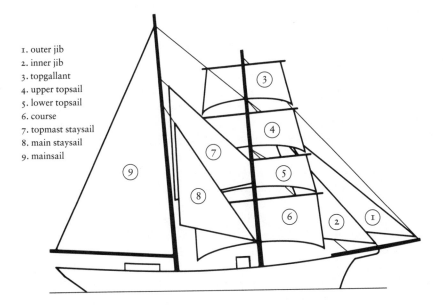

1. outer jib
2. inner jib
3. topgallant
4. upper topsail
5. lower topsail
6. course
7. topmast staysail
8. main staysail
9. mainsail

Albatross's rig conversion from a North Sea pilot schooner *(top)* to a brigantine (hermaph-rodite brig, *bottom*). The original gaff mainsail rig was replaced by a marconi rig in 1958. (Jim Sollers, based on sketch by Howard Chatterton)

such changes would have a grave effect on any vessel's stability, yet there is no record that countermeasures were implemented.

After the work on the *Albatross* was completed, inclining experiments were performed at Moore Shipyard by a naval architect, W. P. Hincks. The tests indicated that, indeed, the center of gravity had risen. The vessel's *metacentric height* (GM) had diminished from 2.81 to 2.02 feet (see Stability section in the appendix for details on metacentric height and center of gravity). Whether Hincks, Gann, or anyone else involved ever commented on these figures is not now known. Since no steps were taken to counteract the effect of conversion, it's reasonable to assume that the new metacentric height was deemed acceptable. Metacentric height is an important measure of stability, but its usefulness is limited to measuring *initial* resistance to heeling forces. It does not shed light on a vessel's performance under more extreme angles of heel or her point of no return.

The results of the work were evidently pleasing. The accommodation and galley were better laid out for voyaging. The increased sail area gave her better performance in light air, and the new square sails were well suited to long trade-wind passages. The inclining tests indicated that "in a 25-knot wind she would heel so that her deck [edge] was level with the water with all sail set." Gann wrote later, "This was subsequently proven to be a surprisingly accurate prediction." We do not know what point of sail (which has significant bearing on the angle of heel for a given wind condition) the prediction was based on, nor did Gann specify the point of sail at the time of his observations. Going to windward will generally induce the maximum heeling moment. The speed of the vessel combines with the speed of the wind, creating a maximum apparent wind, and with the sails sheeted in toward the centerline, the heeling energy is at its greatest. In contrast, when sailing downwind a vessel will sit virtually upright because the wind is no longer coming from the side. A person on deck will feel considerably less wind because the ship is moving with it. Naval architects typically base stability calculations on a beam wind with the sails sheeted in flat, but Gann's comments may have applied to windward performance, which would be the best test of initial stability and general responsiveness to heeling forces. The forces required to induce *deck edge immersion* are of interest because that is the point at which a vessel's ability to resist heeling forces begins to diminish. Deck edge immersion is also the point by which sailors in large-displacement hulls generally reduce canvas. Under the conditions described, it would appear that the converted *Albatross* stood up well under fresh conditions with full sail, and thus felt very solid. Gann had at least one heavy-weather experience in the *Albatross* in the Pacific Ocean and felt the vessel performed well. He praised her seakindly qualities often in *Song of the Sirens*, writing, "our decks seemed as steady as a liner's." But such a feeling does not always equate with a stable ship.

In 1956 the *Albatross* voyaged from San Francisco to Hawaii and French Polynesia. This was another adventure cruise made with a crew of friends and acquaintances. The voyage ended back in Honolulu in December 1956, where the vessel remained for the rest of the year. In March 1957 she rode out a famous tsunami at Honolulu: "*Albatross* and another large yacht took their finger piers with them, damaging several small boats nearby. Surges associated with this tsunami lasted for 30 hours after the initial wave and the wave height was estimated at 32 feet at Pololu on the Big Island." The *Albatross*, it turns out, suffered no more than a broken whisker stay.

Twilight for the Gods was filmed in Hawaiian waters during 1957. Gann had sold his screenplay to Universal Pictures on the condition that the *Albatross* be chartered for the filming and that he be captain. Since he was not licensed for Hawaiian waters, a "paper captain," George Atcheson, was hired as mate. The newly rerigged *Albatross* made for a sufficiently dramatic movie set. The plot called for the ship to burn and be scuttled. At great effort several tons of cement were loaded aboard to create the impression of sinking while smoke billowed from the decks and the sails hung in tatters. After the filming the ship sailed back to the West Coast. In San Diego the gaff mainsail was replaced by a *marconi*, or jib-headed mainsail without reef points. The *Albatross* carried on to Europe, visiting England and Norway before arriving in Copenhagen for the wedding of Gann's eldest son. It was Gann's intent to put the ship up for sale upon completion of the film, and in late 1958 he sold her to another American, Captain Christopher B. Sheldon.

A Return to Sail Training

Captain Sheldon took possession of the *Albatross* at Lisbon. Sheldon hailed from Connecticut and had been looking for a suitable vessel with which he and his wife, Dr. Natalie Alice Sheldon, could launch an innovative shipboard educational program known as the Ocean Academy. Sheldon had sailed from a young age before embarking on an extensive academic career. Then, at the age of thirty, he completed a circumnavigation on the *Yankee* with Johnson. A year later he bought the *Albatross*. Sheldon was smart, he had been around the world with a master in the trade, and he knew what he wanted to do with the *Albatross*.

Though the *Yankee* was larger and somewhat different from the *Albatross*, both were North Sea pilot schooners of a proven design. Both had been modified to carry square sails, and both had been sailed extensively offshore with crews of mixed experience. Based on what was known, a decision to put the *Albatross* to work in blue-water sail training might be taken with a high degree of confidence in the vessel's ability to execute. That she had been used for sail training under Rotterdamsche Lloyd further supported her suitability for Sheldon's purpose. By 1958 she was a very different vessel, however.

The newly purchased *Albatross* came with the stability data commissioned by Gann and approved by Hincks after the rig conversion. Years later, Sheldon reflected on his acceptance of the data:

> When I bought the ship, after he had converted her into a brigantine, Ernie Gann said he'd had stability tests on it and he showed me the figures. I did not take the figures to a naval architect. I just accepted his word.

Although the vessel had performed satisfactorily up to that time, and her stability was approved by a naval architect, there was much that was not known about the cumulative effects of years of changes. Among other questions, no one knew how the ship might handle an extreme angle of heel. The scope of voyaging proposed for the *Albatross* with the Ocean Academy did not differ significantly from that for Gann's cruises: temperate latitudes in summer, tropical latitudes in winter, and avoid the hurricane season between. The main difference lay in that, under the Ocean Academy, the voyages involved young students on a program, rather than pleasure cruising with friends.

Sheldon's concept of the Ocean Academy was rooted in his own experiences aboard school ships and was designed with his and his wife's special qualifications in mind. Sheldon was thirty-three years old when he launched the Ocean Academy. He had an impressive academic background, with degrees from Princeton Theological Seminary, the University of Lima, and a doctoral degree in Spanish from the University of Madrid. His wife was a Cornell graduate and a physician who had also sailed aboard the *Yankee* as ship's surgeon. In addition to Captain Sheldon's experience with the *Yankee*, in 1941 he had been a student on an earlier sailing school vessel, the schooner *Morning Star* out of Annapolis. The Ocean Academy drew upon each model: as a school, the program incorporated the academic structure of the coastwise program aboard the *Morning Star*, but as an oceangoing venture it embraced the extended voyaging and exotic destinations for which the *Yankee* was renowned. Naturally, the project was infused with the Sheldons' own vision, as well as the unique contributions of each participant. Shortly after the fatal voyage, Sheldon described the program in the following terms: "What we had was a sort of apprentice system, which has existed for centuries, mostly in Europe, where boys pay to learn to sail and learn the sea. We were actually a tutoring service, with apprentice seamen. I did not think of the boys as passengers, but as crew."

The Ocean Academy was geared toward high school students, many of whom came from private schools. The Ocean Academy advertised in *National Geographic* and elsewhere. Captain Sheldon taught Spanish, navigation, and seamanship; Dr. Sheldon taught biology. The remaining professionals consisted of George Ptacnik (cook), Richard Langford (English teacher), and John Perry (math teacher). Fourteen students aboard made a ship's company of nineteen. Although mastery of maritime skills was integral to the experience, the Ocean Academy was not manifestly a vocational training course but rather an interdisciplinary academic program for mostly college-bound high school students. Its concept of an academic curriculum combined with nautical studies and the physical demands of seamanship remains the model for many sail training programs today.

Upon taking ownership of the *Albatross*, Sheldon made a shakedown cruise from Lisbon through the Mediterranean, the Red Sea, down the coast of East Africa, around the Cape of Good Hope, and on to the United States. The *Albatross* remained under Panamanian registry, but Mystic, Connecticut, became her home port, while the Ocean Academy maintained an address in Darien, Connecticut. Because the *Albatross* was a foreign-built hull, the Jones Act barred her from carrying passengers under the U.S. flag (the 1984 Sailing School Vessels Act later exempted sail training ships). Under a foreign "flag of convenience," such as Panama's, it was—and still is—possible to carry American passengers without meeting U.S. regulations, as long as the ship does not operate from U.S. ports. At the time, no U.S. Coast Guard regulations accommodated operations such as the Ocean Academy. Even the *Yankee*, another foreign-built hull, was forced to use increasingly creative legal arrangements to conduct her voyages in the 1950s for the same reasons. Only by special federal dispensation did the *Yankee* carry on as long as she did under the U.S. flag.

Under the *Albatross*'s new ownership, modest adjustments were made to the below-decks layout to facilitate her role as a school ship. The modifications made by Gann above decks were retained, and with good reason. For training purposes, a brigantine rig is far superior to a gaff schooner rig. Square sails are more labor-intensive and demand more teamwork than self-tending fore-and-aft sails. The greater manning was a factor in the demise of square rig, which for the most part preceded the decline of the coasting schooners. Most fore-and-aft schooners have boomed sails that self-tend on travelers, leaving only headsails and a few kites, if fitted, for the crew to handle. Square rig, however, involves bracing the yards around for each new tack, plus the tremendous amount of work aloft shaking out and furling square sails, as well as the additional maintenance of the gear. On a training ship, where hands are generally plentiful, the more work, the bet-

The *Albatross* under the Ocean Academy. Late in Gann's ownership, the gaff-rigged mainsail was converted to a very handy marconi rig. (Courtesy Christopher B. Sheldon)

ter. Square rig is also superior to fore-and-aft rig for the trade-wind passages the *Albatross* expected to make. One of the key failures of the giant multimasted schooners built in New England and the Canadian Maritimes was that, whatever the manning economies they afforded, they performed poorly off the wind on long ocean passages compared to square rig. The *Albatross*'s brigantine rig was a superb choice for offshore sail training and voyaging.

Among other changes made under Sheldon, the old U-boat engine was replaced with a more modern and compact Caterpillar diesel. This new engine was considerably lighter. Sheldon estimated that there was a net removal of approximately two tons from the engine room in the process of upgrading. Of the old engine he said, "the flywheel alone weighed about 3,500 pounds." When the new engine was fitted, the ship was found to be down by the head, resulting in a need for ballast to bring the ship back to proper trim. Pilot schooners operating on the Dutch coast were often obliged to anchor and were well-equipped to do so. This may have contributed to the amount of weight carried in the bow of the *Albatross*, but the weight of the square-rigged foremast when combined with a relatively fine entry would have also contributed to a tendency to trim by the bow if not compensated for with weight aft.

Sheldon also added stunsails (studding sails) on the foremast, similar to the *Yankee*. This involved the placing of stunsail booms and additional ironwork, blocks, and running gear onto the forecourse yard, and a lesser amount of gear on the topyard. The sum effect of the added sails and the changed engine was to remove weight down low in the vessel and add weight aloft. Although these changes were relatively minor compared with those wrought by Gann, they added to the cumulative effect on stability. People familiar with both the *Yankee* and the brigantine *Albatross* have commented on how much less freeboard the *Albatross* possessed even though she was only marginally smaller. Film footage of the *Albatross* sailing during the Ocean Academy period clearly shows her rolling deeply and recovering slowly.

FINAL VOYAGE

The students joined the *Albatross* in Bermuda on 29 September 1960. The outward leg of the voyage took them to the Galápagos Islands by way of the Caribbean, Central America, and the Panama Canal. In the Galápagos the crew commemorated their visit by spelling out the date of their visit with stones beside a similar monument made by earlier visitors from the *Yankee*. On the homeward voyage, the vessel called at Progreso, Mexico, on the Yucatán Peninsula en route to the Bahamas. By now it was spring in the Northern Hemisphere, an auspicious time to transit the Gulf of Mexico before hurricane season. Leaving Mexico, the *Albatross* sailed north of the normal rhumb line so as to give Cuba a wide berth: regional tensions were running high with the collapse of the Bay of Pigs invasion only two weeks earlier.

Four days out to sea, on the morning of 2 May 1961, the *Albatross* entered an area of squally, unsettled conditions, not unusual for the tropics at any time of year. Winds had been light in the preceding days, and the vessel motored much of the time. Bill Bunting, the first mate, had the dawn watch and remarked that they had been "drifting for hours, not using our auxiliary engine in order to save a dwindling fuel supply." Sheldon also recalled the status of bunkers and water: "We were very low on fuel and [at] less than half our water supply. Normally we would have been motoring."

In early May in the Gulf of Mexico, nautical twilight (first light) comes at around 0430. Those on the dawn watch, therefore, had a chance to view the sky and developing weather conditions soon after coming on watch. The English teacher, Richard Langford, stood the dawn watch with Bunting and described lightning and "a long black squall line north of us" during the watch. He recalled making a log entry, "lots of celestial fireworks up north—squall coming." But he also later wrote, "We did not think it was dangerous, and hoped it might bring some wind." Bunting recalled distant lightning and sensed that the weather was deteriorating, but he described it as a "slowly gathering gray rather than a dramatic, dark, fast-moving squall line, much less the boiling clouds of a typical tropical squall." Nevertheless, he felt uneasy and was relieved when Captain Sheldon came on deck later in the watch with his sou'wester in hand, indicating that he intended to stay.

At about 0800, the change of the watch, a lone thunderbolt of extraordinary intensity struck close by the ship. Gieg wrote:

> There was a blinding blue flash, and all at once the air around us was filled with the sort of metallic acid smell that most people call ozone. . . . Skipper was as startled as the rest of us but he recovered instantly. "All hands stay out of the rigging and keep clear of the masts," he ordered sharply.

Bunting recalled the lightning coming out of a gray—not black—sky. The question of whether to take in the topgallant came up, but Sheldon quashed it: "Nobody goes aloft in this lightning." There was no obvious visual indication of wind in the offing, and the startling proximity of the lightning seemed to introduce an unnecessary risk to laying aloft. But a change was in the air, and many felt it. The change of the watch was duly executed at 0800. Bunting headed below for breakfast and Captain Sheldon stayed on deck. As Sheldon recounted later:

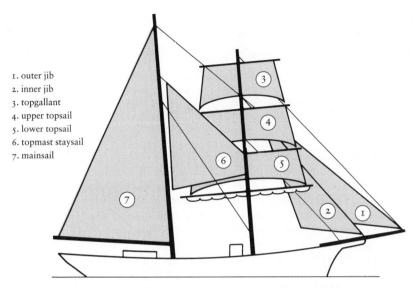

1. outer jib
2. inner jib
3. topgallant
4. upper topsail
5. lower topsail
6. topmast staysail
7. mainsail

Albatross's sail configuration at the time of loss. (Jim Sollers, based on sketch by Howard Chatterton)

There was some squall activity in the distance, and we had one crack of thunder and lightning fairly close to the vessel—but still no wind. And then the weather seemed to get brighter again. About 0830 a beam breeze came up and we set about 70% of our sails. We had everything up except the big forecourse and our main staysail.

Survivors' accounts vary slightly on the particulars of the sails set, but all reports agree that the *Albatross* was carrying close to full press of canvas in basically light conditions.

Although accounts vary, an hour or more into the watch it became apparent to those on deck that a squall was approaching. Sheldon described it:

I saw what looked like a light squall coming—just a grey uniform cloud approaching from windward, and we went into our normal procedure for squall activity. We had been through many squalls and we were used to them. We shut the hatches, all except for the main hatch, which was protected by a hood. I told the helmsman to put the ship off a point so if the squall hit us we would already be off the wind a little bit, and I myself went to the main sheet, ready to let the sheet out.

The sail plan remained unchanged. Sheldon later explained that the squall did not appear exceptionally threatening until it arrived, at which point it was too late to reduce sail.

There was no warning. She heeled us over to about 45 degrees immediately. I let the main sheet out but the boom hit the water and the mainsail did not spill. I sent crew members forward to cut the halyards on the mainsail and the staysails. The ship hesitated at a 45 degree angle and then just slowly sank down on her side and I remember thinking to myself, "she's just dying." That's the way it felt.

Survivor Chuck Gieg's account in *The Last Voyage of the Albatross* captures the same scene on deck in the vicinity of Sheldon and the helm:

... the sky had grown considerably darker; yet the wind hadn't changed much and there was still no rain. Then I heard someone call out: "Here it comes!" Several hundred yards away the surface of the water had taken on that telltale fuzzy appearance that means a heavy rain is coming towards you. . . . Then it hit in a solid sheet. With it came a slight puff of additional wind, and I saw Tod tighten his grip on the wheel.

The rain eased off after a few minutes and settled down to a steady drizzle. We began to heel over a little more sharply. Then, without any sign of warning we began to heel at an alarming angle, much farther than the sturdy old *Albatross* had ever heeled before. I saw Skipper head for the mainsail sheet to let out the boom and spill some air from the big sail[,] which seemed to be pulling us over.

I had been confidently waiting for the ship to right herself to get back on an even keel. But now I saw that she would never make it. The *Albatross* had heeled over to a ninety-degree angle and was lying flat on her side. The whole starboard half of the ship was under water, and so were her tall masts and all her sails. Her five thousand square feet of canvas, dragging in the sea, had brought our forward motion to a dead stop. . . . There was no logical explanation for what had happened to us with such terrifying suddenness.

The brevity of Sheldon's account captures the awful speed with which the capsizing occurred:

And in a few seconds' time it was all over. There was nothing we could do about it. The ship downflooded through the main hatch that was open and through several ventilators, and she filled very quickly and sank within 60 seconds.

Meanwhile, down below, where over half the ship's company was, a different hell was breaking loose. Books, canned goods, typewriters, scuba tanks, and all manner of objects that had in the previous seven months at sea shown no inclination to leave their assigned positions suddenly began to tumble about the living spaces. Water found its way in, slowly at first and then in torrents. Langford wrote, "Suddenly the *Albatross* lurched heavily to starboard and a thick stream of green water poured in on me." The ship heeled over until the walls were horizontal and ladders were positioned at crazy, unfamiliar angles.

Flying objects and disorientation were only part of the peril faced by those below. The most daunting task was fighting the tremendous weight and force of the ocean invading the same apertures that represented escape routes. Those strong enough and quick enough were able to haul themselves out against the water pouring through the open main hatch. But where hatches were submerged, the weight of the water against doors acted like a lock. A group of five students and instructors moved forward toward a closed hatch. Unable to swing the doors open, one of the students, Bob Brett, "broke the doors out by sheer strength." Several in the group were able to follow him. In the main cabin, where the largest hatch was located, the water rushing in was too much for some to fight. Daylight filtered down through the water and the submerged skylight, turning the cabin an eerie green.

Rick Marsellus, a student, had an idea to escape through the dumbwaiter shaft that led to the galley house on deck. Bunting, the mate, broke out the panel leading to the shaft and, with Rick and student Chris Corstine pushing on his feet, he was able to reach the deckhouse. Though still trapped inside, he had made it to deck level, with about a foot of airspace remaining. He battered at the deckhouse door in vain until a pocket of escaping air propelled him against it headfirst, "like a pile driver." Bleeding and barely conscious, he drifted up to the surface through the tangle of rigging and sails in time to see the last of the rig disappear beneath the waves. Rick and Chris were right behind, but time had run out. Back aft, Chuck Gieg and Tod Johnstone dove down alternately to try to open the charthouse doors. Gieg could feel the handle being turned from the other side, but the water pressure was too great and the ship was sinking too fast.

In the group that broke out through the closed forward hatch, Langford was last in line. His time was running out, and the compartment was rapidly filling with water. As the point approached where the spaces aboard the ship were nearly full of seawater, the pressure inside and outside the vessel equalized, and the force behind the torrent of inflowing water ceased. In the darkening interior as the ship plummeted through the water column, Langford discerned the outline of the hatch nearby and, taking a last lungful of air, made his way out. He reached the surface barely conscious from what he later estimated to have been forty feet down.

The *Albatross* sank approximately 100 miles north of Cuba and 180 miles west of Key West, Florida. Four students, George Ptacnik, and Alice Sheldon were lost. Christopher Sheldon believes that one of the students who perished, John Goodlet, became entangled while cutting the lashings on the boats. If so, his sacrifice was the salvation of the survivors. The U.S. Coast Guard report recounted events in the immediate aftermath of the squall: "The two life boats broke their lashings and floated free in a swamped condition. One of two inflatable life floats also surfaced as the

Albatross sank. The life float was inflated and used by the survivors until the life boats were bailed out. The survivors then entered the life boats and under the direction of Captain Sheldon set sail to the mainland of the United States." Whatever he may have been feeling at the time, Captain Sheldon pulled the situation together and kept it together. Later, he would visit the families of each of those who were lost.

The thirteen survivors were picked up at around 0800 the next day by the *Gran Rio*, a Dutch freighter bound for Tampa. The Bay of Pigs invasion two weeks earlier made the captain of the *Gran Rio* reluctant to take the castaways aboard. One student wrote, "They questioned us for about 30 minutes, then threw rope netting over and we climbed up." They were discharged at Tampa on 4 May 1961.

POSTMORTEM

There is no debate that the immediate cause of the casualty was the squall that struck the *Albatross*. Equally self-evident is that the vessel was unable to stand up to, or recover from, the gust. This is related to stability. But how strong was the wind, and how willingly did the ship lay over? Did other fac-

Rescued crew of the *Albatross* arriving in Tampa, Florida. (Burton McNeely/Timepix)

tors contribute to the ship's vulnerability to a knockdown? Given that she had sailed many thousands of miles as a brigantine, not all of it in good weather, we might be justified in concluding that the squall must have been of extraordinary power to lay low such a proven vessel—in other words, that it was an act of God. Another possibility is that the *Albatross* had a hidden flaw that required a special communion of circumstances to reveal itself. In the aftermath of any disaster we pore over the details in hopes of finding a clear explanation or an intimation of impending doom. It is almost a relief when some detail is uncovered among the evidence and the testimony that clarifies all. Since there was never an investigation into the *Albatross*, the best we can do is examine what is known and try to match it with what makes sense.

Structural Integrity

Structural failure is often considered a likely suspect in maritime casualties involving the rapid sinking of older vessels. The coast guard thought as much, as reflected in its report: "It is further noted that this vessel is some 40 years old. In view of the age of the vessel and the extreme rapidity with which she sank, it appears highly probable that a critical structural failure occurred in the hull[,] possibly in the way of the mast step or steps."

In the absence of background information, this was perhaps a reasonable supposition at the time. Given *all* the available information about the *Albatross*, however, structural failure due to age alone seems unlikely. Ships of all ages get into trouble for all sorts of reasons. It may be true that rust never sleeps, but structural problems have as much to do with construction, design, materials, and maintenance as with the mere passing of years. On balance it may be fair to say that an older hull is more susceptible to problems than a newer hull. Ships don't improve with age without a lot of help. Yet there are many examples of older vessels providing reliable service long past what some might consider possible, just as there are examples of new vessels foundering on maiden voyages. Although accurate comparisons are hard to make, there are some good examples.

The wooden cargo ketch *Ceres* was launched in Britain in 1811 and saw nearly continuous service until 1936, a span of 125 years. She is said to have transported military stores from Britain to Spain for Wellington's army during the Peninsular Campaign of the Napoleonic wars, yet she was still sailing the year Hitler remilitarized the Rhineland and placed all of Europe on a war footing. The *Maria Asumpta*, which we discuss later, was launched in 1858 and sailed continuously for 137 years. We also know that a multitude of hardworking wooden Baltic traders of the same period as the *Albatross* were still sailing decades past the forty-year point. Additionally, a number of North Sea pilot schooners of the same period as the *Albatross* were actively sailing at the time of her capsizing, thus indicating the longevity of those hulls. Many of the Maine passenger schooners continue to sail well past the hundred-year mark. In contrast, having been constructed with all the benefits of contemporary regulations, the yearling topsail schooner *Dayspring* foundered in 1985 on her way home to Maine from the Caribbean due to what was thought to be a sprung plank. Certainly, older hulls require more upkeep, but clearly many antique vessels ply their trades and meet demanding regulations in many parts of the world.

Neither the quality of the *Albatross*'s original construction nor the history of her upkeep supports the idea that the hull was deteriorated. She still met survey standards for Bureau Veritas (an independent society that sets marine safety standards), which classed her for "unlimited ocean service." Accounts of the survivors, including those interviewed by the coast guard, do not allude to flooding due to hull failure. Survivors who were below decks at the time of the squall describe having to struggle against water cascading down through the hatches in order to escape, but they do not describe water entering through a rent in the deck or hull. The *Albatross* was indeed flawed, but there is no evidence that structural failure was the cause of her loss, and age alone cannot make it otherwise.

Watertight Subdivision

The *Albatross* is the only of our five casualties that was designed with watertight subdivisions. Records indicate that she was fitted with four watertight bulkheads and five compartments. Watertight doors connected the three largest compartments, but Sheldon averred that at sea the watertight doors were typically kept open to facilitate ventilation and movement below. This is an unfortunate—though by no means unusual—practice that facilitated rapid flooding below decks. Yet the captain, the mate, and some naval architects doubt that intact watertight subdivision would have changed the outcome in this case. The reasons offered vary slightly but can be summarized as follows:

1. If water downflooded through multiple points, the ship would have flooded just as quickly and completely in separate compartments as she did with the watertight doors open and the compartments communicating. Though Sheldon believed that all but the main hatch was secured, people did escape through the forward hatch after forcing it open and allowing water in. Richard Langford, the English teacher, wrote, "the sea roared into the ship through every hatch." Langford could not know if the ship was indeed flooding through every hatch. We do know that the aft hatch could not be opened despite efforts to do so, and that the mid-

ships skylight was secure; nevertheless, he obviously had the impression water was getting in through multiple points.

2. By all accounts, the main hatch and engine room ventilation were unsecured. Sheldon believes that flooding in these areas alone may have been sufficient to sink the ship because they represented such a large proportion of the ship's buoyancy, even if the rest of the ship had been watertight.

3. The lack of stability was so complete that the buoyancy of the hull, even if it had not been diminished by immediate flooding, was insufficient to right the vessel.

Any of these, if true, support the notion that if a ship is laid on her beam ends she may sink for reasons other than structural failure. Watertight subdivision is clearly not an antidote against sinking, but had the *Albatross*'s not been neutralized by the open doors and hatches, at the very least it could have substantially slowed the sinking and contributed to the survival of the people, if not the ship. It is evident that in extreme conditions such as this one, watertight doors cannot be rapidly secured. Indeed, watertight doors that are open at the moment of a knockdown, a collision, or some other rapidly developing and dire circumstance, are ultimately useless as a means of limiting flooding.

Weather

The *Albatross* is one of four weather-related casualties discussed in this book and one of three that have come to be associated with abrupt, localized wind events. But what was the wind that caught the *Albatross*? Was it part of a cold front, or was it caused by convective activity akin to a microburst? Features of each formation were noted, but the annals of seafaring are full of instances of particular weather patterns failing to conform to their textbook descriptions.

Strong cold fronts occur in many parts of the world, and the Gulf of Mexico has a reputation for violent cold fronts known as *northers*. According to the Coast Pilot, northers develop between October and April when cold continental air masses invade the warm waters of the Gulf of Mexico. They typically last one or two days but can persist as long as four days. They are characterized by heavy squalls and showers, with local winds up to 50 knots on occasion, and can result in large, sudden temperature drops. In the nineteenth century two U.S. naval vessels, the sloop of war *Hornet* in 1830 and the corvette *Albany* in 1854, were lost with all hands in the Gulf of Mexico, presumed capsized by northers. In 1846 the U.S. navy brig *Somers*, famous for the controversial suppression of a potential mutiny some years earlier, capsized while on blockade duty during the Mexican War. Described as "overrigged," the *Somers* was giving chase under the command of Lieutenant Raphael Semmes. Semmes later became one of the most renowned naval officers of the century for his devastatingly effective command of the Confederate commerce raider CSS *Alabama*. His description of events aboard *Somers* is not dissimilar to what befell the *Albatross*:

> We were under topsails, courses, jib and spanker. It did not appear to be very violent, nor was its approach accompanied by any foaming of the water or other indications. . . . But the brig being flying-light, having scarcely any water or provision . . . she was thrown over almost instantly. . . . The brig was filling very fast, and her masts and yards lying flat upon the surface of the sea.

According to some sources, high winds were reported in Florida around the period the *Albatross* was lost and were said to be the product of cold front activity with which northers are typically associated. The prescribed season set forth in the Coast Pilot for northers had ended a few days earlier, but this is not a strong argument against a norther knocking down the *Albatross*. Unlike microbursts, cold fronts are large systems that are usually well defined even if they are not particularly strong. Even when the strength of a cold front is inaccurately forecast, it still tends to follow a familiar and recognizable pattern. The squall that took down the *Albatross* did not resemble that pattern in the slightest.

Though the squall that struck the *Albatross* did indeed approach from the north, in some respects it behaved more like a strong convection cell of a type that produces a microburst. Normally the stronger the cold front, the greater the temperature differential between the existing air mass and the cold air invading behind the front. Though survivors experienced chill and discomfort in the lifeboats due to exposure—the speed of the sinking caught some of them wearing nothing but their underwear, and certainly they weren't dressed for an open-boat voyage—yet their accounts make no references to a notable drop in temperature, such as might be expected in the wake of a strong front. As we know, northers will typically blow for a day or more—before shifting and subsiding. However, reports from the *Albatross* crew consistently describe light air in advance of and calm behind the squall. The drizzle, lightning, and overcast sky survivors observed could indicate a frontal approach, but they could equally apply to an area of active convection.

The language and nature of microbursts have become muddled, even among sailors, in the years since the term first came into use. The same phenomenon has been termed a *white squall*, the phrase Sheldon used with the boys in the lifeboat with him. It is variously known as *wind shear, down-*

burst, and *downdraft.* Microbursts are associated with the pronounced convection that often accompanies a trough or thunderstorms. They occur in conjunction with cumulonimbus and thunderstorm formations when cooling air rapidly descends from a great height. When this mass of descending air hits the earth's surface, it deflects outward in all directions in a radial pattern, like water spattering from a pail onto a brick sidewalk. When the vector of deflection coincides with the orientation of existing surface winds, it may produce an aggregate velocity much higher than either wind event taken separately. Wind velocities commonly associated with microbursts may be as little as 25 to 30 knots, but they can range much higher. In summer months, intense convection has been known to produce afternoon squalls with winds up to 70 knots on the Great Lakes and the East Coast of the United States, even when there is no frontal activity in the area.

Unlike large storm systems, microbursts have a localized nature that makes them difficult to forecast. Atmospheric conditions at a given time may be determined to be ripe for microburst activity, but over a large swath of ocean a microburst might occur anywhere—or not at all. Microbursts have been studied in detail ashore in connection with a number of aircraft disasters in the 1980s. The impact of a microburst is more readily documented ashore because investigators have more in the way of physical evidence. In the wake of microburst activity on land, trees have been found cast down in a circular pattern like a deck of cards splayed out. At sea, the ephemeral and local nature of microbursts makes them difficult to document or substantiate. In the aftermath of incidents such as the one experienced by the *Albatross,* all that remains is water in motion—and a space briefly occupied by a ship. It is difficult to confirm that the *Albatross* was struck by a microburst, but much of what we know points in that direction.

Whatever the cause of that wind, we must wonder what degree of intensity was required to knock the *Albatross* down. The question of wind strength bears consideration because there is reason to believe it may not have been abnormally strong. A squall of such strength that no vessel or crew could be expected to survive points us toward the act-of-God approach to disaster at sea. But a wind that is something less than phenomenal causes us to consider factors relating to seamanship, the sail plan, and stability. Descriptions appearing in periodicals and newspapers at the time characterized the squall as a "blast" of wind striking with "savage fury." One article estimated the wind to be 150 miles per hour, but this does not seem credible. Such reports do not mesh with the accounts of survivors, leaving us to ponder the possibility of media hype.

Chuck Gieg's account, for instance, contains no mention of wind strength, and his remark that "there was no logical explanation" is at odds with the notion of a phenomenally strong wind, which would, indeed, constitute a logical explanation. Recalling the incident years later, Gieg stated: "We had an old threadbare t'gallant flying that we fully expected to blow out. We had made a new one to replace it." But the old canvas topgallant and the other sails held, again suggesting that the wind was not of phenomenal strength. David (Tod) Johnstone, the helmsman at the time of impact said, "I never even felt a wind on deck." This is consistent with Sheldon's own recollection. Thirty-five years after the fact he mused: "There was no tremendous amount of wind on deck. The wind must have been aloft. The water was calm before and afterward."

The U.S. Coast Guard report based on interviews with survivors in Tampa refers to a "sudden squall of gale force." It is quite possible that the term *gale force* was loosely employed with no thought to its more strict definition under the Beaufort Scale, which corresponds with force 8, or 34 to 40 knots (see the Beaufort Wind Scale in the appendix). Although a force 8 wind might justifiably be regarded with alarm, and precipitate action to reduce sail, such conditions are not normally considered perilous to a vessel of the *Albatross*'s size and design. The coast guard's description, therefore, must be regarded as approximate.

With respect to the idea that the blast of wind was never at deck level, it is generally true that a given wind will be felt more strongly aloft than alow because friction with the earth's surface will modestly reduce the speed of air flow closer to the water. A 35-knot wind recorded by an anemometer at the masthead 75 feet aloft might feel closer to 30 knots on deck. However, the idea of a dramatic difference in wind strength between aloft and alow with a rig of the *Albatross*'s height does not correspond with general experience, at least not in open waters away from obstructions. More to the point, T. Theodore Fujita, who is credited with coining the term *microburst* and a leading researcher on the subject, believes that where the phenomenon has been studied ashore, the maximum winds are found very close to the ground. Their close proximity to the earth's surface is a characteristic of microbursts that hampers early detection by radar.

This idea of a killer wind aloft while relatively mild conditions prevail on deck may seem aberrant but is worth looking at. As noted earlier, the sea is renowned for providing exceptions to man-made rules. In 1888 the full-rigger *A. G. Ropes* was dismasted from the topmasts up in the western North Atlantic by a "whirlwind" that struck aloft while the wind on deck was reportedly never more than about six knots. A variation on this phenomenon affected a British frigate in the Potomac River during the War of 1812; it reportedly had a jib torn away while the quarterdeck was "in complete calm." And the following incident was recorded by Lemuel Norton aboard the *Vigilant* out of Castine, Maine, in 1805:

On our homeward bound passage, off the Western Islands, we encountered what is sometimes termed a white squall, such a one as none of us had ever seen before. We were standing along with a moderate breeze from the southeast, our topgallant sails furled, all other sails set . . . the wind began to veer south and west, with drizzly rain. I had the care of the captain's watch on deck and happened at that moment to be at the helm myself. . . . All at once I felt her settling on one side, no wind scarcely to be felt on deck, yet I perceived that topmasts were bending and the sails appeared to be full. In a moment the brig righted and everything was as before. . . . All at once she took another lurch, and settled rapidly on to one side. All hands were on deck as quick as possible and notwithstanding every topsail sheet was either cut or let go instantly . . . such was the violence of the squall that we came very near to running under water.

We can never establish the velocity of the wind on that day in 1961 with total certainty, nor can we discount the possibility that an incident similar to those incidents just described befell the *Albatross*. Whether it was a microburst or some other wind phenomenon, we are left to consider the prospect that *Albatross* was laid low by something less than a wind of extraordinary velocity. Based on survivors' descriptions, nothing more than 30 knots may have been felt on deck, and certainly nothing approaching what we might normally think of as ship-killing conditions. Instead, the capsizing may have been precipitated by a convergence of factors that, taken individually, were not catastrophic until combined with the ship's changed stability profile. In any event, the incident illustrates the capacity for the forces of nature to ambush the mariner.

Bearing Off

The *Albatross* was sailing slowly at the time of the squall's impact. She had just started to gather way after a period of light and flukey wind. Bunting said that by the time he went off watch at 0800 the sails were no longer slatting but had begun to fill again. This is of interest because a lack of boat speed reduces rudder control, and this may have exacerbated the impact of the squall. In 1932 the German sail training barque *Niobe* was lost in the Baltic Sea with sixty-nine hands under similar circumstances:

It was a hot summer's day, and prior to squall impact she had been in light force three, with little angle of heel. However, the master had taken the precaution of furling all the upper sails in readiness for the expected increase in the wind force. The squall was witnessed by the Masters of a nearby steamer and the nearby manned light vessel, neither of whom had seen anything unusual in the sky, and both of whom were stunned by the speed with which the vessel rolled over and sank. The Captain had attempted to luff up, with his Petty Officer helmsman almost anticipating the order, but squall impact caused her to lose all way and knocked her over before the rudder movement could take effect.

Notwithstanding the *Niobe*'s attempt to luff up, a standard response for a square-rigger that is already off the wind is to bear farther off and run with it. As the *Albatross* heeled radically and began to flood, Langford, who was belowdecks, hollered in fear and frustration: "Put her off—why don't they put her off? They'll sink us!" This is exactly what those on deck were attempting, and for good reason.

Sudden wind increases are often accompanied by equally sudden wind shifts. If the wind abruptly comes ahead of a square-rigger, she may be caught aback, thus putting her in irons. In such case, not only is the vessel deprived of steerageway and rudder control, she risks being dismasted because square-riggers are not rigged to withstand great pressure on the forward side of their sails. The masts are heavily supported from the sides and from aft by shrouds, but they are relatively lightly supported from ahead by a few stays. Running before the wind minimizes the chance of getting caught aback and dismasted, but, more important in this case, running mitigates the effect of the capsizing forces as the longitudinal buoyancy of the hull increases its resistance to heeling. Running before the true wind also reduces the force of the apparent wind by the speed of the ship. Once a vessel is before the wind, it is able to more readily transmit the heeling energy of the squall into the forward motion of the hull.

The speed with which the bearing-off maneuver is executed is partly in the hands of the officer in charge, but it is also a factor of steerageway. As seen in the *Niobe* case, too little headway in a squall situation may be deadly because the ship is slow responding to her rudder. The flow of water past the *Albatross*'s rudder may have been insufficient for the vessel to answer her helm in time to achieve relief from the squall. Indeed, the heavy application of rudder could have stalled her further, almost creating a tripping effect. At any rate, without adequate steerage a helmsman cannot quickly bring a ship off the wind, no matter how speedy the response to an order.

The film *White Squall* made much of the helmsman's incorrect response to the master's order to bear away from the wind. The coast guard report and eyewitness accounts, including Sheldon's, affirm that the helmsman's initial reaction was to bring the ship up into the wind, contrary to orders and to what the situation called for. However, both Sheldon and Bunting expressed doubt as to whether this momentary lapse on the part of the helmsman affected the outcome. Far more serious problems were at work by this point.

Obviously, a vessel cannot spend all its time running downwind at the first sign of bad weather. However, if there is doubt about the strength of the impending squall, early action to bear off can be an effective course until sail can be reduced and a fuller assessment of the situation made. Was the *Albatross* as far off the wind as she should have been? Given the speed of events, the level of confusion as she heeled alarmingly, and the possibility of a shifting wind, any answer would be grossly speculative. It is clear, though, that the deck watch was not able to get the *Albatross* before the wind in time to prevent what happened.

Sail Area

In addition to bearing off, a common tactic in squalls is to shorten sail preemptively. Unlike storms that build gradually, squalls are characterized by abruptness, and this is their chief danger. The more sail that is set, the more time is required to reduce sail. The effort involved with handling sail can be a deterrent to action. Of the four weather-related casualties discussed in this book, the *Albatross* had by far the greatest proportion of her sail set at the time of her loss. Options short of reducing sail include flaking out halyards and sheets, securing hatches and watertight doors, briefing the watch on a plan of action to reduce sail quickly, and calling extra hands on deck. The degree of precaution exercised will vary with prevailing conditions and the officer's sense of the ship's vulnerability. Because there is often little in the visual aspect of an approaching cloud to indicate whether it will "pack a punch" or cause the breeze to fall flat, an officer will typically rely on reports from previous watches, prior experience, and a general assessment of the vessel and the crew's limitations. This often boils down to little more than a hunch, though the advent of small-ship radar has provided a valuable tool for judging the speed of a squall's approach. The speed with which a squall travels generally correlates with its strength. All other things being equal, fast-moving squalls tend to hit harder. Even on a training ship, where manpower is generally in good supply, it is impractical to strike and reset sail with the approach of every cloud on the chance that one will be dangerous. However, intense lightning activity is usually a reason to bring in the kites and move to a more conservative sail plan.

The *Albatross*'s total sail area of 5,000 square feet was not extreme for the vessel's size and, in fact, compared closely to other trading brigantines of similar size. Approximately three-quarters of this sail area was set at the time of the squall. Given that the vessel was low on fuel, continuing to sail under light-air conditions made sense in order to conserve fuel for when it was really needed. Evidently, those on deck saw little reason to preemptively reduce sail right up to the moment of impact. The prospect of wind was welcomed, and the ominous signs reported by the dawn watch had largely dissipated.

The presence of lightning was described earlier as a deterrent to striking sail. Chuck Gieg commented: "She had eleven sails flying when we were hit. Skipper had just given the order to take in sail when the lightning began to happen. Our spars and rigging were all steel and he cancelled the order." When asked about this later, Sheldon explained that the lightning was a separate and earlier concern; the need to reduce sail was not obvious until the capsizing had begun.

There are indeed risks in laying aloft amidst lightning, but there is no particular risk in *striking* sail, which can be done via the running rigging without leaving the deck. Though the lightning may not have been related to the amount of sail area at the time of the squall, it is still relevant to the conflict captains can face between the safety of the individual and the safety of the ship. At what point does a threat to the ship, and everyone in it, outweigh the threat to the individual who, by putting himself or herself in harm's way, may secure the safety of all?

Given the recent dearth of wind for the *Albatross*, the choice to wait and see what the rising breeze brought before changing sail must have seemed reasonable. Although that choice proved devastating in this instance, bearing off the wind while retaining the sail plan cannot be categorically viewed as an inadequate response. A lack of danger signs is consistent with the notion that the squall that sank the *Albatross* was not what would typically be viewed as ship-killing magnitude.

One lesson of both the *Albatross* and the *Niobe* is that little warning may be all the mariner gets. Since a sailing vessel's intact stability is essentially immutable once she encounters a sudden weather change, getting the vessel well before the wind early and reducing sail are among the only recourses left to the square-rigger sailor. Preemptive action will always be a matter of on-scene judgment, but the knowledge of microbursts and wind phenomena recommend a conservative approach to sail area, particularly if the stability of a vessel is not well-understood.

Sailors can attest that appearances are frequently misleading when it comes to squalls. Ugly skies can bring a dead calm while innocuous-looking puff-balls can leave one gripping the weather rail. In deciding what action to take in advance of a squall, what I call the 30-Knot Rule can be a useful rule of thumb for guiding on-scene judgment, when prevailing winds are light and a vessel is carrying a generous sail plan. My experience has shown that even run-of-the-mill squalls with no particularly menacing features will often run up to 30 knots, even if only briefly. Under the 30-Knot Rule, the mariner assesses the existing sail plan in light of the approaching weather, with an eye toward which sails would not normally be set in a 30-knot breeze, which sails would be especially difficult to strike in 30 knots, and which sails would hamper maneuverability. The captain then takes action accordingly. The value of the rule is that it helps the captain make quick decisions on sail reduction when faced with the inconclusive visual clues that often precede squalls. The rule is applied with due regard to the skill of the crew, sea room, and other considerations. Had the 30-Knot Rule been applied aboard the *Albatross*, some reduction of sail may have resulted when those on deck became aware that a squall was approaching. Whether that reduction could have prevented the capsize is another matter entirely.

Qualifications and Experience

The role of qualifications and experience aboard the *Albatross* is a sensitive but important issue, as in any casualty case. No amount of experience is a guarantee against mishap at sea, but if we are interested in understanding how practices have evolved from the early days of the tall-ship renaissance, then we need to consider past practices, which include the approach to manning.

Of the five adults aboard the *Albatross*, several had previously been to sea. However, Captain Sheldon was the only licensed mariner and the only one aboard with a broad sailing background. The students were essentially green at the outset of the voyage, though some had sailed before with their families. The Ocean Academy held, as many experiential learning programs do, that prior sailing experience among the students was neither necessary nor perhaps even desirable. Sheldon firmly believed that the kid who had never seen the ocean or been on a boat, but had the desire and didn't get too seasick, was the best raw material from which to build a sailor. As on any training ship, everyone aboard had duties and participated in all aspects of shipboard life. The students who showed ability adopted watch officer responsibilities, a task to which Sheldon evidently felt they were equal. This approach had been used aboard the *Yankee* with older participants, and it seemed to work. Sheldon stressed the importance of keeping the captain informed and calling him when in doubt, no matter how often that might be. He found that he could trust his young lieutenants to do this.

At the time of the incident, the students and teaching staff had been aboard the *Albatross* together for over seven months. When compared to a career sailor, this amount of experience may be shallow in respect to evaluating weather patterns and weighing the range of risks that a vessel encounters at sea, but this was not their responsibility. What the ship's company, students and faculty alike, had attained in that time was intimate familiarity with the vessel and proficiency in their duties at any time of day or night. This is the most that can ever be expected of trainees. To the extent that the students and faculty had warning of the squall, their response must be regarded as very nearly professional and certainly not contributory to what happened. The reaction of the helmsman at the time of the squall is not regarded as a significant factor, though it was clearly unfortunate at so critical a moment. Imperfect helmsmanship stands as an example of the kind of mistaken reaction that must be expected aboard a sail training vessel and that sufficient experienced officers are engaged to anticipate and counteract.

The first mate, Bill Bunting, is described as a "crack sailor." Although there were other student watch leaders, Bunting's responsibilities went beyond running a watch. Bunting had come aboard at Mystic and made the voyage out to Bermuda as delivery crew. He was enrolled in the Ocean Academy as a student, but the program didn't officially start until the other students joined at Bermuda. When the professional mate engaged for the program left suddenly in Bermuda, Bunting was made first mate. At fifteen, Bunting was younger than one might expect for such a position of responsibility, but he had previously sailed in the *Yankee* and had considerably more experience than the other students. He was serious and competent, so much so that Sheldon hired him back as mate for a later venture with the schooner *Verona*. On one occasion at Curaçao in the Dutch Caribbean, Sheldon put Bunting in charge of the *Albatross* for a daysail while he and others went aboard another vessel to get photographs. When the capsize occurred, Bunting was off watch and belowdecks and therefore played no role in the response on deck. Given the broader definition of a seafaring officer's duties, Bunting's youth is conspicuous, not in connection with the casualty, but as a reflection of the times. In the years since this casualty, it has become typical on oceangoing educational vessels to carry, in addition to the captain, two or even three licensed professional mates.

Most sailors would agree that Captain Sheldon's action to bring the vessel "off a point" and to ease the main sheet was normal and appropriate in a squall. Most of the hatches were closed, though weatherboards were not necessarily fitted. Other possible measures to prepare for a squall would have included reducing sail, installing weatherboards in the hatches, closing watertight doors below, and bearing off even farther. Some of these precautions would be reasonable only if one suspected a truly dangerous encounter, as opposed to an ordinary squall. Even with a forecast for foul weather, it is common to secure the deck progressively as conditions warrant rather than taking all conceivable precautions the moment the sky darkens. As it was, some measures were deferred. Although the fact that the *Albatross* was not shortened down supports the idea that there was little warning, it is also an indication of the master's confidence in the vessel. This confidence was based on his experience up to that point, but not on an understanding of the *Albatross*'s stability characteristics.

It is unclear what the exact licensing requirements were at the time

Sheldon obtained his Panamanian yacht master certificate. But since Panama is a flag-of-convenience nation, these are thought to have been minimal and, in any event, less than what would be required under the U.S. flag both then and now for a comparable operation. But in looking at qualifications, the standard that matters is whether there was a deficiency in the credentials that actually contributed to the casualty. This does not seem to have been the case.

A license is a valuable credential because the sea-time requirement involved establishes a certain minimum level of experience. Also, passing the exams implies a mastery of standard information such as the Rules of the Road, a mastery of navigation techniques, and an appreciation for the priorities of the regulatory body issuing the license. None of these things had any bearing on what happened to the *Albatross*. Seamanship and judgment are matters of experience and character that fall outside the licensing process. A license to operate big ships does not by definition guarantee a good captain.

Even had Sheldon and Bunting and another mate or two undergone the equivalent U.S. Coast Guard licensing procedure, the outcome would likely not have been different. Even the 2002 requirements for obtaining Ocean Master's certification for auxiliary sailing vessels in the United States do not examine sailing ship captain candidates in depth on any salient area of specialized knowledge pertinent to large sailing vessel operations. Proficiency in squall tactics, heavy-weather sailing, prudent seamanship in respect to carrying sail, and most important, sailing ship stability are still matters of experience and self-education that are not addressed by the licensing process. If any fault can be ascribed to Sheldon, it was not as a sailor but as an owner for not knowing more about the ship's stability. Even in this matter, however, he acted within the prevailing standards of the day.

Stability and the Point of No Return

Whatever squall tactics the master had at his disposal, the real Achilles' heel for the *Albatross* was her deficient stability, which made her vulnerable to knockdown. The circumstances of having little steerageway, slack tanks, and a full press of canvas placed the *Albatross* in the position of a rare worst-case scenario for a squall. Regardless of the many other circumstances of 2 May, the *Albatross* passed her point of no return—the point at which a vessel cannot recover from the forces heeling it, like a saltshaker tipped too far—far sooner than she should have, far sooner than she would have without the modifications, and far sooner than would be allowed under today's regulations in the United States for an oceangoing sail training ship. Although some of the changes made to the *Albatross* over the years may be lost from the record, the most significant ones are known to us (see table next page).

Date	Agent	Change	Result
1949	Rotterdamsche Lloyd	the addition of first deckhouse (aft)	added weight above the center of gravity
1949	Rotterdamsche Lloyd	the accommodation for many more people than originally intended, along with their personal gear, and the appropriate volumes of ship's stores and water	significantly increased movable (as opposed to fixed) weight below decks, reducing freeboard and thereby reducing overall buoyancy
1955	Gann	the construction of the boat gallows and the placement of two heavily built wooden boats approximately six feet above the deck	added weight above the center of gravity
1955	Gann	the addition of second deckhouse (amidships) for galley and accoutrements	added weight above the center of gravity
1956	Gann	the transformation of the rig from a straight schooner to a hermaphrodite brig/brigantine	added significant weight well above the center of gravity
1960	Sheldon	the replacement of the heavier MAN U-boat engine with the lighter and more modern Caterpillar engine	removed weight below the center of gravity
1960	Sheldon	the addition of stunsail gear aloft	added weight above the center of gravity

Though the changes outlined in the table are cumulative, the rig conversion is regarded as the most serious because it both raised center of gravity and reduced freeboard by putting more weight aboard. It also enabled the *Albatross* to set the vastly increased sail plan carried on the morning she sank. The first mate believed that the weight of the wooden boats high above the deck also contributed significantly to the stability condition; he recalled the vessel listing noticeably whenever one of the boats was hoisted for launching.

In addition to the six factors in the table, the *Albatross* was low on water and fuel when the squall struck. This loading condition echoed that of the brig *Somers*: in both ships, it raised the center of gravity by reducing weight down low in the vessel and, in the case of the *Albatross*, exposed the ship to the destabilizing influence of free-surface effect. Considering the *Albatross* in her original form offers perspective on the difference between the spartan pilot schooner and the modified brigantine:

> The *Albatross* class of pilot schooners were in a very different service than vessels on ocean routes. They were primarily station keeping vessels intended to be handled by small crews. This mission would encourage modest sail area, a fact which has probably contributed to the good reputation of the model for Sailing School Vessel type service. The pilot schooners also carried very little in the way of consumables so that their stability was fairly constant.

The original *Albatross* was the product of many years, perhaps centuries, of practical experience. Her design was carefully balanced and motivated by function. It seems obvious enough now that the changes made to her over successive ownerships compromised this original seaworthiness, but in what ways and by how much? The answers eventually came to light through research conducted for a purpose quite different from understanding the *Albatross* for her own sake.

A Discovery

In the early 1980s, the naval architecture firm of Woodin and Marean in Boothbay Harbor, Maine, was engaged to develop stability criteria for the nascent Sailing School Vessels (SSV) regulations initiative in the United States. The U.S. Coast Guard and the Council of Educational Shipowners, an association of organizations engaged in activities not unlike the Ocean Academy, were tasked with creating these regulations. As part of this process, Woodin and Marean made a stability study of the *Albatross*. The *Albatross* was singled out for special attention because of the similarity of her design to two other American school ships seeking certification under these new regulations. One of these we already know, the sister ship *Tabor Boy*, built in 1914. The other was the *Westward*, a yacht built in Germany in 1961 and modeled after the North Sea pilot schooner design, with a strong resemblance to the *Yankee*. Both vessels were based in the United States and carried young trainees on ocean voyages. After the *Albatross* sinking, the U.S. Coast Guard had obvious reservations about this type of vessel, yet there was also ample evidence of its seaworthiness. The burden of proof lay with those seeking certification, and the key was to demonstrate that the *Albatross* was an exception rather than a rule and that the rig conversion was responsible for her becoming that exception. The study looked at three things: the original plans from the vessel's construction in 1921, the stability data compiled in 1949 when Rotterdamsche Lloyd equipped her for sail training, and the results of the 1956 inclining at Moore Shipyard in California. Roger Long, a naval architect at Woodin and Marean at the time, described their approach:

> We have recently obtained a very complete set of plans and calculations for the *Albatross* from the widow of W. P. Hincks, the cognizant Naval Architect during the 1956 conversion to a Brigantine. This material includes the report of an inclining experiment conducted at the completion of the conversion and it is now possible to make a fairly definitive assessment of the vessel's stability characteristics.

Using Hincks's data, Long and others were able to gain insight into the *Albatross* far beyond what Hincks had accomplished. The figures in the table opposite summarize the results.

These figures reveal a vessel much compromised by the modifications of 1956. The center of gravity had migrated upward by nearly a foot, resulting in a decrease in the range of positive stability by nearly half, from a stalwart 110 degrees to a marginal 57 degrees and possibly less. The increase in displacement by approximately five tons meant the vessel sat lower in the water than intended, a condition that had been casually noted by observers. The diminished freeboard is reflected by the somewhat smaller angle of heel needed to achieve deck edge immersion and downflooding. However, judging from the figures, by the time downflooding occurred on 2 May, the vessel had already exceeded her range of positive stability and was committed to capsizing. In light of this, an extreme squall may not even have been necessary to capsize the vessel, and this would be congruent with the eyewitness accounts we have already seen. It is worth noting that the vessel was originally designed with a range of stability of 110 degrees, without any regulatory requirement at the time to do so, and far exceeding that now required by law for comparable operations in the United States. It was simply considered proper and obtainable. This is important to bear in mind when looking at the *Marques* and the *Pride of Baltimore*.

Faced with this extraordinary reduction in stability, it is reasonable to ask why Hincks approved the vessel for ocean sailing after calculating the effect of the modifications. Assuming that the inclining and calculations were properly executed, no explanation may be completely satisfactory, but a few things should be kept in mind. One explanation relates to how Gann's converted *Albatross* was to be used. Gann's plan for the ship was not sail training or passenger carrying, but rather private yachting and filmmaking. Had Gann intended to carry young people to sea for hire, a different approach to the conversion and the calculation of stability may have been employed. A better explanation may lie in Hincks's approach to calculating the *Albatross*'s stability.

	1949	*1956*
GM (corrected for free surface)	2.81 feet	2.02 feet
vertical center of gravity	7.99 feet	8.78 feet
displacement	159.09 tons	164.29 tons
heel angle to deck edge	16.84 degrees	15.85 degrees
downflood angle	58.43 degrees	57.20 degrees
range of positive stability	110 degrees	57.0 degrees

Hincks, like most of us, was a product of his times. He did not calculate the *Albatross*'s point of no return. Instead, he relied on a commonplace, and relatively simple, procedure for calculating *initial* stability. Though initial stability has its place, the stability assessment made in the aftermath of the conversion was not in-depth enough to tell Hincks, Gann, and ultimately Sheldon what they needed to know to avoid disaster. Given the broad capabilities of today's computer programs for stability work, it is easy to find fault with the relatively simplistic approach taken by Hincks, though at the time it was standard procedure. Though commonsense standards of good practice existed, there was no statutory point of reference, and it would be another ten years before this began to change. In addition, we should not overlook the fact that Hincks simply did as much as the client requested and was willing to pay for. An unfortunate consequence was that the *Albatross*'s vulnerability was in a sense masked by Hincks's professional stamp of approval until one morning in the Gulf Mexico when that disguise was abruptly torn away. This leads to the discussion of the quiet yet profound impact the loss of the *Albatross* eventually had on the renaissance of traditional sail in the United States and elsewhere.

REPERCUSSIONS

The first constructive impact of the *Albatross* tragedy came with the publication of "On the Stability of Sailing Vessels" in 1966. The paper was the work of two U.S. Coast Guard officers, J. G. Beebe-Center and R. B. Brooks. Privately researched and published, the paper is considered the seminal work on the stability of large traditional sailing vessels in the United States and a point of departure for the eventual development of sail training regulations in both the United Kingdom and the United States. It was written with an awareness of the *Albatross* and with a view to addressing the problems of regulating the growing and diverse fleet of traditional sailing vessels.

Beebe-Center and Brooks made early connections among the loss of the *Albatross*, the growth of traditional sail and training activities, and the need for appropriate regulations that go beyond the persistent application of initial stability. Reliable methods for calculating ultimate stability that emerged in the late nineteenth century were seen to hold solutions for avoiding tragedy, but the decline of commercial sail blunted their impact: "At the very time it became possible to approach the problem [of sailing ship stability] in a logical manner, the need for the results dwindled. Yet casualties among large sailing vessels still occur." The renaissance of traditional sail provided a motivation to reexamine conventional methods and develop better means of assessing sailing ship stability:

> Large sailing vessels, historical replicas and new designs are being built in increasing numbers. The present day Naval Architect, faced with designing a large sailing vessel has the alternative of using the old standards, sometimes out of context, or of casting about for bits and pieces of information from which he can build confidence in the stability of his design under sail.

Though the authors speak to designers of new vessels, their comments are just as pertinent to converted or restored vessels such as the *Albatross* and the *Marques* that might be modified and put to new purposes.

The limitations of commonly used stability assessment techniques, including those applied to the *Albatross*, were central to the argument constructed by Beebe-Center and Brooks. GM, the distance between a ship's center of gravity and the metacenter, is only a measure of a vessel's *initial* stability at small angles of heel up to approximately 10 degrees (see Stability, in the appendix). GM was for many years the most important point of reference in calculating stability. It remains useful, particularly for motorized vessels and other kinds of craft that do not normally operate at large angles of heel and are not typically vulnerable to heeling forces associated with sailing vessels. Obviously, the shortcoming of this method is that it does not give any indication of the vessel's *ultimate* stability. It also does not give insight into a vessel's theoretical righting-arm characteristics (GZ) over the full range of heeling angles. Yet a sailing vessel in its normal mode of operation is quite exposed to large angles of heel and to knockdown forces in a way that motor vessels are not. Thus, a measurement of GM is insufficient grounds on which to base the safety of a sailing vessel with regard to stability.

Although the value of righting-arm data has long been recognized, prior to the advent of computer programming the calculations were laborious and expensive. Such data were typically applied to new construction of some significance, such as naval vessels or a new class of merchant ship, but not always to other types of vessels. Beebe-Center and Brooks noted that because righting-arm data were difficult to obtain, the method "was often used in the analysis of casualties but not [as] part of a general design tool."

There is a certain irony that the method of analysis that would best avoid a stability casualty was often employed only after it occurred. Beebe-Center and Brooks also noted that changes to a vessel, or to its purpose, can be a recipe for disaster if not fully evaluated and understood.

> Caution must be used when evaluating the stability of replica vessels of a previous era. Local preference [and] special service requirements . . . influenced their designs. The modern designer will do well to analyze the full stability picture of any such vessel.

This point is relevant not only to the *Albatross* case, but to all replica projects involving designs from another era.

Computer programming was already revolutionizing naval architecture when Beebe-Center and Brooks's work appeared in 1966. They observed that as a result of such advances righting arm data had become "readily available," but there was still a great reliance on classical methods, partly because of the convenience of calculating GM.

Despite the recognized value of the Beebe-Center and Brooks work, the loss of the British barque *Marques* over twenty years later was a product of circumstances agonizingly similar to those surrounding the *Albatross*. In some respects the lapse was even more glaring, given the passage of time and given that all the relevant principles had been reasserted. Beebe-Center and Brooks noted that "it is usual to specify and obtain a positive righting arm at 90 degrees of heel for oceangoing yachts." In doing so they offered a standard decades before it became required for certified sailing vessels. It was not regarded as a fresh concept even then.

Beebe-Center and Brooks are also credited with spearheading the "population analysis" approach to statutory stability criteria. Righting arm data taken alone are of limited value without a recognized stability criterion reflecting prevailing attitudes of seaworthiness and acceptable risk. The population analysis method looked at the stability characteristics of a wide range of existing vessels within a category of activity and vessel type. Ideally, samples would include both known casualties as well as "successful" vessels. By identifying patterns from among a field of active vessels, low-risk vessels might be distinguished from high-risk vessels on the basis of their respective stability characteristics. Regulations can then be designed to eliminate vessels whose characteristics resemble those of past casualties, while accommodating existing designs that have not shown problems. The advantage of such an approach is that it should result in realistic regulations based on actual vessels, rather than a theoretical criterion that no existing vessel can meet. Of population analysis Beebe-Center and Brooks wrote: "it is an idea rooted in common sense. Take a look at the record, measure a few significant things, and draw a line between what worked and what did not."

The *Albatross* figured into the population analysis study that led to stability criteria for sailing vessels operating under the U.S. Coast Guard's regulations for Small Passenger Vessels (SPV) in 1968. SPV was a new regulatory category designed to provide the relatively stringent protections normally accorded paying passengers while recognizing the limited resources of smaller vessels (less than 100 gross tons). The methods applied were "virtually identical" to those outlined by Beebe-Center and Brooks.

The Albatross *and the Sailing School Vessels Act*

As Beebe-Center and Brooks foresaw in 1966, traditional sailing vessels and sail training activities did indeed take off. As sail training activities blossomed in the United States during the 1970s, many operators pointed out that trainees are distinct from passengers in that they receive instruction that enables them to contribute to the operation of the ship in ways that conventional passengers do not. This, and other differences, were not accommodated by the existing SPV regulations. By 1982, the Council of Educational Shipowners had succeeded in securing passage through Congress of the Sailing School Vessels Act (SSVA), and work had begun on drafting criteria for educational sailing vessels. Roger Long, a naval architect who was deeply involved with drafting stability criteria for the SSV regulations, described the loss of the *Albatross* as a watershed in the regulation of American sailing vessels and one that had been "widely cited since as the type of accident [that] can befall a sailing vessel and [that] stability regulations are intended to prevent." But one of the difficulties with developing stability regulations is that population analysis surveys had historically been hampered by the inability to obtain hard data on known stability casualties. The SSV process struggled with this problem until Hincks's 1956 test data of the *Albatross* resurfaced after his death. Population analysis was then employed, and this time the *Albatross* featured prominently among the casualty samples in the database.

For obvious reasons, Tabor Academy and the Sea Education Association (SEA), the respective owners of the *Tabor Boy* and the *Westward*, had a stake in the outcome of the regulatory process. Yet the ghost of the *Albatross* loomed over it disconcertingly:

> The fact that the *Albatross* was sailing as a school ship and is of a type still considered excellent for this service makes her loss especially interesting at a time when stability regulations for Sailing School Vessels are being proposed and developed. This unfortunate vessel was built to the same hull lines as one of the vessels in the current U.S. school vessel fleet and is similar in hull type and proportions to another so that her stability characteristics are of more than academic interest.

Regulations excluding the *Tabor Boy* or the *Westward* on the basis of a partial similarity to the *Albatross* would render fruitless the very regulatory reform their respective organizations had spearheaded. On the other hand, the coast guard could not easily endorse regulations that would certify two vessels that bore such a close resemblance to one that sank in a squall with multiple loss of life. Because the Beebe-Center and Brooks study, which by this time was enshrined in the Small Passenger Vessels regulations, had specifically referred to the *Albatross*, the relationship among these vessels could not be ignored.

The stability data that emerged from the Hincks material proved decisive. It identified the specific problems with *Albatross* and established a distinction between her and North Sea pilot schooners in general. The comparison to her earlier self was convincing evidence that her demise was attributable to the rig conversion and not some inherent design flaw in the boat class.

> The *Albatross* class makes an excellent study case. Here we have a class of sister ships with a long and successful operating history as pilot schooners. When one of the vessels was modified so as to have 10% more potential heeling moment, 28% less initial stability, and 45% less range of stability, it was lost.

In this way the *Albatross* arose from the depths of obscurity to play a key role in shaping future conduct of the very activity she was engaged in at the time of her loss. It is a tribute to the appeal of that activity that within two decades of her loss, operations akin to the Ocean Academy were prolific enough to warrant their own code of standards in the United States. But the key to using the tragedy of the *Albatross* constructively lay in devising regulations that were realistic, practical, and did not serve merely to stifle in the name of safety. The regulatory ideal in this case was to eliminate high-risk designs, or severely restrict their operations, without obstructing the popular interest in traditional and historic sailing ships. Though the efficacy of the SSV regulations is not beyond debate, it is clear that the loss of the *Albatross* ultimately added to knowledge, and that knowledge had an important bearing on the present stability regulations. Long wrote: "There is no question that our proposed criteria would have eliminated the converted vessel from the SSV fleet most decisively."

The eighty-eight-year-old gaff schooner *Tabor Boy* and the forty-one-year-old staysail schooner *Westward* met the new criteria in due course and have continued to operate as sail training vessels. Their rigs are more conservative than that of the 1961 *Albatross*, but in certain respects they closely resemble the more seaworthy *Albatross* of 1949. Although both vessels had to undergo modifications as part of the coast guard approval process, the SSV regulations enabled them to operate as certified school ships despite a relationship to the ill-fated *Albatross*.

LOOSE ENDS

Whatever insight has been gained into the loss of the *Albatross* by exploring so many aspects of her operation, the paramount issue in her demise remains stability. Other variables such as the difficulty in getting the ship before the wind, or the amount of sail set at the time, or the effect of diminished consumables on stability are transitory circumstances that increased her vulnerability. The chief value in illuminating that fatal synthesis may be to help us understand how the *Albatross* sailed so extensively as a brigantine without capsizing sooner. Another piece of that explanation must certainly be that she was well handled by those who sailed her, even if they were unaware of her flaws.

Stability. One revelation concerns the flawed reliance on initial stability and the need for deriving full stability data when putting a sailing ship into service. The failure to do so resulted in a poverty of understanding that led directly to loss of the *Albatross*. Initial stability is not related to the survivability of a vessel in a catastrophic knockdown situation. Recognition of this relationship has grown enormously since the *Albatross* was converted to a brigantine. Unless Sheldon insisted on a stability investigation of a higher order, any number of naval architects at the time may have simply confirmed that the ship had sufficient initial stability.

Modifications. We cannot discuss the loss of the *Albatross* without addressing the potential for a sound design to be utterly compromised through changes to the vessel. Vessels can be safely modified, but only if the impact of the change is assessed and understood in light of the purpose of the ship. When the purpose of modifications is to maximize the dramatic effect of a sailing ship for a Hollywood movie, particular caution is warranted should the vessel then be put to sail training or anything else.

A ship with many past lives faces increased odds of being modified for the worse as she moves farther from her original purpose and the people who knew her first. In the absence of a periodic investigation and a load line (Plimsoll mark), modifications can have a cumulative effect unknown to the trusting souls who go to sea aboard her. A vessel may be unwittingly undermined as time goes by and incomplete records come to reflect normal human fallibility. That said, age alone is not a determinant of serviceability. A well-built and properly maintained vessel may remain seaworthy indefinitely. Although the *Albatross* fell victim to an approach to calculating stability that has been overtaken, she herself was not outmoded.

The Illusion of Safety. Beyond all reason, it seems that aesthetics influence the way people feel about ships. The impression of the *Albatross*'s stability was so convincing that, even after she capsized and sank in a wind-related event, one survivor described her as the "ultimate in seaworthiness and safety." Another claimed, "She was as seaworthy as she was beautiful." A third wrote, "She was a rugged ship, and we were all confident that she could take anything in her stride." Such statements of confidence can only be squared with what actually happened by the reasoning that the vessel *felt* much safer than she actually was. A tragic and recurring theme among sailing ship casualties is the dangerous misconception that one can "feel" stability. Deficient stability was not evident to those aboard the *Albatross* until a worst-case scenario unfolded because it is imperceptible in any useful way to the sailor standing on deck: "If a vessel is found to be tender, the prudent Master will carry less sail. Such a vessel may, nevertheless, be quite safe from flooding or capsizing. Conversely, as has been learned at much cost in human life, a vessel may feel quite stiff and still be at risk of flooding or capsize."

Sea trials are invaluable for confirming designed capabilities in many areas, but because trials never test a vessel at large angles of heel, ultimate stability is not one of those tested capabilities.

In the absence of properly derived stability data, a history of successful voyaging is not always an indication of safety, even with heavy-weather experiences factored in. For the *Albatross* it appears to have only been a matter of time until circumstances revealed her flaws. Those who find the complexities of stability mysterious may easily misconstrue a large vessel that has an extensive voyaging history with a sound vessel. The issue of misplaced confidence is noteworthy because it is conspicuously present in the case of the *Marques* under nearly identical circumstances. In the case of the *Albatross*, Long wrote, "It is apparent from the accounts of the disaster that over confidence in the vessel may have delayed taking action, which could have saved her." In fairness to Captain Sheldon, and given his deep personal loss, it is unthinkable that he would have taken the *Albatross* to sea had he been aware of her true stability condition. His confidence in her, although ultimately unjustified, was understandable. But it raises the question: what does the average sailing ship captain of today know about sailing ship stability? The answer is, probably not enough.

The Licensing of Sailing Ship Officers

The regulatory approach in respect to sailing ship stability in the years since the *Albatross* was lost has been mixed. Stability standards have been established for the ships themselves, which is a significant step. However, the people responsible for the ships continue to be largely left to their own devices to figure out what they need to know. This system is essentially unchanged from the one Captain Sheldon knew the day the *Albatross* went down. Stability remains the purview of the naval architect hired by the owner, on whom the captain relies. There is no aspect of the licensing process in the United States that requires sail-endorsed officers to demonstrate an understanding of sailing ship stability in a manner pertinent to the management of the vessels they serve. The sailing endorsement exam focuses on naming the parts of a sailboat and does not consider in detail the finer points of seamanship with respect to professional sailing ship operations. The examining of U.S. officers-in-sail is simplistic and therefore facilitates more of the same. Fortunately, the safety record has been good, but this owes little to the exam process.

Squall Tactics. Another lesson arising from this case pertains to the nature of squalls. Heavy weather, unlike squalls, imposes its demands on a ship's stability gradually. As a storm develops, the master and crew generally have time to assess and respond to deteriorating conditions by reefing sails, securing hatches, altering course, and so forth. Under such circumstances, a true test of a vessel's ultimate stability may never be precipitated, despite many encounters with fierce weather. Therefore, the brief and sudden squall may be more dangerous to a sailing vessel than the well-forecast storm. Under light conditions, the 30-Knot Rule can help guide decisive action in respect to sail area in the onset of a squall. At the very least, the *Albatross* illustrates the speed and totality of a stability casualty, and the lack of forewarning that may accompany it. When a vessel's stability is of a low order, the master's handling must be conservative in the utmost. When a vessel's true stability characteristics are not even known, then the master is in danger of not taking appropriate action to preserve the ship.

Watertight Subdivision. Although structural failure does not appear to be an issue in this case, there is reason to believe that watertight doors left open contributed to the speed of the flooding. If subdivision is intact (that is, the watertight doors are closed), then downflooding may occur through one or two hatches and still prevent a rapid sinking such as the *Albatross* experienced. In the event of a catastrophic knockdown or a collision, watertight subdivisions that aren't intact are useless: crew cannot be expected to handle the doors effectively under such circumstances. Opening and closing watertight doors while routinely moving about a ship may pose certain inconveniences, but those inconvenient doors exist for a purpose. When an extreme situation arises, one hopes the doors are positioned to advantage, rather than the opposite.

Watch Below

Many years after the fact, the first mate reflected on the loss of the *Albatross*:

> In hindsight, obviously things should have been done differently, but that is
> not to say that people were not alert and trying to respond correctly to condi-
> tions as they perceived them. Given what we now know about the *Albatross*'s
> stability problems, it is apparent that she had been skillfully handled through
> many previous squalls. What was a tragedy on the *Albatross* would likely
> have been a bad scare on another vessel.

The need to appreciate a vessel's stability characteristics is abundantly
clear. When the mission becomes the carriage of young, inexperienced people in an environment renowned for its hostility and unpredictability, this
duty acquires an even greater urgency. The loss of the *Albatross* was probably not an act of God in the sense that the forces unleashed were beyond
what could ordinarily be considered survivable. Had well-designed stability
criteria existed and been applied, the *Albatross* might still be sailing today.
The criteria embodied in the SSV regulations that require a range of positive
stability to 90 degrees is the *Albatross*'s sad gift to future sailors. When
asked about the safety of sail training in general, Captain Sheldon opined
that it was a reasonably safe activity. "You have to live life," he said. When
asked what the single most important development was in sail training
practices that might have saved his ship, he replied without hesitation, having ships with the ability to withstand a 90-degree knockdown.

The *Marques*, rigged as a barque, charges along before a fair breeze. (PPL)

Marques
1917–1984

BUILDER: Unknown, in Valencia, Spain

RIG: Levant schooner, Polacca brigantine, barque

HULL: Wood

SAIL AREA: 7,500 square feet

LOA: 87.55 feet

LWL: "About 72 feet"

SPARRED LENGTH: 117 feet

DRAFT: 9 feet (register); 10.5 feet maximum; 8 feet mean draft at time of loss

BEAM: 23 feet (register); "found to have probably been 24.28 feet" by other records

TONNAGE: 85 gross tons; 57.82 gross registered tons

POWER: Twin 6-cylinder Gardner diesels, 127 horsepower each, driving twin screws

FLAG HISTORY: Spain, Britain

*I*N JUNE 1984 the British sail training vessel *Marques* was participating in a tall-ships race from Bermuda to Halifax when she was bowled over by a squall and sunk in a matter of seconds. The incident occurred during the first night at sea after leaving Bermuda, and most of the nineteen people who were lost were trapped below. The nine survivors were picked up after daybreak and returned to Bermuda.

At many levels within the broader endeavor of traditional sail, questions of seaworthiness, responsibility, and liability were brought sharply into focus in an unprecedented fashion. In Britain and around the world, regulatory agencies and sail training organizations scrambled to reassess their standards and procedures in the hope of heading off another such incident. The investigation brought to light a tragedy in the classical sense, whereby the outcome was foretold but, through human nature and happenstance, the warnings of the Cassandras were ignored.

CONTEXT AND FALLOUT

For a host of reasons—including timing—the loss of the *Marques* illuminated the renaissance of traditional sail and sail training in the worst possible light. The fallout is still felt. Unlike the *Albatross*, which was a low-profile enterprise making a solitary voyage to remote destinations, the *Marques* was lost while participating in a series of high-profile international tall-ships races and events. The races were organized by the American Sail Training Association (ASTA) and its British counterpart, the Sail Training Association (STA), and sponsored by Cutty Sark Ltd. The 1984 program was scheduled to culminate in the celebration of the 350th anniversary of Québec City. It was the premier maritime event of the summer in North America and the first major tall-ship event in North America since the U.S. bicentennial eight years earlier. Naturally, the races and festivals were designed to celebrate tall ships in a manner that would best promote sail training and attract public participation. The *Marques* put sail training in the spotlight, all right, but not in a manner intended.

By nature and necessity, the maritime world has long been characterized by an international flavor. The *Marques* herself was a creature of this on several counts. She was Spanish built and British owned and flagged; the captain was American, the mates were British; the remaining crew were British and Antiguan; the trainees were Antiguan and American; the sail training instructors were assigned by ASTA. Like the Olympic Games, tall-ship events are conceived as an opportunity to build on an inherent internationalism to foster camaraderie and friendly competition while upholding pride in national maritime traditions. All the participants are goodwill ambassadors for the larger venture, while spectators enjoy a glimpse of a world that for the most part fulfills its function somewhere over the horizon. The loss of the *Marques* altered this happy image for a time, and perhaps permanently in some respects. The tragedy extended beyond the ship itself and ignited a spate of legal actions on both sides of the Atlantic, though liability was never established in a court of law. To say the least, the atmosphere of enthusiasm and cooperation that brought about the 1984 program was dampened and strained as organizers and participants wondered what they had gotten themselves into.

Compounding the negative publicity was the *Marques*'s recent history, which reflected badly both on the renaissance of traditional sail in general and on sail training in particular. At the time of the *Marques*'s sinking, traditional sailing activities had been gaining momentum for nearly three decades. Yet the picture that emerged from the *Marques* study suggests an accident waiting to happen. Her operators exacerbated her fatal shortcomings while, despite warning signs, a reputable maritime authority (the British Department of Transport) approved her for oceangoing sail training only months before her loss.

About the fallout from the *Marques*, it was noted shortly after the disaster, "When a government department is embarrassed, other people always suffer." While reform did and generally does involve some suffering, it was not as great as that experienced by those who lost friends and loved ones aboard the *Marques*.

Another matter of timing that influenced the impact of the casualty relates to the fact that the sinking coincided with the unveiling of new regulations for sail training vessels in the United States. These Sailing School Vessels (SSV) regulations had been in the works for some years and were shaped, as we know, in part by the loss of the *Albatross*. Problems such as those that afflicted the *Marques* had been freshly approached in the United States just as counterparts in Britain were grappling with the same issues. This coincidence of purpose contributed to a fruitful dialogue and exchange of ideas regarding the safety and regulation of sailing ships in the postcommercial era.

Finally, in the midst of the *Marques* investigation, news came that the American topsail schooner *Pride of Baltimore* was lost at sea on her way home from Europe. Although the *Pride of Baltimore* was technically not a sail training ship, she was a well-known historic replica whose authenticity and ambitious voyages epitomized one facet of the renaissance of traditional sail. Her loss added fuel to a fire already burning in Britain, and contributed to a sense of urgency regarding the safety of tall ships on both sides of the Atlantic.

The pattern of developments shared by the *Albatross* and the *Marques* can only be described as uncanny. The deleterious rig expansions for film work, the changes of ownership, inconstant missions, and the misplaced confidence bolstered by each squall successfully weathered show how seaworthiness may be compromised with the best of intentions. Despite its celebrated internationalism, a certain provincialism regarding matters of stability may have afflicted the resurgence of traditional sail, as seen through this case, though three decades after the loss of the *Albatross* this argument seems more strained. Ultimately, the vessel's unchecked drift into sail training ended up costing lives. More than any other case considered in this book, the story of the *Marques* is a parable for the way in which the renaissance of traditional sail has contributed to the venerable process whereby safety at sea is improved through tragedy. Sweeping generalizations cannot be made about the sail training industry because of the *Marques*. Her story is worthy of the telling precisely because it is extraordinary.

The *Report of the Formal Investigation* (the *Report*) is the principal source of facts in this case and is widely cited in this chapter. The investigation and proceedings exceeded the original estimated time frame of six weeks and ultimately spanned a year and a half. The record suggests that, at least initially, the Department of Transport was not eager to investigate the loss of the *Marques*. Sixteen months passed before an investigation was convened, and only then largely due to persistent pressure from families of the victims. At one point, Lord Napier of Ettrick, who was in Bermuda at the time of the race, raised the question in the House of Lords inquiring into the "inordinate delay," and a former partner in the *Marques* also pressed for an investigation. The request for an investigation was finally approved.

THE HISTORY

The *Marques* was built in Spain as a smallish cargo schooner in 1917; she was an unremarkable craft in her day. Her prosaic task was to carry general cargo to and from small ports in the western Mediterranean. Although steam had largely supplanted sail in the deep-sea trades in the aftermath of World War I, many coastal and "short-sea" trades thrived in sail up to World War II in the Mediterranean and elsewhere. Local trades involved small enough volumes that they were adequately served by vessels of the *Marques*'s size as long as shippers were willing to accept the inconveniences associated with sail transport. At the same time, the economics of investing in steamers of comparable size were prohibitive. The following synopsis of the *Marques*'s early history appeared in the official report of the inquiry that followed her loss:

> In 1928 she was fitted with an engine and single propeller. She continued to trade, but during the 1930s is thought to have been badly damaged in the Spanish Civil War. In 1945 she was largely rebuilt and it appears probable that much of her keel and many of her frames were replaced. She resumed carrying cargo between the Spanish mainland and islands. In 1958 the ship was described as "a sailing and motor vessel with two masts." In 1960 she was fitted with two Kelvin engines and twin screws. Two years later the documents record that her mainmast was removed "as she was no longer used as a sailing ship."

The *Marques* must have been among the very last auxiliary-sail coasting schooners carrying cargo in Europe, as such vessels were thought to be essentially extinct by 1960.

Cargo Schooner to Pleasure Yacht

In 1972 an Englishman named Robin Cecil-Wright purchased the *Marques* in Spain to "further his interest in film-making, and for cruising with his family." John Perryman, who advertised himself as a naval architect, was engaged to survey the vessel. Perryman found some decay but felt that, though old and in need of work, the hull had been well maintained and was generally sound. A limited refit was undertaken in Spain, which included reinforcing the inner structure of the hull with steel to resist further hogging, and installing ten ferro-cement tanks in the hold. Although Perryman was not engaged to conduct a stability survey, he suggested that an additional thirty-five to forty tons of ballast be shipped, since the vessel would no longer have the weight of a cargo to lend stability. This recommendation was not followed. Instead, Cecil-Wright decided to rely on the weight of these new cement tanks and their liquid contents. The free-surface effect makes using tank space that contains consumable liquids, such as freshwater or fuel, in lieu of ballast a questionable approach to maintaining the stability of any vessel.

Cecil-Wright found the vessel's rig "insufficiently interesting for film work," so the *Marques* underwent a conversion to a Polacca brigantine, in keeping with her Mediterranean origins. Upon completion of the work, the *Marques* carried on her foremast a topgallant, topsail, and a course, along with three headsails. The mainmast carried a gaff mainsail and a gaff topsail, and there were three staysails between the masts. The vessel was not engaged in commercial activities, so no stability assessment was required and none was conducted in connection with these changes.

In 1974 the *Marques* was registered in London as a Wood Pleasure Yacht, a status the authorities evidently regarded as compatible with commercial film work. Cecil-Wright managed the *Marques* from his home in Cornwall under the business name China Clipper Society. Although the *Marques* was not a clipper in any respect and had no connection to China, the name had a certain ring.

Pleasure Yacht to Film Star

Over the next two years the *Marques* participated in a number of film projects around Britain, including the popular television series *The Onedin Line*. In 1976 the BBC contracted the vessel for a project re-creating Charles

Darwin's famous voyage to the Galápagos by way of the Strait of Magellan. This project represented a significant expansion of the China Clipper Society's sphere of operations. The role called for the *Marques* to play the part of HMS *Beagle*, a three-masted barque, even though the *Marques* was a two-masted brigantine. The China Clipper Society overcame the problem in the following manner:

> The *Marques* was re-rigged and refitted as a 3 masted barque with topgallants, topsails and courses on the fore and main masts. A mizzen mast was added. No professional advice was sought when making these changes, which increased the top weight and the sail area. Additionally a heavy structured low poop house was constructed for cosmetic purposes. . . . The original cargo hatch was redesigned for the voyage by the BBC Design Department.

At the request of the BBC the Department of Transport assigned an inspector, Mr. Longbottom, to examine the vessel during the refit in the spring of 1977. Although he found the vessel's structural condition adequate, his report included the following:

> It would appear that no information on the stability characteristics of the vessel is available. Having particular regard to the change of rig and the extent of the voyage . . . it is *strongly* recommended that a competent consultant be engaged to lift the lines, prepare hydrostatic and cross curves of stability, and carry out an inclining experiment and investigate the power to carry sail [emphasis added].

Longbottom was not ambiguous. He considered it "only sensible to take these measures, when nothing was known of [the vessel's] stability characteristics." The BBC charterers relayed Longbottom's recommendation to the China Clipper Society, who assured the BBC that stability data would be obtained. Appledore Shipyard estimated the cost of the work, which would take two weeks, to run about £3,000. The inspector's recommendation was considered valid in principle, but with the conversion work already behind schedule, the China Clipper Society decided not to do the stability work after all. Despite the society's prior assurances to the BBC, the *Marques* proceeded to sea without stability data. Thus, seven years before the *Marques* was lost, the crucial issue of stability was formally raised by a qualified inspector—and shelved.

Though the data were not required of a pleasure yacht by law, Longbottom's recommendation to secure them was rooted in experience and commonsense. But the race to complete a radical rig alteration, an alteration that could only challenge the vessel's stability, displaced the commonsense obligation to understand the effect of that alteration on stability. The ship then bustled off to sea, which as events ultimately proved, was the worst place a vessel so altered could be.

From Film Prop to Sail Training

During preparations for the BBC Darwin project, former Royal Navy officer Mark Litchfield joined Cecil-Wright in the operation of the *Marques*. Litchfield soon became a partner in the China Clipper Society and was appointed captain for the second part of the Darwin expedition that brought the vessel home to England by way of Panama. In the course of her twenty-thousand-mile voyage, the *Marques* experienced winds up to force 8 winds (34–40 knots; see the Beaufort Scale in the appendix). The vessel was said to have "stood up well," and this convinced Litchfield that she was "sound and stable." As with the *Albatross* and other ships, a measure of successful performance at sea became the basis for sweeping confidence, despite the absence of supporting data or an unbiased assessment. Back in Britain in 1978, the *Marques* continued to do film work, but her sail training debut came when she was chartered on short notice to participate in a Tall Ships Race from Britain to Oslo. Litchfield sailed as master, though the sail training program was handled by the charterers.

In 1979 the *Marques* underwent another refit. To improve the chartroom and "reception conditions," a new poop house was constructed that extended the full width of the vessel and stood approximately twice as high as the earlier deckhouse. At some point in this process, a decision was made to locate a battery bank on deck forward of the aft deckhouse. Although this was not a unique arrangement, the significant weight of the batteries above the center of gravity is not inconsequential. These changes merited the same consideration as adding masts, topmasts, and yards as far as stability was concerned. John Perryman, who had been the consultant for earlier modifications, was consulted informally during this refit, but neither he nor a trained naval architect was engaged to consider the effect of these changes on stability.

For the rest of 1979 the *Marques* engaged in a variety of promotional ventures, film jobs, and charters throughout the British Isles. The charters were primarily booked through the Demarco Gallery in Scotland. Under the regulations of the time, a passenger certificate was not required as long as the vessel remained in home waters and did not carry more than twelve passengers. The rules that applied to the *Marques* allowed *non-cargo-carrying sailing vessels of less than 80 net registered tons to operate in British waters* without a Loadline Certificate or a Loadline Exemption Certificate. Nevertheless, at one point during the summer of 1979, the local Department of Transport Ship Surveyor notified the Demarco Gallery in writing that the *Marques* had no passenger certificate and that she was subject to geographical operating restrictions and passenger limits. Though the *Marques* did not require a passenger certificate to do what she was doing, the inspector evidently felt the charterers should understand that the vessel they were hiring was an unknown quantity to the Department of Transport. He also informed the Demarco Gallery that the China Clipper Society had not obtained the stability data recommended by Longbottom in 1977. The motivation for this communication did not come out in the later inquiry, but it was more likely an exercise of due diligence on the part of a department representative rather than a manifestation of some extraordinary prescience or knowledge of sailing-ship stability.

With winter approaching, the China Clipper Society made plans to operate natural-history cruises in the Canary Islands for groups of passengers from Britain. Cecil-Wright duly notified the department of these plans. Once the ship was in the Canary Islands, paying guests flew down to join her. Some were signed on as passengers and others were regarded as paying crew. Though no prior experience was required, they had shipboard duties, including watchstanding. Inexperienced people paying money to stand watch and help with the operation of a sailing ship under supervision pretty well describes the basis of modern sail training.

Upon the *Marques*'s return to Britain in the summer of 1980, the Department of Transport's Marine Directorate informed Cecil-Wright that, under the terms of the Merchant Shipping Act of 1967 (Load Line Act), the vessel needed either a Load Line Certificate or a Load Line Exemption Certificate when operating beyond British coastal waters.

The capacity to grant a Load Line Exemption reflected a provision in the International Maritime Organization's (IMO) convention allowing national authorities to exercise discretion within their jurisdiction under special circumstances. The protocol for granting an exemption required that the Department of Transport obtain a thorough understanding of the vessel it was exempting, including an extensive structural survey and a stability assessment. Obtaining either certificate would have been a costly undertaking for any vessel but especially so for a historic vessel such as the *Marques*, which was not designed or built to meet contemporary safety regulations. The department clarified that it was not the vessel's classification that determined the need for certification (the *Marques* was still officially registered as a "pleasure yacht"), but rather "the use to which she was being put." The department acknowledged that it was "often difficult to determine when pleasure activities ended and business began," but explained that the carriage of fare-paying passengers while abroad was a matter of concern. The department continued to view the commercial aspects of film work as separate from accepting payment to take people sailing. Indeed, at the conclusion of another season of chartering with the Demarco Gallery in British waters, the department approved the *Marques* to voyage to the Mediterranean for a refit and "filmmaking."

Extending the Rig Farther

In 1980 the China Clipper Society signed a film contract for the movie *Tai Pan*. On the basis of that contract, the society purchased in Spain a second vessel named the *Ciudad de Inca*, formerly the *Maria Asumpta*. The *Ciudad de Inca* was described as a "hulk" at the time of her acquisition, so the new owners set out to rebuild and rerig her at a shipyard at Barbate in southern Spain. According to the subsequent investigation, this is the point at which Mark Litchfield was considered to have adopted responsibility for all management and operating decisions made by the China Clipper Society, though Cecil-Wright was technically still a partner until March 1983.

The *Marques* joined the *Inca* at Barbate for the winter of 1981. During this time the *Marques*'s rig was substantially renewed and extended even farther. The foremast and mainmast were heightened by eight feet to take royals (square sails above the topgallant), and stunsails (studding sails) were added. By now the *Marques* had gone from a schooner to a brigantine, to a barque, to a more extreme barque fitted with stunsails. Still no ballast had been added as per Perryman's original recommendation, nor had her stability been analyzed in keeping with Longbottom's recommendation, both of which would have been appropriate precautions even before the latest modifications to the rig and the aft deckhouse. Meanwhile, the contract to film *Tai Pan* appeared to have fallen through.

With the rerig complete, the *Marques* spent the summer of 1981 cruising the western Mediterranean with groups of people who had flown in from Britain. The investigation never addressed how this activity squared with the concerns expressed by the department after the winter natural-history cruises in the Canary Islands, or with filmmaking, which was the basis of approving the Mediterranean cruise.

At one stage that summer, the vessel experienced a powerful *mistral*, a Mediterranean squall. By Captain Litchfield's reckoning it blew as high as force 12, around 65 knots. It was daylight at the time and the vessel was carrying nearly full sail, though the royals had been struck in anticipation of the squall. Litchfield bore off and later estimated the angle of heel at 40 degrees, saying that the rail went under one to two feet. Other eyewitnesses put the angle at less, but regardless, the squall was of a high order. Though there was some difference of opinion regarding how quickly the bearing-off maneuver was accomplished, the investigation concluded that it was fairly prompt and averred that this may have been crucial to the vessel's survival. Rather than prompting Litchfield to pursue a fuller understanding of the

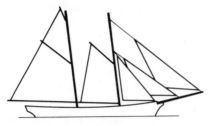

Cargo schooner (1917)

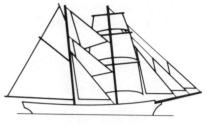

Polacca brigantine (1972)

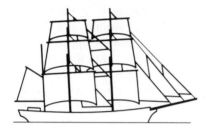

Three-masted barque (1977)

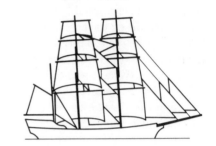

Enlarged poop deck (1979) and mast extensions to take royals (1981)

A re-creation of the rig conversions of *Marques*. (Jim Sollers, based on sketch by Howard Chatterton)

vessel's stability characteristics at the next haulout, the squall had the opposite effect:

> This experience [with the *mistral*] gave Mr. Litchfield even greater confidence in the vessel's stability and was subsequently used by him as the best evidence of the vessel's stability when he was seeking a Load Line Exemption Certificate.

From November 1981 through January 1982 the *Marques* was hauled out at Barbate, Spain, again for maintenance and repair. The hull underwent significant work, including a new keel, new forefoot, and comprehensive refastening below the waterline where planks had softened around the iron spikes. A number of planks were said to have been replaced, as well. The film contract for *Tai Pan* having come to naught, British Electric Traction (BET) expressed interest in using both of the China Clipper Society's vessels for a promotional drive in Britain during the summer of 1982. As part of the agreement, BET required a written professional opinion affirming the vessels' seaworthiness. Perryman was engaged to provide this certification and thus surveyed the *Marques* in Barbate. His overall impression was favorable: with proper maintenance "the vessel should be capable of giving many good years of service."

In a separate matter later that year (May 1982), Perryman conducted an inclining experiment of the *Marques*. Inclining experiments are by nature subject to a variety of errors, both external and internal. Customarily, known weights are moved from side to side while the naval architect measures the effect on a pendulum or series of pendulums hanging on the centerline. Three pendulums are the industry standard for an inclining conducted for official purposes. As with taking star sights, the purpose is to average out errors. Wind on the rig or a dockline left too tight can skew the results. Weight that is free to move, such as a standing gaff that is not vanged down tight, or uncertainty about the weights themselves, can introduce errors. Inclining is a useful but imperfect procedure. This was the first and only occasion that the stability of the *Marques* was measured in any fashion while owned by the China Clipper Society. It was not done to determine the stability characteristics of the *Marques*, but rather as "some check" on the *Ciudad de Inca*.

The *Ciudad de Inca* had a Spanish stability booklet, and Perryman wanted a basis for checking those data. The *Report* explained that because in Perryman's view the two vessels had somewhat similar dimensions, and Litchfield had expressed total confidence in the *Marques*, an inclining of the *Marques* might lend insight into the characteristics of the *Ciudad de Inca*. It was not made clear why, if the *Ciudad de Inca* was the point of interest in this exercise, she herself was not inclined. The results of Perryman's inclining produced a metacentric height (GM) of 3.76 feet, which was then written up as a Certificate of Statical Stability. Though an inclining was not requested by BET, the results were included in the Certificate of Seaworthiness that Perryman provided based on his hull survey. The certificate stated that "the statical and sailing stability characteristics of the vessel, as rigged, was comparable with that of contemporary craft." The experiment did not include any righting-arm curves (GZ), and there was no recommendation by Perryman to obtain full stability data. After discussions with Perryman, Litchfield logged that the ship's GM was "very high and thus . . . very stable. Bore out my belief."

Far from arresting the chain of missed opportunities in respect to understanding the *Marques*'s stability, Perryman's inclining bolstered opinion at China Clipper Society by providing quasiscientific evidence of the vessel's stability. Yet the inclining experiment was clearly not conceived of as a precision exercise, and the investigation concluded the following:

> This document [the Certificate of Statical Stability] had to be treated with extreme caution: the vessel's draught was not a direct measurement; the displacement was an estimate based on "probable" prismatic coefficient and only one pendulum had been used, so there was no check for errors in measurement. There could be doubts about the accuracy of the weights of the three drums of water used as inclining weights.

Most important, it stated, "Mr. Perryman was not testing the *Marques* for her stability." The court stated that this, coupled with other considerations, "leads us to reject Mr. Perryman's inclining experiment."

Sail Training as a Mainstay

By 1982, the transition from film work to sail training seems to have accelerated for the China Clipper Society. By this time the two ships had absorbed considerable investment, much of it based on expectations for the *Tai Pan* film contract, and were increasingly operated as a business. The original concept of a pleasure yacht and filming no longer characterized the activities of the China Clipper Society. Both vessels returned to Britain for the summer of 1982 and successfully participated in the Clipper Challenge, the publicity event organized by BET. Daylong races were held between British ports with teenage students who signed on as crew and received instruction from the professional crew. The close resemblance of this activity to passenger-carrying aroused misgivings within the department: "At both district and headquarters level, representatives of the Department were not happy with the situation presented by the Clipper Challenge." One inspector wrote the Marine Directorate (the maritime division of Department of Transport) expressing concerns about taking schoolchildren to sea aboard vessels that had never been surveyed or formally certified for such work. In response, the Marine Directorate acknowledged that students who signed on as crew for sail training instruction were "akin to passengers," but also noted that the authority of the department in this case was limited to lifesaving and firefighting equipment. It is recalled that under the Load Line Act, sailing vessels of less than 80 net registered tons that were not carrying cargo could legally operate within British coastal waters without complying with the requirements for a Load Line Certificate or a Load Line Exemption Certificate. In other words, with the exception of firefighting and lifesaving equipment, the vessels were essentially unregulated. Only if the *Marques* proposed to conduct sail training activities beyond British coastal waters could the department require compliance with the terms of the Load Line Act.

In response to the concerns expressed by its own officials, the Marine Directorate issued a memorandum instructing inspectors to monitor future activities of the vessels. It also reminded inspectors that the vessels could not be required to undergo a survey because of the exemption that applied to their present activities. The China Clipper Society was again notified through official channels, including the Senior Ship Surveyor of the Load Line Section, that any sail training outside U.K. waters would necessitate either a Load Line Certificate or a Load Line Exemption Certificate, and the requisite structural survey and stability data. Litchfield responded to the

Marine Directorate by stressing the "worthwhile purpose of youth training" aboard the vessels and the need to operate outside British waters during winter months in order to be financially viable.

At this point it is clear that the authorities were alert to the China Clipper Society's tendency to press the boundaries of the existing regulations. It is also apparent that the inadequacy of the Load Line Rules for regulating the China Clipper Society's new activities contributed directly to the restraint the authorities adopted toward the *Marques* and the *Ciudad de Inca*. Sail trainees seemingly occupied a nether zone between passenger and crew that had not yet been resolved.

The Load Line Exemption Certificate

Early in 1983 Captain Litchfield contacted the American Sail Training Association (ASTA), proposing to operate in North America with U.S. trainees aboard. ASTA stipulated that the vessels would first need to be certified by the national authority under which the vessels operated. In March 1983 the Department of Transport reminded Litchfield yet again of where the law stood on overseas sail training operations. The Bristol office was instructed to "keep the vessels under surveillance." Litchfield was also informed that, if he were to seek a Load Line Certificate, a survey would take several weeks and would entail, among other things, deriving full stability data and partially dismantling the ships for inspection. Meanwhile, the China Clipper Society went ahead with plans to conduct sail training voyages in the United States. What happened next is a matter of the official record:

> In Bristol Captain Martinez [district representative of the Marine Directorate] became aware of an advertisement in the national press offering places for 750 pounds for a voyage across the Atlantic. Persons who were accepted were to be signed on as crew and receive sail training. Captain Martinez asked Mr. Litchfield what his intentions were and was told of the plans to operate from cities in the United States. Captain Martinez told Mr. Litchfield that the vessels would have to obtain Load Line Certificates before they could depart, and reported the matter to the Marine Directorate.
>
> On 9th June a meeting was held chaired by Mr. John of the Marine Directorate and attended by, amongst others, Mr. Litchfield. Mr. John, having heard Litchfield's account of the vessels made it clear that it was the Department's view that the ship required a Load Line Certificate for the planned trans-Atlantic voyage. Mr. Litchfield stated that this would mean at least the partial opening up of the vessels, which apart from the heavy cost would do the vessels irreparable harm. Mr. John replied that . . . in his opinion the proposed voyage was not a pleasure cruise and he warned Mr. Litchfield that if he failed to comply . . . the Department would be forced to

consider prosecution. Mr. Litchfield was concerned at what he saw as the inflexible attitude of the Marine Directorate. He discussed the situation with a number of people and organizations in an attempt to find a way of operating the vessels without the need for a Load Line survey. There appeared to be no solution.

At that time the Marine Directorate set out the details of the structural survey, since the vessels had never been surveyed by British authorities for any type of commercial work. It was further stated that the vessels would need to be "inclined in the presence of . . . a Department Surveyor."

By this stage the China Clipper Society had been repeatedly apprised of the requirements for offshore sail training, going as far back as the summer of 1980. The *Report* pointed out that the extensive reconstruction work done in the winter of 1982 at Barbate had afforded an excellent opportunity to view the structural integrity of the vessel since a number of planks were removed for replacement and refastening, and other structural work was done. The *Marques* had hauled out on other occasions since that time, during which the lines could have been lifted and her stability calculated without incurring the expense of a special-purpose haulout. In light of this, the *Report* criticized Litchfield for paying "insufficient attention to the regulatory requirements." The *Report* also mentions a document in which "Mr. Litchfield refers to keeping as low a profile as possible as far as the DTP [Department of Transport] was concerned."

The Department of Transport may have indeed shown itself to be inflexible in certain respects until David Mitchell, Parliamentary Under-Secretary of State for Transport, became involved in July 1983. Yet based on the record, the approach of the China Clipper Society leaves the impression it was not keenly interested in compliance except to the extent necessary to secure charters. The China Clipper Society had invested substantially in its two ships for filmmaking and perhaps was surprised to discover, when its interest changed to deep-sea sail training, that the certification process for that activity was more demanding and costly than anticipated. The society seems to have adopted the view that the worthwhile nature of sail training activities conducted on its historic ships entitled it to special regulatory consideration.

In the years since the accident, many have privately wondered what role Mark Litchfield's family connections may have played in this case, including the fact that his father, John Litchfield, had been a member of Parliament. The investigation produced no evidence of undue influence, but Litchfield's persistence, as documented by the investigation, conveys a hope of finding an alternative route to certification, and this is exactly what came to pass.

After Mr. John of the Marine Directorate took a hard line against what he saw as a blatant attempt to stretch the interpretation of a pleasure yacht,

Litchfield wrote his member of Parliament, Andrew Rowe. In his 1 July 1983 letter he described the value of being able to offer a sail training experience aboard these two historic vessels, and the predicament the project now faced. Rowe, in turn, forwarded the letter to David Mitchell, Parliamentary Under-Secretary of State for Transport, in hopes that the department "might find a way of saving the unusual venture."

The request received prompt attention at the highest levels. On 13 July Dr. Cowley, the Surveyor General, met with Mr. Holstead, a department surveyor, to discuss how to proceed in respect to the Minister of Transport's interest in the case, and "to decide whether as a matter of policy the Department could take the unusual procedure of accepting the survey of a private surveyor retrospectively." To Dr. Cowley's knowledge such a measure was without precedent, but he "anticipated that the Minister would probably want to accede to the owner's request" that such a course be allowed. Cowley advised Holstead that if the minister favored this course of action it could be acted on if the following conditions were met: "Holstead would have to interview the surveyor and be satisfied with the surveyor's competence, [confirm] that he carried out a proper survey, and that the surveyor realized his responsibility. The surveyor would have to sign a declaration taking responsibility for the condition and seaworthiness of the ships." The investigation report stated: "Mr. Holstead appreciated that he would have to act with caution."

A meeting held the next day included Holstead and Captain Jestico, Chief Examiner of Masters and Mates. As anticipated, the Minister for Transport inquired if it would be possible to accept the findings of a private surveyor, Perryman, even though they were more than a year old. Although it was considered a "most exceptional course," Holstead agreed to interview Perryman to ascertain his competence and to determine if his 1982 survey could be accepted in lieu of the normal procedure.

The interview on 18 July established Perryman's credibility in respect to wooden vessel construction. Holstead agreed that the GM of over three feet was high, but he did not "probe" how the inclining test had been conducted. The *Report* stated: "Not very much time was spent on stability, since Mr. Holstead knew that the *Marques* had no stability data. He was impressed by Mr. Litchfield's encounter with the mistral . . . and admitted that his knowledge of sailing was limited."

Perryman was shown the written declaration he would be required to sign:

> It is my professional opinion that both the *Marques* and the *Ciudad de Inca* are now in such safe and seaworthy condition and possess such adequate stability to enable them to sail on transatlantic voyages and to operate within the following geographic limits . . . for the next two years.

Holstead reported back to the Surveyor General that he had "no qualms" accepting Perryman's survey.

The next day another meeting was held with Captain Jestico that focused on manning and crew qualifications. Litchfield agreed to submit the qualifications of anyone he intended to hire as master or mate for approval by Jestico. A few days later Litchfield submitted a list, which Jestico approved, thus clearing the way for the issuance of the Load Line Exemption Certificate. Perryman signed the declaration, with a caveat reflecting his concern about the state of the timbers beneath the ferro-cement tanks. "We can not go on squeezing extra months out of a Declaration," he wrote. Perryman's earlier recommendation for 30 to 40 tons of ballast was not raised, nor was Longbottom's recommendation to acquire full stability data. The issue of stability was essentially dropped.

While preparations went ahead for the voyage to North America, the ships were visited by department inspectors to observe work being done and inspect firefighting and lifesaving equipment. In October 1983 while the ships were at Plymouth, Inspector Darlow observed that the freeing ports on the *Ciudad de Inca* had been permanently secured, and he ordered them reopened. The *Marques* had a similar arrangement whereby gunports served as freeing ports. These were functional when the inspectors were aboard, and a crew member informed them that the decks did not flood at sea. Longbottom himself resurfaced for the final inspections but does not appear to have raised the issue of stability in an official capacity at that point. The Load Line Exemption Certificate was duly issued on 25 November 1983.

With the Exemption Certificate in hand, the China Clipper Society had accomplished all it had hoped for. It avoided the expense of surveying and obtaining stability data for not one but two ships. Over the concerns of its own officials, the British Department of Transport sanctioned the use of these ships for offshore sail training, which in turn enabled the China Clipper Society to access the U.S. market via ASTA.

Missed Opportunities

Judging from the record, all parties to the certification process focused on the structural integrity of the *Marques* at the expense of stability. The owner showed a keen desire to avoid a structural survey due to the expense and delay, both of which would increase if problems were found. Perryman's credibility with the department was largely predicated on his knowledge of wooden sailing ship construction and maintenance, as well as his recent involvement with the *Marques*. His caveat to the declaration indicated that the framing beneath the cement tanks was his greatest concern.

Likewise, the department's representatives focused on structural issues and manning. The *Report* states that "not much time was spent on stability" because the *Marques* lacked the data and there was a general lack of familiarity with the topic in respect to sailing vessels. Reports of the recent hull work, Perryman's unverified inclining, and Litchfield's sailing experiences were taken as proof of the vessel's overall soundness.

The failure to require stability data was a missed opportunity for several reasons. Litchfield's petition, which was the basis of the approval process, spoke of "irreparable harm" to the hulls and costs estimated at £100,000 for a conventional survey. Making approval conditional on stability analysis would have amounted to a compromise solution that would avoid the great expense of dismantling the hull, while addressing an area of obvious importance—an area that the authorities admitted to understanding only incompletely with respect to sailing vessels. Acquiring righting-arm data would have involved slipping the vessel to take her lines, but no one who intended to eventually fulfill the requirements would consider this unreasonable, particularly if it were timed with a routine haulout.

The department had every good reason to require stability data and none to waive it. Through Longbottom's recommendation the department had formally noted the need for stability information for the *Marques* because she had been greatly altered. The China Clipper Society had implicitly acknowledged the utility of the data when it assured the BBC it would get it. Perhaps most important, the terms of the Load Line Exemption required stability data and that a department surveyor participate in the process. Admittedly, the stability criteria then current were not particularly useful to sailing ships: research conducted retrospectively showed that the *Marques* may have met the righting-arm requirement (designed for merchant ships) but not the angle at which maximum righting arm occurs. We cannot say conclusively how these data would have affected what followed, but insisting on stability information would have given the department hard data on a vessel that had proved elusive to regulate, and it would have sent a strong message that some level of compliance could and would be insisted upon. It would also have given subsequent captains valuable insight into the nature of the ship beneath their feet. In light of the China Clipper Society's sustained efforts to avoid the normal exemption process, the insistence on stability information may have been as worthwhile as the information itself. Instead, in the course of deliberations, the lack of stability data aboard the *Marques* became the rationale for not dwelling on the matter.

Seeking a Load Line Exemption through political channels was a legitimate course of action, but in acceding to the request for special consideration the department failed to fulfill its function and ultimately did itself no favors. In a significant departure from their own procedures, the authorities gave their seal of approval to a vessel they had never surveyed, and did so on the hearsay of its owner and his hired private surveyor. According to the *Report*, at no point did department representatives inspect the hull out of the water or even crawl through the bilges to check the condition of the framing. Compared with the partial dismantling of the hull that would have been required in the normal exemption process, such measures cannot be regarded as onerous and would have been appropriate. While there is good reason to believe that structural failure did not precipitate the loss of the *Marques*, the lack of follow-through on the part of the department once Under-Secretary Mitchell became involved hurt everyone.

In view of the department's well-documented involvement with the *Marques*, and the byzantine path that led to her Exemption Certificate, her loss six months later with nineteen lives was a regulator's worst nightmare. Unlike other tragedies, which may occur beyond the pale of familiarity, the path to the *Marques* tragedy was marked with red flags.

That regulations reflecting the special nature of tall ships and sail training did not exist in Britain at the time the *Marques* was seeking certification was clearly frustrating for both the China Clipper Society and for the authorities who had misgivings about the operation. Ironically, under the existing regulations, the authorities could not insist on a Load Line survey or stability data as long as the *Marques* conducted her activities in British waters, though even this had raised concerns. But when the proposed activities of the *Marques* came to involve long-range sail training on ocean waters, the authorities finally had the regulatory tools to exercise more stringent oversight. Instead of using them, however, they provided a gaping loophole through which the *Marques* sailed.

Transatlantic

The process of acquiring the Load Line Exemption Certificate had disrupted the original plan for the *Marques* to cruise the east coast of the United States in 1983. However, Litchfield had succeeded in obtaining approval to operate abroad, thus satisfying the key prerequisite for ASTA's cooperation. At the end of November, when work on the *Marques* and the *Ciudad de Inca* was nearing completion, Litchfield decided on short notice that the ships should sail due to an impending legal action by his former partner, Robin Cecil-Wright. In a bizarre and prophetic last-minute incident, Cecil-Wright obtained a court order to prevent the vessels from sailing, claiming they were unfit for sea. With the lock gates open and crew standing by the docklines, Longbottom detained the ships until matters could be resolved. Most of the items of concern were deemed to be "trivia," and the whole exercise was seen as a stratagem in Cecil-Wright's legal wrangling with Litchfield. Thus, on 2 December 1983, with the few remaining projects of importance completed, the ships were allowed to sail for the Caribbean.

On the passage to the Canary Islands, Litchfield commanded *Ciudad de Inca* and Captain John Adams commanded the *Marques*. Off Morocco the ships encountered heavy weather, which Adams estimated at force 10 at its peak. During a particularly heavy squall the lee rail went under and the vessel heeled to an angle of "about 40 to 45 degrees," about which Adams reported feeling "no undue concern." The *Marques*'s gunports, which functioned as freeing ports, were damaged during the gale. Repairs were carried out in Tenerife, and the gunports were "sealed by securing timber across them" to prevent further damage. One opening was left on each side aft near the deckhouse.

Another peculiar incident occurred in Tenerife when one of the trainees, Philip Graf, aborted his plan to sail to the Caribbean in the *Marques* and abruptly left the ship. An ASTA member, Graf took the unusual step of writing ASTA a strongly negative report of his experience aboard. Upon learning that ASTA was planning to work with the China Clipper Society, he wrote a second letter:

> There is an unnecessary hazard in sailing these ships. I have never been on vessels where less care was taken to ensure the safety and comfort of the ship's company. I strongly urge that the vessels be thoroughly and periodically inspected and an understanding reached [as to] . . . what ASTA expects and demands in respect to safety, comfort, education, leadership, routine and discipline.

ASTA took the letters seriously. However, when ASTA's commodore, Vice-Admiral Tom Weschler, pressed the matter with Graf, it became evident that his concerns were related more to management than to the seaworthiness of the vessels. Graf had experienced the rough weather on the way down from England and felt the ships handled it well. Rough weather will reduce the standards of comfort and cleanliness on any ship, though Graf used the words "safety" and "hazard" in describing his concerns. Graf's unflattering assessment of the China Clipper Society's operation cast doubt on the professional management of the *Marques*. Given what ultimately came to pass, this incident might be seen as a portent, as did Cecil-Wright's last-minute claim that the vessels were unseaworthy. Few would doubt a connection between professional management and safety at sea, and it may not be incorrect to view Graf's specific complaints as parts of a larger problem. Still, Graf's was the only complaint, and it was not directed at the ship itself. As a result of his letters, ASTA insisted that the China Clipper Society provide "disciplined, orderly, clean and safe ships," and it secured the right to place its own sail training instructors aboard the ships to insure the quality of the educational experience. In Tenerife there was a change of command. Captain Adams shifted to the *Ciudad de Inca*, and Captain Martin Minter-Kemp, an experienced transatlantic sailor, took command of the *Marques*.

The original plan for the ships was to operate day charters in the British Virgin Islands for the winter and then link up with ASTA for the tall-ships races in the summer of 1984. However, in the course of the transit a decision was made to go to Antigua, instead. Stuart Finlay, a paying guest aboard *Ciudad de Inca*, was in charge of a maritime center in Antigua and thought it might be possible to employ the vessels as training ships there. When the ships reached Antigua, however, the maritime center was found to have become "largely moribund" due to a lack of funding. Without the anticipated revenue source, the vessels turned to passenger daysailing and Finlay recruited some Antiguan trainees who participated in the sailing and maintenance of the vessels.

When Captain Minter-Kemp's commitment ended in March 1984, Stuart Finlay became a candidate for the position of master of the *Marques*. He had never been master or a watch officer in a square-rigger before. The transatlantic passage in the brig *Ciudad de Inca* was his first experience with such a vessel. He had, however, pursued a sailing career for some years and had wide experience with yachts, both offshore and coastal. Finlay held a U.S. Coast Guard license for auxiliary-sail vessels, a copy of which was submitted to Litchfield. As part of the review, Finlay skippered the *Marques* for a five-mile trial run in the presence of Captain Minter-Kemp, who was satisfied with his performance. Both Adams and Minter-Kemp supported his candidacy, though Minter-Kemp did so only for the purposes of day chartering in Antigua and was not consulted in respect to the upcoming tall-ships race. In April Finlay's qualifications were submitted to Captain Jestico, the chief examiner of masters and mates for England's Department of Transport, who approved him to sail as master of the *Marques*. Soon after, both vessels proceeded to San Juan, Puerto Rico, to participate in the first leg of the ASTA-organized Tall Ships Race to Bermuda.

Bermuda

Donald Treworgy, an astronomer from the Mystic Seaport Museum, had been assigned to make the passage from San Juan to Bermuda as an educator on behalf of ASTA. Although Treworgy was not a professional sailor, he was a consummate celestial navigator and had made a number of offshore voyages in a variety of vessels. Due to a communications mixup, his arrival at the ship in San Juan had been completely unexpected by Captain Finlay. Despite this inauspicious beginning, Treworgy reported afterward that the voyage had gone well and the ship had seemed well run. For the most part it had been a fair-weather passage. There were no ASTA cadets aboard for the San Juan–Bermuda leg and no formal sail training program, but Treworgy taught the Antiguan trainees navigation as time and interest allowed, and the trainees all stood deck watches.

Reviewing the navigation equipment when he came aboard in San Juan, Treworgy was disappointed to find many of the charts uncorrected and up to seven years old. The *Marques* was fitted with radar, VHF radio, and an RDF (radio direction finder), but she carried no electronic position-fixing equipment such as loran or satnav (satellite navigation). For celestial work there was but one sextant aboard, a plastic training sextant. Although plastic sextants can produce surprisingly good sights, their accuracy is compromised by temperature changes and lower quality construction compared to metal-framed sextants. A metal one had reportedly been removed before the voyage. When the Race Committee at Bermuda discontinued the race from San Juan due to time constraints, it requested that the racing ships call in an electronic fix so they might determine a winner based on best performance up to that point. With no electronic position equipment aboard, Treworgy took a five-star fix with his own sextant and turned in his calculations, which were accepted. The *Marques* arrived at Bermuda on 29 May 1984, having won the first leg of the race on corrected time.

Treworgy's participation on board the *Marques* proved fortuitous from a navigational perspective on more than one point. Prior to joining the ship, he and his Mystic Seaport Museum colleague, Susan Howell, had difficulty getting information about the China Clipper Society ships and the navigational equipment aboard, which would have helped them decide what materials, equipment, and teaching aids to bring. When Treworgy set out to join the ship he still did not have clear answers to these questions, so he had packed along a few additional items, including a metal sextant and a battery-operated upper-sideband receiver. He discovered on arrival in San Juan that the ship's single-sideband (SSB) radio was not functioning. A replacement part was said to be in transit but hadn't arrived before the ship sailed. Fortunately, Treworgy had been able to connect his receiver to the existing antenna. This became the ship's only source of weather information and radio time ticks necessary for accurate celestial positions. The accuracy of these positions became critical when the ship lost its taffrail log spinner (a key piece of dead-reckoning equipment) two days out of San Juan. Since there was no spare spinner on board, dead reckoning aboard the *Marques* instantly became a more precarious exercise.

Though now considered laborious, celestial navigation is a well-proven system with tried-and-true techniques. Given the times and the territory, the lack of electronic position-fixing equipment aboard the *Marques* was not a deficiency. Loran coverage did not extend to the waters between the Caribbean and Bermuda, and satnav was far from common. But certain precautions are incumbent on the master who chooses to depend solely on celestial navigation with trainees and novice crew on board. Among these are ensuring the means to dead reckon and to obtain accurate time. Backup equipment such as additional sextants and taffrail log spinners, along with some duplication of expertise among the officers in the use of the equipment, are also normal precautions. It would appear, however, that the *Marques* was scantily equipped to rely on celestial navigation techniques. Had those aboard the *Marques* needed to transmit emergency information or obtain medical assistance by radio, they would have been out of luck. The odds of such a contingency were demonstrated when on that same leg the *Ciudad de Inca* had to call in a helicopter medical evacuation for a trainee.

In respect to first impressions of the *Marques*, the record is decidedly mixed. Treworgy was struck by the large number of hatches, in particular the size of the main hatch amidships. The main hatch was a converted cargo hatch shaped like a large fore-and-aft rectangle between the foremast and the mainmast. The coaming had been modified for eight teak gratings: two forward and two aft, port and starboard. The gratings accounted for most of the hatch space, but between the forward grates and the aft grates a companionway ladder led to the hold from the deck on the starboard side. The coaming was cut lower where the ladder met the deck to facilitate access. An athwartships sliding hatch covered the companionway descent. The gratings were made watertight by a system of tarpaulins that were battened and wedged around the perimeter of the coaming, and then lashed as they would have been when the vessel was a cargo schooner. When conditions at sea permitted, the sliding hatch was opened and the tarpaulins left off to allow ventilation. Keeping the hatch open improved living conditions below decks, and the high coaming usually prevented water on deck from sloshing below.

When briefing the ASTA instructors who replaced him in Bermuda, Treworgy shared his observations regarding the hatches. Speaking after the fact, Stuart Gillespie, one of the oncoming instructors, agreed that the hatch arrangement was unusual in his experience. He added that he had the impression that the *Marques* was overrigged. The main hatch also caught the attention of Admiral Sir Rae McKaig, who was inspecting the fleet at Bermuda. When he inquired about it, he was assured that it was "properly closed at sea."

On Friday, 1 June, two counselors, Gillespie and Howell, and ten trainees went aboard the *Marques* by arrangement with ASTA. The trainees were briefed on the ship's routine, watchstanding, and emergency procedures and received a general shipboard orientation. In accordance with race

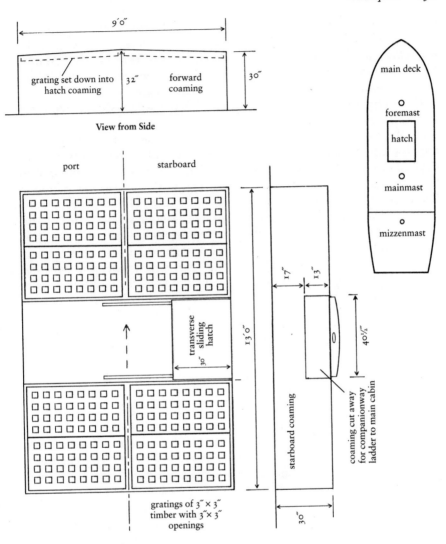

9′0″

grating set down into
hatch coaming

32″

forward
coaming

30″

View from Side

main deck

foremast

hatch

mainmast

mizzenmast

port

starboard

transverse
sliding
hatch

30″

13′0″

17″

13″

40½″

starboard coaming

coaming cut away
for companionway
ladder to main cabin

30″

gratings of 3″ × 3″
timber with 3″ × 3″
openings

View from Above

Details of the *Marques*'s central hatch.
(Jim Sollers, based on description
appearing in the *Report of the Formal
Investigation*)

rules, ASTA officials in Bermuda inspected the *Marques*'s safety equipment. The faulty SSB radio underwent repairs at Treworgy's insistence. The inspection found that one of the life rafts was expired. The Marine Directorate in London granted permission to defer servicing of the life raft, at which point ASTA signed off on the prerace inspection report.

On the morning of 1 June, a captain's briefing addressed, among other things, the weather to be expected after the start of the race on Saturday, 2 June. Weather is expressed in a variety of ways, among which the most important to sailors are surface *forecasts* and *analysis*. Forecasts are *predictions*, whereas *analysis* depicts the actual situation at a given point in time. Weather information was supplied by the U.S. Naval Air Station in Bermuda and included maps prepared by the U.S. Naval Oceanography Command depicting 24-hour, 48-hour, and 72-hour surface forecasts for the local waters around Bermuda. The forecast called for a slow-moving (5–10 knots) cold front followed by weak high pressure to pass through the area from west to east early on Sunday morning, 3 June. The front was expected to bring scattered showers and possibly thunderstorms, with southwest winds force 4–6, shifting northwest with the frontal passage and subsiding. The forecast maps indicated a 1008-millibar low-pressure system near Cape Cod with an associated cold front sweeping down from it in a southwesterly arc. To the west of the cold front, a dotted line curved southwest from the low to a point approximately 300 nautical miles northwest of Bermuda. The significance of the dotted line on the forecast map was not discussed at the meeting. It has since been referred to as a *secondary trough line*, but the well-defined cold front approaching from the west was of more immediate concern and therefore was the focus of discussion. Wind arrows in the vicinity of the dotted line indicated maximum winds of 25 knots: breezy but not menacing. The High Seas forecast from the U.S. Weather Bureau did not warn of a secondary trough or any severe disturbance. The low-pressure system near Cape Cod was forecast to move northeast and out of the area in advance of the racing vessels, presumably dragging any related activity with it. The forecast was not ideal, since once the wind shifted to the northwest the course to Halifax would be close-hauled, but it indicated nothing that posed a threat to the fleet.

On Friday night, 1 June, the night before the race, winds up to 35 knots and heavy showers buffeted the anchorage at Hamilton, Bermuda. The cold front forecast for Sunday morning had arrived. It was stronger than forecast but, perhaps more important, it was about thirty hours ahead of schedule. The surface analysis map from 2000 local time Friday night shows that, indeed, a low-pressure center had developed immediately northwest of the island and was down to 1000 millibars (map 1).

A sharp kink in the cold front and a tightening of the isobars associated with a gale center correspond with the unexpected intensity of the weather the night before the race. Perhaps of greater interest is the fact that the same map showed that the low-pressure system near Cape Cod had moved southeast, not northeast, and had deepened to 997 millibars.

That night both the *Marques* and *Ciudad de Inca* dragged anchor, and the latter damaged her rudder and withdrew from the race. The next morning, after some deliberation and review of more recent weather information, the Race Committee unanimously agreed to start the race as scheduled. The forecast distributed in Bermuda was essentially unchanged from the previous day. The surface analysis from that morning shows that the cold front had moved very quickly and was far to the east of Bermuda (map 2). The secondary low-pressure center that appeared in map 1 near Bermuda was nowhere to be seen. Although forecasts continued to call for the primary low pressure near Cape Cod to move northeast, it had not budged. It was hovering just off Nantucket and was down to 990 millibars.

In the aftermath of the casualty, the decision to start the race was challenged in an article appearing in the *Royal Gazette* in Bermuda. Jim Travers, deputy meteorologist in charge of the Forecast Office at the National Weather Service (NWS) headquarters in Washington, D.C., later recalled that "there were gale warnings all the way down to Bermuda the day of the race. It would have been a little bit difficult to ignore that something was out there." Travers added that if the NWS had been consulted— as it had been with other ocean races going to Bermuda—it would have warned of the severity of the system that was developing north of the island and cautioned against starting the race. Oliver Pemberton, a spokesperson for the Tall Ships Race organizers, defended the decision to sail, saying that forecasts from the Royal Canadian Navy indicated "clear sailing." He also pointed out that it was typical to use forecasts provided at the port of departure. Pemberton said, "You can't start looking at weather conditions at Halifax five days down the road, otherwise you might never start the race." But Travers was not talking about five days out: he was talking about less than twenty-four hours.

FINAL VOYAGE

The race started at 1500 on 2 June under clear skies, with a west wind of force 4–5 and a confused sea left from the night before. The forecast had called for the wind to shift northwest after the front, but this did not happen because the low pressure of the Cape Cod was not moving as expected. Twenty-eight people were aboard the *Marques*: six trainees from Antigua, ten trainees recruited through ASTA, *(continued page 136)*

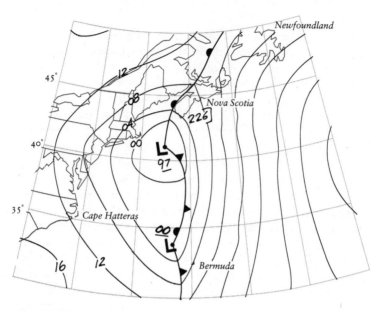

Map 1. National Weather Service Surface Analysis, Friday, 1 June 1984, 2000 hours Bermuda Time. Strong winds the night before the race. (NWS, redrawn by Jim Sollers)

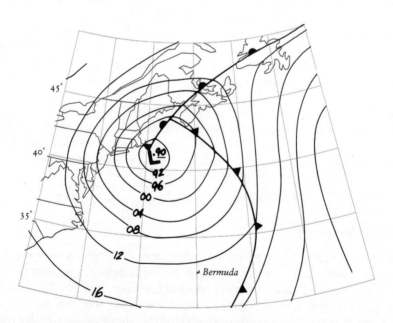

Map 2. National Weather Service Surface Analysis, Saturday, 2 June 1984, 0800 hours Bermuda Time. Decision to start the race. (NWS, redrawn by Jim Sollers)

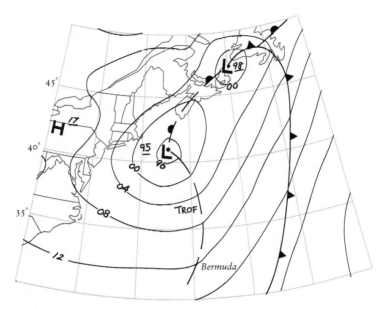

Map 3. National Weather Service Surface Analysis, Saturday, 2 June 1984, 2000 hours Bermuda Time. Just before sunset, wind picking up. Decision to shorten sail. Trough first appears on weather map. (NWS, redrawn by Jim Sollers)

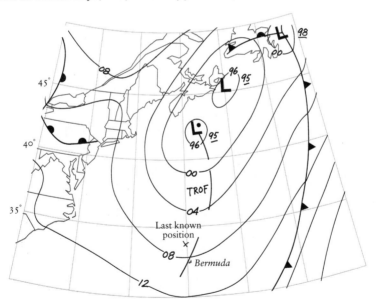

Map 4. National Weather Service Surface Analysis, Sunday, 3 June 1984, 0500 hours Bermuda Time. *Marques* sank forty minutes earlier, approximately 34° N, 65° W, 80 miles north of Bermuda. (NWS, redrawn by Jim Sollers)

Some of the crew of the *Marques* in Bermuda before her final voyage. Standing, from left: Denis Ord (chief mate), John Rudd (Cutty Sark representative), Captain Stuart Finlay, Aloma and Christopher Finlay, Robert I. M. Cooper (third mate), Andrew Lindsay Freeman (engineer), Gillian Shaughnessy (cook), and John Philip Sefton (deckhand). Seated, from left: Peter Messer-Bennetts (second mate), Augustus Nathaniel (trainee/deckhand), and Oswald Alexander Cole. (Courtesy Donald Treworgy)

(continued from 133)   the two ASTA counselors, Captain Finlay, his wife Aloma and sixteen-month-old son Christopher, plus the regular crew of seven.

By 2000 the ship was steering north-by-west true. The wind had increased to force 5–6 and was a point or two abaft the beam. The first mate, Denis Ord, had the watch. While it was still daylight, sail was reduced in response to freshening conditions: the fore and main topgallants, main topgallant staysail, outer jib, and main course were all taken in. Many of the trainees and some of the crew were seasick. On the weather analysis map for this period, a dotted line has appeared curving southeast from the low-pressure system and back to a point near Bermuda (map 3). The line harkens back to the forecast maps distributed at the captain's meeting. By this time, it has been labeled "TROF" and represents a new band of low pressure extending from Cape Cod to Bermuda.

By midnight a steady force 6 was blowing. The mizzen was taken in and the mizzen staysail was set. The second mate, Peter Messer-Bennetts, relieved Ord, and from midnight on the vessel carried the following eight sails:

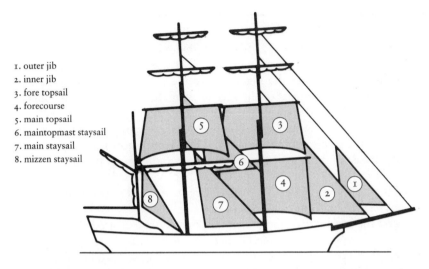

1. outer jib
2. inner jib
3. fore topsail
4. forecourse
5. main topsail
6. maintopmast staysail
7. main staysail
8. mizzen staysail

Marques sail configuration at the time of loss. (Jim Sollers, based on sketch by Howard Chatterton)

Foremast: outer jib, inner jib, fore topsail, forecourse

Mainmast: main topsail, maintopmast staysail, main staysail

Mizzenmast: mizzen staysail

Ord recalled that Finlay received a forecast after midnight from the Portsmouth (Virginia) Coast Guard Station calling for west winds, 15 to 25 knots, becoming northwest, 10 to 20 knots with scattered showers and thunderstorms. Based on this information, the fleet could continue to expect conditions to moderate as the wind gradually shifted ahead. However, as Messer-Bennetts's watch progressed, the wind increased to force 7, with skies mostly overcast with occasional showers. According to Ord, who was on deck at times during this period, the ship was rolling to leeward 20 to 25 degrees, with the occasional sea coming over the rail. Had the *Marques* possessed a weather fax machine, Captain Finlay would have seen that the gale near Cape Cod that had been crouched like a batter in the batter's box was now swinging the trough line like a baseball bat right through Bermuda and the waters north of it.

At 0300 on 3 June the Portsmouth station issued an updated verbal forecast, but it cannot be verified that the *Marques* received it. The report described a 995-millibar gale center located 150 miles east of Cape Cod moving northeast at 20 knots. The report stated that in the southeast quadrant, within 600 miles of the center, winds were expected to be 25 to 40 knots, seas 8 to 12 feet. It is possible that at this point the forecasts were catching up with developments. The synopsis stated: "east of cold front frequent heavy thunderstorms . . . with possible hail and waterspout activity. Exercise caution in vicinity of cold front." If this was the cold front that passed through Bermuda the night before the race, it was long gone and located some 300 miles east of the race area by this time and of no concern to the fleet. Though the front had moved on, the *Marques* remained just inside the 600-mile radius that was reported to contain force 8 conditions. Meanwhile, the gale center to the north did not track northeast at 20 knots. It wobbled east and then dipped to the south and then wobbled east some more. Out in front of the pack, the USCG barque *Eagle* had been knocked down by a 70-knot gust well before midnight. And there was still no mention of a secondary front or a trough.

During the last hour of the midwatch, the sky had cleared so the helmsman was able to steer by the Big Dipper. The vessel was charging along on a beam reach. Those who were not sick remember it as "exhilarating." The record states that "some time towards the end of the middle watch Mr. Ord [first mate] suggested to Peter Messer-Bennetts [officer of the watch] to call some of the permanent crew so as to be ready to take in the forecourse." With so many green hands, both in terms of seasickness and experience, trainees alone were insufficient for this task. But since the wind eased soon thereafter, Ord "did not press the suggestion."

At 0400, when Robert Cooper's watch took over, a light rain had resumed. The tarpaulins on the main hatch, which had been open for ventilation, were drawn over the hatch from port to starboard and the battens were wedged into place by hand to hold until the rain passed. Since the intent was only to keep rain out, the covers were not lashed down, nor were the wedges fitted and driven home as they were designed to be. Most of the battens were steel, but at least one was wooden, and that is what one survivor recalled using that night.

Many of the trainees on Cooper's watch did not report for duty at 0400 due to seasickness. Witnesses reported a brief lull in the wind followed by a sudden and powerful blast that heeled the vessel sharply to starboard as she sailed along on the port tack. Survivor Stuart Gillespie, who was off watch, recalls hearing a roar and thinking that it was a coast guard support aircraft making a flyby. The ship then began to heel dramatically and accelerate. Estimates of the squall's strength range up to force 11 and 12. According to the *Report*, the helmsman responded quickly: "[Philip] Sefton at the wheel had not needed any order. He had immediately started to turn the wheel to starboard. He got two turns on but was forced to let go in order to grab the port side bulwark rail."

Sefton described the sea transformed before his eyes: "You actually saw the sea itself just turn milky white, absolutely white, like a bath of milk." When the forecourse entered the sea, the vessel came to a stop, and water poured in over the bulwarks. Survivors recall the vessel hesitating and even recovering slightly. With the freeing ports secured, boarding seas were trapped on deck and water entered the hull through the main hatch. To facilitate intermittent ventilation, the tarpaulins had not been fully battened and wedged, leading the investigation to conclude that it was "very probable" that the tarpaulins were displaced by the seas, particularly where the buoyant wooden batten was used.

The vessel sank approximately 80 miles north of Bermuda, "within 30 seconds to a minute, certainly no more than two minutes." The majority of those below decks were lost. There was no time to transmit a distress call, and the ship's emergency position-indicating radio beacon (EPIRB), which was stowed below, went down with the ship. Of the ship's company of twenty-eight, only nine survived. Lost were Captain Finlay and his family, Messer-Bennetts (second mate), Gillian Shaughnessy (cook), Benjamin Bryant (deckhand), Susan Howell (ASTA instructor), and twelve trainees.

Three of the four life rafts surfaced and inflated properly. The fourth emerged still secured in its bracket, which had torn free of the ship. Seven survivors ended up in one raft, which Ord took charge of. Andrew Freeman, the engineer, ended up alone in a raft. Stuart Gillespie survived by clinging to the overturned inflatable dinghy. Flares discharged from the rafts were sighted by the Polish sail training vessel *Smuga Ciena* at around 0430. Another Polish vessel, *Zawisza Czarny*, got word of the distress signals from *Smuga Ciena* and proceeded to the area. The *Zawisza Czarny* recovered eight survivors and a body. Gale-force conditions continued throughout the morning, and one last survivor was recovered by helicopter from HMCS *Assiniboine*. The surface analysis map from 0500 local time showed the trough passing right through the fleet (map 4). Maps from later that morning show the gale forming two centers and spreading across the entire swath of ocean between Bermuda and Nova Scotia.

POSTMORTEM

As with the history of the *Marques*, the investigation is the starting point in establishing the main considerations in this casualty. In the United Kingdom, the Merchant Shipping Acts provided for a formal investigation of shipping casualties where determined to be beneficial to the safety of future activities. In cooperation with the Wreck Commission, a Court of Inquiry held hearings between October 1985 and June 1987. The investigation was instigated not by the Department of Transport but by Shirley Cooklin, the mother of Benjamin Bryant, one of the lost crew. Cooklin was unable to afford legal representation for the process, but an attorney, Rupert Massey, accepted the job at no fee. Over the investigation loomed the prospect of legal action among the various parties, but the Court of Inquiry was not established to decide liability among parties. It was called upon to answer certain questions, make certain judgments regarding responsibility, and make recommendations in the interest of safety. In carrying out its mandate, the court wrote that "reasonable foresight is the standard to apply." With issues of liability long settled, it is easier to approach the matter from the perspective of a sailor and a captain.

We have already seen how difficult it can be to establish all the facts with total certainty. As the *Report* pointed out, "it is always possible to take issue with assumptions." Nevertheless, in any discussion of a casualty, at times there may be no choice but to rely on reasonable assumptions. This is what the investigation did and what we must do here, as well.

Safety Equipment

Safety equipment was one area where the department had held the *Marques* to existing standards as a condition of certification, and by all accounts she was properly equipped. In this case the life rafts were the most crucial component of the ship's safety gear. Essentially, they performed to expectations and appear to have saved all the lives they could have. One life raft did not inflate because the mounting bracket tore free of the ship before the hydrostatic release could activate, and the *Report* noted the importance of securely mounting rafts in the future. The raft floated to the surface, where survivors could have manually released it had it been necessary. However, three other rafts inflated as designed and provided sufficient capacity for the small number of survivors.

The discovery of an out-of-service raft by ASTA inspectors in Bermuda had created an unforeseen need to obtain a service deferral from the Marine Directorate. Life raft servicing is a basic chore of shipboard operations everywhere, and keeping current is a matter of simple record keeping. Though the need for a deferral occasionally arises, there was nothing unforeseeable about the raft expiry in this situation, and the *Marques* had not been engaged in the type of operations that made servicing a practical impossibility. Though the expiration did not impact the casualty, it reflects on both shipboard and shoreside management. High turnover in senior positions, as aboard the *Marques*, can contribute to poor record keeping and losing track of key maintenance dates. Meanwhile, shoreside management was not on top of the situation, either.

A serious failure was that the ship's EPIRB went down with the ship because it was stowed belowdecks rather than in a float-free position.

Though this did not lead to loss of life, it was a misguided arrangement that was not unique to the *Marques* at the time. With no requirement to stow EPIRBs in a float-free position, it had become commonplace on many vessels to protect them from the elements by stowing them in an interior space near a hatch or opening. An identical situation arose when the *Pride of Baltimore* was lost in 1986. The potential for sudden and catastrophic disaster makes a strong case for equipment that deploys automatically. The situation with the EPIRB highlights how easily priorities can become misaligned.

Structural Integrity

The possibility of structural failure was dealt with at length by the investigation but was ultimately dismissed. Structural integrity received attention partly because the unorthodox channels through which the *Marques* received her Load Line Exemption Certificate meant that her structural condition was never established beyond doubt. Also weighing in were Cecil-Wright's last-minute claims of unseaworthiness as the vessel was about to sail from England. In the aftermath of the sinking and prior to the investigation, two carpenters who had done reconstructive work on the *Marques* in Spain spoke publicly about the poor condition of the hull. One, Robert Smith, said, "We were levering off 25-foot planks from the hull with no trouble at all." The other, Tom Gavin, spoke of spongy timbers: "I was doing repair work that in my opinion should have been replacement work. But that could have cost hundreds of thousands of pounds." Such remarks resulted in an enduring aura of uncertainty about the true condition of the hull, despite the fact that the investigation later assembled a considerable amount of evidence supporting the seaworthiness of the hull.

The concerns of both the Department of Transport and Perryman in 1983 focused on the condition of the timbers beneath the ferro-cement tanks because they had not been inspected for a decade. However, in light of the documented maintenance efforts of previous years, the investigation ultimately found that "the *Marques* was in a proper state of repair . . . for participation in the race from Bermuda to Halifax." To support this finding, the investigation produced calculations showing that the rate of inflow through the main hatch alone was adequate to sink the vessel with the speed with which she was lost. Additionally, none of the survivors reported observations consistent with hull failure. Sefton, the helmsman, remembered observing from the water that the rig remained intact as the vessel sank. Although there are always suspicions about strength when older hulls are involved, the case for structural failure in this instance remains unconvincing.

Design Integrity

As an exempt vessel, the *Marques* did not operate under any particular design criteria for commercial vessels. Design criteria for sail training vessels did not exist in Britain at the time. There are, however, some common-sense design issues to consider: the main hatch, the freeing ports, and to some extent the lack of watertight subdivision. The problems with the main hatch and the freeing ports were ultimately found to be secondary to deficient stability, but they are significant features in any vessel's seaworthiness and appear to have been ill considered aboard the *Marques*. To ignore them here on the premise that insufficient stability was the greater evil would be a disservice to sailors everywhere.

MAIN HATCH

The main hatch measured nine by thirteen feet. A former cargo hatch, it was monstrously oversized for the new purpose of allowing people to come and go from the deck. The hatch coaming was fairly high: 30 inches along the sides fore and aft. The athwartships coaming sloped upward from each side to an apex amidships 32 inches high. A portion of the starboard coaming had been cut down to 17 inches where the companionway ladder arrived at the deck level. There is no mention of weatherboards having been fitted at the top of the companionway on the night of the casualty, so it was ill luck that under the force of the squall the ship heeled to starboard—the side most vulnerable to downflooding.

The method for securing the hatch carried over from when the vessel worked cargo. Although when Admiral McKaig had asked about it in Bermuda the crew had said it was secured at sea, it is evident that the vessel routinely sailed, even in fairly rough weather, with the hatch partially unsecured. In addressing this issue, the *Report* made the following comments:

> Having become the practice for the sake of ventilation when at sea to leave the tarpaulins off, it is not surprising that the tarpaulins were not fully battened down and properly wedged when the gratings were covered because of the rain. . . .
> . . . Without proper ventilation there would always be a tendency to leave the tarpaulin off and to be casual on occasions when replacing it.

It can be easily imagined that the rougher the weather, and the sicker the trainees, the greater the desire for ventilation.

The opinion that the hatch posed a danger was not universally held, and the department itself was not especially concerned by the hatch. However, there was a history of observations to the contrary. It would seem that at least some people perceived a chink in the armor of seaworthiness, even if they could not always articulate why. Susan Howell, the ASTA instructor who was lost with the ship, had been disturbed by the hatch arrangement. From Bermuda she telephoned her brother, a naval architect, to discuss it. Stan Hughill, the renowned chanteyman and former Cape Horn sailor, once reportedly declined an invitation to sail on the *Marques* in Britain, saying, "I wouldn't get aboard her even at the dock." His comment was evidently followed by a colorful opinion of the main hatch, the freeboard, the deckhouse, and the rig, as well as his own experiences with cargo hatches in sailing ships. If nothing else, hatches designed by moviemakers should be suspect.

Historically and still, cargo hatches are designed to be secured for the duration of a voyage, not opened and closed with the weather. In the past, ventilation of the hold was not a consideration at sea because it was used for cargo, not accommodation. In consequence, securing a cargo hatch was a deliberately cumbersome process that was typically carried out only once per voyage, before leaving port. Using a cargo hatch for living quarters makes it possible to indulge the desire for fresh air below. By its mere existence, the main cargo hatch on the *Marques* invited the crew to choose between comfort and watertight integrity in a way that ultimately compromised the ship.

The investigation regarded the failure to secure the hatch as "a reservation to a finding that all seamanlike precautions had been taken." But it also considered the issue to be essentially "a problem of design and not seamanship." Although design was indeed at the heart of the problem, there are implications for the standards of seamanship, management, and regulatory oversight affecting the *Marques*.

A hatch is essentially a hole in a ship. In the cargo trades, there is a fundamental and age-old understanding that when the hatches give way, the ship is doomed. For this reason great emphasis has always been placed on the securing of hatches. Even the most unobservant merchant mariner would recognize the danger of going to sea with open hatches. The description of the procedure for securing the hatches of Cape Horners like the *Pamir* amply demonstrates the significance of this aspect of seamanship. The importance of securing cargo hatches is not merely of historic interest. In 1987 the British cross-channel ferry *Herald of Free Enterprise* foundered with the loss of two hundred lives because the loading doors, that ship's equivalent of a cargo hatch, were not secured before heading to sea. The investigation into that case showed that management had pressured the crew to sail ahead of schedule and did not devise a system to protect against leaving the doors open. Although the crew of the *Marques* may have been experienced in sailing, rigging, or other relevant skills, it is evident that there was a failure to appreciate the significance of that hole in their ship. In consequence, a habit was formed that was inimical to their own well-being.

It went unchecked voyage after voyage despite the avowed professionalism of the crew. The arrangement had stood a long time, leading to an all-too-common condition whereby things are accepted as they are found under the presumption that they had been properly considered by someone who knows best.

In fairness to the crew, if they were inclined to correct the hatch situation, there was nothing they could have done about it without the owner's consent other than batten the hatch and suffer below. In terms of management's role, retaining a cargo hatch design on a sail training vessel points to an alarming ignorance of the implications. The manner of the transition at China Clipper Society from filmmaking to sail training resulted in an "authentic" feature that had grave consequences.

Considering that the Department of Transport inspectors were familiar with the *Marques* as well as with the standards applied to other types of vessels where passenger safety was considered paramount, it is surprising that no department concerns regarding the main hatch are noted in the *Report*. It is possible that any questions the department posed to the crew regarding the hatch met with the same explanation that was given in Bermuda: that all was properly secured at sea. If so, it can only be said that regulatory authorities are supposed to know better. The department was in a position to set the conditions of the Exemption Certificate. Had it required a redesign of the main hatch, precedent suggests that the China Clipper Society would have made an outcry about the cost and the historical nature of the ships. But regulatory authorities earn their keep by using experience and knowledge to promote safer operations within the powers they are granted. This did not happen in the case of the hatch, though the problem was reasonably transparent and not prohibitively expensive to rectify.

The investigation was correct to point out that the survival of the *Marques* cannot be assumed had she been fitted with a different hatch arrangement. Efforts to re-create the *Marques*'s stability characteristics during the investigation suggested that she passed her range of positive stability at about the same time downflooding began. But these calculations also showed that if the main hatch had been secured after 4 seconds, the *Marques* would not have sunk for an additional 10 to 15 minutes. Since the fatality rate in this case was closely linked to the speed of flooding, the ramifications of those additional 10 to 15 minutes for survivability are enormous.

The bottom line is that the degree of human intervention required to activate the hatch closure system on short notice, combined with the assumption that any sailing vessel can suffer a knockdown, made such a hatch inappropriate for an active sailing vessel carrying trainees. A possible exception could be a dedicated replica ship with limited operations (typically defined by waters, season, numbers of people, duration, and sometimes even daylight). Paradoxically, an inanimate cargo, with no preference for fresh air, would have been safer aboard the *Marques* than were the human beings. The folly of this was not foreseen, but it was foreseeable.

FREEING PORTS

The freeing ports on the *Marques* were essentially doors in the bulwarks. They replicated gunports and in this sense served two purposes: nineteenth-century appearances and a means for rapidly draining large amounts of water from the deck. The ports were hinged at the top and secured by a lanyard at the bottom. When acting as freeing ports, they swung open as the vessel rolled to leeward, thus permitting water on deck to drain away. On the voyage to the Canary Islands, a number of the gunport doors were damaged. Despite the authorities' order to reopen the equivalent ports on the *Ciudad de Inca* in England, a month later in Tenerife all but two of the *Marques*'s gun doors were sealed to prevent further damage at sea—thereby disabling them in their critical function as freeing ports.

For a variety of reasons the capacity to shed boarding seas quickly is essential to seaworthiness. This is why it has long been dogma that freeing ports be kept clear, particularly in rough weather, and regardless of the inconvenience. Sailors who ignore this fact have always done so at some risk.

The experience of the *Marques* and the *Ciudad de Inca* suggests that using authentically styled gunports as freeing ports brings certain operational responsibilities that are not always clearly spelled out to captains. With the *Marques*, there appears to have been a lack of awareness on many parts regarding the consequences of disabling the freeing ports. The decision to seal them without a compensating means for shedding water not only went against good practice, it reversed a situation the department had recently addressed on the *Ciudad de Inca* as being pertinent to seaworthiness.

Freeing ports that incorporate doors are inconvenient and susceptible to damage, even when they are designed without a dual purpose. Freeing port doors are notoriously annoying, especially on steel ships, because the doors clatter and clang incessantly as they swing open and shut with the roll of the ship. They are typically located in the waists of a ship, where water collects. Traditionally, on commercial vessels this was some distance from the living quarters, which were generally all the way forward or all the way aft. Not so aboard today's sailing ships. With passengers, trainees, and crew living the entire length and breadth of contemporary sailing ships, the temptation to silence the freeing ports is continuous. This has led some designers to do away with freeing ports altogether and to substitute larger scuppers fitted with mesh or a grill to prevent the loss of objects into the sea.

Another reason for doing away with freeing ports that have doors relates to the effect solid bulwarks can have on stability. High bulwarks that don't allow water to flow through to the deck act like a vertical extension of the hull in respect to the buoyancy. A solid bulwark has the effect of increasing the righting arm and the point of deck edge immersion up until the cap rail submerges and water abruptly floods over the bulwarks and is trapped on the weather deck. At this point three things happen almost instantaneously, all of them bad:

1. The righting arm abruptly diminishes to its true and lesser nature based on the actual deck edge and buoyant volume of the ship.

2. The vessel's center of gravity rises due to the large amount of water trapped on deck.

3. There is a large free-surface effect resulting in a further virtual rise in center of gravity.

The bulwarks serve an important purpose, but without adequate freeing ports they can have the effect of "deceiving" a ship into thinking it has higher freeboard, and therefore more buoyancy and a longer righting arm, than it really does. Fishing vessels are notorious for closing freeing ports while handling a catch on deck, and any number of them have disappeared as a consequence. Gunports or any other type of door arrangement that requires human intervention in order to function as intended in a time of crisis should not be categorized or counted on as a freeing port.

There is little to suggest that properly functioning freeing ports alone would have saved the *Marques*, but they are a part of the *Marques* story that deserves mention. Both the main hatch and the freeing ports provided a false choice between convenience and safety. In both cases the former was taken at the expense of the latter, presumably in part because the risk was not appreciated, but more importantly because the option was available.

WATERTIGHT SUBDIVISION

The absence of watertight subdivision aboard the *Marques* presents a slightly different situation. By contributing directly to the speed with which the vessel flooded, and therefore to the high number of fatalities, it was undoubtedly the most crucial design deficiency aboard the *Marques*. Not all vessels have subdivision and not all are required to, but the benefits in delaying or preventing foundering had been established for over a century by the time the *Marques* received her Exemption Certificate. The absence of subdivision was probably one of the best reasons for limiting the *Marques*'s area of operation with fare-paying trainees. Unlike stability, which is essentially invisible to the naked eye, the absence of watertight bulkheads was plainly visible. However, when compared with the other design issues aboard the *Marques*, the lack of subdivision would have been by far the most problematic to address. Unlike the hatches or the freeing ports, retrofitting a wooden ship for watertight bulkheads is monumentally complicated and expensive because it affects every shipboard system. For this reason it is rarely undertaken. The *Marques*, however, was not retrofitted, and its operations were not restricted.

Although good sense and precedent argue for watertight subdivision, from a management point of view it is not the type of project one undertakes unless required to do so. From a seamanship point of view, not a thing could be done about it other than staying ashore. Although the Department of Transport had the authority to require subdivision, the whole point of applying for the Exemption Certificate was to avoid enormous expenditures that might make the vessel more seaworthy but financially unsustainable. Requiring watertight subdivision or limiting operations would have defeated the purpose of the exemption process from the perspective of the China Clipper Society.

The main hatch, the freeing ports, and the absence of watertight subdivision illustrate the problems that can arise when converting a historic vessel to a modern purpose. Arcane design arrangements aboard the *Marques* added to her vulnerability, and not purely in hindsight. In the case of the main hatch, it appears that no one involved was able to draw the line on authenticity. Once the ship left England and the eyes of the inspectors, it was up to the sailors to keep the freeing ports open. Good, creative design can do much to eliminate false choices. The role of design in the context of the renaissance of traditional sail is crucial in reconciling conflicts between practical needs and historical authenticity, while providing an appropriate level of safety at sea.

Weather

In terms of weather patterns, the race from Bermuda was scheduled for a propitious time of year. The North Atlantic high pressure was filling in for the summer, and the chances of an early hurricane were virtually nonexistent. Because the race brought an uncommonly large number of sailing vessels into that patch of Atlantic, the investigation was able to draw on many accounts to establish a reasonably complete picture of conditions on the night the *Marques* was lost.

It is evident, for example, that by the early hours of 3 June all the vessels were experiencing conditions in excess of those forecast, and there was no sign of abatement. Aboard the *Marques* the barometer was steady at 1010 millibars from midnight onward, with a slight decline by 0400. Other vessels reported pressure dropping between 2 and 4 millibars through the same period, probably due to differing positions relative to the advancing isobars. Notable differences were recorded for the upper limit of observed wind strengths. In some cases the maximum winds compared closely to those aboard the *Marques* prior to the squall, force 6–8. In a few cases more extreme squall activity was reported, with gusts well above 50 knots. As early as 2215 on the night of 2 June the *Eagle* was knocked down approximately 55 degrees from vertical for about three minutes by a squall estimated at 70 knots while cadets were aloft furling topgallants. On the bridge a "puzzling drop in the barometer" had been observed, and a dense "bull's-eye" squall was detected by radar bearing down at a speed of approximately 45 knots. Said one of the officers, "I knew we were going to get slammed." The incident was serious, but the injuries aboard the *Eagle* were only minor. Other vessels experienced difficulties and in some cases damage.

Taking all this as well as survivors' testimony into account, the investigation concluded that the *Marques* was struck by "a good Force 11 or Force 12." The investigation also concluded that the most likely explanation for the squall was a microburst of 30 to 40 knots superimposed over force 7 surface conditions. The result was a far higher aggregate wind speed on the order of 65 knots. The possibility of coincident wind vectors is supported by the fact that there was no appreciable change in wind direction when the squall struck the *Marques*. This matches the experience aboard the *Eagle*. Though not definitive, other weather features and observations at the time were compatible with a microburst.

The possibility of a waterspout was considered, based on a reliable sighting of one by a yacht some 200 miles to the west at about 0230, and there had been waterspout warnings in connection with the earlier front after it passed to the east. But because no waterspout sightings were reported in the vicinity of the fleet, it was set aside as less likely. In the end, the difference may be academic for a sailor. Both phenomena are potent, highly localized, and ephemeral. By day waterspouts may be readily spotted up to a few miles off; nevertheless, neither waterspouts nor microbursts give much in the way of advance notice. It was the *Marques*'s misfortune to be in the line of fire for a squall of "the worst and most destructive type." Without questioning the alertness of the crew, the incident underscores the importance of maintaining a weather eye at all times, regardless of data coming from other sources, especially in unsettled conditions, and especially when the weather is developing into something other than that forecast. It also demonstrates the difficulty of spotting such a gust at night. One of the few precautions vessels can take is to properly brief the lookouts, who are often the least experienced members of a watch, on what to look for and the importance of their role. Another is to maintain a radar watch despite concerns that doing so may cause unnecessary wear and tear on the unit.

Perhaps the most difficult aspect to understand about the weather on the night the *Marques* was lost appears to have been the fleet's complete lack of foreknowledge. The pattern of gale-force winds encountered is now attributed to the trough associated with the low-pressure system east of Cape Cod. The first trace of that trough was the dotted line that appeared on weather forecast maps reviewed at the captain's briefing. Due to other considerations, including the prediction that the low pressure would track away from the race, the significance of the dotted line was not discussed, so no one in the fleet was certain as to what it represented. Other warning signs included a slight deflection of isobars and the early arrival of an unexpectedly strong cold front in Bermuda that did not correspond with predictions.

According to the *Report*, the first synoptic chart to indicate a disturbance did not appear until 0300 on 3 June, though as seen, surface analysis maps show a trough at 2000 on 2 June (map 3) and in every map after that. The race was well underway at this point and the vessels were committed to sailing; however, it is notable that word of this trough did not reach the fleet. The 0300 (3 June) High Seas radio forecast from Portsmouth gave the first indication of stronger weather for the area: up to force 8 within 600 miles of the low pressure in the southeast quadrant. But there was still no mention of the trough or of the highly unstable disturbance to come. The *Report* therefore concluded that there was nothing in the forecasts to give warning of the severe conditions encountered. Since even the maps depicting the trough did not indicate its ferocity, this is probably a fair assessment. However, the Race Committee's take on the weather forecast was at odds with the statements by Travers of the National Weather Service in Washington, D.C., and this was not addressed in the *Report*. We have to believe that the race would not have been started in the face of force 8 forecasts; therefore, despite what was known on the U.S. mainland, it may have been a case of necessary information not getting where it was needed. Instead, the race was started based on the relatively benign forecast in the hands of the Race Committee. A more in-depth consultation with upstream weather sources on the mainland may have proved fruitful, but this is a matter of debate.

The *Report* identified the inadequacy of general-purpose High Seas forecasting for detecting highly localized phenomena as a major problem, and it recommended "dedicated forecasts" for future tall-ship races. Although this is helpful, a more versatile and transcendent conclusion for the practical sailor pertains to the importance of independent decision making. An alert sailing captain is constantly reevaluating and cross-checking information in light of what is being seen and heard on-scene. Prerace briefings are valu-able and necessary forums for disseminating information, including weather forecasts, but prudent captains—who normally operate indepen-dently, anyhow—will guard against the herd mentality in these situations.

We can never know what hunches or misgivings may have visited the various skippers and officers as the weather deteriorated that night, but those aboard the *Marques* were not alone in having to weigh a changing sit-uation. As seen with the experience of the *Eagle*, those aboard the *Marques* were not the only ones caught unawares, although on the *Eagle* at least the radar delivered some sense of an impending threat. But since the forecast gave no inkling of what was to come, in hindsight the best clue that all was not well may have been the fact the weather forecasts had been significantly in error for over twenty-four hours.

Platitudes regarding the fickleness of weather are numerous and true. Forecasting has always involved margins of error and it will likely continue so for the foreseeable future. Nevertheless, the arrival on Friday, 1 June, of a cold front in Bermuda some thirty hours ahead of schedule, with more punch than expected, signaled that the situation had been misread. From that point on, a large margin of error was in play, regardless of the meteoro-logical explanation offered. From then on a higher degree of caution may have been called for. Thus, the real weather lesson arising from this incident relates not to dedicated forecasts, but to the danger of persisting with a plan based on prescribed information, such as a forecast, long after the observed situation has changed. When forecasts fail to materialize, it is time to con-sider the possibility that something unforeseen is brewing and to examine the vessel's situation accordingly. As with lookout, early detection depends not only on alertness but on sharing information so those on watch can be at their most effective.

Also on the matter of sharing information, the *Report* notes that the *Eagle* was struck by a violent squall approximately six hours before the *Marques* was lost under similar circumstances. As we also know, other ves-sels experienced squalls on the order of force 10, 11, and 12 during the night. Yet the *Report* contains no record of any attempt by any vessel to alert the fleet of the fierce local conditions, either directly by VHF radio or through the safety escort *Assiniboine*. There may have been reasons that seemed compelling at the time for not issuing an urgency call, but clearly the presence of hurricane-force winds constituted crucial information for all participants. The investigation correctly recommended that future tall-ship races include in communication instructions and at captain's briefings the need to report "any situation which from its nature or unexpectedness can be foreseen as a potential danger to other competitors." We cannot say what other vessels might have done differently had they been aware of gusts to 70 knots as early as 2215 on Saturday, 2 June, but there is little doubt that such information would have been met with interest.

Unsettled weather and violent squalls are not uncommon in the waters north and west of Bermuda. The Gulf Stream and the accompanying temperature contrasts make the area known for breeding intense cellular activity. It is impossible to predict where and when a microburst may strike, especially at night, but in a general way squall activity comes with that territory. The *Report* recognized this when describing the microburst: "Though this coincidence is rare, it is a known phenomenon and cannot be dismissed as a freak wind or Act of God. Downdraughts (microbursts) are not unique to these waters, but it would seem that particular alertness is required . . . in the waters North of Bermuda."

Had the fleet received forecasts calling for force 8 conditions, preemptive shortening of sail may have prevailed among the fleet, rather than betting on an imminent improvement. Still, even with the knowledge of a rough night ahead, no one would have sailed their vessel in anticipation of a force 12 blast. Yet only one vessel was lost that night. It is under such circumstances that seaworthiness and survivability are put to the test and, unfortunately, the *Marques* failed.

Sail Area

Decisions regarding sail area are one aspect of sailing over which the individuals aboard exert virtually complete control, but the amount of windage and the weight of the *Marques*'s rig were a direct result of the conversions of the late 1970s. In any discussion of her sail area, these seat-of-the-pants conversions must be regarded as the root issue. A sail or two less on that particular night may not have made much difference. Nevertheless, the issue of sail area bears consideration.

At the time of the squall the *Marques* had eight sails set, about 35 percent of the working canvas, plus the windage of the rig. Changing the mizzen for the mizzen staysail at 2200 would have improved the balance of the helm and eased the motion, but it was not a significant reduction of sail area. The record states that by 0400 on 3 June all three mates (Ord, Messer-Bennetts, and Cooper) had considered taking in the forecourse, but for one reason or another each chose to defer action. The *Report* took the view that "there was nothing unreasonable in waiting to see whether the expected improvement would materialise." In determining what was a reasonable amount of sail, the investigation turned to Captains Litchfield, Minter-Kemp, and Adams, all of whom held that the vessel could be "safely sailed" in force 7 conditions with the amount of sail set at the time, but they concurred that "the time had arrived when it was prudent to consider taking in the forecourse." Though the Exemption Certificate surely convinced many people to accept the vessel as they found it, it is difficult to accept the word of former captains regarding what was truly a "safe" amount of sail for the *Marques*, given how little they understood of her stability and her other flaws.

For what it is worth, the investigation produced computer models showing that even a substantial reduction of sail, the forecourse and both topsails, would have had little influence on the outcome under force 12 conditions. However, a force 11 scenario introduces the possibility of a less extreme situation from a meteorological standpoint. Naturally, the theoretical nature of these models makes it difficult to know with certainty what difference less sail would have made, and how much less sail would have made a difference. The models simply represent an educated guess. The most that can be said is that without the forecourse the ship may have heeled more gradually, which in turn may have made a difference to other efforts to control the ship, such as bearing off.

The amount of canvas the *Marques* had set on the night of her loss was not especially conservative for force 7–8 conditions, but it has also been described as not excessive in the context of her total sail area. It has often been pointed out that the *Marques* was participating in a race for which she had already set a high standard by winning the first leg. The notion that the vessel was being pushed hard is difficult to lay to rest, but it does not correspond with Treworgy's descriptions of Captain Finlay's command style on the first leg from San Juan, during which "the race seemed almost secondary to the comfort of those aboard." If racing tempts a skipper to accept a little more risk in exchange for a little better performance, then this type of bargaining is not unique to the *Marques*. It is the nature of racing itself. All captains need to watch for the point at which racing and safety begin to conflict and decide whether they will sail their vessel differently from the way they would on an ordinary transit, or not. A better appreciation of the *Marques*'s stability may have prompted the officers to act decisively on the concerns they obviously shared in respect to sail area, but it appears that action would have been limited to the forecourse. Further sail reduction would have come about only if these same officers were capable of setting aside blind confidence in past performance. Clearly, once the squall struck it was too late to reduce canvas. The knowledge that the mates considered reducing sail but hesitated reminds us of the old sailor's dictum, "If you are thinking of shortening sail, then it is time to shorten sail." Some would have carried less sail; few would have carried more.

Even if sail area did not play a decisive role in the loss of the *Marques*, it invites us to review broader considerations in respect to carrying sail on training ships. A sail training ship in its normal mode of operation relies on inexperienced trainees; therefore, the sail plan customarily incorporates a margin of safety reflecting this fact. Factors in this margin of safety may include time of day, experience of the crew, how long trainees have been aboard, proximity to navigational hazards, prevailing conditions, and the likelihood of squalls. The ever-present potential for the unexpected to occur is fundamental in any margin of safety. This was echoed in the investigation's finding that a microburst is "a known phenomenon" and not an act of God. Given that it happened the first night at sea with green trainees who could not be relied upon for much, and given that the vessel was in low visibility with other ships around and moderately rough conditions in excess of the forecast, the situation called for a particularly large margin of safety and a conservative sail plan. But establishing an appropriate margin of safety is a function of experience. Although those aboard could not have known this, the *Marques* as a barque under reduced canvas carried an amount of sail close to what she would have carried as a bald-headed cargo schooner under full sail, and it is unlikely that a cargo schooner would have carried full sail in force 7 conditions. But then a cargo schooner would not have had her hatches open or have been rigged for moviemaking.

Qualifications and Manning

The investigation considered the formal qualifications of the master and mates of the *Marques* to determine what role, if any, they played in the casualty. As if the *Marques* was not already dogged by enough dubious arrangements, several irregularities in licensing were revealed that illustrated a lack of diligence on the part of the China Clipper Society. However, the court determined that the qualifications aboard the *Marques*, irregularities and all, did not contribute to the casualty.

The least significant manning discrepancy relates to the number of deckhands aboard. The requirements called for three deckhands, one of whom typically handled engineering duties. When the *Marques* sailed from Bermuda, only two deckhands were aboard due to the unscheduled departure of one of the crew. To address the shortfall, two Antiguan trainees filled in as deckhands. Promotion resulting from being in the right place at the right time is commonplace in the marine trades, so that such a thing happened scarcely warrants mention except for the pattern of which it is a part. There is no evidence to suggest that the trainees who stepped up were not equal to the job.

A second discrepancy occurred in respect to the qualifications of Denis Ord, the chief mate. Ord had fifteen years in the merchant marine and held a Royal Yachting Association Yachtmaster Certificate. Many countries do not have an equivalent to the Yachtmaster Certificate in Britain, but the

process for obtaining it is rigorous, making it a highly appropriate credential for sail training vessels. A Yachtmaster's Certificate can be used in commercial application.

When Litchfield forwarded Ord's credentials to the Marine Directorate
for approval, the class of Yachtmaster Certificate that Ord held was not
specified. Captain Jestico, Chief Examiner for Masters and Mates, assumed
that Ord possessed an *ocean* certificate, when in fact he held the lesser *offshore* endorsement. Jestico's assumption was based on the fact that both he
and Litchfield knew that the vessels were operating on ocean routes; therefore, without special petition, only an ocean certificate would fulfill the
needs of the proposed activities. Jestico testified that he would not have
approved Ord had he understood that he lacked an ocean certificate—not,
at least, without making further inquiry into his experience. Jestico allowed
that Ord's level of experience probably would have been found to be sufficient to qualify him for the position of chief mate on the *Marques*, but the
Report added that the miscommunication demonstrated "a lack of awareness of the significance of a qualification required by law, as a measure to
ensure greater safety."

The most mysterious discrepancy pertaining to qualifications involved
the captain's U.S. Coast Guard license. The photocopy submitted by
Litchfield to the Marine Directorate was not a copy of the one the U.S.
Coast Guard had on file at Boston. The copy Litchfield submitted for
approval stated that Finlay was licensed to operate auxiliary-sail passenger
vessels "of not more than 100 gross tons upon the waters of the Atlantic
Ocean." The license on record with the coast guard stated that he was
restricted to vessels of 60 gross tons, on the "waters of the Atlantic Ocean,
not more than 100 miles offshore between Great Boars Head, New
Hampshire, and Cuttyhunk, Massachusetts." In terms of operational scope,
the difference is significant. Upon closer examination it appeared that the
photocopy had been altered and was "not a true copy of the original."
Expert evidence established that the photocopy submitted by Litchfield was
made on a type of paper available in the United States but not in Britain.
Nobody who was questioned about it, including Mark Litchfield, could
account for the discrepancy, and witnesses testifying on behalf of Captain
Finlay asserted that an attempt to deceive in this matter was not in his character. Unable to resolve the mystery fully, the investigation moved on: its
duty lay in determining "whether the appointment was made on proper and
adequate grounds."

Not surprisingly, Jestico stated that he would not have granted approval
for Finlay to be master based on the original license. Litchfield was faulted
for not verifying the license or checking references, but ultimately the
Report concluded that "Finlay ran the ship well . . . and acted in a perfectly

proper and seamanlike manner. Since his conduct was that of a prudent master any fault in his appointment is not causative of the loss."

Irrespective of this conclusion, the issue of licensing reflected on the hiring practices at China Clipper Society. No matter how much informal experience a sailor may have, the trainees and passengers who put their trust in the crew are entitled to be led by people who have taken the time to obtain the proper credentials as well as the experience. Although a license does not trump experience when the chips are down, the demanding process of obtaining a license and upgrading it for ocean service reinforces the solemn responsibilities of an officer. The number of discrepancies aboard the *Marques* suggested a lack of diligence on the part of the ownership.

Contributing to the problems with licensing was a system favored by the Marine Directorate for approving masters and officers for sail training ships on a case-by-case basis. By employing regulations that in some cases called for unlimited masters and mates aboard relatively small sail training ships, the directorate deliberately used a standard was "seldom capable of achievement." The reason for this was to make it necessary for owners to apply for exemptions, thus enabling the directorate to exert "better control" over the selection process. Regardless of the performance by the officers aboard the *Marques*, in terms of verifying credentials this procedure did not accomplish its intended purpose in this case. The system cannot be faulted for not uncovering an altered document or poor record keeping by other parties, but accepting comparable experience in lieu of a specific qualification by definition opened the process to interpretation. The Marine Directorate was not widely experienced with traditional sail, yet without a licensing structure that was directly linked to actual commercial sailing activities, the directorate had to rely on information supplied through the owners for the approval of people the owners wanted to hire. The absence of a statutory licensing structure that reflected the needs of commercial sailing vessels is further telling of the unconventional and ill-defined place these ships occupied in the spectrum of maritime activities in Britain at that time.

Experience

The sea is a notoriously hostile environment that routinely mocks our efforts to master it. The disappearance in the Southern Ocean of the new and exceptionally well-equipped and well-officered five-masted training barque *København* in 1928 illustrated all too clearly how going to sea in a well-found, properly manned sailing ship carries no guarantees of safe passage. In more recent times, modern vessels of all types equipped with all the latest advantages end up at the bottom of the sea or broken up on the rocks. Experience reduces risk, but risk is still present. As we shall see, there is little in the loss of *Marques* that indicates inexperience contributed directly to her capsizing. Yet at the same time, inexperience did touch the *Marques* in crucial ways.

If action taken under duress is an indicator of experience, the performance of the crew on duty showed good instincts in every respect. The helmsman attempted to bear off without awaiting an order that, when it came, confirmed his action. Cooper, the mate on watch and the most junior of the mates, struggled in vain to cast off the course sheet even as it submerged. Perhaps most important, he had the presence of mind to call down the main hatch "All hands on deck!" before the ship succumbed. Ord was by the lee rail and was dumped in the water before he could react. However, his long seagoing career came into play when he took charge of the primary survival raft: he directed bailing, deployed sea anchors, and fired the flares that were sighted by the rescue craft. In very rough conditions Cooper courageously left the raft and swam a line over to another raft that turned out to be empty. The two rafts were tied together to enlarge the target for search-and-rescue parties. The engineer, Andrew Freeman, found himself alone in a leaking raft but managed to keep it bailed and also set off a parachute flare. It is difficult to say what more any of them could have done once the squall struck. As far as is known, Captain Finlay and Messer-Bennetts, the second mate, never made it on deck.

That all three mates considered taking in the forecourse could be construed as a failure to act decisively on a misgiving due to inexperience. It can just as easily be explained as a uniform perception, right or wrong, that the ship was carrying an appropriate amount of sail for the breeze based on previous experience and the forecast.

In terms of general background, the level of experience among the officers was mixed, as one might expect. In addition to his Yachtmaster Certificate, Ord had the most overall time at sea, with fifteen years in the merchant marine before pursuing a sailing career. However, he had been on the *Marques* only since Antigua. The second mate, Peter Messer-Bennetts, was twenty years old, but in his short career he had sailed on the *Marques* in 1980 and 1983 and therefore was quite familiar with the vessel and had sailed under different captains. The third mate, Robert Cooper, was only eighteen years old and was said to be a competent sailor. Clearly, the two junior officers were less seasoned in terms of general seagoing experience, and by the standards of many sail training programs today they might accurately be considered too young to lead and teach trainees effectively. But this is of no consequence in how the vessel came to be lost. The record shows that they were effective watch leaders and energetic in maintaining the vessel, which was their primary function.

Captain Finlay was an accomplished yachtsman and sailing instructor.

He had navigation experience and evidently possessed many qualities looked for in a captain. However, his command of the *Marques* was unquestionably a significant leap to a complex and relatively unfamiliar type of vessel. He earned his command of the barque on the relatively idyllic sailing grounds of the Caribbean after an uneventful trade-wind passage as a trainee. His experience with sizable traditional rigs was limited to a short time as a second mate aboard the U.S. staysail schooner *Westward* two years earlier. In January he was a trainee aboard the *Marques*; by May he was the master in a tall-ship race. By virtually any standard of commercial tall-ship operations, both then and now, Finlay had considerably less experience in square rig than would normally be expected of a skipper carrying paying trainees on ocean routes. Yet it is clear from much that has been said and written, and from the testimony of surviving crew, that his handling of the ship was careful and seamanlike. Finlay has been described as alert and available to the mates for questions, and was frequently about the ship during the night. Treworgy related that on the trip from San Juan to Bermuda Finlay unofficially deputized him to be the celestial navigator. Treworgy was a recognized specialist in this area and had more time to devote to it than the master, who had many duties aboard his still relatively new command. But by Treworgy's own account, Finlay closely watched his technique and checked his work for accuracy before entrusting him with these duties. He also requested additional sights when approaching Bermuda to ensure a safe landfall. If this anecdote can be applied to Finlay's general approach to his job, he demonstrated appropriate care and an effort to compensate for his inexperience with diligence while getting to know the barque through the eyes of a captain. One known exception to this diligence was the departure from San Juan without a functioning high-frequency radio. The vessel was wholly reliant on celestial navigation, which in turn requires access to accurate time and the ability to estimate a position by dead reckoning. The lack of redundancy aboard the *Marques* became apparent in this case, but, more important, the lack of a radio transmitter meant there was no way to communicate in the event of an emergency. This is not a minor oversight for one who accepts command. But the race was starting and the failure to appear was deemed the greater sin, whereas more experience might have argued otherwise. Thus, if there is anything to say about the level of experience on board the *Marques* it would be the willingness to accept certain dubious features of the vessel as they were found, including equipment, but not so much in the handling of the vessel at the time of her loss.

The willingness to accept deficient features is seen in the fact that in varying degrees Finlay and his officers were in positions to influence practices regarding the freeing ports and the main hatch. They could have acted on these only if equipped with the confidence of knowledge necessary to challenge a convenient but ultimately dangerous status quo. Additionally, that stability data were not aboard represented a crucial gap in the master's ability to know his ship. Was Finlay willing to take responsibility for trainees and a vessel he barely knew because he felt his experience had rendered stability data superfluous? It seems more likely that his experience did not extend to an appreciation of just how important those data were to knowing his ship. Other British sail training ships had stability data for the very reason it was considered important.

In accepting things as they were, Finlay and his mates were in good company. By the time they came aboard, all these questionable issues had been approved, institutionalized, or both. Given that the *Marques* lacked many safety features that a more carefully conceived sail training vessel would have had, and given that her rig had been greatly modified to unknown effect, Finlay and others before him were probably more out of their depth than they knew.

Life on any ship has a flow and rhythm, and a way of doing things that everybody who is part of it understands. Playing a part in that rhythm is a source of satisfaction to crew and makes for a happy ship. But there is a tendency when going aboard a ship to accept things as they are found, such as freeing ports nailed shut. Unlike an inspector, a person joining a ship is making a new home. Crew members, officers, and even the captain want to maintain harmony, and the owners don't want to hear about problems. Instigating change, even when justified, is difficult. Too often the illusion of well-being is maintained by the mantra, "We just do it that way." Sometimes the explanation is good, and sometimes it isn't. So it is not surprising that certain aspects of the *Marques* were built on the false premise that someone somewhere in the chain of responsibility had carefully considered all of it, and that it had been found to be safe. Therefore, when we contemplate the issue of experience aboard the *Marques*, it isn't so much in connection with sailing the ship from one place to another. Instead, the question of experience turns on the ability to recognize and act on a potentially hazardous practice in a timely fashion.

Some of the deficiencies we have discussed may well have drawn the attention of her captains and crew, but their concerns were blunted by the Exemption Certificate and the stamp of approval it represented. If inexperience led those aboard to accept questionable practices, then the same might be said for the process by which the *Marques* received that certificate. The investigation broached this when it criticized Holstead, the department surveyor, for approving the exemption process without stability data:

> He knew there was a high GM but no GZ curve. On the file was Mr.
> Longbottom's recommendation, and the Rules required the provision of sta-

bility information . . . *he ought not to have been prepared to approve a Load Line Exemption Certificate without insisting on stability data being obtained and information provided for use by the master* [original emphasis].

In the meeting with Perryman and Litchfield, Holstead conceded that "his knowledge of sailing was limited," and the investigation noted that he "did not have first-hand knowledge of the vessel." Unfamiliarity, not only with the *Marques*, but with traditionally rigged sailing vessels in general, led to insufficient emphasis on the significance of sailing ship stability, and instead the focus remained on the more tangible issue of structural integrity.

Another player whose experience was brought into question was Perryman, the naval architect. Though Perryman advertised himself as a naval architect and had considerable knowledge of wooden ship construction and draftsmanship, the *Report* discovered that he "had no formal academic qualifications and was not a chartered engineer." The *Report* further found:

> His reliance on a vessel's GM . . . ignores all that can be derived from knowing the righting arm . . . at all angles of heel. He knew the story of the vessel's conversion and that the additional top weight was likely to have adversely affected her stability by lifting the center of gravity. His survey in 1982 reminded him of the . . . absence of solid ballast. As the expert he purported to be, he ought not to have left Mr. Litchfield with the impression that a high GM necessarily meant that the vessel had good stability over the full range of angles of heel. *Mr. Perryman knew or ought to have known that he did not have the information to justify a declaration that the vessel possessed adequate stability for world wide operation* and ought to have required the vessel's stability be fully investigated [original emphasis]. The fact that the DTp [Department of Transport] did not require this . . . does not excuse him from his duty as the owner's Naval Architect.

Questions of experience extend to the performance of shoreside management, as well. Although Litchfield may well have been a capable sailor and captain, his role as the principal behind the China Clipper Society must be viewed differently. The issues of the poor hatch design and the disabled freeing ports have been considered in other contexts, but shoreside management also shared deeply in those arrangements. Having commanded the *Marques* in the tropics himself, Litchfield had personally experienced the ventilation problems and the temptation to seek relief by opening the hatch at sea. In light of the delicate process that produced the Exemption Certificate, he was also aware that the Marine Directorate had required the *Ciudad de Inca*'s gunports be reopened, and that approval of the *Marques* was likewise predicated on the gunports being serviceable as freeing ports. Finally, he was in Tenerife when the *Marques* repaired and sealed the damaged gunport hatches and should have been aware of that action.

The investigation also confirmed that shoreside management was unprofessional by not verifying Finlay's license:

> The princip[al] indication of [Finlay's] ability to command was the Coast Guard license to which Mr. Litchfield chose to pay scant attention. It is our considered view that Mr. Litchfield *ought to have taken and considered references . . . and ought to have verified the copy license* [original emphasis]. . . . We consider the latter was necessary not only as a verification of the copy, but also as an assurance that the licence had not been suspended or revoked since it was issued.

The large volume of communications notifying the China Clipper Society of the need to obtain either a Load Line Certificate or a Load Line Exemption leaves an unambiguous record of regulatory guidance. The absence of progress toward compliance indicates a management approach that did not prioritize either the letter or the spirit of the marine safety regulations, prompting the *Report* to conclude that the China Clipper Society "chose to pay insufficient attention to the regulatory requirement."

The final and most significant respect in which shoreside management contributed to the error chain related to stability. Although Perryman was faulted for not urging a full stability assessment, the *Report* also concluded that "Mr. Litchfield was party to ignoring Mr. Longbottom's recommendation."

> Thereafter he [Litchfield] never instructed an expert to consider the matter even when the vessel's use changed to carrying larger numbers of persons, many of whom were inexperienced. . . . Mr. Litchfield's own knowledge of the theory of ship stability was very limited, yet he had not instructed Mr. Perryman to consider the vessel's range of stability, nor had he informed him of Mr. Longbottom's recommendation. Mr. Litchfield cannot shelter behind the opinion of an expert whom he had not instructed to consider the relevant matter. *Mr. Litchfield as the owner was in breech of his common law duty of care* to those who would sail in the *Marques* in that he failed to instruct an expert to obtain the vessel's full stability data and advise him of any necessary action [original emphasis].

Taking a comprehensive view of vessel management, from details such as the foreseeable expiry of the life raft in Bermuda, to major issues such as stability and the appointment of a master, in ways both large and small shoreside management participated in significant oversights. When the *Marques* was a pleasure yacht the responsibilities of an owner were minimal, requiring little experience or time. These responsibilities became extensive and demanding for the owner of an oceangoing sail training vessel, however. The drift from one type of operation to another appears not to have been accompanied by a commensurate transition in the standards of management.

Stability

Despite the range of issues affecting the *Marques*, the evidence is preponderant that she was essentially a stability casualty. When the squall struck, she heeled until her righting arm vanished, which coincided closely with the angle of downflooding. She laid over, filled, and sank. Little is known of her stability characteristics prior to her loss, and her true hull proportions are uncertain. The absence of these details makes it impossible to set out the precise cumulative impact of the rig conversions as we did with the *Albatross*. Their stories are similar, though, and familiarity with the *Albatross* makes it easy to imagine the deterioration of the *Marques*'s stability. She was transformed from a schooner to brigantine, then to a barque fitted with royals and ten stunsails, and the deckhouse was added for film work. Additional water, stores, systems, facilities, and sundry gear for sail training continued to raise the center of gravity while reducing freeboard. As with the *Albatross*, there was the steadfast reliance on GM in place of full righting-arm data, and with the *Marques* even this figure was subject to doubt. Finally, satisfactory performances in rough weather on previous occasions were accepted as proof of stability, rather than as anecdotal. Using dimensions from 1966 found on file in Spain, the investigation endeavored to derive full stability data for the *Marques* retroactively. This effort resulted in the following figures:

Maximum righting arm: 25 degrees

Angle of downflooding: 60 degrees

Range of positive stability: 57 degrees

The only commercial stability criteria in Britain at the time were established for merchant ships. They called for a righting arm to 40 degrees of heel and a maximum righting arm at 30 degrees. Though the *Marques* failed only the maximum righting arm, she bore no resemblance to the motorized merchant ships the criteria envisioned. Not only did her figures not measure up to what has become the statutory standard for commercial sailing vessels in the years since, they did not approach the characteristics of many certified sailing vessels that were on file with the Department of Transport even at the time.

In establishing the role of stability in this case, the investigation used language only too familiar in the wake of the *Albatross* story:

A vessel may appear comfortable and responsive up to quite large angles of heel, yet be deficient in her range of stability. . . . The real lesson is that a vessel must have both adequate stability for comfortable sailing in steady conditions and must have a sufficient margin to survive severe gusts and squalls. In order to be assured [of this] a theoretical assessment of stability is essential.

A Point of Controversy

Spreading the criticism among Litchfield, Perryman, and Holstead, the investigation denounced the absence of stability data aboard the *Marques*. The following passage sums up the court's view in respect to reasonable foresight and the significance of stability:

> The *Marques* used as a sail training ship . . . could be expected to carry up to 30 persons, many of them young and of limited sailing experience. It did not need calculation to know that if this vessel capsized onto her beam ends, she would not recover. . . . Reasonable care therefore demanded a high standard of forethought so that the vessel did not unexpectedly capsize. . . . Having regard to the risks involved, experiences should not have displaced the good sense of Mr. Longbottom's recommendation made in 1977 that full stability data should be obtained.

Despite this, the court reached a final conclusion that may strike some as contradictory:

> It was not the fault of any person or persons that the *Marques* had insufficient stability to resist the said squall, but if judged by the knowledge and experience now available, the stability of the *Marques* would be found to have been inadequate and the vessel unseaworthy for sail training in non-coastal waters.

As in the *Pamir* case, this inquiry failed to make everyone happy. Because of the above conclusion, the investigation has often been dismissed privately as a "whitewash" despite the careful research on which it is built. The explanation that generally accompanies this sentiment holds that the *Marques* received her Exemption Certificate through an unorthodox, last-ditch effort that entered the halls of power through the side door. If the exemption process had been condemned as improper, so the argument goes, then the ramifications at the Department of Transport might have been truly significant. The reasoning runs that since the department was involved at a high level, political expedience called for exoneration, which in turn necessitated the same treatment for anyone else involved.

The investigation took a two-step approach to dissipating fault. First, it was pointed out that the significance of righting-arm calculations and ultimate stability was not sufficiently appreciated in Britain at the time to be considered an industry standard. Holding individuals to a standard of practice that, however sensible, was not codified in law was thought unreasonable. Second, the investigation noted that even if full stability data had been obtained for the *Marques*, it would not have prevented the casualty because it would not have resulted in a determination that the *Marques* was unseaworthy. The stability criteria that existed in Britain at the time were designed for power vessels and bore no relationship to the needs of a sailing vessel.

The handling of personal responsibility in this case was a judgment call. The court showed itself willing to give the benefit of the doubt to those in positions of responsibility, and many people who lost family members believed it was wrong to do so. Although the inquiry was ultimately conservative in terms of assigning personal culpability, it lambasted key players where it found them to have failed in their duties. More important for the future of traditional sail, the *Report* made it abundantly clear that the *Marques* represented a major failure of the regulatory system that warranted immediate and drastic reform.

Although there is evidence that the standard practices of the day in respect to sailing ship stability in Britain had not caught up with the United States and that the emphasis on deriving righting arms was uneven, there is also evidence to the contrary. In addressing the view of sailing ship stability in Britain's naval architecture community at the time, the court considered the views of two American naval architects. William M. Peterson (USNR), whose sister (Susan Howell) was lost in the sinking, and Roger Long essentially argued that there was no excuse for the *Marques* to have gone to sea without full stability data and a far better range of stability than that she was found to possess. The court judged their views as useful for the future but essentially the product of an indigenous situation in the United States:

> Both Mr. Long and Commander Peterson have practiced in a different environment to the United Kingdom. The loss of the *Albatross*, the work of Beebe-Center and Brooks, and the stringent United States Coast Guard regulations applying to the considerable number of passenger yachts off the eastern seaboard have resulted in an earlier awareness of the need for a higher standard of stability and the potential dangers of converted vessels.

Although a self-taught naval architect of Perryman's caliber practicing in a narrow niche may not have been exposed to the range of methods and concepts that form the substance of naval architecture, as it turns out, interest in solving the problems of sailing ship stability was neither recent nor uniquely American.

As early as 1868, GZ curves were used by the British Admiralty to predict stability performance for naval vessels. In 1870, after the "arrogantly sparred" battleship HMS *Captain* capsized in a squall with the loss of over five hundred lives, righting-arm GZ predictions became compulsory for all new Royal Navy designs. Sir William White's *Manual of Naval Architecture* first appeared in 1877 and explored methods and principles for the calculation of GZ. It was published and regularly revised through 1894. Sir

Edward J. Reed's *Treatise on the Stability of Ships* was published in London in 1885, adding to the body of knowledge on the subject of stability. The loss of two Royal Navy sail training ships—the HMS *Eurydice* in 1878, a year after White's work appeared, and the HMS *Atalanta* in 1880 with a loss of approximately six hundred lives—ensured that stability work for large sailing vessels continued to be refined through the end of the nineteenth century. The woes of converting vessels to sail training were experienced early on, as both the *Eurydice* and the *Atalanta* were converted to sail training from other purposes. Though the need for understanding sailing ship stability diminished with the passing of sailing merchant ships and warships, history shows that principles of hull proportions, resistance to knockdowns, and the concept of dynamical stability (the sudden application and the absorption of heeling energy) were well understood by the late nineteenth century.

Although the need to relearn the lessons of the past seems to be a hallmark of these casualties, interest in sailing ship stability was not completely relegated to the days of commercial and fighting sail. After the loss of the converted sail training barque *Niobe* in 1932, the *Gorch Fock* class of sail training barques was conceived. Five of these barques were built in Germany in the 1930s, and three of them are still in active sail training service around the world. The class incorporated stability design standards later described as having "set the benchmark for future development." Since the German barques were a new class, part of a government project carried out in the shadow of a disaster, the high degree of care taken with their design is not surprising. For its part, the first conversion of the *Albatross* to sail training in 1949 was a private-sector affair conducted on a much smaller scale. Even so, the standards employed by Royal Rotterdamsche Lloyd Steamship Line in that instance included righting-arm curves and wind heel analysis so as to understand the effect of changes far less dramatic than those made to the *Marques*. Such diligence was exercised in the absence of a statutory requirement; therefore, it appears to have been motivated by common sense and professional management rather than compliance. The *Report* itself recognized that stability minimums as a means to achieve greater safety were not news in Britain:

> It is common knowledge in naval architecture that the GM only gives an indication of stability at small angles of heel. That lesson had been turned into statutory form by 1967 for powered ships, and there is no reason to assume that the same lesson does not apply to sailing ships. Indeed it can be said that since sailing vessels heel to greater angles there is a greater need to know the strength and range of the vessel's stability.

We should also recall that Longbottom, who "strongly recommended" obtaining full stability data, did so not because of some special knowledge of traditional sailing ships, sail training, familiarity with the *Albatross* case, or the American experience. Longbottom was a department inspector, not a stability specialist or a researcher. His was a commonsense recommendation in light of the fundamental duty that a ship be fit to carry out her intended purpose.

Even closer to the time of the *Marques*'s conversion was the Fastnet disaster of 1979. The loss of seventeen people in a yacht race profoundly refocused interest in yacht stability in every sailing nation in the world—especially in Britain. In response to Fastnet 1979, the Department of Transport tasked the Wolfson Unit at Southampton University with conducting stability research in an effort to mitigate future incidents of that type. Although we have seen ample evidence that the regulatory structure in place at the time the *Marques* received her exemption left much to be desired, the conclusion that Britain was bypassed by special developments in sailing-ship stability elsewhere is debatable. Other evidence suggests that the limitations of metacentric height and the value of righting arm data for sailing vessels were not such obscure doctrine at the time.

In terms of a workable criterion appropriate to sail training vessels, there is evidence that this too was not an area where naval architects and regulators in the United States were uniquely positioned to know what an acceptable righting arm should be. The Sailing School Vessels (SSV) regulations in the United States, which required full stability data and a righting arm to 90 degrees, predated the loss of the *Marques*. They were the outgrowth of an expanding industry that had pressured the authorities to develop appropriate regulations, but similar processes were afoot in other countries, most notably Australia. These initiatives were not always precipitated by a tall-ship casualty. Some seventy years before the *Marques* was lost, pilot schooners were being built in the Netherlands with righting arms to 110 degrees, not because it was required but because it was thought to afford the appropriate margin of seaworthiness. And in 1966, Beebe-Center and Brooks considered a positive righting arm to 90 degrees for oceangoing yachts to be "usual" rather than a radical new American standard. According to the investigation's own research, all but one of the British sail-training vessels that had stability data on file with the Marine Directorate had righting arms in excess of 90 degrees.

Nevertheless, the court took the view that the existence of full stability data would not have led to improved stability because an adequate range of stability was "largely a matter of naval architectural opinion in the United Kingdom in 1983." In maintaining a conservative interpretation of what should have been known of stability, the *Report* advanced the following conclusion:

> Had the stability data . . . been available in the United Kingdom in 1983, it could not reasonably have led to the conclusion that the vessel was unseaworthy. . . .
> . . . The failure to provide stability information, which rendered the *Marques* unseaworthy *did not cause her loss or the loss of any persons on board* [original emphasis].

Not all agreed with this reasoning, but this point is burdened by conjecture. If Perryman knew that the righting arm was only 57 degrees, he *may* have been less willing to sign a document stating "the *Marques* possesses such adequate stability to enable her to sail on trans-Atlantic voyages and to operate worldwide." The Marine Directorate, knowing that all but one British sail training vessel (the *Eye of the Wind*) had righting arms at 90 degrees, *may* have reconsidered the exemption process once they knew more about the *Marques*. Though clearly not proactive in this area, Litchfield *may* have reevaluated his confidence in the vessel when faced with a definite and unimpressive figure. In short, at any number of other points along the way the stability data *may* have triggered a rethinking of the plan.

In respect to the role of the sailors themselves the *Report* maintained that, had stability data been on board, action to reduce sail would have been limited to the forecourse, which alone would not have saved the vessel:

> To suggest that they should have done more . . . is reading too much into the effect of the [stability] information which they ought to have had, and the known experience of the vessel.
> Given the hurricane strength of the squall [the chance of survival] is a mere possibility and quite insufficient to support a finding that the loss was caused by the lack of stability information.

This conclusion, although speculative, may be justified. An exceptionally conservative master who was trained to interpret stability data might well have sailed the *Marques* with the degree of caution that she warranted. But it also seems that, given what we know about the renaissance of traditional sail, that person would have been exceptional. This is not because sailing ship captains are a reckless breed, but because the study of sailing ship stability rarely intersects the typical path to command. The exposure to stability, such as it is, is more often limited to the basics of weight added, removed, or relocated and does not normally address wind heeling energy or how to read a stability booklet for a sailing ship. Except for the fact that 57 degrees is an obviously limited range of stability, many licensed small-tonnage captains would not have been comfortable interpreting the data.

In sum, the *Marques* operated at what some would consider an inordinate level of risk. Paramount among these risk factors was the lack of stability, but this was only one manifestation of multiple problems. Although many of the problems affecting the *Marques* may be attributed to circumstances within the China Clipper Society, it is also evident that the authorities contributed to a full-blown maritime disaster by not fulfilling their function as a bulwark against marginal operations. While it is only too easy to criticize government agencies for their shortcomings, in this case the blunder had truly monumental consequences. The Department of Transport's particular miscalculation in this case seems to have reflected a general unreadiness to handle the public's newfound fascination with traditional sail. As the *Report* observed, "So far as the DTp [Department of Transport] was concerned there had been no casualties or general cause for concern in the United Kingdom." Although individual officials may have been aware of tall-ship activities expanding in Britain, the *Marques* showed that the system for coping with them was broken. Despite the involvement of professionals, the operation of the ship itself was also dogged by a quality of amateurism that presumed too much. The findings of the investigation may well have been appropriate to that forum, but those active in sail training and traditional sail need to consider the gray areas closely because their goal should be not to seek exoneration, but rather never to be the object of an investigation in the first place.

REPERCUSSIONS

The loss of the *Marques* has influenced tall-ship safety more than any other single event in the renaissance of traditional sail. As one writer put it, "Indeed, it was this disaster that really touched off the resurgence of official interest and research." The loss of the *Marques* resonated for years to come not only in Britain but internationally. It has cast a shadow over all subsequent tall-ship races and any project that involves the adaptation of older vessels and designs for training or passenger purposes. Above all, it generated momentum for the creation of regulatory regimes tailored to the realities of large traditional sailing vessels. This story is replete with missed opportunities, but the sail-training industry and regulatory authorities alike in Britain were aggressive in their effort to glean the most from the tragedy.

Recommendations

The *Report of the Formal Investigation*, issued on 23 April 1987, set forth a series of recommendations for regulatory reform: "The loss of the *Marques* has demonstrated an urgent need to establish a safe and acceptable standard of stability for sail training ships." The *Report* pointedly noted the inadequacy of the Load Line Rules for sailing ships and the IMO resolutions that produced them. The absence of full stability data and wind heeling moments were among the weaknesses specifically cited. The *Report* added:

> Confidence in the accuracy of any stability information provided to a ship is necessary to ensure that the information is not ignored by the mariner who considers that his sailing experience alone is sufficient.

The seriousness with which the *Report* viewed the matter was underscored by the recommendation that new stability criteria apply to all sail training ships regardless of when they were built: " 'Existing Ship' exemptions, commonly found in Merchant Shipping legislation, ought not apply to a matter so fundamental as a safe standard of stability in a sail training ship."

Other significant recommendations are condensed here:

1. Watertight subdivision: The difficulties in wooden sail training ships of fitting new watertight transverse bulkheads . . . are appreciated, but in the interest of safety it is considered that every effort should be made to overcome these difficulties wherever possible.

2. Hatches: All hatch openings should be on the center line and open in the fore and aft direction. This case has shown the risks inherent in the use of boards and tarpaulins to provide watertightness over a hatch, upon which ventilation in the main cabin is dependent.

3. Freeing ports: Retain all freeing ports in working order and unobstructed. Load Line Exemption Certificates should expressly state that they are granted on condition that the freeing ports, which should be defined, are kept in working order and unobstructed.

Recommendations for the conduct of future tall-ship races included communications, obtaining weather reports, and especially the need for participating vessels to share information regarding potential navigational hazards.

The Merchant Shipping Notice

Following the *Report*, the department issued an interim Merchant Shipping Notice, "The Stability of Sail Training Ships." The notice acknowledged the expanding role of traditional sail and identified provisional standards addressing elements of the *Marques* casualty.

> Although sailing ships are not, in general, used nowadays for the carriage of cargo, they have become increasingly popular for taking young people to sea

for training in seamanship, character building, expeditions and Tall Ships races. . . . However, the growing number of sail training ships, and a recent casualty involving such a ship, has made it necessary for the Department to consider further the question of developing standards appropriate for this type of ship.

The criteria established by the notice called for "a substantial range of stability" based on "standards achieved by existing United Kingdom sail training ships" and taking into account "standards applied by two other countries" (Australia and the United States). The required range of stability was set at 90 degrees for vessels up to 24 meters, and this was eventually extended to larger vessels. Further to the lessons of the *Marques*, it was required that hatches be of the minimum number and size appropriate to the proper working of the ship, and that they be capable of rapid closure in emergency. The notice reiterated the importance of locating hatches on the centerline of the ship and orienting them in a fore-and-aft direction rather than athwartships. Adequate means for shedding water from the deck was addressed, with the additional warning that "on no account should these openings be closed." For vessels of the *Marques*'s size the following measures were also taken:

> The Merchant Shipping (Load Line Exemption) Order, 1968, which previously exempted sailing ships of under 80 net tons, which were employed in the coasting trade and did not carry cargo, has been revoked. The Owners of ships to which the Load Line Regulations apply are required to submit stability information to the Department for approval.

The prompt striking down of the old law is the best evidence that the authorities recognized the inadequacy of the previous system. Although a step in the right direction, the notice was only a starting point.

Stability Research and the Work of the Wolfson Unit

Even before the investigation was completed the department commissioned the Wolfson Unit for Marine Technology at the University of Southampton to do stability research as "a basis for informed discussion." Even before the Fasnet disaster, the Wolfson Unit had become the first point of contact in technical matters of design and stability. This mandate was expanded to include the development of requirements that had "a more technical basis than those currently in existence."

Building on work that emerged from the SSV process in the United States, the Wolfson Unit adopted the standard calling for a minimum range of positive stability to 90 degrees. The research also broke new ground on the influence of dynamic wave action and downflooding on vessel stability.

A wind tunnel was constructed around a pond in which scale models of the barque *Lord Nelson* and a 56-meter three-masted staysail schooner were subjected to wind gusts of varying velocity and apparent direction.

A significant innovation emerging from the Wolfson Unit was the concept of a "safe heeling angle." The safe heeling angle was an attempt to establish a measure of reserve stability that corresponds to a particular angle of heel for a given vessel. A master could readily ascertain from an inclinometer when a sail reduction is appropriate in order to preserve a margin of stability that the safe heeling angle represents. This approach applies equally to all weather conditions and provides a technical basis to the intuitive process that has always been part of sail change decisions by masters. One of the primary concerns of the Department of Transport in developing new stability standards was "to avoid . . . dictating to the master how to sail his vessel; in particular, the type of rig to set in the prevailing weather conditions." The determination of a safe heeling angle is to enable a vessel to be rigged with sufficient sail area to be sailed effectively in the wide variety of conditions experienced in long-distance voyaging by emphasizing the angle of heel and its relationship to a safe margin of stability rather than the height of the rig. This helps avoid an inflexible restriction on maximum sail area that is a handicap in light wind conditions and irrelevant under storm conditions when sail is reduced, anyway. The fact is, short canvas is not synonymous with safety: a vessel that is perennially undercanvased endures longer passages and increased risk of exposure to foul weather. The sailor's adage "a fast passage is a safe passage" reflects the need to have adequate sail area to make use of light airs. Though the concept of safe heeling angle has not been embraced by the U.S. Coast Guard, some certified U.S. vessels have been provided with stability letters that set out sail combinations for different conditions of wind strength. Such an approach reflects the principle of safe heeling angle and, although it does in a sense impinge on the master's discretion, it is an improvement over being sent to sea with a stumpy rig that begins to perform only in half a gale. The extent to which a safe heeling angle can account for sudden and substantial increase in wind force is still limited, but it has been regarded by some as an advance over earlier approaches to design and stability.

New Regulations

The intent of the research conducted by the Wolfson Unit was to pave the way for new, improved regulations for British sailing vessels. The new regulations were created in three stages. Between 1990 and 1997 three different regulatory initiatives were crafted to address the diversity of large sailing vessels and their activities. All three codes incorporated the stability research of the Wolfson Unit. The regulations for small commercial sailing vessels were introduced with the following: "The primary aim in developing the Code has been to set standards of safety and protection for all on board and particularly for those who are trainees or passengers. The level of safety it sets out to achieve is considered to be commensurate with the current expectations of the general public."

The introduction to the 1997 code also articulated a fundamental truth regarding these ships: "It is important to stress that, whilst all reasonable measures have been taken to develop standards which will result in the production of safe and seaworthy vessels, total safety at sea can never be guaranteed."

Licensing and Manning

The case-by-case exemption system used for the masters and chief mates aboard the *Marques* remained in place until 2002, when it was superceded by the international Standards of Training, Certification and Watchkeeping for Seafarers (STCW 95) protocols. The benefit of the exemption system for vessel owners was the flexibility it afforded in finding crew. The drawback was the inherent inconsistency that occurred when a given Department of Transport official attempted to weigh the conglomeration of one candidate's experience against the conglomerations of previous candidates' experience. The lack of a clear standard allowed the department to interpret and the applicant to bluff. The weapon of choice in this duel of ambiguity was, naturally, paperwork. Captain Mark Kemmis-Betty, a veteran sail training master in Britain, utilized the exemption system with regularity and offered the following appraisal of how it worked: "Generally, if you sent in enough pieces of paper with the application you would get the exemption."

The *Marques* casualty revealed the existing licensing system in a less-than-reassuring light. Although the system that ultimately displaced the old one was not solely motivated by the loss of the *Marques*, it was a factor. As of 1997, a new licensing system was codified for the manning of square-riggers in Britain. Though it was years in the making, the Manning Scale for Commercially Operated Square Rigged Sailing Vessels over 24 Metres addressed virtually all the licensing and training concerns that arose in connection with the return of traditional sail and the loss of the *Marques*. The scale is perhaps the first manning schedule specific to traditional sail to emerge since the days of commercial sail. The regulations lay out the grade and number of licenses required aboard square-riggers. Additionally, there is a requirement for a fourteen-day apprenticeship aboard a given vessel before a master or mate may assume responsibility. The code also calls for every vessel owner to create and submit for approval an in-house assessment system that addresses fundamental aspects of a square-rigger's operation. Among the evolutions required to be addressed are wearing ship, tacking, heaving-to, setting and striking sail, reefing, operating in heavy weather, coping with squalls, and the effect of knockdowns. If traditional sail is to have a future and hold its own as a profession, these are the topics toward which commercial sailing license exams should incline. Of the reformed system, Kemmis-Betty remarked: "The new system of certification and manning is a great improvement and gives a proper career structure for sail training. At least some good has come out of the loss of the *Marques*."

Professional Literature

The loss of the *Marques* spurred interest in sailing ship stability not only in the public policy arena, but throughout the international community of naval architects. Soon after the incident, a steady flow of papers and articles on the subject began to appear in the professional literature. These studies addressed the types of problems facing traditional sailing ships operating in a modern era. In particular, from 1984 onward any serious discussion of sailing ship stability, in either a theoretical or regulatory context, was conducted against the backdrop of the *Marques*. In 1986 Tsai and Haciski published "The Stability of Large Sailing Vessels," which focused primarily on the U.S. Coast Guard training barque *Eagle*, but the impact of the *Marques* was still felt: "Recent interest in the design and operation of large sailing vessels, either historical replicas . . . or new sail-equipped tanker designs has raised the search for satisfactory stability analysis method, and for a set of satisfactory stability criteria."

Sail Training Organizations in Britain and the United States

The *Report* acknowledged the role of ASTA in the development of sail training regulations in the United States and urged a similar process in Britain. Sail training groups were encouraged to collaborate with one another and with the Department of Transport to create suitable regulations, a process that eventually bore fruit.

In the United States the incident brought about the total suspension of ASTA-sponsored tall-ship races while the organization defended itself from legal actions arising from the deaths of trainees. In 1994 ASTA was cleared of the last of these suits and has since resumed a leadership role in North America, including the organization of tall-ship races. Nevertheless, a decade filled with important developments on the American sail training scene had passed, and a new generation of traditional sailors had come up in the meantime. ASTA has supported the professionalization of the sail training industry in North America in a variety of ways, including providing sail training officers with financial assistance for required training courses.

International Sail Training Safety Forum (ISTSF)

The ISTSF is perhaps the best example of an industry-led response to the *Marques* sinking. The Safety Forum has its roots in an impromptu meeting of captains in Québec in 1984 shortly after the *Marques* was lost. After sporadic meetings, it eventually became an annual event held on alternate sides of the Atlantic in conjunction with sail training conferences. The forum has been regularly attended by representatives of Argentina, Australia, Canada, Chile, Denmark, Germany, the Netherlands, Norway, Oman, Poland, Sweden, the United Kingdom, the United States, and Venezuela, and less regularly by many other countries. The forum provides, literally, a forum, and is a clearinghouse for developments in marine safety that are relevant to tall ship operations. Although it is not a policy-creating body, the forum is essential to the exchange of information, which in turn can guide the direction of future policies. At the opening remarks in 1993, the forum was described as "a sign of the maturing—one might almost say the professionalization—of sail training, and the shock of the *Marques* has had a great deal to do with it." Should momentum develop for an international sail training safety standard, the ISTSF would likely play a central role in it.

LOOSE ENDS

No casualty did more to propel the professionalization of sail training in the postcommercial era than the loss of the *Marques*. That the world of sail training and tall ships has changed since May 1984 is largely due to the clarity the investigation brought to problems affecting the *Marques*. Based on what we now know, from many standpoints the *Marques* may be fairly held up as an example of what not to do. Yet the *Marques* was not the only vessel ever to suffer from oversights and mistakes of the type that dogged her, and therein lies a potent warning.

The loss of the *Marques* reinforced the lessons of the *Albatross* in respect to modifying a vessel to unknown effect and to the illusory security represented by measures of metacentric height. After reviewing the *Albatross* and the *Marques*, it is obvious that vessels whose stability characteristics are not properly understood may be accidents waiting to happen, regardless of past performance. It seems unlikely that the excuse of ignorance in this matter could ever hold water again where a certified vessel is involved.

The rediscovery of traditional sail could never proceed without the vision and the energy of nonsailors, yet the vision cannot be brought to fruition without the guidance of professionals. Paying a pittance to starry-eyed deckhands with visions of palm trees and dolphins does not transform them into professionals. Professionalism must be defined by experience, of course, but also by a mastery of relevant knowledge. Until the licensing process for tall-ship sailors reflects the unique nature of the work, tall-ship sailors will never measure up in the eyes of regulatory authorities, and they will always be studying for an exam that was developed with conventional maritime activities in mind.

Emerging from the broader issue of safety is the question regarding the type of vessel appropriate to sail training. Some schools of thought strictly advocate purpose-built sail training vessels, pointing to the ease of incorporating safety measures at the design stage, as well as the excellent safety record for such vessels in recent times. In the years since the *Marques* was lost, historic vessels in many countries (both restorations and replicas) have been turned to sail training and passenger work while meeting the more stringent regulations of the post-*Marques* world. There have been no design-related casualties of significance among such vessels. Nevertheless, the *Marques* provided a drastic example of the problems that can arise when an older vessel of historic interest is turned to a purpose other than that for which she was built, without a comprehensive assessment. It is the role of effective regulation to eliminate or restrict vessels that possess characteristics that are known to be likely to kill people. The *Marques* case has ensured continued debate over the safety of converted vessels for sail training vis-à-vis purpose-built sail training ships.

Problems with the *Marques* were not limited to the ship itself, to regulatory issues, or to seamanship: shoreside management also played a role. Although the underpinnings of modern tall-ship activities are frequently humanistic rather than vocational, organizations that run these types of ships need to think of themselves not only as nonprofits dedicated to lofty and compelling goals but as shipping companies with all the duties, obligations, and expenses that go with owning and operating ships. "Safety First" is a worthy but unhelpful mantra that can easily obscure the actual issues.

The easiest thing in the world in this case would be to cite the loss of the *Marques* as an act of God and leave it at that. But at every step of the way more experience, more knowledge, and a greater respect for the sea could have protected this ship from what happened. In discussing the impact of the *Marques* at the 1993 Safety Forum, Captain David V. V. Wood, former master of the USCG barque *Eagle* and executive director of ASTA, said, "Sail training seems actually to have become a kind of 'industry' with the attendant need for standards of professionalism, and attention to safety is very much a part of that." The story of the *Marques* reinforces the recognition that sail training and the renaissance of traditional sail must be guided by professional judgment, though they thrive on youthful exuberance and high-flying dreams. The loss of the *Marques* was a loss of innocence for the entire endeavor just when it was enjoying unprecedented success. It stunned many advocates, as well as people in positions of responsibility, and it continues to influence the conduct of traditional sailing activities everywhere.

Fair weather sail drill on the *Pride of Baltimore* in the Virgin Islands days before the loss. Both stunsails and the ringtail are set. The length of the headrig in proportion to the hull is evident, and the helmsman is clearly visible at the tiller. The topgallant yard and sail as well as the main gaff topsail and stunsails were sent up from the deck each time they were set. (Courtesy Robert Foster)

Pride of Baltimore
1977–1986

DESIGNER: Thomas C. Gillmer

BUILDER: Melbourne Smith, International Historical Watercraft Society, Baltimore

RIG: Two-masted topsail schooner, Baltimore clipper style

HULL: Wood

SAIL AREA: 9,523 square feet

SPARRED LENGTH: 137 feet

LOD: 89 feet, 9 inches

LWL: 76 feet, 8 inches

DRAFT: 9 foot, 9 inches

BEAM: 23 feet

TONNAGE: 67 gross registered tons

DISPLACEMENT: 121 tons

POWER: Caterpillar 85-horsepower diesel

FLAG HISTORY: United States

*T*he early 1980s witnessed what seemed an inordinate number of tall-ship casualties. Vessels of all types are lost in all times, of course, but in those years it almost seems as if there was a sort of thinning out of vessels that had come into service during the renaissance of traditional sail. Many of these casualties were older vessels, but many were new. An element of romance had propelled all of them onto the high seas, where they encountered difficulties.

In 1981 the schooner *John F. Leavitt* was abandoned off Cape Cod on her maiden voyage from

Massachusetts to the Caribbean. Built the year before as an engineless replica of a New England coasting schooner, the *Leavitt* was laden with a cargo of lumber. Her owner was attempting to prove that this mode of transport could be viable once again. The venture was ill prepared for winter in the North Atlantic, and when the weather turned rough, problems arose. The skipper called in a Mayday, and the ship was abandoned though still afloat. In April 1982 the three-masted topsail schooner *Sophia* was lost with one person off North Cape, New Zealand. The *Sophia* was a sixty-one-year-old Baltic trader, American owned and Bahamian flagged. She had become home to what was in effect a sailing commune, in which people bought shares and participated in the work and the adventure of sailing around the world regardless of prior experience. In rough weather with her bilges full of water she was rolled by a sea and didn't recover. In October 1984, a few months after the *Marques* went down, the restored American cargo schooner *Isaac Evans* capsized in a sudden squall associated with a cold front. The *Evans* was part of a substantial fleet of schooners, some restored, some purpose-built, that carry passengers along the scenic Maine coast. When she came to rest on the bottom of Penobscot Bay, her pennant was still fluttering above Maine's icy autumn waters. There were no fatalities, and the schooner was sailing again the following season. In 1985, the Swiss-flagged topsail schooner and sail training vessel *El Pirata* went down in a Bay of Biscay gale. In the spring of that same year, the brand-new American topsail schooner *Dayspring* took on water and was abandoned at sea while returning to Maine from her first season chartering in the Caribbean. Then, on 14 May 1986, the topsail schooner *Pride of Baltimore* met with a powerful squall in the North Atlantic that caused her to capsize and sink with the loss of the captain and three crew.

A replica of the Baltimore clipper type, the *Pride* was returning from a goodwill tour of Europe. By 1986, the loss of the *Pride* may have looked like part of an alarming trend, particularly to regulators, yet some people thought these ships had always been and would always be dangerous, and they loudly said so each time one was lost. Although the *Pride* did not carry passengers or trainees, she was an international celebrity, and her loss reverberated far and wide, shattering any complacency in the effort to resurrect the glorious sailing ships of the past.

The Pride's *Role in the Renaissance of Traditional Sail*

The *Pride of Baltimore* was a representation of the fast and able Baltimore clipper privateers of the War of 1812. She carried a complement of twelve paid sailors, including the captain, but had no berthing for additional people. The *Pride* was a "sailing goodwill ambassador" for the city of Baltimore, which meant that, unlike a passenger ship or a sail training vessel, she best filled her role when in the limelight. Operating in a way that garnered maximum media exposure, the *Pride* earned a place in the public's imagination that few vessels ever achieve. In her nine-year life the *Pride* sailed over 150,000 nautical miles and made hundreds of official port visits. Tens of thousands of people went aboard her in ports ranging from Poland to British Columbia and from Newfoundland to Venezuela.

Most tall ships entering service in the early 1980s set out to execute some form of educational training or passenger-carrying mission. The *Pride* was different. She was conceived as a centerpiece for an urban waterfront renewal project in downtown Baltimore. As the container revolution in shipping rendered Baltimore's Inner Harbor obsolete, local politicians and boosters saw an opportunity disguised as a problem. The old warehouses were razed and the docks reconfigured for public access and tourism, and the result was a successful paradigm for waterfront redevelopment that has been copied the world over. Constructing the *Pride* on the quay in the midst of this redevelopment drew both locals and visitors to the formerly derelict waterfront and helped establish a new pattern of activity for the downtown area. Originally the *Pride* was intended not to voyage internationally but to lay dockside as part of the new waterfront scenery and only occasionally sail. While she was still under construction, however, the idea took flight that the ship could promote the city better by sailing than by sitting at the dock. Ultimately, the *Pride* sailed to three continents, two oceans, and a multitude of islands, ports, and seas. Because public relations was her stock in trade, the *Pride* made friends wherever she went. Perhaps more than any other tall ship, the *Pride* became a centerfold for the renaissance of traditional sail.

Although the *Pride* did not have a structured educational program, there was an important educational strand to her mission. As a reasonably authentic replica of an 1812 privateering Baltimore clipper, the vessel embodied a remarkable but little-recognized chapter in American history. This history was transmitted through every aspect of the vessel's operation: sailing, maintenance, and dockside interpretation. Her designer, Thomas C. Gillmer, described her as an experiment in nautical archaeology. The *Pride* became a mobile publicist for all tall-ship activities, including sail training, because few of the thousands who went aboard her failed to inquire how they too could sail aboard such a ship.

The *Pride* was connected to the larger revival of tall ships in other important ways. Her captains and crew were part of a free flow of talent between the *Pride* and the fleet of traditional sailing vessels operating in the United States at the time. Pay scales, background, and experience levels were comparable from ship to ship. At any given time a typical *Pride* crew combined a spectrum of experience from seasoned officers to green deckhands. However, the *Pride* was a demanding ship to sail, therefore even the deckhands usually brought prior experience with them. Sea time acquired aboard the *Pride* often paved the way to positions on other traditional vessels because of the exceptional opportunity the vessel offered to gain traditional rigging skills and offshore experience. In this sense the *Pride* was a training ship for sail trainers.

The *Pride* frequently interacted with sail training vessels at home and abroad. For example, in 1985 she participated in crew exchanges with sail training ships from Britain, Norway, and Sweden. The *Pride*'s administrative organization was also affiliated with the American Sail Training Association, and several people connected to the *Pride* have held leadership positions with ASTA.

But the greatest relevance of this case to the traditional sail movement is in what it says about the relationship between the authenticity of a replica vessel and the purpose to which it is put. A variety of historic sailing vessels have been built or restored in recent decades—some for long-range voyaging, some for more limited operations, and others still for use only as stationary dockside exhibits. Although the authentic oceangoing vessels of two centuries ago were serviceable and durable, they could not satisfy current marine safety expectations. Therefore, all projects involving facsimiles of historic vessel types are inevitably compelled to strike a balance between authenticity and contemporary expectations, chief among which is safety. The story of the *Pride* sheds light on this balance.

A Trilogy

As with the *Albatross* and the *Marques*, the loss of the *Pride* was precipitated by the sudden onset of extreme weather. In all three cases the situation deteriorated too fast for effective countermeasures or for a coherent abandon-ship response. The circumstances of the *Pride*'s loss closely resemble those that befell the *Marques*: both vessels were sailing under reduced canvas in moderately rough conditions when the weather abruptly and catastrophically deteriorated. Like the *Marques* and the *Albatross*, the *Pride* lacked effective watertight subdivision, which led to rapid flooding. All three vessels were similar in tonnage. But by far the strongest thread tying the cases together, in terms of both policy and practice, is that none of them possessed adequate stability or resistance to downflooding to survive the knockdown forces they encountered. The *Pride* possessed far better stability than either of the other vessels, yet it was not sufficient to save her.

Replicas and Replicas

Despite similarities to the earlier casualties, two unique aspects to the loss of the *Pride* form a prism through which we must view the case. First, the *Pride of Baltimore* was essentially a new vessel, and the only replica casualty considered in this book. A high degree of historic authenticity—with all the attendant aesthetic considerations, uncertainties, and limitations—was incorporated into the vision and implementation of the enterprise from its inception.

Second, of the ships in this book, only the *Pride of Baltimore* was replaced by another replica of the same type, the *Pride of Baltimore II*. Here we have a situation in which tragedy and circumstance posed in concrete terms what is normally a purely hypothetical question: if we had to do it all again, what would we do differently? The *de facto* answer is a fully operational replacement vessel built by the same organization for the same basic purpose. This vessel has now sailed much more widely than her predecessor.

The spirit and shape of the first *Pride* runs strong in the *Pride II*, yet in fundamental and deliberate ways the two vessels are different creatures. Many of these differences are direct responses to the loss of the first vessel. Others represent a more evolved approach to the vessel's mission and shipboard life. Still other differences between the two ships reflect budgetary realities, regulations, changes in technology, and, yes, ideas in vogue at the time. *Pride II*, for instance, was designed for a 20-ton chunk of lead in her keel to improve stability and internal capacity.

HISTORY

The Baltimore Clippers

When the *Pride of Baltimore*'s keel was laid, roughly 165 years had passed since the high-water mark of the Baltimore clipper privateers. The *Pride of Baltimore* sought to replicate the American privateering vessels from the War of 1812, a period during which the Baltimore clippers are said to have reached their "highest degree of excellence." The Baltimore clippers, including the *Pride*, were characterized by low freeboard, sharp entry, great deadrise, and a pronounced rake to the masts. The maximum beam was well forward, resulting in the classic *codfish head–mackerel tail* configuration. The keel tended to run straight but with considerable drag, meaning it was significantly deeper aft than forward. The main result of all this was that Baltimore clipper hulls were fast, weatherly, and maneuverable.

The rigs were lofty for the size of the hull and can fairly be described as "extreme." The typical Baltimore clipper could set a phenomenal amount of sail as compared with an ordinary trading vessel of similar tonnage. The headrig on the *Pride of Baltimore* alone represented nearly a third of her total sparred length. The rig type of choice that accompanied privateers' sleek hulls was the topsail schooner (square topsails rigged on the foremast). However, there were many variations on this theme, and it was not uncommon for a vessel to undergo changes in the rig during her life. Double-topsail schooners (square sails on the mainmast as well as the foremast), brigs, and brigantines all appeared on sharp-built Baltimore clippers. Howard Chapelle, one of the foremost maritime historians to document the Baltimore clippers, wrote about the shipwrights who built them:

> Having no method of putting their designs on paper and checking the elements of such designs, either mathematically or by the eye, they were often led, like later yacht modelers and builders, to great extremes due to the . . . tendency of such a builder to attribute speed of sailing to certain elements . . . considered to be absolutely necessary in a fast vessel.

Though extreme sail area had no direct bearing on the loss of the *Pride*, even her naked rig presented considerable windage. The investigation into her loss noted the following: "A full suit of sails for the 122-ton *Pride* amounted to nearly 10,000 square feet of sail. By comparison, the Coast Guard's 1,816-ton training vessel *Eagle* has 21,350 square feet of sail."

To understand the advent of the Baltimore clippers and their unusual characteristics, one must look at the historical milieu that produced them. As a hull type, the Baltimore clippers did not appear overnight but were part of a gradual and distinctly American development. As a rig type, the distinguishing characteristics of the Baltimore clipper privateers evolved in response to an unstable political situation in the Atlantic Ocean starting in the late eighteenth century. A near-constant state of war among European powers, as well as the American Revolution, created a need for vessels that could evade naval blockades, outsail pursuers, and capture lightly armed but valuable commercial prizes. Whether it was as privateers in the service of patriotism or smuggling, as pilot schooners, or as slave traders later, the Baltimore clipper type excelled at operations requiring speed.

During the Napoleonic Wars, geopolitical tensions in the Atlantic intensified into prolonged and open warfare during which U.S. relations with both Britain and France were strained to the breaking point. American merchant shipping was jeopardized by these two belligerents at a time when the U.S. Navy was too weak to offer a credible deterrent—the British navy alone built more ships each year than the U.S. Navy possessed in total. Mer-

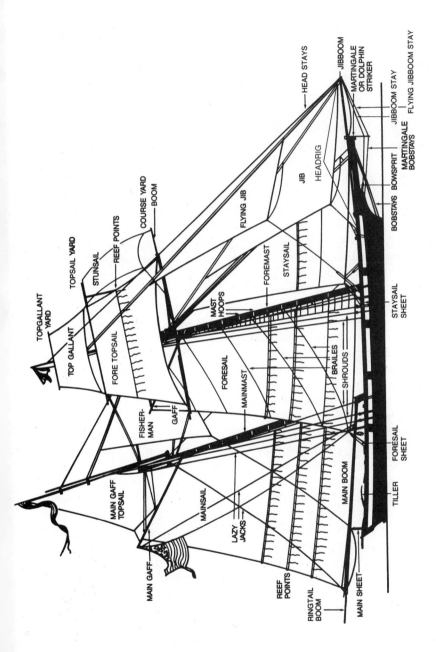

TOPGALLANT YARD
TOP GALLANT
TOPSAIL YARD
STUNSAIL
REEF POINTS
COURSE YARD
BOOM
HEAD STAYS
JIBBOOM
MARTINGALE OR DOLPHIN STRIKER
JIBBOOM STAY
FLYING JIBBOOM STAY
MARTINGALE BOBSTAYS
BOWSPRIT
BOBSTAYS
FLYING JIB
JIB
HEADRIG
FORE TOPSAIL
FORESAIL
FORESAIL STAYSAIL
FOREMAST
MAST HOOPS
STAYSAIL SHEET
FISHER-MAN
GAFF
MAINMAST
BRAILES
SHROUDS
MAIN GAFF TOPSAIL
MAINSAIL
LAZY JACKS
FORESAIL SHEET
MAIN BOOM
TILLER
MAIN GAFF
REEF POINTS
RINGTAIL BOOM
MAIN SHEET

Basic rigging and sail plan of *Pride of Baltimore*. Note how the foresail overlaps the mainsail. This additional sail area could mean the difference between escape or capture for a privateer in the War of 1812. (NTSB *Report*) chant ships of the neutral United States were subjected to search and seizure by both Britain and France, and American sailors were removed from U.S. ships and pressed into the service of the British navy. Meanwhile, foreign privateers proliferated. This situation led to friction and protest, followed by a declaration of war against Britain in June 1812. A blockade of U.S. ports by the British navy quickly followed.

Under this situation, speed under sail became synonymous with survival at sea, and so the Baltimore clipper design was in its element. Vessels of the Baltimore clipper type were built along the length of the eastern seaboard, but the Chesapeake Bay region, and Fells Point at Baltimore in particular, are credited with much of the design innovation and construction. Their low freeboard granted them proportionally less cargo capacity than might be found in trading vessels of comparable length where speed was a lesser priority. The trade-off was balanced by their sailing qualities. Thomas C. Gillmer, designer of both the *Pride of Baltimore* and her successor, the *Pride of Baltimore II*, described Baltimore clippers as "truly the first all-American contribution to shipbuilding and design." Efficient cargo carriers or not, Baltimore clippers enabled goods to travel under hazardous circumstances. They prevented the strangulation of the American economy while raising the stakes for British merchant shipping and stretching the Royal Navy more thinly.

The qualities that made Baltimore clippers so effective at avoiding predators also made them excel as privateers, and this became their real contribution to the national war effort. President Madison stepped up the policy of issuing "Letters of Marque and Reprisal," which authorized private shipowners to fit out armed vessels and prey upon the shipping of hostile nations with the official sanction of the U.S. government. This policy remains a classic example of a private-sector solution to a public problem, since Baltimore clippers "rendered a service to a nation that her navy was unable to do and which her government was unable to afford."

According to one source, American privateers, many of them Baltimore clippers, were responsible for the capture or sinking of more than 1,700 enemy ships in the two-year conflict. Other sources cite lower but nevertheless impressive figures. The effect on insurance rates for shipping inflicted particular pain on British commerce.

Baltimore clipper privateers made an art of "cutting out" and capturing merchant ships sailing in convoy, often in plain view of a powerful but cumbersome naval escort. One tactic involved luring the naval escort away from the convoy by offering a tempting downwind chase that favored the large square-riggers. Having drawn the escort some distance away, the more weatherly Baltimore clipper could then beat its way back up to the undefended convoy, leaving the naval escort powerless to intervene. At times

American privateers cooperated with one another as well as with U.S. naval ships. Privateers took on the occasional British naval vessel, but generally speaking they avoided slugging matches with the enemy. The hit-and-run tactics refined by American privateers were an effective form of guerilla warfare on the high seas.

One Baltimore clipper that gained particular notoriety was the *Chasseur*, under the command of Captain Thomas Boyle. In a single five-and-a-half-month cruise in 1814 she is reported to have captured forty-five British prizes. Upon her triumphant return to Baltimore she received the sobriquet "the Pride of Baltimore," which was bestowed on her successor 163 years later. Boyle is renowned for the audacious proclamation that he directed to have posted to the door of Lloyd's of London, declaring that "all of Britain was thenceforth under a state of strict and rigorous blockade." An audacious and improbable boast for a single ship, Boyle's proclamation nevertheless had the desired effect on insurance rates, which skyrocketed and discouraged trade vital to the British.

The havoc wrought by Maryland-built privateers led to British retaliations throughout the Chesapeake Bay during the War of 1812, including efforts to destroy shipyards on both sides of the bay, as well as a major assault on Baltimore in September 1814. The level of activity in Fells Point by this time was such that shipyards were able to launch a vessel within ninety days of laying the keel. The British attack on Baltimore failed, but the incident inspired a poem, which was put to an air then popular. Today we know this song as "The Star-Spangled Banner."

It might be said that Baltimore clippers were shaped by geopolitics as much as the sea. In the aftermath of the War of 1812, these swift and weatherly ships passed into other risky services, including various South American revolutions and the slave trade. Many features of the Baltimore clippers lived on in other incarnations, including pilot schooners, revenue schooners, and various other fast cargo schooners. As Pax Britannica descended across the Atlantic Ocean, however, the need for the extreme Baltimore clippers of the privateer style waned and passed into history. They had not been built as long-term investments, thus "these hastily built vessels did not enjoy long lives." Also, although considered one of the fastest vessels afloat, they were demanding to sail:

> Over sparring was always common and the clipper schooners and brigs built for the privateering and naval services had this fault almost without exception. But they were safe if in the hands of an officer who was acquainted with their handling; in the hands of an unskilled commander, however, their antics, as described by eyewitnesses, were hair-raising to say the least. These long-sparred vessels, in spite of this, do not seem to have suffered capsizing as often as one would have expected.

The Baltimore clippers, like many vessels of their time, were sailed by large and seasoned crews. Privateers in particular carried large crews for the purpose of putting aboard their prizes. Sending down yards and topmasts for bad weather as if reefing a sail was a form of seamanship almost unimaginable to today's tall-ship sailor. Ships of this period weren't bound by schedules, so they could be sailed as conservatively as conditions warranted: vessels simply arrived when they got there, or they didn't. This is in contrast to the expectations of today's tall-ship fleet.

Construction of a Replica

Funds to build the *Pride of Baltimore* were appropriated by Mayor William Donald Schaefer and the City Council of Baltimore in 1975. An announcement in the *Baltimore Sun* in September that year solicited bids to build a replica:

> The City of Baltimore wishes to have built as a public attraction on the shores of the Inner Harbor an authentic example of an historic Baltimore Clipper ship. The ship is to be between 85′ and 90′ length on deck, fully operable, capable of being sailed, and equipped with replica cannon. Wherever practicable, the construction materials, methods, tools, and procedures are to be typical of the period.

Melbourne Smith of the International Historical Watercraft Society prepared a bid with designer Thomas Gillmer, and that proposal was accepted.

Rather than building the ship in an existing shipyard with limited public access, the *Pride* was constructed in full view of passersby at an improvised shipyard beside the promenade at Baltimore's Inner Harbor. The story of the Baltimore clippers in the War of 1812 was compatible with patriotic themes of the American Bicentennial, and the project quickly came to symbolize the city's downtown renewal.

Despite the large numbers of Baltimore clippers a century and a half earlier, little documentation and no existing examples survived into the late twentieth century. Early American shipbuilding was largely an intuitive craft whereby individual shipwrights interpreted hand-carved half-models by eye. Builders tended to use rules of thumb rather than plans, and they left little in the way of records. In consequence, building the *Pride* was a research project before it became a shipbuilding project:

> We were regenerating something that had been laid to rest long past. Consequently, there were questions that could not be answered as to her structure, shape, and rig. . . . It was rather like reading a book or a manuscript in which every so often a word is missing, so one must replace the missing words with some of one's own that will result in a sensible statement.

Research conducted as part of the design process relied upon literature, period works of marine art, and, ironically, detailed British Admiralty records of captured American privateers. The outcome was a composite design, which Gillmer described as "an honest attempt to produce a vessel that would be typical and retain the best historic features within the size limitation."

Construction on the *Pride* started in April 1976. Structural members were fashioned from dense tropical hardwoods, including Cortez, Santa Maria, and bulit tree. The keel was fashioned from a single thousand-year-old tree of lignum vitae. Yellow pine (pitch pine) went into the hull planking and the deck. Though much of this wood was not native to Maryland, nor would it have been used in construction of local Baltimore clippers, it had the advantage of being extremely rot resistant, and therefore more durable.

During construction, the scope of operations envisioned for the vessel was revisited: "Although it was originally planned to sail the *Pride* only in protected waters, about halfway through construction it was decided to extend the range of the vessel and do ocean sailing to foreign ports and represent the City of Baltimore."

Such a project perhaps seemed too significant an effort for a static dockside exhibit, whereas an active sailing program might maximize the potential of this unusual resource to promote Baltimore abroad. As part of this conceptual shift an auxiliary engine was installed, which, in the designer's words, was "too underpowered to drive the hull as a powered vessel and too large to fit properly into the small space available." The *Pride* was also fitted with a generator and batteries for essential lighting, a VHF radio, and some navigation equipment, but few other modern amenities.

The hull was launched by crane at Baltimore's Inner Harbor on 27 February 1977 with thousands looking on. She was commissioned on 1 May and set sail for Bermuda. By most reports this was a harrowing experience as the ship taught the sailors how much they had to learn about a Baltimore clipper. Due to time constraints, her distinctive top-hamper (the yards and square topsail gear) was not put in place until August, when the vessel returned to Baltimore.

As with the design phase, sailing the *Pride of Baltimore* involved rediscovering what had once been common knowledge but had since lapsed into obscurity. The *Pride*'s rig possessed features not typically found aboard vessels in the traditional sailing fleet from which her captains and crew were drawn. Captain Peter Boudreau, who helped build the *Pride* and was mate on the maiden voyage and later master aboard her, described the process:

> Nobody had any experience with a genuine Baltimore clipper. . . . The peculiarities of that type of vessel make her very difficult to sail. . . . We started out slowly and carefully. While we practiced tacking and jibing, we kept the sail area reduced so we could handle it. Often we were dealing with only two sails.

Among her unusual features was a loose-footed foresail that overlapped the mainsail and brailed into the foremast. Much like a headsail passing around headstays, the clew of the foresail had to be passed around the mainmast when tacking, after which a new sheet was reattached each time. In a fresh breeze this maneuver required three-quarters of the modern-day crew. The fore staysail and the foresail were designed to be reefed by means of a detachable bonnet up to the first set of reef points, a technique not seen since the nineteenth century. Additionally, the vessel carried two stunsails (studding sails), a decksetting topgallant yard, and a ringtail that extended the mainsail in much the same way a stunsail does square sails. The mainsail was set by means of an unusual clew outhaul arrangement and was rigged with a tricing tackle for hauling up the tack to depower the vessel in close quarters. The main gaff topsail hoisted from the deck on a *jackyard* (spar) that came to rest nearly parallel to the main topmast and to extend it even farther. In true privateer fashion the lower masts were independently stayed, although a spring stay hung between the mast caps as a backup. The mainmast was supported by a pair of running forestays that were alternately tensioned and eased off for each new tack, much like more conventional running backstays, which she also had. The headrig ultimately utilized a system of lateral spreaders on the whisker stays, which proved to be necessary for the strength of the headrig. The extreme rake of the masts introduced a number of rigging considerations that are not typically factors aboard other traditional sailing vessels. This led to the elaborate use of hand-stitched leather to protect components of the rig. As called for, the *Pride* was fitted with working cannon, and she was steered by means of a seven-foot tiller. The original suit of sails was cut from flax and cotton of a quality nearest to the traditional type that could be found. Even within the context of the renaissance of traditional sail, the *Pride* was exceptionally intricate, arcane, and committed to the past.

Form and Function

The construction of the *Pride* served its purpose as a magnet and a focal point for Baltimore's waterfront renewal. Less clear was how the completed vessel would serve the city. As the original public bid required, the ship was "capable of being sailed," but how far and for how long, and on what basis would the scope of operations be determined? Historical authenticity was an overriding consideration in design and construction, yet a modern public relations mission would impose a different set of requirements.

In keeping with the original concept for an authentic replica, the *Pride* had not been built to meet U.S. Coast Guard regulations for passenger vessels. These regulations would have introduced some very different features and assumptions that were not necessarily compatible with the original vision. Foregoing the certification process meant that not as much was known about the ship as would have been for a vessel certified to carry passengers or trainees, and that operations were unrestricted. Although she was publicly owned, the regulations governing the *Pride* were essentially the same as those that govern private yachts, thus allowing a tremendous operational latitude.

In 1978, after the ship had been operating for about a year, the *Pride* organization approached the coast guard and consulted with the designer over the possibility of obtaining coast guard certification. The investigation addressed this:

> The designer believed that *Pride* was not suitable to meet all the requirements for an inspected vessel to carry passengers even though he thought it would meet the stability requirements and the mechanical and safety requirements. The vessel was constructed without watertight bulkheads and had a relatively low freeboard and any alteration in the design would detract from its authenticity as a historic vessel. The operators, nevertheless, submitted plans and information to the Coast Guard, but after several questions were raised by the Coast Guard concerning additional stability calculations and structural changes, the matter was not pursued.

Although any number of changes to safety equipment and machinery, and to some extent even major alterations to hatches, were within the realm of possibility, the vessel's freeboard, a critical factor in stability and downflooding, was essentially immutable. Retrofitting watertight bulkheads is costly and would only partially satisfy requirements for certification. The rig could be reduced, but at a certain point the vessel would no longer possess the distinctive look of a Baltimore clipper. A new rig that reduced or reapportioned the sail plan was an expensive and frustrating option. In practical terms, once the vessel was designed and built, it could not obtain certification, and never did. She was what she was. The *Pride* remained classified as a documented yacht, and her mission developed accordingly. Unlike the stiuation with the *Marques,* the coast guard declined to entertain a more creative approach to certification, and the Pride organization declined to pursue one.

Had certification been obtainable, it would undoubtedly have led to increased opportunities for the vessel, but passenger carrying proved not critical to the success of the public relations mission that had evolved for the *Pride.* The main service the ship rendered to the city was through hosting dockside receptions, gaining media exposure, and opening the ship to the public. This remains the case for the *Pride of Baltimore II*, which, though fully certified and hence more versatile, relies upon passenger-carrying activities for a relatively small portion of its revenue stream. The success of the

Pride showed that a goodwill ambassador ship can fulfill its function through port visits, where passenger carrying is an enhancement but not a necessity.

The tension among historical accuracy, safety, and practicality makes an important theme throughout the renaissance of traditional sail, and the certification process figures largely in that tension. Certification is costly but also desirable because it not only increases the level of safety, but it increases earning potential through the ability to carry people for hire. Certification always involves compromises of historical authenticity, though in the case of the *Pride* many important compromises, such as the installation of machinery, had already been made. Even without certification as a goal, the *Pride* underwent extensive retrofitting and modifications in the course of her life.

Voyages and Mission

The *Pride* operated three years under the direct authority of the City of Baltimore before Pride of Baltimore Inc., a separate nonprofit entity, was created in 1980 to manage and operate the vessel under the direction of an executive director and a board of directors. Maryland-based corporate and government entities used the vessel extensively to establish and maintain commercial and cultural partnerships in cities the ship visited. Like her forebears, the privateers, the *Pride* prospered in a niche that blended public- and private-sector interests.

The scope of the *Pride*'s voyages was impressive. By the time of her loss she had sailed farther afield than any U.S.-flagged tall ship of recent decades, with the possible exception of the U.S. Coast Guard barque *Eagle*. The *Pride* traveled extensively up and down the eastern seaboard and throughout the Caribbean basin, including parts of South America. She made two voyages through the Canadian Maritime Provinces and into the Great Lakes. In 1983 the *Pride* traveled to the West Coast of North America by way of the Panama Canal, as far north as British Columbia, and back to Baltimore. The conservatism that guided the initial process of learning to sail the *Pride* was evident in many of these voyages when the topmast and spars associated with the square topsail (fore top-hamper) were left on deck for open-water passages during hurricane season. The West Coast voyage significantly expanded the *Pride*'s sphere of operations and introduced the possibility of voyaging even farther afield.

More distant voyaging became a reality on 31 March 1985, when the *Pride* set sail for Europe on a two-year campaign. The vessel was scheduled to visit Northern and Western Europe the first year, followed by Mediterranean ports in 1986, with a winter layover in Spain. The *Pride* crossed the Atlantic by way of Bermuda and the Azores to Baltimore, Ireland, and was said to be the first Baltimore clipper to cross the Atlantic in a century and a half. Under the command of Captain Jan C. Miles, the crossing was made in April, which can resemble a winter month on that route. Indeed, there was plenty of wind and the vessel made a fast passage, but conditions seldom exceeded 30 knots and she encountered no difficulties.

The itinerary included ten countries from Sweden to Spain, with a visit to Poland while that country was under martial law. If public interest and media exposure are any measure of success, the 1985 tour was highly successful. Nevertheless, a decision was made to cancel the second part of the European tour and bring the schooner home early to participate in the Statue of Liberty celebrations in July 1986. Rising tensions in the Middle East and North Africa coupled with a number of terrorist acts targeting Americans convinced Pride of Baltimore Inc. that the Mediterranean segment of the campaign posed an unnecessary risk to a high-profile mission that could succeed only by courting the public eye.

FINAL VOYAGE

The *Pride* wintered over in Málaga on the Mediterranean coast of Spain, where a partial crew conducted maintenance while awaiting finer weather. In March 1986 they sailed for home under the command of Captain Armin E. Elsaesser III. Elsaesser had been with the organization consistently since 1980 and had spearheaded much of the long-term planning for the ship and the mission in that period. After a stop at Madeira, the *Pride* crossed to Barbados in seventeen days. Once in the Caribbean, the maintenance effort resumed as the vessel proceeded up through the Antilles to the Virgin Islands. Realizing that a trade-wind passage is not a complete education in sail handling, Elsaesser conducted sail training drills in the Virgin Islands in preparation for the last leg home. On 11 May, the ship took departure from St. John, bound for Baltimore.

After two days at sea marked by intermittent motoring, a sailing breeze finally filled in from the east. At 2300 on 13 May, the engine was secured and a double reef was taken in the mainsail. Other sails carried at this time were the foresail, staysail, and jib. The vessel was beam reaching in force 6 conditions, steering north-northwest on a starboard tack.

With the exception of the aft cabin, all hatches were secured, a necessity that arose readily on the *Pride* when conditions built above force 5. The forward hatch was a hinged affair with a substantial coaming. This was closed to keep out spray, though it is not clear if any mechanism secured this hatch. The main hatch, the engine room hatch, and the lazarette hatch were all secured by a traditional cargo hatch arrangement utilizing grates, tarpaulins, and battens. The coamings of these three hatches rose approximately seven inches above the deck, making it relatively easy for water on deck to slosh below if the hatches were not fully battened. The aft cabin hatch, the one that was open, ran on fore-and-aft slides like a conventional yacht hatch. Though the weatherboard was in place, the hatch was not secured because it was necessary to leave some sort of access to the deck and, with the exception of the forward hatch, the other hatches were inoperable from below once battened.

Another reason for battening the hatches early was that, once water was on deck, it did not always drain away readily. Instead of continuous scuppers at deck level, the outboard perimeter of the vessel was described by *waterways* that formed a solid sill around the entire weather deck. Circular drain holes pierced this sill in several places and scuppers were cut in the bulwarks above it, but the arrangement did not facilitate the rapid draining of wate. Even after additional drain holes were added in the winter of 1985, the deck tended to hold water. Although the gunport hatches were capable of passing large amounts of water, these were generally closed at sea. For all these reasons, the hatches on the *Pride of Baltimore* had been secured early as the weather built on 13 May.

On the morning of 14 May, the weather built to force 7–8. Around this time, the dawn watch put the weatherboards into place for the aft cabin hatch. At around 1130, all hands were called to reduce sail. Captain Elsaesser took the helm and bore off to a broad reach, steering a northwesterly course to facilitate sail handling. The jib was struck and triced up to prevent it from filling with seawater and stressing the jibboom. An order was give to furl the foresail, but before it could be executed it was changed: the standing gaff foresail was instead lowered to the deck, gaff and all. Elsaesser and the first mate, John "Sugar" Flanagan, conferred and agreed that sail was sufficiently reduced for the conditions. The staysail and the double-reefed mainsail were the only sails that remained set. Flanagan described the situation: "There was a line of squalls on the quarter and overcast skies on the beam. None of them appeared unduly threatening, and we were comfortable with the way the ship was handling and the amount of sail up."

Flanagan went below through the aft hatch to update the deck log while Elsaesser continued on with the broad reach rather than returning to the earlier course. By the time Flanagan returned to the deck, Elsaesser had evidently become aware of an approaching threat and ordered him to stand by the main sheet. Flanagan described what happened next:

> We were suddenly hit by a wall of wind and water with wind speeds of 70 knots and more. I let out the main sheet, Armin had the helm all the way up and we were trying to fall off. There was a call to ease the stays'l sheet. In what appeared to be slow motion the boat started laying over to port and in less than 60 seconds the boat was over on its side.

As the vessel heeled farther and farther, the rudder lost its bite on the water and eventually became ineffective.

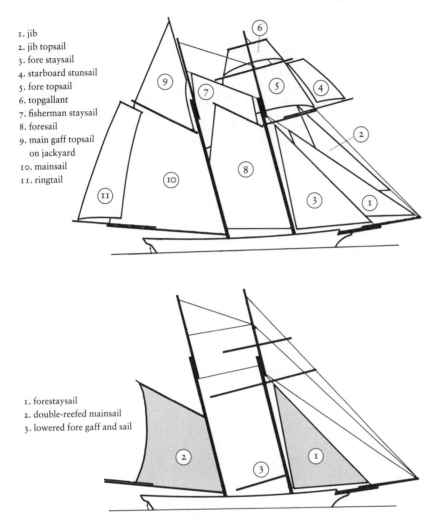

1. jib
2. jib topsail
3. fore staysail
4. starboard stunsail
5. fore topsail
6. topgallant
7. fisherman staysail
8. foresail
9. main gaff topsail
   on jackyard
10. mainsail
11. ringtail

1. forestaysail
2. double-reefed mainsail
3. lowered fore gaff and sail

Pride of Baltimore's sail plan *(top)* and sail configuration at the time of loss *(bottom)*. (Jim Sollers)

The aft hatch was offset to the port side of the cabin trunk, the same side to which the vessel heeled under the squall's impact. The sea poured into the ship through this point. The only person not on deck at the time, the cook nevertheless managed to escape through the hatch against the torrent of seawater flooding in. Farther forward, a crew member attempted to release the staysail sheet, but it was cleated to leeward, the normal position, and already submerged:

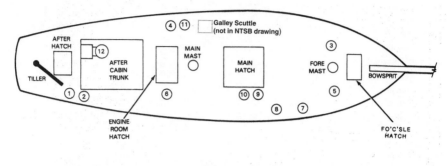

Crew position at the time of loss. Eleven of the twelve crew members were on deck and the wind was abaft the beam. Note the location and size of the hatches. (NTSB *Report*)

I remember . . . taking a deep breath and putting my whole head down . . . and feeling for the sheet. I felt the vessel go over on her side . . . I saw light and swam up to the surface . . . it was a bit of a swim. When I surfaced the ship was definitely on her side and the next thing that happened . . . was the fore-mast hit the surface of the water in front of my eyes.

Elsaesser called for a head count and ordered the crew aft toward the rafts. The crew moved by whatever means possible, some clambering along outboard of the starboard bulwarks, which by this time were nearly hori-zontal. The vessel sank at approximately 23 degrees North, 67 degrees West, righting herself as she went down. With the ship gone, the crew's troubles were just beginning.

Given the speed of events, the ship's two EPIRBs went down with her. One of these was stowed just inside the fully battened main hatch and was utterly inaccessible from the deck. The other was just inside the aft hatch but was neither retrieved nor was situated to float free of the wreck. There was no time to send out a distress signal or prepare to abandon ship. Sur-vivors' estimates of the time it took for the vessel to sink ranged from less than a minute to five minutes.

The ship had two six-person life rafts stowed all the way aft beneath the tiller. The first mate dove to release them, but the wildly swinging tiller made it dangerous to approach. The hydrostatic releases then activated and the rafts came to the surface and inflated. The blast that knocked over the ship had not subsided in the slightest. One raft became caught in the rigging and tore; the other inflated normally but then malfunctioned:

It blew its valves and deflated. So we were left with two deflating liferafts in conditions where one could barely see 50 feet in blowing sea and rain and where communication was difficult to impossible.

The squall lasted fifteen to thirty minutes before returning to force 7–8 conditions.

In the melee, three people did not reach the rafts. Captain Elsaesser was seen swimming nearby at one point but disappeared into the spray and sea. One crew member, Jeannette (Nina) Schack, was sighted floating in the water, apparently lifeless. A third crew member, Vincent Lazzaro, disappeared in the confusion of the sinking and was not seen again. Nine people congregated around the untorn raft. The hand pump proved ineffective, so the survivors resorted to blowing up the raft by mouth. The coast guard investigation stated that the cook, James Chesney, "almost singlehandedly blew up the undamaged raft by mouth over a period of about four hours." Meanwhile, the survivors struggled to stay afloat without flotation devices. The ship's carpenter, Barry Duckworth, had swallowed a large amount of water and was incapacitated. Though the others tended to him for several hours, he perished before the raft was ready for boarding.

The eight survivors boarded the underinflated six-person raft about six hours after the sinking. They drifted for four days, seven hours, the heaviest occupants sitting in seawater the entire time. The raft's meager supplies were slightly augmented by flotsam from the wreck, though a valuable five-gallon jug of "emergency water" salvaged from the wreck was tainted with salt water. Rations consisted of one quarter of a biscuit and two ounces of water a day. A small amount of rainwater was collected. In the words of the first mate, "The days were barely tolerable, the nights were hell."

During the time the raft was adrift, one aircraft and six ships were sighted, including a cruise ship on the first day that passed within two miles. Flares were fired but drew no response. When the supply of flares was exhausted, the survivors resorted to waving yellow rain gear by day and signaling with a flashlight by night. On 19 May at about 0200, at a range of more than two miles, watchstanders aboard the Norwegian tanker *Toro* spotted a blinking light, which they realized had a repeating pattern. The pattern spelled S.O.S. The *Toro* stopped and rescued the *Pride*'s eight survivors. The raft was slashed and allowed to sink. In the end, it was not the satellites, the flares, the international orange, or the specially sealed nickel-cadmium batteries inside the EPIRBs that saved the day. It was a malfunctioning life raft, a flashlight, and an alert crew member on a passing ship that saved what remained of the crew of the *Pride of Baltimore*. The importance of maintaining a sharp lookout is usually emphasized in terms of the safety of one's own ship. This incident dramatically demonstrated how lookout can bear on the survival of others.

As with the *Albatross* and the *Marques*, the loss of the *Pride* was precipitous. The *Pride* had not maintained a daily communications schedule with the home office on this last leg, nor was she in the thick of a tall-ships race surrounded by potential rescuers. Thus it was not until receiving a call from the *Toro*, four and a half days after the sinking, that anyone at home learned what had taken place.

POSTMORTEM

Although the *Pride* was not a commercial carrier by any description, the incident was deemed significant enough to warrant an investigation by not one but two federal agencies: the U.S. Coast Guard (USCG) and the National Transportation Safety Board (NTSB). This was not a joint investigation, although the two investigations were conducted simultaneously. This degree of official interest probably has more than one explanation, but the notoriety of the *Pride* certainly ensured a greater than normal public interest. The ongoing debate regarding the safety of traditional vessels may have led some to believe that the loss of the *Pride* might prove to be a test case of sorts against such ships. Also, that the entire crew got off the ship alive, yet there was still a 33 percent mortality rate in a matter of moments, was of obvious concern to all.

Nine days of joint hearings were held in Baltimore. These investigations differed from the *Marques* investigation in several ways. The *Pride* investigations convened mere days after the incident, on 23 May 1986. In contrast with the *Marques* investigation, which didn't start for more than a year after the loss and then dragged on for nearly two years, the USCG and NTSB issued their reports five and eight months after the accident, respectively. The fact that the *Pride* was not certified made the investigation more straightforward in some respects, if no less tragic. The prompt airing of conclusions is a critical element of the investigative process. Had they been disseminated sooner, some of the conclusions arising from the *Marques* case—concerns regarding EPIRBs, hatches, gunports, watertight subdivision, and stability—might have found a ready ear aboard the *Pride* as plans were laid for sailing transatlantic.

The two investigative reports contain an inevitable degree of duplication and share many of the same conclusions. Neither found gross negligence or misconduct of any kind to have caused the loss, but neither was completely uncritical. Twice the length of the USCG report, the NTSB report offers more in the way of background and policy issues pertaining to uninspected vessels. Its conclusions and recommendations are more sweeping. While acknowledging that the *Pride of Baltimore* exceeded the limited coast guard requirements for lifesaving equipment for uninspected vessels, the NTSB report criticized the regulations themselves as applied to all uninspected vessels, such as the *Pride*, that operate on ocean waters.

These conclusions regarding the inadequacy of uninspected vessel requirements held the seed of a potentially far-reaching policy impact, but the U.S. Coast Guard report was less adamant. As an enforcement agency, perhaps the USCG had a better understanding of the practical difficulties of creating workable regulations for such a diverse category of vessels. The coast guard report primarily confined itself to establishing the facts, though the coast guard did initiate an important stability study, comparing the *Pride*'s stability with statutory stability criteria under the Small Passenger Vessels (SPV) regulations and Sailing School Vessels (SSV) regulations of the time.

Authenticity: Hull and Rig

As fondly as the *Pride* is remembered by many, the vessel's less flattering characteristics were well-known to those who sailed her. In particular, elements of the hull and rig flexed and shifted dramatically in a seaway, earning her the nickname the "Flexible Flyer." When sailing to windward it was not uncommon to see a steady stream of seawater passing one's bunk on its way to the bilge and back into the ocean by way of the hourly pumpout. Bilges were typically pumped by hand, but a crew member recalls on one occasion running the mechanical bilge pump twenty minutes each hour to keep pace. In terms of the rig, by the time the *Pride* sailed for Europe in 1985 she was on her third jibboom, one of which broke in conjunction with the fore topmast failing; on another occasion a bowsprit was replaced. These experiences may have been common enough aboard the privateers of old, but, if so, they represented a level of authenticity with which Pride of Baltimore Inc. was not entirely comfortable. Changes to the ship began to be made. Though all vessels go through a process of working out the kinks and addressing unforeseen needs, the process with the *Pride* went beyond what might be considered typical or desirable, and it continued throughout her life. There were good reasons for this ongoing reassessment: little was known of the original Baltimore clippers or of what an oceangoing goodwill ambassador mission might entail.

Despite the issues that hard use brought to light, structural failure was never considered a realistic factor in the *Pride*'s loss. She may not have been tightly built, but she did not come apart at the time of the capsizing, and all the evidence from the investigation confirms this. Though a vessel's youth is no antidote against structural problems, she was only nine years old at the time of her loss. In terms of the life expectancy of her components, she was still quite young and had been well maintained. It is nevertheless appropriate to the greater good of traditional sailing activities to understand some of the problems the vessel experienced, as well as what was done to correct them.

The tremendous size and power of the rig certainly caused many difficulties aboard the *Pride*, though the most significant upgrade was redecking the midships area. At the time the deck was laid, two different styles of planking were employed. They met abruptly approximately five feet aft of the mainmast. A single transverse plank ran across the ship, a dividing line between the two zones. Forward of that point, the vessel was ship-laid (planks run straight fore and aft the length of the ship and are nibbed into the covering board or margin plank). Aft of that point she was yacht-laid (planks follow the curvature of the covering board and butt into a king plank). The mixing of planking styles meant that all the butts of the deck planks were concentrated in one area of the deck, resulting in a weak point. The ship flexed alarmingly at this point, which became known to the crew as the "hinge." Although there is ample precedent for designing ships with a "break" in the deck, this is typically associated with elevating the aft deck to keep it drier, provide more buoyancy, and afford more room below. In such instances, the entire structure compensates for the lack of longitudinal strength in the deck. This was not the case with the *Pride*. In 1983, prior to the *Pride*'s West Coast trip, the deck was pulled up and relaid to distribute the plank butts more evenly and introduce more uniformity of strength.

One crew member who also helped build the boat likened the masts to gigantic pry bars acting on the ship as she sailed along. To address this, additional bracing was installed below in the area of the mast partners. Similarly, the headrig generated enormous loads, which also required corrective measures. The jibboom dislodged the heel block, requiring reengineering, and spreaders were added to support the jibboom better. The bowsprit also transferred tremendous loads to the hull, causing movement and leakage: "the thrust actually tumbled over the forward deckbeam that the heel was against." The deck beam was actually trying to rotate in position in response to the forces of the bowsprit pushing back into the ship.

As time went on, the *Pride*'s rig and structure were reinforced with ironwork and steel to provide stiffening. A gammon iron was added to reinforce the traditional gammon lashing that held the jibboom and the bowsprit together. At the time of her loss, the *Pride* was on her third set of chainplates, each larger than the last, in an ongoing effort to distribute the load of the rig over a wider area of the hull. Steel hanging knees and lodging knees were installed through the midships sections to counteract racking stresses from the rig. The occasional short plank and some rather approximate joinery didn't help the situation, but over time many of these issues were addressed as part of the overall effort to make the vessel more suitable for her assignments. As a chain is only as strong as its weakest link, it is possible that these efforts simply chased the weak point or points from one place to another, but this was preferable to doing nothing to address obvious problems. Though in a sense a ship is never finished, many of the most significant concerns had been addressed by the time the ship sailed for Europe. In some respects, the *Pride of Baltimore* was actually a much better vessel by the time she was lost than at any previous point in her life.

In sum, although structural integrity was not a factor in the loss of the *Pride*, significant retrofitting was part of her history. That the *Pride* was still new when this augmentation process began speaks to the way in which the priorities of authenticity and of a sustainable modern mission cannot be assumed to be automatically compatible. On the contrary, they must be deliberately woven into an appropriate compromise. At this writing, the *Pride of Baltimore II* is five years older than the first *Pride* was at the time of her loss and has voyaged far more extensively. That such modifications have been relatively minimal for *Pride II* seems to indicate a more realistic connection between the ship and its ultimate purpose.

Design

Design is a broad and encompassing subject, the discussion of which is limited here to a few points of particular relevance to the renaissance of traditional sail. The *Pride* amalgamated certain signature design features aesthetically appropriate to an authentic Baltimore clipper. This was the mandate given to the designer. Some of these features warrant discussion in their own right, whereas others are interesting in light of other casualties in this book.

CARGO HATCHES

The cargo-style hatch closures aboard the *Pride* were fully secured at the time of capsizing, and this did not contribute to her rapid demise. However, in light of what we learned in the *Marques* about this arrangement, it warrants discussion here. Three of the five hatches on the *Pride* used a traditional cargo hatch system not unlike that on the *Marques*, though with much lower coamings. Each rectangular hatch had either gratings or boards that rested flat inside the frame of the hatch and were flush with the top of the coaming. U-bolts protruded from the coaming at intervals. Specially made tarpaulins fit snugly over the entire hatch and coaming. Where the tarpaulin came down over the outside of the coaming, small openings in the material lined up with the U-bolts, allowing the bolts to pass through the material. Wooden battens with gaps cut to accommodate the

U-bolts were placed against the face of the coaming, sandwiching the tarpaulin against it. Tapered wooden pegs fit into the eye of the U-bolt outboard of the tarp and the battening, securing it all into place. All this took time to execute; therefore, if the weather looked threatening, prudence argued for securing the tarpaulins early. As with the *Marques*, however, the ventilation and light that the main hatch admitted to the primary living space encouraged the crew to leave the grating and the tarpaulin above the ladder off or partially off as often as conditions allowed. The starboard aft corner of the hatch, where the companionway ladder reached the deck, was often left ajar so the crew could come and go from the main cabin without transiting through the engine room and the aft cabin to get to the deck by way of the aft hatch. Once the tarpaulins were battened and wedged into place, it was not really possible to get out of the ship through those points. With the gratings properly positioned, cutting one's way through the tarpaulin in an emergency was not an option. Leaving the grates out might make cutting one's way out possible but would defeat the design of the hatch system.

That the *Pride*'s loss occurred in daylight with only one person below was, therefore, a grace because escape options were limited. The situation underscores the folly of pairing cargo hatches with human beings: when left open to facilitate ventilation and access, cargo hatches expose the ship to downflooding, but when properly battened they eliminate escape routes for people. All hatches represent a point of vulnerability to some extent, but cargo hatches are especially problematic for a working ship with people living where the cargo once did. Had the squall struck during the night, with

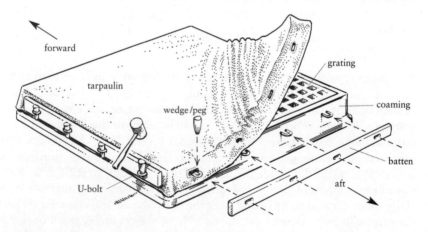

A view from aft of the main hatch on *Pride of Baltimore*. A companionway ladder led to the deck beneath the starboard aft grating. (Jim Sollers)

two watches in their bunks, as it did for the *Marques*, those trapped below would have stood as little chance of surviving as well-lashed cargo.

OFFSET HATCHES

Like the *Marques*, the *Pride* was fitted with a hatch offset from the ship's centerline. When a ship is heeled to the same side as the offset hatch, this feature results in downflooding at a lesser angle of heel than if the hatch were on the centerline. Unfortunately, this is what happened to the *Pride*. The NTSB report even speculated that "if the vessel had heeled to starboard, rapid downflooding may not have occurred and the vessel may have recovered." This presumes that she had the stability to recover. In addition to the aft hatch, the *Pride* was fitted with a second offset hatch. This was the galley scuttle located above the diesel stove amidships, just forward of the mainmast and about six feet off the centerline also on the port side. The galley scuttle was not mentioned in the investigation reports, nor was it shown in drawings of the ship appearing in the reports. As originally conceived, the galley cook station was a brick oven that was a "near duplicate" of one found on the wreck of a privateer schooner sunk in Penobscot Bay in 1779. It was located farther forward in the hold and on centerline. For various reasons the brick oven was deemed impractical. A more modern diesel stove was fitted on the port side where a small galley was created, and the brick oven was eventually dismantled. A small rectangular scuttle was built above the diesel stove with an aft-sloping saltbox lift hatch that could be opened for light and ventilation. The scuttle integrated a stovepipe known as a Charlie Noble that stood about three feet above the deck. The scuttle was located in the lowest part of the deck, which was frequently awash, but the sides were high enough that water could not readily enter it; the lift hatch could be closed if conditions warranted. The status of the lift hatch at the time of the knockdown was not addressed in the reports. Those survivors spoken with are uncertain on this point, but it has been said that the conditions on deck preceding the knockdown did not preclude having it ajar for ventilation, and the stove was in use for lunch preparation. Whether the scuttle was open or not, once the ship was on her side and the Charlie Noble was submerged, water could have entered the hull through it. There is no reason to presume that the galley scuttle determined the outcome, but it may go some way toward explaining the rapid flooding of the ship, which so amazed everyone.

Problems with offset hatches and hatches that open athwartships were recognized by the *Marques* investigation report and addressed in subsequent regulations in Britain. Naval architect P. G. Winch made the following comment regarding centerline hatches: "My opinion is that 'when there's a will, there's a way' and I am sure that near-centerline accommodation hatches and doors can be arranged in the vast majority of new sailing craft of all sizes, and maybe in all of them." Centerline hatches can be more safely left open in bad weather, while the arrangement makes a downflooding situation less likely to occur in the first place.

WATERTIGHT BULKHEADS

As with the *Marques* and the *Albatross*, the lack of watertight subdivision aggravated the speed of flooding and the loss of buoyancy. Her designer wrote, "it was perhaps one element of authenticity in her design, specifically her open space below deck, that resulted in her rapid flooding and loss." Watertight bulkheads were never seriously considered for the *Pride* because they would have amounted to an egregious compromise of historical authenticity, though the decision to create an engine room resulted in a need to construct partitions, anyway. As long as stability was adequate and the other openings were secure, it is conceivable that watertight subdivision may have limited flooding to the aft cabin. In such a scenario, the vessel could have stayed afloat for some time, albeit in a semiswamped condition.

FREEBOARD

The *Pride* had a reputation for being a wet boat. This was true not only of her bilges, but also on deck. Though typical of the Baltimore clippers, her low freeboard caused problems in the Baltic Sea in August 1985. With winds to around 40 knots, a succession of short, steep seas characteristic of the Baltic filled the amidships deck to the top of the bulwarks. Seven crew members, who were on the leeward side trimming the foresail sheet, were lifted bodily over the bulwarks while the ship drove on. Most of the crew were able to wrap some part of their body around a piece of the ship or rigging, thus only one person became separated from the ship. That person was later recovered, but the incident demonstrated the downside of the *Pride*'s low, lean profile and the tendency for water to collect on deck. Though not common, there are tales of ships much larger than the *Pride* losing entire watches of a dozen or so crew overboard while they were hauling on the lee braces in heavy weather. This, of course, would be unacceptable aboard today's tall ships.

STEERING SYSTEM

The use of a tiller on the *Pride of Baltimore* occasionally attracted criticism for being unmanageable and difficult to control by a single person. When *Pride II* was being built, the USCG took the position that a wheel was a necessity if the crew size were to stay at twelve, the same as the first *Pride*. The ship was fitted out with a wheel though many who sailed the first *Pride* using the tiller did not find particular fault with it while sailing. Though the *Pride* did not necessarily track well, this was unrelated to the tiller. Experience with both steering systems suggests that the wheel gives some mechanical advantage over a tiller, but under moderate to heavy conditions a gun tackle was normally rigged to the tiller, which helped compensate for the additional resistance. Smaller people with less leverage seemed to struggle with either system under strong conditions unless the captain made an effort to balance the sail plan. The wheel is primarily handier for close-quarters maneuvering because it saves the helmsman from running back and forth across the aft deck as rudder commands come fast and furious, but this is purely a question of convenience.

An issue related to steering is the *rudder's* effectiveness. As we know, the vessel was not designed to have an engine, and the later decision to install one was accompanied by a choice to locate it on the centerline rather than offset it. Although a centerline propeller confers advantages, it also resulted in the need to cut away the rudder and rudderpost to create a propeller aperture. The reduction in the surface of the rudder, as well as the turbulence associated with that location, could cause the rudder to "stall at relatively modest loads."

ACCOMMODATION

As the *Pride* expanded her sphere of operations, her accommodation also underwent significant upgrading in the course of successive refits. The following partial list of examples gives a general idea of the scope of this transition:

hammocks were replaced by built-in bunks, each with an electric light

a brick solid-fuel oven in the middle of the hold was replaced by a new galley with a diesel stove and day tank

a new generator was installed

electrical systems were expanded for radar, electronics, and other amenities

a shower was installed along with a hot water heater

water storage capacity was increased with the addition of another tank

refrigeration was added

Some of these modifications were linked to safety, but most were motivated by the simple recognition that the facilities initially put aboard were inadequate for the role the vessel had come to serve: long-range voyaging. These details demonstrate how the priority placed on authenticity was reconciled with functionality as the vision for the ship expanded and became clearer. Though great effort was expended to restrike the balance between these considerations, certain features were more or less immutable. These were addressed only when the *Pride of Baltimore II* was built. Many of these changes found aboard *Pride II* were dictated by the Small Passenger Vessels (SPV) regulations under which she was built. Still, since the mission of the second vessel picked up where the first left off, it is hard to imagine that these changes would not have been adopted by choice, given the increased understanding of the balance between form and function that emerged from nine years of operating the first vessel and from its loss.

Sail Area

At the time the *Pride* was lost, the wind was building to 30 knots, and the master had gone to a much-reduced sail plan: a double-reefed mainsail and a forestaysail. This is conservative by any measure, but the NTSB report did consider that the *distribution* of sail area may have posed a problem: "The amount of mainsail set probably caused the vessel to respond slowly to the helm when the master was attempting to turn downwind." It also stated that "the time taken to make a decision and execute the maneuver was too great or the vessel failed to react to the rudder action."

Given the conditions prior to the fatal squall, the *Pride* could not have reduced sail area by much more without causing her to wallow with insufficient canvas in a building sea. The wind was essentially from a favorable direction for the desired course, so there was no good reason to heave-to. Practically speaking, this left the master with two possible maneuvering responses to the squall: either luff up into the wind or bear off and run before it. A third option, easing the sheets, was attempted in conjunction with bearing off, but by then the ship was already *in extremis*. Cutting away the rig or halyards was an extreme measure that was theoretically feasible since the ship was rigged with deadeyes and lanyards. But given the speed of events, it was only practical if it had been considered and trained for in advance.

LUFFING UP VERSUS BEARING OFF

The choice to bear off with the *Pride* rather than luff up has been viewed by some as crucial to the outcome. The merits of each course of action deserve discussion.

Bearing off to run before a gust is a normal response for sailing vessels of all types, particularly with the wind aft of the beam already, and especially for vessels with square sails set. Luffing up to spill the wind is a tactic more readily employed by fore-and-aft rigged vessels, particularly when the wind is already forward of the beam. Luffing up is especially useful in protected waters, where there is little risk of burying the bow in a head sea. Luffing up gives temporary relief from heeling forces, but there are some drawbacks as well, especially offshore. For one, luffing up generally incurs some loss of steerageway. This can be aggravated when there is a substantial sea running that can stop a ship dead and throw her back on her rudder, risking damage or putting her in irons. At night, when it is difficult to "read" the sails, this is a distinct possibility. Bearing off generally preserves greater maneuverability as long as there is sea room to do it.

Luffing up also risks injuring crew and damaging sails should gear start to flog in a squall's shifting breeze, especially if the sheets are already eased for off-the-wind sailing. Bearing off and keeping the wind aft, on the other hand, will hold the sails steady and in some cases make reducing sail easier. When luffing up, a vessel will tend to pitch and leap about in a seaway, making a particularly unstable platform for the crew to effect the desired sail changes. Additionally, unlike modern yachts, traditional vessels such as the *Pride* carry a long bowsprit that is vulnerable to damage when plunged into a head sea. The *Pride*'s headrig was particularly long and low, and had a history of breaking under just such circumstances.

In a square-rigged vessel, luffing up brings the additional risk of being caught aback. Though there is evidence that luffing up was a squall tactic used by square-riggers, it was typically employed when already close-hauled and hard on the wind, not when off the wind. On this occasion, the *Pride* was not carrying any square sails, so luffing up was an option that could theoretically have been executed without fear of being caught aback. However, the schooner already had the wind nearly three points abaft the beam, making bearing off the logical course of action as long as the vessel could be made to answer her helm. The investigation found no fault with the attempt to bear off.

SAIL PLAN

The *ability* to luff up or bear off is a separate issue, hinging on the sail plan and the balance or imbalance the sails create with the hull and rudder. There are many options when reducing sail on a rig as complex as the *Pride of Baltimore*'s, but it is customary to reduce progressively from the extreme ends of the rig toward the center where the rig is strongest, where the heeling arm will be least, and where the crew will be less exposed in further sail handling in deteriorating weather.

A schooner's response to a given sail plan is predictable. In general, sail area located forward will fight against efforts to luff up, and sail area aft will fight against efforts to bear away. The latter is particularly true in a gaff schooner, which concentrates sail area aft so as to improve windward performance. Even with the mainsail reefed down, a schooner will frequently experience *weather helm*, a tendency to round up into the wind. This is especially true in a gust.

Elsaesser's order for the mate to stand by the mainsheet suggests that he was aware of an approaching gust that might significantly exceed the prevailing conditions. Under the sail plan chosen, the vessel would have been reasonably well-balanced for resuming the beam reach with the conditions experienced up to that time, as confirmed by survivors. However, with the mainsail set at this point of sail, even in its double-reefed state, the vessel would have resisted bearing off in a sudden blast, and this appears to be what happened.

Under such circumstances, the speed of events is bound to be disorienting and therefore difficult to reconstruct, but it seems likely that when the squall struck the vessel wanted to round up. In response, maximum rudder was applied to drive the ship off. The opposing forces canceled each other out, and the vessel ended up with the wind more or less on the beam, the point of sail most vulnerable to a knockdown. In any event, she never got before the wind, and the propeller aperture in the rudder would not have helped in this situation. It is impossible to conclude that bearing off with a different sail plan or luffing up with the same sail plan would have prevented what happened, because regardless of the choices made the ship was facing a very serious situation. It can be said, however, that exchanging the double-reefed mainsail for sail area in the center of the rig, such as a reefed foresail, would have aided the ship in answering the helm in the way the master intended. With the foresail set, the main boom would not have dragged in the water and prevented the sail from spilling the wind. The loose-footed foresail would have spilled the wind more readily. One seasoned sailor and nautical writer who researched the event wrote the following:

> At the time there was talk that no vessel could survive such a severe microburst. Had I believed that, I never would have thought about going to sea, because such blows are not uncommon. I am convinced that if *Pride* could have been turned into the wind or away from the wind, and her companionway hatch could have been closed, or if she had been fitted with watertight compartments, she would have survived.

The sail plan may or may not have changed the outcome, but other masters-in-sail would do well to contemplate the ramifications of these variables in the event they are faced with a similar situation.

Weather

The USCG investigation described the phenomenon that struck the *Pride* as a microburst associated with thunderstorm activity, with estimated wind speeds of 70 to 80 knots lasting ten to twenty minutes. Visibility went from 2 to 3 miles down to 50 to 75 feet with the onset of the squall. The NTSB report described the same event as a "gust front" producing winds "probably greater than 60 knots . . . for a duration of 15 to 30 minutes." This slight discrepancy between the two reports over a key point of information is curious given that they relied upon the same sources. Nevertheless, it was established that the squall did not differ in direction from the prevailing wind, thus supporting the microburst concept of one wind source being superimposed on another, and bringing about a much greater velocity. There is no mention of the wind having a downward component such as might be expected if a microburst dropped directly on the ship.

Forecasts had called for showers and thunderstorm activity, but nothing extreme. The National Weather Service (NWS) issued the following forecast for the *Pride*'s location on the morning of 14 May 1986: "Wind east to southeast 15 knots. Sea 3 to 5 feet. Wind and sea higher near scattered showers and thunderstorms east of 70 degrees, West. Widely scattered showers or thunderstorms elsewhere."

This forecast prompted investigators to conclude that such an extreme squall could not have been anticipated. NWS satellite photos examined later confirmed that thunderstorm activity in the area on the day of the casualty was consistent with conditions that produce microbursts. That such phenomena are highly localized and brief simply reaffirms the difficulty of forecasting them, leaving sailors to contemplate how best to prepare for such dangerous, unpredictable, yet well-established phenomena.

In the aftermath of the accident, the NTSB recommended that the NWS improve efforts to identify microburst activity and include warnings of the "potential for rapidly developing high winds in the vicinity of thunderstorms." These recommendations have been implemented to some degree, but the practical limitations of identifying and forecasting such phenomena remain significant. The similarity of circumstances surrounding the losses of the *Marques*, the *Albatross*, and the *Pride of Baltimore* stand as a warning that such events are well within the possible and not at all unique. When microbursts occur during times of limited visibility, the opportunity to respond is severely hampered. Though coastal operations come with a different and possibly more intimidating set of hazards, sixteen years after the loss of the *Pride*, the ability to receive localized weather forecasts of equivalent detail to those available near shore simply does not yet exist for most vessels in ocean operations. This is important to realize when considering ocean operations.

Qualifications

As an uninspected vessel that carried no passengers, the *Pride* was not subject to licensing requirements. Her masters were always licensed, however, and it was customary for the watch officers to have licenses, as well. On the return trip from Europe, an unusually high proportion of the ship's company held USCG licenses. Captain Elsaesser held two licenses, a Master of

Sail upon Oceans for 250 gross tons and an Ocean Operator license for auxiliary-sail vessels up to 100 gross tons. These licenses represent a level of certification well above what would have been required had the *Pride* been a passenger vessel. Five other crew members held licenses as well, including all three watch officers, so half the crew held some form of master's or mate's license. Two of the three officers had ocean certificates, and another member of the crew had a Third Mate license from the U.S. Merchant Marine Academy. By any measure there was a high proportion of licensed crew aboard, especially in light of the fact that none were required. It is unlikely that any comparable traditional sailing vessel operating in the United States would have surpassed this level of licensing at the time. As discussed in the *Albatross* chapter, the licensing process in the United States barely touches on issues critical to sailing ship operations. Proficiency in sailing a vessel like the *Pride* would have come almost entirely from experience alone. The level of certification in this case, however, indicated a substantial professional commitment among the crew.

Experience

In the context of the day, the crew aboard the *Pride* was also highly experienced, both in offshore sailing in traditional vessels generally and aboard the *Pride* in particular. Captain Elsaesser had been master aboard the *Pride* on a rotational basis since 1980. He had sailed as master aboard five other vessels, including schooners, had over twelve years "in all phases of small boat and ship operations," and also spent time in the U.S. Navy. The USCG report described him as "an experienced, competent, professional sailor, who was safety conscious and was not one to overpower or show off a boat."

Elsaesser's activities on the day of the squall suggest that he was intuitively aware of a threatening situation, which bespeaks of experience. As with the *Marques*, the conditions preceding the microburst were well in excess of those forecast. As also seen in that case, the disparity between the forecast and the reality may have been the best and only warning that something was amiss. Whereas in the *Marques* case it might be said that the disparity between forecast and presquall conditions were given insufficient weight, in this case there is every reason to believe that the master was concerned about the disparity. Differences of opinion regarding the distribution of sail area aside, the master acted decisively to prepare the ship for bad weather by reducing sail to a very conservative plan. Perhaps most telling was that he also ordered the foresail lowered to the deck. The foresail on the *Pride of Baltimore* was rigged to a standing gaff that normally remained in the hoisted position. The sail was typically struck by brailing it into the mast like drawing a curtain. Lowering the whole affair represented additional work and a level of preparation that was atypical for the conditions the ship had experienced to that point, for it meant that the sail was no longer readily available when conditions improved again. Lowering it, however, would improve the vessel's overall stability because of the weight represented by the gaff, sail, and associated running gear. All of this, along with descriptions of Elsaesser's behavior that day, suggest he was very much preoccupied with the weather and the vessel's ability to handle what he evidently sensed was out there.

As far as the rest of the crew's experience is concerned, they had all gone to sea before. Half the crew had sailed aboard the *Pride* prior to this trip in some capacity, some extensively. All three watch officers had sailed aboard the *Pride* before and had over twenty-five years' experience among them. Although not everyone aboard shared this depth of experience, the breadth of experience exceeded that found aboard virtually any other American traditional sailing ship of comparable size at the time, including the certified vessels.

Taken as a whole, it is quite likely that there is less experience aboard the traditional sailing vessels of today than there was aboard their forerunners in the days of working sail. But if the ships are to sail at all, then it must be at the hands of contemporary sailors, and the *Pride* had as seasoned a captain and crew as was likely to be assembled at the time. It may always be said of such a disaster that another sailor might have done something heroically different, but this is a form of self-flattery or self-flagellation, not a standard of seamanship. Given the speed of events, it is hard to see what greater experience might have done to relieve the vessel once the squall struck. A different sail plan in advance of the squall is another matter, but ultimately it remains an unknown quantity.

Safety Equipment and Procedures

Due to circumstances peculiar to the *Pride*, discussion of safety equipment and procedures is especially worthwhile. As an uninspected vessel, the *Pride*'s requirements in this area were minimal. She voluntarily exceeded those minimal requirements in significant ways, however, and in specific instances met the more stringent standards for Small Passenger Vessels (SPVs) and Sailing School Vessels (SSVs). The NTSB report found that the crew was generally "adequately equipped, trained and drilled in the use of firefighting and emergency equipment." Despite this affirmation, the case brought to light some noteworthy problems for the benefit of future operations. The speed with which the *Pride* sank and the subsequent reliance on survival equipment highlighted the need for emergency preparations that anticipate a sudden, catastrophic casualty. Although the *Pride* was well-supplied with safety equipment, most of it went down with the ship.

Harnesses. The experience of the survivors revealed that the safety harnesses issued to crew had a crucial design flaw that could not have been anticipated. When the vessel went over, several crew who were clipped in to avoid being washed overboard were flung beyond the reach of the clip at the far end of the tether that attached them to the ship. The harnesses were fitted with a clip only at that end of the tether, so they could not disconnect themselves from the sinking ship. The second mate, Joseph McGeady, used his rigging knife to cut four people free, and the investigation noted that "the cutting of the harness tethers probably saved several lives." It was recommended that harnesses be fitted with clips at both ends of the tether, and this is now the practice aboard a number of other American traditional sailing vessels.

Sheath Knife. The situation with harnesses also underscored the utility of a sheath knife as an article of safety equipment. The sheath knife, along with a marlinspike, has long been considered required personal gear aboard sailing vessels, but in recent years some sail training programs for at-risk youth viewed knives and marlinspikes as potential weapons and discouraged the practice of professional sailors wearing them on duty. Because of the general risk of entanglement on a sailing ship, a means for cutting away gear is of great importance and needs to be readily accessible. This incident is a reminder that a sharp, ready blade has no substitute in an emergency, and its potential value outweighs the risks of its misuse.

Float-Free Personal Flotation. Although the *Pride* exceeded requirements for personal flotation (life jackets, immersion suits), virtually all of it went down with the ship. Float-free stowage for this type of equipment was required for SPVs and SSVs, but not for uninspected vessels. Without the lifejackets and immersion suits that were stowed below, the survivors expended crucial energy to keep themselves afloat until the raft was ready for boarding. In a colder climate, the effect could have been catastrophic. In the aftermath, the USCG resisted recommendations by the NTSB that uninspected vessels be required to stow personal flotation and immersion suits in float-free positions, on the basis that this was not practical in some types of uninspected vessels.

Wearing safety gear is generally impractical when sailing under normal conditions. The equipment is cumbersome and can actually be dangerous until such time as it is actually needed. Buoyant work vests or harnesses fitted with a CO_2 cartridge and an inflatable bladder can help, but crew often resist wearing them under ordinary circumstances. Life jackets that are positioned to float free improve the chances that at least some of the equipment will be retrieved and used when the need arises. For all that was known about the advantages of float-free flotation, not having such an arrangement was more than just a pity. The incident points to the importance of incorporating a good idea, whether it is required or not.

Float-Free EPIRBs. The inability to deploy EPIRBs because they were stowed below was a circumstance shared by the *Marques*, the *Pride*, and unfortunately a great many other vessels in the early years of EPIRBs. Although the two units aboard the *Pride* were positioned near hatch openings, there was not time enough to get them. The EPIRB located inside the main hatch could not have been retrieved without unbattening the hatch, or worse still leaving it unsecured.

The survivors of the *Albatross* twenty-five years earlier were actually better equipped to remedy their situation than the crew of the *Pride*. The *Albatross* survivors set sail for the coast of Florida in their longboats. They had food and water for two weeks and were making good progress when they were picked up. The *Pride* survivors, however, drifted helplessly in a partially inflated, undersized raft with insufficient supplies, separated from their EPIRB while coming to grips with the discredited assumption that it would summon help if ever such a situation arose.

The comparison between the *Albatross* survivors and the *Pride* survivors draws attention to a transition in the approach to survival at sea in the latter decades of the twentieth century. Historically, survival at sea required boats with some means of locomotion (sails, hand-crank propellers) as well as supplies for a prolonged voyage, during which survivors attempted to get to land or into the shipping lanes, where rescue might occur. The present approach, toward which the *Pride* was oriented, involves staying in one place and allowing automatic electronic satellite communications to summon rescuers. This approach is now pervasive. At the time, however, uninspected vessels such as the *Pride* were not under any particular pressure to stow EPIRBs in float-free positions. In consequence, the system on which the abandon-ship procedure was premised was rendered ineffective. In the years since, not only has the technology improved, but the training and the understanding on the part of those using it has, as well.

In view of these problems regarding float-free equipment, the NTSB report found that "the master . . . failed to develop emergency procedures for the vessel and the crew in the event of a knockdown." Although it is not possible to realistically train for a microburst, the criticism relates to the value of equipment that automatically deploys and to discussing knockdown scenarios with the crew.

By contrast, in 1993 the *Pride of Baltimore II* became certified under SOLAS (Safety Of Life At Sea), the most widely recognized international form of certification for a commercial vessel. The SOLAS-approved life rafts with which the ship is fitted contain a variety of self-deploying rescue equipment, including category 2 406 MHz EPIRBs, emergency VHF radios, and thermal protection suits, in addition to flares and other typical life raft equipment. As part of the SOLAS requirements, the vessel also carries search-and-rescue transponders (SARTs) and a separate category 1 406 MHz EPIRB on a hydrostatic release. For emergency communication there is an Inmarsat C and a digital selective calling (DSC) radio, both of which are fitted with a push-button distress feature. All the ship's small boats are connected to hydrostatic release mechanisms and are stowed with extra food and water during offshore transits. Much of this equipment was not available in 1986, and some of it would have still been neutralized under the circumstances. A philosophy of preparedness may be as important as the equipment itself.

Life Rafts. The life rafts were a significant safety equipment issue in the loss of the *Pride*. These were stowed aft with a hydrostatic release system that functioned as intended. However, the malfunction of the relief valve in the untorn raft nearly cost the lives of those who had survived the initial sinking episode. The rafts had been serviced in Spain just before the voyage at a certified manufacturer's service center. Although not USCG approved, they were of a type considered to be "adequate for the rigorous require-ments of ocean service" and were commonly used aboard oceangoing yachts. The NTSB pursued the matter of the rafts with particular thorough-ness, performing tests on the same raft type and visiting the service center in Spain where the rafts had last been serviced. The results were inconclusive. The tests showed that the valves malfunctioned only if the reassembly was grossly inadequate. The operating manager of the Spanish service center communicated his low opinion of that particular type of valve assembly but insisted that the raft was properly serviced and that he had never witnessed a valve failure of the type that occurred. No definite explanation for the malfunction has ever been provided. The NTSB recommended that the manufacturer replace that valve arrangement in favor of ones not as vulner-able to unseating, and this was done. Despite the problems with the life raft, it must be recognized that the raft still did its job. As the mate, Sugar Flana-gan, said, "It was a good raft. It saved our lives."

Daily Communication. Perhaps the most significant criticism regarding safety procedures arising from either investigation was the lack of a daily communications schedule between the ship and the office:

> The failure of the operator to require and the master to initiate a daily radio communications schedule is a serious omission. This omission did not con-tribute to the deaths of the four crewmembers. However, it did prevent more timely notification of search and rescue forces.

On the eastbound trip to Europe in 1985, a daily radio communica-tions schedule had been maintained through a marine operator using the single-sideband radio. This was an arduous but effective procedure. The communications schedule was modified to every third day on the return trip as far as the Caribbean, then it was dropped altogether because shore-based telephone service was readily available. The call-in schedule was not reestablished for the final transit home. Although this may seem a glaring deficiency in light of longstanding communications policies in the commercial shipping world, the daily radio check-in was not historically a uniform practice aboard the *Pride* or among many other American traditional sailing vessels operating off the eastern seaboard in the mid-1980s. This aspect of professional ship management was slow to be adopted by vessels associated with the renaissance of traditional sail, undoubtedly partly because of the expense. When the *Pride of Baltimore II* became operational, the organization notified the NTSB of its new policy:

> The Captain is to report into the office once during every 24 hours while underway by the best available means possible and give current position, speed, course, weather and a 24 hour estimated position. The Captain shall call the office by landline from every port upon arrival.

Subsequent advances in technology, especially the reduction of antenna size, have made satellite communications for traditional sailing vessels simpler, cheaper, and more practical.

Reviewing the various issues arising from equipment and procedures, it is fair to say that some though not all of the problems were foreseeable. An important lesson is that, in preparing for the worst, it must be assumed that some portion of one's preparations will quite likely be neutralized by the overwhelming nature of the emergency. Therein lies the strength of the argument for redundancy and flexibility in developing emergency procedures.

Stability

DEVELOPMENTS ABOARD THE *PRIDE OF BALTIMORE*

Since the *Pride* was in fact a stability casualty, investigators spent considerable effort trying to understand her characteristics and her history. The earlier stability casualties in this book were plagued by some combination of lack of awareness, lack of statutory incentives, or, in the case of the *Marques*, an unwillingness to consider the matter in depth. In contrast, the *Pride*'s stability received considerable attention beforehand. Though not required for the *Pride*, stability criteria designed with large traditional sailing vessels in mind had by this time become available in the United States as a point of reference. Ultimately, the USCG investigation showed the *Pride* to have a positive righting arm to 87.7 degrees—quite high—yet it also showed that she could not have met stability regulations for SPVs or SSVs except under a greatly reduced sail plan that bore no resemblance to a Baltimore clipper.

Of the loss of the *Pride*, the USCG report wrote that "the proximate cause of the sinking was a sudden and extreme wind that heeled the vessel beyond its range of stability and knocked it down." As with the *Marques* and the *Albatross*, a stability booklet with righting arm data had never been prepared for the *Pride* while she was sailing. However, the *Pride* was inclined on three occasions in her life: once during the original fitting-out in 1977, and then twice in the seven months leading up to the voyage to Europe.

Date of Inclining	Mean Draft	Displacement (long tons)	Height of Center of Gravity above Keel (KG)	Metacentric Height (GM)
11 April 1977	9′2.25″	99.80	9.14′	6.08′
22 August 1984	9′6″	120.10	9.75′	5.55′
8 March 1985	9′3.5″	112.55	9.42′	5.78′

In each case the inclinings were conducted by the designer and were carried out for the purpose of calculating metacentric height (GM). The NTSB report made the following observation about the available data:

> No dynamic stability calculations were made to compare heeling energy with righting energy under various conditions of sail. The designer believed they were hypothetical and of no particular value as far as the design was concerned although under Coast Guard regulations, these calculations would be required.

Upon the *Pride*'s return from the West Coast in November 1983, Gillmer noticed that the vessel was sitting low in the water. In August 1984, two months after the loss of the *Marques*, he conducted an inclining experiment on the *Pride*. In light of the planned voyage to Europe and the recently loss of the *Marques*, such interest was justifiable. The first inclining in over seven years of operation revealed adverse developments in the vessel's stability: displacement had increased, KG was higher (the distance between the keel and the center of gravity—see Stability section in the appendix), and GM had dropped to 5.55 feet. Normal soakage may have accounted for some increase in displacement, but the accumulation of weight aboard was a more significant factor. Rare is the vessel that carries less gear as time goes by. As the vessel voyaged farther and longer, and the operation became more elaborate, she carried more equipment, supplies, and paraphernalia. This negatively impacted her freeboard and center of gravity, as the 1984 inclining showed. Over the years, modifications such as the addition of an iron capstan, water barrels, a wooden boat on deck, a steel gangway atop the boat, an inflatable boat atop the gangway, and the steel reinforcement beneath the deckhead gradually raised the center of gravity. The new water tank, the refrigeration unit, and the built-in bunks in place of hammocks all added weight below and increased displacement. The latter items may not have affected the center of gravity greatly, but cumulatively these changes and many lesser ones hastened the point at which deck edge immersion and downflooding could occur and eventually wrought a transformation in the vessel's stability profile. This development prompted the designer to recommend that an effort be made to winnow the contents of the ship to regain freeboard and to also try to lower the center of gravity overall.

Through the winter of 1984–85 the ship was laid up in Baltimore for maintenance and upgrading in preparation for the impending voyage to Europe. This created an opportunity for the crew to empty the ship and reassess what was being carried aboard. The following steps were taken between August 1984 and the vessel's departure in April 1985:

Weight Removal
public relations material: visual display and pamphlets
souvenirs: T-shirts, trinkets, and printed matter
miscellaneous spare rigging gear: blocks, line, hardware
miscellaneous wood stock
miscellaneous maintenance supplies: paint, solvents, coatings, etc.
general "housecleaning"
canvas from old or spare sails—uncertain quantity
spare hawser
split-log bilge pump from on deck amidships

Weight Lowering
repacking ballast in bilges to reduce its volume into a lower position
cannon barrels and carriages stowed belowdecks for long transits
new topmast backstays with reduced diameter both lowered and removed weight

The weight removed appears to have amounted to a major housecleaning rather than any single weight of significance. Most of the items came from inside the ship, though the smaller wire size on the backstays amounted to a slight removal of weight aloft.

In March 1985, while still rigging up for the European voyage, the third inclining was conducted using the ship's cannons for weights. According to the investigation, the results of the third inclining were adjusted to account for the top-hamper, which was not aboard at the time of the test. The results of this test indicated that freeboard had increased and that GM had improved to 5.78 feet. The change in displacement indicated that 7.55 tons had been removed from the vessel during the seven months between the second and third inclinings. The center of gravity of the 7.55 tons removed calculates out at 14.7 feet above the baseline, a point well above the deck level.

Gillmer gave the results of the latest inclining to the master along with a warning in respect to GM: "Don't return to 5.55 feet." Yet on all vessels the matter of minimizing weight aboard must be balanced against the need to be prepared to handle maintenance, repairs, and emergencies. The ship was still not fully ready for sea at the time of inclining, thus provisions, crew effects, tools, galley equipment, books, spare parts, rigging, and maintenance supplies came aboard before departure. A large hawser weighing several hundred pounds and a small quantity of public relations material were stowed belowdecks in the main hold. In light of this reaccumulation, the investigation surmised a "most probable" displacement of 122 long tons at the time of capsizing. This was the same operating displacement the designer estimated in 1980, and somewhat more than the August 1984 inclining, which had raised concerns.

Once in Europe, the practice of stowing the cannon barrels belowdecks was continued on the open water legs, but when operating coastwise they were lashed on deck. The public relations materials went back aboard, along with a souvenir inventory. Fewer stores were carried through this period since port visits were frequent.

The investigation indicates that prior to returning from Europe there was again an interest in improving the vessel's stability: "Captain Elsaesser appeared to be well aware of the *Pride of Baltimore*'s stability conditions and had recommended in a letter to the Executive Director dated 8 March 1986, that further evaluation be conducted after the *Pride of Baltimore* returned from Europe."

The cannon carriages, public relations material, and other gear unnecessary for the return voyage were shipped back to the United States. The cannon barrels were stowed belowdecks for the transit. At least one barrel of diesel fuel weighing about 370 pounds was carried on deck during the final leg. The NTSB report concluded that the removal of excess gear from the vessel before departure indicated that the master had concern about the stability.

EXTERNAL DEVELOPMENTS

Elsaesser's concern was quite likely related to the designer's warning of the previous spring, but it may also have reflected a growing awareness regarding the overall issue of stability in the traditional sailing profession. Although the investigation into the *Marques* had only just commenced when the *Pride* went down, the fact that she had suffered a knockdown made it clear that stability was going to be an issue. Meanwhile, the SSV process in the United States had given great attention to the matter of sailing ship stability, and new regulations were coming into effect. Since that research had been sponsored by a group of American sailing school ship operators (one of which had employed Elsaesser), many were aware of the data.

In 1985, research conducted by the firm of Woodin and Marean Inc. for the SSV criteria was compiled as a "Survey of Sailing Vessel Stability Leading to Modified Regulations." The study conducted a population analysis survey of thirty-eight American traditional sailing vessels, including the *Albatross* and other known casualties. It indicated that the *Pride of Baltimore* possessed a righting arm of only 76 degrees and had downflooding characteristics of a low order relative to other vessels considered. The study did not take into account measures to improve the *Pride*'s stability prior to going to Europe in early 1985. Though the representation of the *Pride* emerging from the study was not nearly as deficient as the stability casualties examined earlier in this book, it was not as robust as those who designed the new SSV regulations believed that a vessel intended for ocean-going sail training should be. The *Pride*, of course, was not such a vessel.

Out of courtesy and concern, the information was passed along to the Society of Professional Sailing Ship Masters, in which Elsaesser was active, and to other interested parties. Although the USCG ultimately adopted the criteria and methodology proposed by these researchers for the SSV criteria, the controversial material was rejected as "prejudicial" in the *Pride* investigation. Gillmer characterized the material as a "troublesome attack on the *Pride*'s credibility" and "contrived criticism, factually and technically incorrect, put forward for inexplicable reasons."

U.S. COAST GUARD TECHNICAL STUDY

As part of the investigation, the USCG conducted its own stability study on the *Pride*. The purpose was to better understand the role that stability may have played in the casualty, but also to determine if there were ramifications for the existing fleet of large traditional sailing vessels operating under the coast guard's rules. The study was approached in two ways. The first was to compare the *Pride*'s stability under various sail plans to the USCG stability criteria for SPVs and SSVs operating on ocean waters and partially protected waters (20 miles from safe harbor of refuge). Although not required to meet these regulations, it was a way of checking how the *Pride* measured up against existing criteria established for marine safety. The second approach was to compare the hull characteristics of the *Pride* to a pool of USCG-inspected passenger schooners in Maine. The first part of the study employed a certain amount of guesswork to deal with uncertainties regarding the *Pride*'s stability condition at the time of loss. A "most likely" displacement of 122 tons and a KG of 9.3 feet were used to conclude that downflooding would have occurred through the aft hatch at 61.4 degrees of heel, and the point of vanishing stability at 87.7 degrees. The existence of such a long righting arm places emphasis on the offset hatch as a fatal flaw because it implies the ship was well on her way to flooding before her righting arm was exceeded.

To compare her performance with SPV and SSV regulations, the study adopted three possible KG values. From the lowest KG (most stable) to the highest (least stable), these values were 8.8 feet, 9.3 feet, and 9.8 feet. The KGs were applied to four different sail configurations:

1. full sail: all canvas, minus the ringtail and stunsails

2. schooner-rigged: main, fore, staysail, jib

3. reduced sail: full mainsail and staysail

4. casualty: double-reefed main and staysail

The results of this process were then compared to the SPV requirements for both ocean service and partially protected waters. The process was repeated for the SSV requirements.

The study showed that when the extremely conservative sail plan that was set at the time of the loss was combined with the "most likely" KG of 9.3 feet, the *Pride* would have met USCG stability criteria for a Sailing School Vessel (SSV) on ocean waters, but not as a passenger vessel (see tables pages 220–21). As a fully rigged topsail schooner, the *Pride* met no USCG stability criteria for ocean waters or partially protected waters at any KG considered. When down-rigged to a straight schooner (no topmasts), the ship met no criteria for passenger vessels for ocean waters at any KG considered; as an SSV, she met the criteria only using the most optimistic KG of 8.8 feet. However, as a straight schooner on partially protected waters, the *Pride* met the criteria for both SSV and SPV under five of the six KG possibilities considered. When viewed in light of the USCG stability regulations, the *Pride* measured up well as a schooner operating on partially protected waters, but not as a topsail schooner operating on the ocean. The USCG regulations do not account for all the realities of sailing ship operations or stability dynamics, but they are widely considered to have brought about a safer fleet in the United States, and they were adopted for the *Pride of Baltimore II*.

The second part of the USCG study compared the *Pride* rigged as a bald-headed schooner (four lower sails) to a sample population of schooners whose technical particulars were on record at the USCG Marine Safety Office in Portland, Maine. Out of concern that some people would falsely conclude that all historic ships were inherently prone to disaster, it was necessary to assess the role of the *Pride*'s hull form in the casualty to determine if its authenticity made it intrinsically unsafe. The study found that in its hull proportions, angle of downflooding, and stability the *Pride of Baltimore* "compared favorably with similarly rigged Coast Guard–inspected sailing vessels." Since the data pool represented successful vessels, the idea that all such hulls were dangerous was discredited.

In her rig and activities, however, the *Pride* was clearly different from these vessels. The exact vessels to which the *Pride* was compared is not public knowledge, but to give perspective to this comparison, the Maine schooners operate almost exclusively in the protected waters of Penobscot Bay between the months of May and October. Many of the vessels do not carry topmasts at all, or only a main topmast. None carry yards. Some of the vessels are quite aged and are operated accordingly. In general, operating certificates are restricted to 20 miles from a harbor of safe refuge. As a sampling for comparison, the Maine schooners therefore represent a far more conservative type of rig and operation than the *Pride*.

REPERCUSSIONS

Policy

By drawing attention to vessels that had no connection to Pride of Baltimore Inc., the coast guard technical study showed how the ramifications of a casualty can extend beyond the organization that loses the ship. For all the publicity it generated, however, the loss of the *Pride of Baltimore* had relatively little impact on the actual regulation of traditional sail, mainly because the prevailing view was that it did not point to any major blind spot in the existing regulations. Indeed, some regulators may have felt that the loss of a famous but uncertified traditional sailing vessel vindicated the extension of their control over such activities, while highlighting the risks faced by uninspected vessels. The two investigations by unaffiliated federal agencies found that the casualty was not caused by negligence or by the action of any person connected to the vessel. They did, however, raise a *(continued page 222)*

PRIDE OF BALTIMORE
Passenger Vessel Criteria

Ship Configuration	Parameter Req. Value	OCEAN SERVICE					PARTIALLY PROTECTED WATERS				
		GM - Wx 6.64	Rt. Arm 90°	Dk. Edge 1.50	DnFlood 1.70	Knockdn 1.90	GM - Wx 3.34	Rt. Arm 70°	Dk. Edge 1.00	DnFlood 1.10	Knockdn 1.25
Condition 1 Full Sail	KG 8.8'	6.6'	97.9°	0.60	0.89	1.16	6.6'	97.9°	0.60	0.89	1.16
	9.3'	6.1'	LESS STABILITY—DEFICIENT				6.1'	LESS STABILITY—DEFICIENT			
	9.8'	5.6'	LESS STABILITY—DEFICIENT				5.6'	LESS STABILITY—DEFICIENT			
Condition 2 "Schooner"	8.8'	6.6'	97.9°	1.20	1.78	2.33	6.6'	87.9°	1.20	1.78	2.33
	9.3'	6.1'	87.7°	1.10	1.55	1.80	6.1'	87.7°	1.10	1.55	1.80
	9.8'	5.6'	75.8°	1.00	1.31	1.30	5.6'	75.8°	1.00	1.31	1.30
Condition 3 Forestaysail & Full Main	8.8'	6.6'	97.9°	1.98	2.95	3.85	6.6'	97.9°	1.98	2.95	3.85
	9.3'	6.1'	87.7°	1.82	2.56	2.98	6.1'	87.7°	1.82	2.56	2.98
	9.8'	5.6'	75.8°	1.66	2.16	2.15	5.6'	75.8°	1.66	2.16	2.15
Condition 4—Casualty Forestaysail & Reefed Main	8.8'	6.6'	97.9°	3.37	5.00	6.54	6.6'	97.9°	3.37	5.00	6.54
	9.3'	6.1'	87.7°	3.09	4.34	5.06	6.1'	87.7°	3.09	4.34	5.06
	9.8'	5.6'	75.8°	2.81	3.67	3.65	5.6'	75.8°	2.81	3.67	3.65

Sailing School Vessel Criteria

Ship Configuration	Parameter Req. Value	OCEAN SERVICE					PARTIALLY PROTECTED WATERS				
		GM - Wx 6.64	Dk. Edge 0.6	Rt. Arm	DnFlood	Knockdn	GM - Wx 3.34	Dk. Edge 0.6	Rt. Arm	DnFlood	Knockdn
				See Ocean Service Plots					See Prot. Water Plots		
Condition 1 Full Sail	KG 8.8'	6.6'	0.6	OK	NO	OK	6.6'	0.6	OK	NO	OK
	9.3'	6.1'	LESS STABILITY—DEFICIENT				6.1'	LESS STABILITY—DEFICIENT			
	9.8'	5.6'	LESS STABILITY—DEFICIENT				5.6'	LESS STABILITY—DEFICIENT			
Condition 2 "Schooner"	8.8'	6.6'	1.20	OK	OK	OK	6.6'	1.20	OK	OK	OK
	9.3'	6.1'	1.10	OK	OK	OK	6.1'	1.10	OK	OK	OK
	9.8'	5.6'	1.00	NO	OK	NO	5.6'	1.00	NO	YES	NO
Condition 3 Forestaysail & Full Main	8.8'	6.6'	1.98	OK	OK	OK	6.6'	1.98	OK	OK	OK
	9.3'	6.1'	1.82	OK	OK	OK	6.1'	1.82	OK	OK	OK
	9.8'	5.6'	1.66	NO	OK	NO	5.6'	1.66	OK	OK	OK
Condition 4—Casualty Forestaysail & Reefed Main	8.8'	6.6'	3.37	OK	OK	OK	6.6'	3.37	OK	OK	OK
	9.3'	6.1'	3.09	OK	OK	OK	6.1'	3.09	OK	OK	OK
	9.8'	5.6'	2.81	NO	OK	NO	5.6'	2.81	OK	OK	OK

Passenger vessel criteria versus sailing school vessel criteria for the *Pride of Baltimore*. The unshaded areas of the tables represent sail area and KG combinations (the height of the center of gravity measured from the keel) under which the *Pride of Baltimore* would meet USCG criteria for Small Passenger Vessels or Sailing School Vessels. (Courtesy Howard Chatterton) *(continued from page 219)*   number of practical safety considerations. The process also highlighted the difficulty of deriving a complete and unambiguous stability assessment after a ship is gone if stability data are not already on record.

Requirements for Uninspected Vessels

Although no regulatory failure or violation contributed to the loss of the *Pride*, the incident delivered ammunition to the NTSB, which was already critical of the requirements for uninspected vessels. The NTSB expressed a degree of outrage that under applicable law there was "no requirement for uninspected vessels to have a compass, fathometer, electronic position fixing device, visual distress signals, or liferafts." Having found that these things were aboard the *Pride* on a voluntary basis, the NTSB report stated:

> If a vessel operator, such as Pride of Baltimore Inc. can recognize the short-comings of the uninspected vessel regulations, it is clear that these regulations need to be upgraded.

The NTSB went on to add the following: "The Coast Guard uninspected vessel regulations are inadequate because they do not require sufficient life-saving and navigation equipment for documented vessels that operate off-shore."

This was followed by a recommendation that the USCG "seek legislation . . . to require uninspected vessels that operate offshore . . . to carry navigation equipment, visual distress signals, and liferafts." Another recommendation urged the coast guard to require the float-free stowage of EPIRBs and life jackets on uninspected vessels, and yet another urged that the existing requirement for offshore fishing vessels to carry EPIRBs be expanded to include *all* uninspected vessels operating offshore.

The NTSB practice of tracking the progress of its recommendations helps in assessing the policy impact of the loss of the *Pride*. As of 1998, twelve years after the *Pride* was lost, NTSB records showed mixed success in the implementation of recommendations to the USCG relating to the *Pride of Baltimore* case. Given the elapsed time, the potential for this casualty to mobilize a policy initiative has probably run its course.

The most expansive recommendation directed the USCG to seek legislation to upgrade lifesaving and navigation equipment for uninspected vessels. That effort was defeated on the floor of the U.S. House of Representatives. However, efforts to expand the use of EPIRBs have been successful. The EPIRBs on Uninspected Vessels Act became Public Law 100-540 in 1993:

Although disappointed that the USCG was unable to obtain the legislative authority to require liferafts and navigation equipment on uninspected vessels, the Board is pleased that the USCG now requires EPIRBs on vessels operating on ocean and coastwise routes. Furthermore, the Board understands that the USCG is addressing the issues of uninspected vessel safety through other means.

The coast guard did not concur with the NTSB recommendation that life preservers be required to be stowed in float-free positions:

> On smaller vessels, such stowage could lead to the loss of the life preservers overboard if a large wave washes over the deck. The regulations already require that the life preservers be readily accessible. A more specific regulation would be difficult to develop since uninspected vessels are of many different types.

For a vessel the size of the *Pride*, stowing life preservers on deck would not have been particularly onerous, and the effect on aesthetics would have been minimal. Such arrangements have been devised for many traditional sailing vessels of comparable size. This situation epitomizes the awkwardness of formulating regulations that seek to impose uniformity where it doesn't exist naturally.

The loss of the *Pride* had some impact on regulations, but it was limited, mixed, and not tightly linked to the renaissance of traditional sail. This is in stark contrast to other casualties examined in this book.

The Renaissance of Traditional Sail

The world of sail training and traditional sail is a small one. In many cases, the practical lessons of the *Pride* case were transmitted informally to other vessel operators. To an extent not easily defined, general practices were indeed altered in response to the incident. One example relates to the proliferation of in-house policies relating to ship-to-shore communications schedules. The impact of the *Pride*'s loss on ship-to-shore communication policy was articulated by Captain Bert Rogers of the Ocean Classrooms Foundation: "there is no question that the loss of the *Pride* was a defining moment for management in respect to communications policy." Rogers said that the loss of the *Pride* forced management to "take a hard look at the informality of the existing situation and has resulted in written, and detailed policies on communications." Such nonstatutory impacts are a product of every casualty, and may be best expressed as a heightened awareness in the wake of disaster. This effect can be significant on an industry-wide basis if properly disseminated. "Awareness," however, has an uncertain duration in the collective memory. If casualty research shows anything, it is the human capacity to forget what has been learned and to repeat mistakes.

The Role of Regulation

A properly designed code of regulations places the minimum burden on a given activity while providing what is considered a reasonable level of protection to the public interest. Regulations do not guarantee safety, and neither does the USCG. Regulations establish a starting point from which other efforts build. Although all regulation is imperfect and expensive, this case offers some of the clearest evidence that the certification criteria available to large traditional sailing vessels have value for the purposes of safety. Anyone intending to build and operate a traditional sailing vessel for any public purpose would do well to bear this in mind for reasons other than revenue. The majority of large traditionally rigged sailing vessels built since 1986 in the United States has been constructed to meet USCG regulations.

Nevertheless, a number of uninspected traditional sailing vessels are engaged in sail training activities in the United States. That the renaissance of traditional sail still includes uninspected vessels, despite the example of the two *Pride*s, simply demonstrates the continuing tension between historic authenticity and prevailing standards of safety.

Society of Professional Sailing Ship Masters

Several recommendations of the NTSB regarding the stowage of lifesaving equipment and the design of harnesses were addressed to the Society of Professional Sailing Ship Masters (SPSSM). The NTSB called upon the society to "disseminate to the members of your society the details of this accident report, including the associated recommendations." The recommendations directed to the SPSSM are the only ones emerging from this case for which NTSB records indicate "Closed—Unacceptable Action." This organization appears to have become defunct around the time of these events. The International Sail Training Safety Forum is probably best positioned to disseminate this type of information in the future, along with national sail training organizations.

Research

The loss of the *Pride* prompted no research into sailing ship stability of an order comparable to that done by the Wolfson Unit in response to the *Marques*, although the Wolfson Unit has considered the *Pride* case in more recent research on "effective stability." In the United States, regulations for SPVs and SSVs already reflected the current thinking on the role of stability in sailing ship safety by both the USCG and private industry, and there was no incentive to revisit the matter. The criteria established under those regulations offer useful guidance but cannot be imposed on vessels operating with uninspected status.

Pride of Baltimore II

Though not a public policy or statutory repercussion, the decision to replace the *Pride of Baltimore* with a new vessel offers a unique opportunity to view the practical impact of a casualty on an actual replacement vessel. In the words of her designer, the overall aesthetics and sailing characteristics of the *Pride of Baltimore II* "would seem to be no less a true Baltimore Clipper." The public relations and promotional mission developed through the first *Pride* could have been fulfilled equally well by an identical replacement, but this course was not chosen. The *Pride of Baltimore II* is a radical departure from the "old boat" in ways that reflect important developments in current safety doctrine. The extent to which the changes are a direct result of the casualty is a matter of interpretation and varies from point to point. One distinction beyond debate between the two vessels are the premises upon which each was built: whereas the first *Pride* was conceived as "an authentic example of a Baltimore Clipper ship," *Pride II* embraces the following recommendation from the NTSB to Pride of Baltimore Inc.:

> Comply with the current Coast Guard regulations for passenger sailing vessels in ocean service in any future design, construction and operation of sailing vessels, including historic sailing vessels.

Compliance with USCG regulations for SPVs is a fundamental difference between the two vessels from which many other differences flow. The above recommendation was made without regard to the future purpose of a replacement vessel, and recognized the value of USCG regulations to the safety of the crew, regardless of who else might be carried aboard. The following lists some of the more significant departures in *Pride II*:

- 50 percent more displacement: 187 tons versus 122 tons
- proportionally less sail area to displacement: 9,707.8 versus 9,523.0 square feet
- watertight subdivision: five watertight bulkheads and six compartments
- increased freeboard
- hatches: no cargo hatches; hatches and coaming height comply with USCG requirements; most hatches are on the centerline
- external lead ballast: 31 percent, roughly 20 tons, of the ship's ballast is external
- internal lead ballast: 43 tons; all internal ballast is secured lead rather than a variety of less dense materials

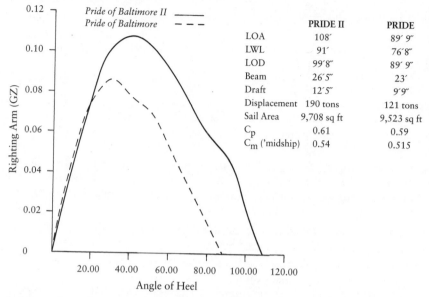

	PRIDE II	PRIDE
LOA	108′	89′ 9″
LWL	91′	76′8″
LOD	99′8″	89′ 9″
Beam	26′5″	23′
Draft	12′5″	9′9″
Displacement	190 tons	121 tons
Sail Area	9,708 sq ft	9,523 sq ft
C_p	0.61	0.59
C_m ('midship)	0.54	0.515

Stability and specification comparison of *Pride of Baltimore* and *Pride of Baltimore II*.
(Andy Davis)

• two engines driving twin screws: propellers are offset; no propeller aperture
• approximately four times more horsepower
• greater fuel capacity
• increased water tankage and watermaking capability

Though *Pride II* is nearly 50 percent larger in displacement, she carries only 2 percent more canvas. Her increased beam not only leads to greater comfort belowdecks, but the added buoyancy magnifies the righting energy by half, which is important in enhancing the stability picture.

It is evident that nine years of operating experience revealed certain limitations of the *Pride of Baltimore*. These were often related to the original commitment to authenticity, and only brought to light as the vessel sailed harder and farther from home. The *Pride of Baltimore II* is superior to the first *Pride*: unlike her predecessor, she was built to be lived aboard, to keep the sea over long distances, and to be sailed hard. Of the replica vessels actively sailing, *Pride II* is among the very best suited to what she does.

Authenticity, like tradition, exists in degrees. There are sailing replicas that are more authentic than *Pride of Baltimore II*, and there are some that are less so. *Pride II* is not a museum piece, nor was she built to be. Some of the less practical touches of historical accuracy were abandoned, though not without debate: the jackyard gaff topsail, the bonnet on the staysail, the cobblestone ballast. Yet the rig and the hull retain the essentials. *Pride II* is a tangible example of one organization's decision to redraw the line of authenticity closer to the priorities and preferences of what had become a well-defined modern mission. She is a plausible representation of a Baltimore clipper but is better suited to the expectations of present-day seafaring.

LOOSE ENDS

Not all aspects of the *Pride of Baltimore* discussed here related directly to the loss of the vessel or the loss of life, but for better or worse a casualty provides an opportunity to look at the way things are done in their entire. In doing so we may derive lessons that can be transferred elsewhere. For instance, the cargo hatches did not play a role in this sinking, yet consideration of them here combines with what we learned from the *Marques* to build a stronger case against them. This is a legitimate and necessary approach if mariners are to perpetuate traditional sail in a changing world.

MICROBURSTS

One source estimated that the incidence of microbursts may exceed 13,000 a year in the United States alone. The *Pride* was struck in broad daylight, and except for the cook, who succeeded in escaping, all hands were on deck and presumably alert to the unfolding situation. Despite the relative preparedness of those aboard, the speed of events highlights the difficulty of detecting such phenomena in the restricted visibility associated with foul weather, and thus the importance of maintaining a weather eye. It also speaks to the need to design traditional sailing vessels for situations in which the skill and experience of the master and crew may be rendered ineffectual, and rehearsed responses become impossible to execute.

EMERGENCY AND RESPONSE

The bottom of the sea is littered with the hulks of ships that disappeared without a trace. But for modern life rafts, even faulty ones, and hydrostatic releases, the *Pride* would have been another such case. Having nearly everyone on deck at the time of the squall was in some ways a best-case scenario for what befell the *Pride*, yet there was still a high casualty rate. Attention to the location and type of float-free emergency equipment should be part of the ongoing internal assessment on any vessel, regardless of formal requirements.

BUILDING REPLICA VESSELS

Embedded in the story of the *Pride of Baltimore* and the *Pride of Baltimore II* is the issue of the appropriateness of building and sailing historic replicas in a modern age. Gillmer addressed this directly:

I believe that the building and sailing of replica ships is a proper and honest inquiry into history. These are valid archaeological experiments and the sources of basic knowledge. From concept through construction and operation, the *Pride of Baltimore*, as well as the *Lady Maryland* and the *Pride of Baltimore II* and other similar historic vessels, are convincing examples of such inquiry and discovery. It is not for the critics of one loss to condemn the reasonable motives that build and sustain such ships.

This statement rings true, although it must be remembered that traditional sail will always attract, not only nautical archaeologists, but people, even paid crew with prior experience, who are not in a position to judge the risks. They will be attracted by the beauty of the ships themselves and the opportunity to live an extraordinary life seemingly beyond reach in these times. In years gone by, sailors of the vessels we now replicate expected very little and got what they expected. That world has changed and continues to change before our eyes. When resurrecting the past, the line between historical authenticity and present expectations needs to be drawn with a weather eye on the future.

SAILING REPLICA VESSELS

It is fortunate for those who are interested in the building and sailing of replica ships that casualties have not discredited endeavors of this type.

Pride of Baltimore II under full sail. (Courtesy Pride of Baltimore Inc.)

The building and sailing of replica vessels is a valuable activity that should continue. Replica vessels may be designed, built, and equipped to modern standards, but these standards do not relieve any of us from recognizing that the sea is inherently dangerous. All vessels have limitations and need to be operated accordingly. Just as with untested new technology, when technology is resurrected from an earlier age, the process of rediscovery can be hazardous. When our experiments result in a loss of life and become front-page news, the larger endeavor can expect to attract criticism, fairly or unfairly.

MISSIONS ABOARD REPLICA VESSELS

An increased awareness of the ongoing relationship between nautical archaeology and modern missions must be counted as one of the impacts of this case. Although the *Pride* was built as a replica privateer, she operated in a historical context and with a mission fundamentally different from those of the original Baltimore clippers. Although the basic configuration of the *Pride* never really changed, "*Pride* the authentic replica dockside exhibit" metamorphosed by degrees into "*Pride*, the international sailing goodwill ambassador." Efforts were made to upgrade the vessel at each stage of her evolving mission, but in retrospect it almost seems that the mission outgrew the ship. Building a vessel in the service of nautical archaeology but operating it as something different will always lead to divergent priorities. This case is but one point of reference for the ongoing challenge of matching historical pursuits to present expectations.

Watch Below

While nothing in the investigation found fault with the *Pride*'s replica status, it would seem impossible to construct an operable replica vessel in the post-*Pride* era without considering the *Pride* story. At the time of the original public bid solicitation in the *Baltimore Sun* calling for an authentic Baltimore clipper "capable of being sailed," no one harbored visions of the *Pride* voyaging as extensively as she ultimately did. Her crew often pronounced with glee that sailing the *Pride* was like riding "a wild black mare bareback through the night." Though *Pride II*'s mission is significantly the same, her very existence sheds a light on the first *Pride* that is of great value to the larger proposition of traditional sail.

The *Pride of Baltimore* and all she stood for were dearly held public property, not only in Baltimore, but everywhere she sailed. For that reason, her loss was a public loss that was accompanied by a public grief. There is a monument to the *Pride* in Baltimore's Inner Harbor, but the most fitting monument is the *Pride of Baltimore II*.

Unlike vessels of a later period, the *Maria Asumpta* carried full topsails. (PPL)

Maria Asumpta
1858–1995

BUILDER: Unknown, near Barcelona, Spain

RIG: Brig

HULL: Wood

SAIL AREA: 8,500 square feet

LOA (SPARRED): 125 feet

LOD: 98 feet

LWL: Unknown

DRAFT: 10 feet, 6 inches

BEAM: 25 feet

TONNAGE: 127 gross tons; 72 net tons

POWER: 2 GEC Dorman 6 LET diesels, 175 horsepower each, driving a single propeller

FLAG HISTORY: Spain, Britain

O N 30 MAY 1995, a small crowd gathered on a cliff top on the serrated coast of Cornwall, England, to watch a beautiful white brig sail into Padstow Harbour. She approached under nearly full sail, an apparition of a distant and awesome maritime past. It was a clear afternoon with a light northwest breeze blowing across the Bristol Channel. A heavy swell roiled at the base of the cliffs. Far below, a jagged spur of rock called Rumps Point projected into the Celtic Sea like a snaggled old tooth.

To those watching from the cliff, it seemed that the brig was steering too close to shore, almost as if to graze the foot of the cliffs. Why was she coming so close? On the ship, the master was also realizing the precariousness of the situation. The tide, the wind,

and the swell were conspiring to set the ship toward the cliffs. The master
fired up the engines to take the ship out of danger. And then the engines died.

Before everyone's eyes the *Maria Asumpta* struck a submerged rock just
off Rumps Point. The masts, yards, sails, and rigging tumbled to the deck
while the hull was pummeled this way and that at the foot of the cliff. Within
minutes the grand old lady of the sea was transformed into kindling. As one
onlooker reported, "the ship was obviously in trouble as she sailed round
the headland. It was clear they weren't going to make it. She was swept onto
the rocks and her bow folded up like cardboard." The lighthouse keeper at
Trevose Head, the next headland down the coast, said, "it did not look like a
sailing ship anymore. It was just crumbling before my eyes."

Amid a heavy surge, many of the fourteen people aboard struggled to
safety from the wreck to the rocks. Others were picked up in the water by
nearby vessels. In the ensuing mayhem, three people died. The casualty
occurred in fair weather and in broad daylight, but the approach left little
margin for error. The prevailing conditions of wind, tide, and swell put the
brig at a grave disadvantage. The ship had sailed into a situation from
which she could only be extricated through the use of her engines. When
the engines failed at the critical moment, the vessel was instantly in peril.
The captain, Mark Litchfield of the *Marques* and the China Clipper Society,
was tried in a criminal court and served time for manslaughter.

Immediately after the casualty, the Marine Accident Investigation Branch
(MAIB) of the Marine Safety Agency under the United Kingdom's Department of Transport was assigned to investigate the incident. The MAIB produced a report under the Accident Reporting and Investigations Regulations
established by the Merchant Shipping Act of 1994, which included the following:

> The fundamental purpose of investigating an accident under these Regula-
> tions is to determine its circumstances and the causes with the aim of improv-
> ing the safety of life at sea and the avoidance of accidents in the future. It is
> not the purpose to apportion liability, nor, except so far as is necessary to
> achieve the fundamental purpose, to apportion blame.

The investigation interviewed survivors while divers surveyed the
wreck and salvaged various components for testing. The report, issued in
January 1996, is the foundation for much of the factual evidence presented here.

HISTORY

In one way or another, all the vessels we have dealt with in this book are
"historic." In this regard, however, the 137-year-old *Maria Asumpta* was

in a category of her own. Promotional literature for the ship stated that "no other ship of her age still regularly sails." The *Maria Asumpta*, like so many sailing vessels, was a fairly ordinary creature in her day. As a result, the documentation of her life is sparser than it would be for a more famous vessel. Over nearly a century and a half of operation, the vessel probably saw everything the sea could offer. She was built in 1858 near Barcelona for transatlantic trading with the vestiges of Spain's New World empire and her former possessions. Of her earlier work, it is said that the *Maria Asumpta* carried textiles to Buenos Aires on her maiden voyage, and "later worked as a slave carrier and a salt vessel." Originally rigged as either a brigantine or a brig, she could carry up to about five hundred tons of cargo. The ship traded under sail until the 1930s, when a single main engine was installed, and thereafter she traded as a "moto-velero," or motor sailer. Her sailing rig was allowed to deteriorate through disuse, and eventually it ceased to exist. She was renamed *Pepita* at some point and then *Ciudad de Inca* around 1953. The vessel continued to work until 1978, but by this time she was making only short Mediterranean trips under power. She had no masts and sported a two-story aft deckhouse, complete with funnel.

Restoration

In 1980 the Spanish owner of the *Ciudad de Inca* was intending to sell the engines and burn the hull when Mark Litchfield and Robin Cecil-Wright of the China Clipper Society appeared and purchased her whole for the price of the engines. The China Clipper Society had earlier restored and was still operating the *Marques* at this time. Their newest vessel was moved to Barbate, Spain, where the following work was undertaken:

> Over 18 months in 1981–82 the ship was stripped and virtually rebuilt. About one-third of her frames were removed and replaced and about half of her outer planking. As suitable timber was unavailable in Spain, 200 tons were shipped from England, chiefly for making new masts and spars.

Keeping the name under which she was purchased, the *Ciudad de Inca* sailed in company with the *Marques* in Britain, Portugal, and the Canary Islands. Projects included film work, promotional activities, and sail training ventures such as the 1982 Clipper Challenge. In late 1983 both ships received Load Line Exemption Certificates from the British Department of Transport and sailed to the Caribbean. In 1984 they joined up with the tall-ships race to Bermuda with trainees aboard—the race that would claim the *Marques*. Suffering rudder damage when she grounded in Bermuda the night before the race, the *Ciudad de Inca* temporarily dropped out of the race but rejoined the fleet in Canada and attended the summer's keynote event, the 350th anniversary celebrations in Québec City.

The vessel stayed in the Canadian waters of the Great Lakes from the summer of 1984 until late 1987. Little documentation has been found about the vessel's activities in Canada, though it was reported that the vessel sank in Kingston Harbour, Ontario, in a winter storm. The threat of legal action arising from the *Marques* sinking had virtually trapped her in Canada: in order to leave Canada, the vessel would have to pass through the U.S. portion of the St. Lawrence Seaway, where she might be seized *in rem* by federal marshals as collateral for impending lawsuits in the United States against the China Clipper Society over the loss of life in the *Marques*. Stories are still told of the ship slipping through the American locks in the seaway in the nick of time. In any case, the *Ciudad de Inca* eventually got out of the Great Lakes and returned to Britain in 1988, where her original name, *Maria Asumpta*, was restored.

In Britain a new organization, the Friends of the *Maria Asumpta* (FMA), was formed to support the vessel, and the China Clipper Society ceased to be an active entity. Captain Mark Litchfield owned the vessel and operated her through a company known as Yalefleet, Ltd. Both Litchfield and Yalefleet were based in Maidstone, Kent, England. Under the FMA, the vessel earned her keep with varied programs still allowed outside the new, more restrictive certification system in Britain. Her activities included promotional visits to festivals and special events, souvenir sales, and film and photographic appearances. Private contributions and membership dues also helped keep the ship afloat.

The revocation of her load line exemption in the aftermath of the *Marques* disaster meant that the *Maria Asumpta* was no longer certified to conduct sail training in the style of earlier years, though the organization was able to carry people to sea through other arrangements.

By buying a membership in the FMA, interested individuals could gain access to sailing privileges aboard her. The ship was thereby able to take nonprofessionals to sea, where they could participate in the running of the ship under the direction of more experienced people. Simon Mason, a businessman who sailed aboard, described his experience: "I was astonished at the number of novices aboard. But we were still expected to work as full crew members, taking the wheel and acting as lookouts." John Howells, the helmsman at the time of loss, was a professional tree surgeon. Another report stated that "twenty-four trainee crew, mostly British teenagers, had already been dropped off at Swansea" before the fatal voyage to Padstow, thus avoiding a potentially much larger casualty. The membership structure enabled a private "pleasure yacht" to avail itself of the participation and support of anyone interested in joining in an informal trainee capacity, without charging on a per-passage basis.

The now-moot question as to whether the *Maria Asumpta* was engaged in sail training was controversial in the aftermath of her loss. Not the sail training community, nor the owner of the vessel, nor the authorities were keen to see this case associated with sail training. Not only was it bad press for legitimate, certified sail training outfits, but "sail training" suggested exactly the sort of commercial activity for which the vessel was not certified. The mere hint of sail training would resurrect questions about the ability of the regulatory authorities to protect the public from harm aboard traditional sailing ships, a very real dilemma in the post-*Marques* world. Despite claims to the contrary, activities aboard the *Maria Asumpta* often resembled what would otherwise be described as *sail training*. The difference was categorical rather than practical.

However one phrases it, part of the *Maria Asumpta*'s purpose and appeal lay in offering a participatory seagoing experience, including the fundamentals of seamanship and sailing. The presence of people from all walks of life seeking a hands-on experience aboard a traditional sailing vessel is virtually indistinguishable from sail training, and no amount of legal posturing changes this. It would appear, however, that this arrangement had begun to run its course for the FMA. At the time of the casualty, Captain Litchfield was actively seeking certification for the *Maria Asumpta* and had been working closely with the authorities to bring the vessel into compliance. Speaking shortly after the incident, Litchfield remarked, "a certificate of seaworthiness was a foregone conclusion."

Winter Refit

In May 1995 the *Maria Asumpta* came out of her winter layup to begin a new season. She had undergone an extensive refit at Gloucester Docks with the goal of attaining certification for commercial sail training operations. Some £50,000 were spent on projects such as an overhaul of the main engines, replacement of tailshaft and bearings, reconstruction of the transom, recaulking the hull, and installation of a new system of fuel lines, valves, and filters.

In the course of the refit, fuel contamination was discovered: rust and freshwater were seeping in around a fuel filler cap. The response was described in a pamphlet supporting Captain Litchfield after his conviction:

> Mark Litchfield arranged an analysis of the fuel by the County Public Health Analyst. Subsequently, in consultation with engineer Jamie Campbell and a

volunteer [Peter Davis], a lecturer from Swindon Technical College, he [Litch-field] decided to discharge all fuel from the tanks. Clean fuel from the top two-thirds of the tanks was pumped into two bowsers ashore while all fuel from the bottom of the tanks was collected into a third bowser and an oil drum. Once settled, the clean fuel from the first two tanks was returned to the ship. The rest was disposed of.

The tanks were cleaned while the fuel was ashore, and 1,800 liters of new fuel was subsequently taken aboard.

Standards of maintenance often fluctuate over the life of any vessel. Most nonprofit organizations running large traditional sailing vessels struggle with difficult choices of maintenance and improvements. In this case, how-ever, there appears to have been a comprehensive effort to upgrade the *Maria Asumpta* at considerable expense so she could meet the Code of Practice for Small Commercial Sailing Vessels and thus gain the benefits of certification for future operations and become more self-supporting.

FINAL VOYAGE

The *Maria Asumpta* weighed anchor off Swansea early on the morning of 30 May 1995 with fourteen people aboard under Litchfield's command. She started out by motor sailing across the Bristol Channel and along its south coast in a south-southwesterly direction (see chart). A west wind was blow-ing force 3–4, too light and too close to the desired course to set the square sails and turn off the engines.

By noon the wind veered into the northwest as forecast, enabling the crew to set square sails and shut down engines. The brig proceeded under sail alone on starboard tack. According to the *Summary Report*, around that time the wind shifted into a more favorable quadrant and the master decided to change the passage plan. Instead of running a course from Hart-land Point straight down to the vicinity of Padstow, he altered course toward the coast and into a shallow bay characteristic of that part of the coast (see chart). The rationale was "to avoid the strength of the predicted tidal flood and to be able to view the coastline more closely." Litchfield commented later, "it was a nice coast and I thought everybody else would like to look at it." A rhumb line was plotted to a waypoint one mile off Tin-tagel Head, and another course was laid to a position just inside Newland, off Pentire Point on the approach to Padstow. The second rhumb line was closer to the wind by nearly three points, or 30 degrees, but the master was confident the vessel could make good the second rhumb line under sail only.

By 1430 it was evident the vessel was running ahead of schedule. The mainsail (main course) was taken in to reduce speed. By 1500 the vessel was

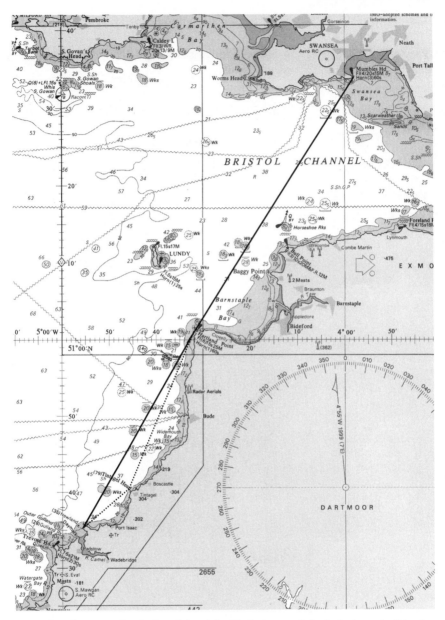

Original track (——) and revised track (·······) for *Maria Asumpta*'s final trip down the Bristol Channel. (British Admiralty Chart, with track information from MAIB, *Summary Report*)

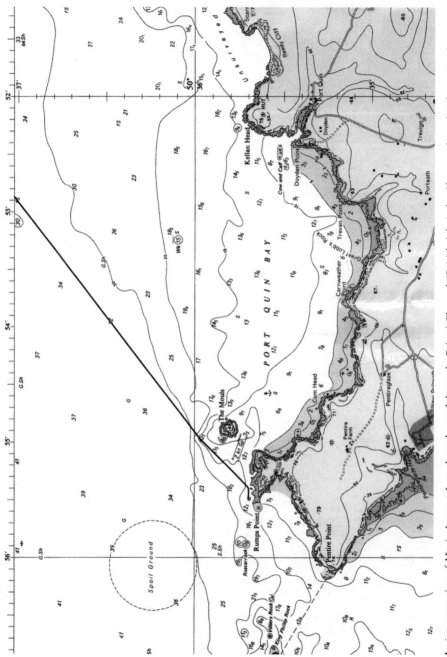

An intrepretation of *Maria Asumpta*'s track made good down the Bristol Channel. (British Admiralty Chart, with track information from MAIB, *Summary Report*)

off Tintagel and slightly inshore of the planned rhumb line. Shortly after passing abeam of Tintagel, the helmsman was instructed to come up to a course of 245 degrees (compass), and the yards were braced sharper in order to sail closer to the wind. Positions were plotted at fifteen-minute intervals. Newland and Gulland Rock were visible to port, as expected. At some point in this leg, the master reportedly shifted to a larger-scale chart and plotted two more positions about eight to ten minutes apart. From these positions it was evident that the vessel was still inshore of the intended trackline and that she would pass closer to the Mouls than desired. At one point Adam Pursar, who was described as a watch leader and "perhaps the most experienced crew member aboard," suggested tacking out to sea, away from the Mouls and Rumps Point. Observing from shore, the Padstow harbormaster called the ship by cellular telephone and advised the master to take a different approach to the harbor entrance from the one he was obviously pursuing. Trevor Platt, the Padstow pilot assigned to bring the ship in, commented: "When I realized where she was I was dumbfounded. She'd have been at least a mile off course. It looked like bad seamanship." Don McBurnie, another Padstow resident, concurred, saying: "It is a tragedy but the standard of navigation and steering comes into question. It mystifies me what it was doing there." Having transited these waters in the past, Litchfield evidently felt the situation was in hand, yet others discerned a disaster in the making.

Appreciating that under sail alone the vessel might be set onto Rumps Point, at approximately 1601 the master ordered the engines started. He instructed the helmsman to "steer as close to the wind as possible without pinching" so that they might clear the coast coming up fast to leeward. The engines were engaged, and the helmsman was ordered to steer 250 degrees. This caused the sails to luff. Approximately five minutes later, when abeam the Mouls at a range of about one and a half cables (0.15 mile), the engines stopped. The master was immediately aware that the brig was in danger. The engineer and his assistant were sent to the engine room to investigate. Other action included calling hands to reset the mainsail and brace the yards around as far as they would go. This latter action is perplexing because one would have assumed that the ship was already close-hauled and that nothing more could be had from the braces. The helmsman at the time reported Litchfield saying, "This could be serious."

The *Maria Asumpta* was now sailing as close to the wind as she could—which wasn't very close—and losing much of the lift that the sails normally provide. Like other square-riggers, which are designed to sail best with the wind aft of the beam, she was not especially weatherly. The bracing of the yards was limited by the standing rigging, so further bracing would have afforded little advantage. A prodigious amount of sail was set at the time: the inner and outer jibs, foresail (course), fore topsail, and fore topgallant; mainsail (course), main topsail, and main topgallant spanker. Even so, the wind was light, so she was unable to generate much boat speed, nor was she at her most maneuverable. Aggravating the situation was the shape of the hull itself. As a former cargo vessel, the *Maria Asumpta* had relatively round bilges and a flat bottom for optimum cargo capacity. With the tide and the swell setting the brig toward shore, these features guaranteed that she would make considerable leeway. A fin-keeled yacht with a fore-and-aft rig could have performed much better under such conditions, though it would still have been a close call. The master had told the helmsman not to "pinch," meaning that he should not steer so close to the wind that the sails would lose all drive, causing the vessel to stall. But by this time the margin between pinching and sailing a course to safety had become negligible. The vessel sailed on.

IN THE ENGINE ROOM the engineer and his assistant were frantically trying to restart the engines. The daytank was half-full, indicating that ample fuel was on hand. The unions on three injector lines on each engine were loosened, as were the air bleed valves on each primary filter. When the engines were cranked over on the starters, no fuel flowed from the loosened injector unions. None of the other cylinders fired, either. Fuel did flow from the air bleed valves on primary fuel filters, and when it splashed on the white, fireproof insulation on the bulkhead it was observed to be "slightly discoloured."

At 1616, approximately five minutes after the engines failed, the *Maria Asumpta* struck a rock at the foot of Rumps Point and was washed onto the unforgiving coast. The surge lifted and slammed the hull onto the rocks. The bow section broke away from the rest of the hull and lodged in the rocks while the rest of the ship began to disintegrate. The situation immediately became chaotic. Survivor John Howells explained:

> At that stage I was more worried about crashing timbers from above than drowning. The foc's'le was the safest place to be since not much would fall forwards. I got my legs tangled in ropes by the rail. The ship was already listing at about 20 degrees, and up to 60 degrees every time the swell hit. The deck was almost vertical at times.

A member of the nearby Port Isaac lifeboat team watched the events from the cliff top: "She was too far in Port Quin Bay and making very little headway. It was only a few minutes before she broke up into matchwood. It was horrible to watch but it was inevitable because she was too far in the bay."

The life rafts inflated automatically but were not used. The life jackets were stowed below-decks, where they stayed. (PPL)

Within minutes she did not look like a ship anymore. (Sam Morgan Moore)

The *Maria Asumpta* didn't stand a chance on such a coast. The surge dragged people back into the sea even after they reached the rocks. The Mouls are visible in the background. The possible escape route into Port Quin Bay was between the Mouls and the cliffs at the upper right. (PPL)

Upon grounding, Litchfield issued a Mayday call and instructed all hands to save themselves and "make land by the rocks." No attempt had been made to pursue a strategy other than sailing clear of the point. No order was given to retrieve life jackets from below or to anchor in advance of the grounding. Though there were numerous instances of people attempting to help one another, the abandon-ship response was uncoordinated despite the fact that approximately five minutes passed between the engine failure and grounding. Pursar, who earlier raised the question about tacking out to sea away from the coast, screamed at Litchfield as he jumped from the wreck, "You bastard. You bastard." The *Times* the next day quoted Litchfield:

> It looked as if we were going to be perfectly safe so we ran up the engines and that was fine. We were then passing shore somewhere between a quarter of a mile and a half mile off. Then the engines failed. They suddenly stopped. We did everything we could to claw her off the rocks but we couldn't. It looked as though we were going to make it and then there was a tremendous thud.

The search-and-rescue services responded immediately upon receiving the Mayday call, but the Mayday did not come until the grounding occurred. The surge and the cold waters were too much for three of the people still aboard the *Maria Asumpta*. (PPL)

It is uncertain what point of land Litchfield is referencing, but his estimation of the vessel's distance from the Mouls was not supported by the investigation.

The speed with which the hull went to bits was astounding to those who witnessed it or who have seen the photos. Though there is no reason to believe the hull was particularly unsound, many of the timbers and fastenings were old and thus vulnerable to the violent contact with the rocks, a force they were never meant to bear. Wood has been shown to be especially susceptible to point impact, and the absence of transverse bulkheads exacerbated the situation. In any event, the ship was quickly a total loss, and it is hard to imagine any other outcome once she struck.

There was a rapid response from search-and-rescue services by helicopter as well as by the local Royal National Lifeboat Institute rescue craft. Nearby fishing vessels and pleasure craft also proceeded to the area to assist. The master and eight others made it ashore from the bow of the vessel, while others went into the sea. The engineer's assistant, John Shannon, drowned in plain view while attempting to get hold of a floating plastic ice chest that was adrift: "It kept on spinning over. Tim had a fix on him and finally saw him slip under. He just couldn't hold that box." The cook, Anne Taylor, was lost when the ship split at the point where she was standing and witnesses saw her "pulled down into the churning sea." The engineer, Jamie Campbell, returned to the ship after getting safely ashore to assist Emily MacFarlane, who had been left behind on the disintegrating foredeck. He got her as far as the rocks, but she was pulled back into the sea by the surge and was lost. MacFarlane had rescued a drowning man who had fallen into the water at the Gloucester docks only two weeks earlier. Another crew member was dragged back into the sea attempting to help the engineer, and they were both picked up by a fishing vessel. It is astounding that so many survived and that none were incapacitated by the tons of spars and rigging that collapsed around them.

POSTMORTEM

The analysis of this case is fairly straightforward: a brig sailed into a tight spot under prevailing conditions that had been working against her for some time. The master turned to the auxiliary engines to correct the situation, but they failed. In the days before engines, vessels lost by similar miscalculation of wind and tide were commonplace. What makes this case different is technology: access to technology gives us different expectations for seamanship. Reasonable or not, we also have an expectation that people should not die this way.

After a six-week criminal trial, the jury concluded ten to two that the casualty was avoidable and a direct consequence of the master's negligence. This was a controversial decision, but the appeal also failed. It has been suggested that in the hands of skilled lawyers, jurors who knew nothing of the sea were led to conclusions that some mariners would have rejected. Furthermore, the public's awareness of Litchfield's experience with the *Marques* may have weighed against him. The criminal conviction hangs over every aspect of this story as we consider the pros and cons of choices, alternatives, and standards of practice that were debated before the jury. The verdict in this case, and any precedent it implies, is purely a British domestic matter, but time will tell if it has ramifications outside Britain.

In my analysis of this case I rely on three main sources: the investigation's *Summary Report*; Captain Frank J. M. Scott, the expert witness for the prosecution and author of *A Square Rig Sailing Handbook*; and a group of sixteen individuals, including several accomplished professional mariners, who presented a pamphlet, *To Whom It May Concern from Friends of the Maria Asumpta*, defending Captain Mark Litchfield's seamanship and reputation after his conviction. Although the primary purpose of the *Summary Report* was to establish the facts, in doing so it also judged the master's decisions, many unfavorably. The other two parties were nearly diametrically opposed. There was virtually nothing in Litchfield's performance that Captain Scott did not condemn as unseamanlike. Conversely, the pamphlet authors found no fault with any of Captain Litchfield's choices or decisions and were adamant that his conviction was a gross miscarriage of justice.

Unlike the stability casualties discussed in this book, each of which involved an element of postmortem guesswork, the loss of the *Maria Asumpta* follows a relatively concrete and identifiable chain of navigational choices, side by side with clear alternatives. The potential dangers in each of these choices were perhaps not obvious to the master at the time, but at least some errors seem obvious upon reconstruction. The master was also faulted for something masters routinely do on both sail and power vessels: rely on their engines to avoid danger. The *Maria Asumpta*, although a pleasure yacht, thus holds lessons for all professional mariners.

Engines

A number of issues emerged from the role of the ship's engines in the loss of the *Maria Asumpta*, not least of which was the question of fuel contamination. Although the *Summary Report* concluded that the fuel at the time of engine failure was contaminated, it also found the degree of contamination insufficient to cause the type of engine failure that occurred. First, the engines quit abruptly without the sputtering or change in rpm that would normally accompany fuel starvation due to clogging. The filters were recovered and found to contain contamination, but not at significant levels. That the engines ran for thirty-six hours without mishap prior to failure does not necessarily refute fuel contamination: clogging of filters can be slow and cumulative, but it can also occur in relatively short order if particulates from the bottom of the tank are drawn up into suspension when a vessel enters open water and seas increase, or as engines draw from lower in the tanks. Either way, the tanks had recently been cleaned and the engines had run without mishap, suggesting that the master had reason to believe the engines were working properly and the fuel quality was acceptable. A consideration for mariners is that, excepting when breakdown occurs from excessive wear, the next most likely timing for engine failure may be after a major overhaul. The disassembly and reassembly of so many parts creates opportunities for error and for stirring potential problems that might otherwise have lain dormant indefinitely. After the *Maria Asumpta*'s extensive engine overhaul, it would have been appropriate to treat the engines with special caution for a period of several weeks. This gives electrical connections an opportunity to adjust to vibrations at different rpm's and sea states, and it allows the engineer and crew to observe any other defects under different conditions.

Although several people testified that the handling of the questionable fuel was proper and should have effectively eliminated any contaminated fuel, it remained an issue in the trial. Peter Davis, the Swindon Technical College consultant, stated after the wreck that he had advised disposing of the *entire* fuel supply and returning none of it to the ship. This was contested by Litchfield's defenders and remains unresolved. The *Summary Report* does not mention microbiological contamination (MBC) as a factor in the alleged contamination, so presumably it was not. MBC, which grows like an algae in diesel fuel and does not "settle out" like water or particulates, can be eliminated only through an industrial filtration and treatment process.

The crux of the matter is that fuel contamination was established by the investigation but rejected as a cause of engine failure. The problem faced by Litchfield, and any captain in such a position, is that the home remedy applied for separating the bad fuel from the good may well have been perfectly adequate, but it failed to dispel the doubt and the insinuation of negligence. Whatever the role of the fuel in the engine failure, the allegation could never be entirely put to rest because of the absence of documentation and sampling to disprove it conclusively or establish due diligence. Perception as well as procedure are part of what a captain must consider in the management of a vessel. Despite elements of professionalism, the operation of the *Maria Asumpta* was essentially—and at times avowedly—amateur. Charitable, nonprofit organizations face the same standards of accountability as do commercial enterprises if a fatal accident occurs and is perceived to have resulted from a cut corner.

The most likely cause of engine failure, according to the investigation, was "the simultaneous and involuntary release of the main engines' fuel pump hold-on solenoids." This conclusion was based on parts recovered from the wreck and by the abrupt nature of the engine failure. The *Summary Report* noted that "the cause of this release has proven impossible to establish but it follows that the engines could have been restarted had these solenoids been re-energized or actuated manually." Whether an engineer with greater training or experience could have diagnosed and rectified this situation in the time available (five minutes) is difficult to say.

Litchfield was specifically faulted for his reliance on the engines to protect his ship after having chosen a course that provided little margin for error. It was also pointed out that he should have started his engines sooner. If the engines had been started sooner, they might have died sooner, thus altering the moment and location at which the master had to react, but since the engine failure was not predictable, this point seems moot. It is a little like saying that if a driver had only had a heart attack *before* getting behind the wheel of a car, he or she would not also have had a car accident. The engines on the *Maria Asumpta* had been run for several hours earlier that day, so there was no specific cause to doubt their reliability and, after all, the engines did start on command. The randomness of engine failure teaches not that sailors should start their engines whenever they see land, but rather that because engine failure can occur at any time with no warning, all vessels should be navigated accordingly. The fallibility of gadgetry dictates that engines be treated with the same healthy skepticism that should attach to all such devices.

The fact that Captain Litchfield was imprisoned raises unique questions. Since an auxiliary sailing vessel has two means of propulsion, what is a sailing master's obligation to operate with special regard to the what-ifs should engine failure occur? In the event of engine failure, is it fair to legally hold sailing shipmasters to a standard of seamanship higher than that applying to captains of power vessels who also have engine failures? In a courtroom, are a sailing vessel's capabilities defined by her sailing qualities, by her horsepower, or by some combination, and how is that combination established? There is no simple and good answer to these questions, but sailors should note that engine failure is a far more common eventuality than hurricanes, white squalls, or microbursts.

Litchfield's particular approach to Padstow left much to be desired, but the fact remains that all manner of vessels place themselves in situations whereby mechanical failure would result in catastrophe. Litchfield's defenders pointed out that the motorized tour boat *Jubilee Queen* routinely passed Rumps Point with up to two hundred passengers as part of her sightseeing excursion, relying on nothing but her engines. The tour boats that operate at the foot of Niagara Falls also come to mind, as do the occasions one is compelled to surf, full throttle, between two foaming jetties before a raging sea in order to seek the shelter of harbor. All close-quarters situations involving shipping, narrow channels, and docking find sailing vessels just as dependent on engines as power vessels to avoid disaster. That a shipmaster should not rely on engines is akin to saying a motorist should not rely on brakes, though no one has yet proposed that cars be fitted with anchors in case of brake failure. Why should it matter that this vessel also had masts and sails?

It is true that sailing vessels, especially the *Maria Asumpta*, have considerable windage and therefore are more vulnerable to set and drift in certain situations. But when one considers the windage of cruise ships, car carriers, ferries, crane barges and other designs arising from specific operational needs, the windage of a sailing vessel is not extraordinary. The real issue is not whether relying on engines is reasonable, but whether the risks of the chosen approach to Padstow received proper consideration.

Equipment

The equipment aboard the *Maria Asumpta*, both navigational and otherwise, was scrutinized by the investigation as well as by the trial lawyers. The expert witness for the prosecution, Captain Frank Scott, raised the point that the master knowingly sailed with an uncorrected and defective steering compass and that comparisons with the standard compass were not a regular practice aboard ship. Also absent was the largest-scale chart available for the waters. A recent survey by the Marine Safety Agency resulted in a recommendation to obtain a hand bearing compass, though this had not been done. Scott also noted that the ship's radar was a relatively simple model lacking some more sophisticated capabilities available at the time, and that the ship did not possess an electronic position-fixing device such as a GPS or Decca, which was standard equipment in 1995—and not only for commercially certified vessels. The radio direction finder (RDF) aboard the ship would not have been useful for close-quarters coastal navigation.

Visual navigation with a lead line, a pair of binoculars, and tide tables is perfectly effective if it is applied methodically, as distinct from mere eyeballing. However, the *Maria Asumpta*'s suite of bridge equipment left something to be desired for a vessel of her capacity and complexity. Doubts concerning the compasses may illuminate the standards of maintenance and navigation practiced aboard, but the ship had sailed extensively around the coast of Britain and elsewhere in Europe for many years under the same management without mishap. British waters are challenging by any standard, so we have to question how defective the compasses could have been. Addressing the shortcomings of bridge equipment in the aftermath of a casualty so clearly linked to navigation is appropriate, but it seems unlikely that a lack of sophisticated equipment contributed materially to the loss of the vessel. Better equipment surely could have helped a navigator who more readily appreciated the unfolding situation. Yet, given what we know, it seems more likely that the overall approach to Padstow, not navigational imprecision, was the real problem. The master's testimony clearly establishes he was not lost: he had chosen to go there and he wanted to be there up until the time the engines failed. In his mind, and in the minds of his defenders, locating the ship so far inshore under the prevailing conditions was entirely seamanlike. Such a view of events leads us to consider that, although marginal equipment did not help matters, it was not the primary cause of the grounding.

A separate equipment issue is that life jackets were stowed below rather than in deck boxes where they could be readily accessed or float free. No order was given to retrieve them after the engines failed, and after the vessel grounded it probably seemed too risky to send someone below to get them. That Litchfield focused on sailing the ship out of danger, however futile, rather than ordering life jackets to the deck is hardly surprising. But his intervention would have been unnecessary if the life jackets had already been on deck. There, they would have provided an immediate alternative to the crew having to claw their way up the rocks amid a breaking swell and swirling wreckage, possibly preventing some of the drownings. As a private pleasure yacht, the *Maria Asumpta* was not required to stow the life jackets in float-free locations on deck. This aspect of the casualty suggests an inadequacy of the regulations pertaining to large pleasure yachts at the time, or the inappropriateness of that designation for the *Maria Asumpta*. In doing only what was required, the operators of the *Maria Asumpta* repeated one of the most regrettable errors of the *Pride of Baltimore* nine years earlier in respect to the stowage of lifesaving equipment. No captain really wants to have done the bare minimum, especially when the flexibility offered by a larger vessel allows for other options. Sometimes experience can point the way toward better methods without awaiting an official requirement. Clearly this is how the jury saw it in this case.

Qualifications

Mark Litchfield held a Royal Yachtmaster's Certificate for ocean operations. In recent decades this license had been considered appropriate for operating vessels such as the *Maria Asumpta* and was common aboard British sail training vessels. As we know, Litchfield sailed extensively aboard the *Marques* and on the *Maria Asumpta* through the Mediterranean, the North Sea, and British waters. He virtually circumnavigated South America on one voyage, and had sailed transatlantic. Notwithstanding the *Marques* disaster, for which Litchfield was not present, by the time the *Maria Asumpta* was lost he had been continuously involved in this sort of work for some twenty years. He knew his vessel intimately, having overseen all stages of her restoration, and he had sailed her in all manner of conditions.

The prosecution pointed out that Litchfield had never been examined on matters pertaining to square-riggers and had no formal square-rig qualifications. The reality is, however, that in Britain at the time, very few masters and mates operating square-rigged vessels had been examined in square-rig techniques. Although he had never been formally examined in square rig, Litchfield probably was more familiar with the *Maria Asumpta* than anyone else. His experience surely must have extended to the perils of tide, lee shore, and engine failure. It seems unlikely then that a lack of formal qualifications alone placed the *Maria Asumpta* in so vulnerable a position, especially since the master had so much to lose and so little to gain.

It is appropriate, however, to point out that since 1993 the Nautical Institute in London has offered a square-rig exam and certificate. The syllabus includes sailing vessel stability, knockdown tactics, passage planning, emergencies, maneuvering a square-rigged vessel, and lee shore considerations. In the first year these certificates were issued, the requirements exempted any master who had held command of a square-rigged vessel for at least two years; Litchfield would have met this criterion. Although this exam remains something of a novelty internationally ten years after its institution, it points the way for the future of traditional sailing qualifications. Even if the lack of formal credentials is of limited significance in the *Maria Asumpta*'s case, at least in Britain an effort is being made to establish meaningful standards of seamanship for traditional sailing vessels. The Nautical Institute's exam still has no equivalent in the United States.

Perhaps of greater relevance in the matter of manning and qualifications is the fact that Litchfield was in many respects on his own. There were people with some experience aboard, and people who knew the ship and knew him, but judging from the record there does not appear to have been a core of experienced people to effectively handle an emergency or materially aid the master once trouble started other than the engineer.

Because the vessel was not certified, there was no requirement for a higher level of expertise.

The lack of professional support is worth discussing in terms of the bridge team management. In his book, *Bridge Team Management*, Captain A. J. Swift specifically deals with the breakdown of situational awareness and the tendency to focus dangerously on one concern to the exclusion of all others. The phenomenon of "coning attention" under stress is well documented and is particularly relevant to this case. As the situation on the *Maria Asumpta* became critical, the master was increasingly alone, single-minded, and overburdened. Scott characterized Litchfield's assessment that "the last part was just a question of sailing and hoping for the best" as a classic case of tunnel vision under stress: "A system by which the master was doing all the navigation exposes him to the full force of the human error side of the 'error chain.' " This was inevitable once things began to unravel. As Swift points out, maritime incidents are seldom the result of a single event but are rather the culmination of a "series of non-serious incidents" forming a chain of errors. If decisive action is not taken to break the chain, the incident will fulfill its logical conclusion. Had another officer been intimately involved with the navigation, that person could have quickly laid out alternative courses of action for the master to consider or raised questions about the proposed passage plan from the beginning. Yet another officer could have directed the sail handling in which Litchfield became involved. A junior officer could have set about organizing an abandon-ship response, issued an immediate Mayday call rather than awaiting the grounding, or stood by the anchors. The lack of support of this type made a bad situation worse. The vessel was being sailed and commanded like the personal yacht it technically was, yet it was an extremely complex vessel to sail. The master sailed into the situation pretty well of his own accord, but part of the tragedy is that he took people with him. When the situation came apart, all the decision making for survival crashed down on the master at once. This is contrary to the tenets of modern seafaring, even when it involves a nineteenth-century sailing ship.

Alternatives After Engine Failure

During the afternoon as the vessel was closing with the shore, the *Maria Asumpta* could have put about onto the other tack at any time and stood out into more open water. This was not done, because there was no sense of danger. When the engines died, those aboard the *Maria Asumpta* still had escape options, though the tolerances of the situation were close. To the person in command, all options may have appeared equally perilous. The possible folly of standing on may have been matched in the mind of the master by the possible folly of abandoning the original plan. Some of these options stood a greater chance of succeeding than others. All were judgment calls and all involved a degree of preparation. What these alternatives also held in common is that by the time the master needed one, it was too late to adequately weigh any of them. Given human nature and the absence of time for due consideration, the decision to persist in a bad plan rather than latch onto another prospect is not surprising. It had become the easiest course of action. But what were Captain Litchfield's options?

ANCHORING

Among the charges leveled at Captain Litchfield was the failure to ready anchors and seriously consider using them. Though we will never know, given the swell, the rocky bottom, the windage of the rig, and the inability of the crew to strike sail before anchoring, any attempt to save the ship by anchoring was unlikely to succeed. Anchoring would have caused the big square sails to come aback, exerting tremendous drag on the ground tackle. The swell would then have lifted the bow, threatening to tear the anchor from any tenuous hold it may have found on the rocky bottom. Thus, attempting to turn head-to-wind and anchor after the engines died may well have been tantamount to surrendering the ship to the coast, though doing so may have bought time and thus saved lives. But, if lives had still been lost despite an anchoring attempt, the master might have stood accused of giving up too easily by not trying to sail the ship to safety. Throwing people into the surf while the ship dragged anchor toward shore might not have made for a strong case in a court of law, either. The fact that only the master can give the order to abandon ship recognizes that in an emergency the faint of heart may panic and abandon ship prematurely, to their own detriment. Perhaps Litchfield should have known his plan to sail clear would fail, but his effort to preserve the ship was rooted in a strong seafaring ethic that warns against leaving the ship before the ship leaves you: the preservation of the ship is often the best means of preserving those aboard it. That said, there is an adage just as old that a ship should never be driven ashore with her anchors still in her hawsepipes, and that is exactly where the divers found them.

SAIL CHOICES

In the analysis Captain Frank Scott provided to the prosecution, the time spent resetting the mainsail after the engine failed was wasted:

> Not only is the main course both partially blanketed by the spanker, but due to the inertia of the vessel at the early stages it will provide more turning moment than forward drive, thus actually degrading performance by giving more weather helm. A jib always performs better to windward. Had the outer

jib been available, that would have been a much better sail to set. By reducing weather helm it would improve boat speed much more quickly.

Scott did not advocate the decision to try to sail clear of Rumps Point, but his point concerns vessel performance and the need to expend effort wisely when time is of the essence. There is no evidence that the *Maria Asumpta* suffered especially from weather helm, but the outer jib was not available and was certainly not ready to use.

TACKING OUT TO SEA

The *Summary Report* offered up the possibility that if the ship had been immediately thrown onto the other tack at the time of engine failure, she may have had enough momentum to complete the maneuver. This is speculative, since the swell may have been big enough and the wind light enough to stymie any such effort. The *Maria Asumpta* was not known for her litheness in tacking even under the best conditions. The report acknowledged that success in this effort would have involved having people prepositioned to handle the lines. This was not done because the possibility of a close-quarters engine failure had not been considered in advance.

JIBING INTO PORT QUIN BAY

An estimate in the *Summary Report* that at the time of engine failure the ship had just passed the Mouls at 0.15 mile (see chart) suggests that the *Maria Asumpta* might have successfully jibed into the gap between the Mouls and Rumps Point and entered the small Port Quin Bay. This would have required a radical decision, however. As with other alternatives, success depended at least partly on people being at sailing stations as the vessel entered confined waters. If the levels of skill and manning aboard were insufficient to execute such a maneuver, that is all the more reason the ship should have been nowhere near the Mouls. Scott was of the opinion that even if the crew was not prepared, immediate action may well have resulted in success despite being "a most untidy maneuver, not in the textbooks." One reason for this optimism is that the same current that was impeding progress on the starboard tack would have been favorable on the port tack and thus may have helped sluice the vessel through the gap between the Mouls and the mainland.

Once she was in Port Quin Bay, the prospects for preserving the ship and those aboard would have improved significantly. The anchoring situation would have been better because the water was half as deep and partially protected from the swell that might have dislodged the anchor or parted the cable in the open waters west of Rumps Point. Nor would the vessel's options in the bay have been limited to anchoring. With a northwest breeze, the vessel should have been able to sail clear of Kellan Head to the east and gain open water. All of this would have bought time for the engineers to diagnose the problem and to hail assistance. This is in stark contrast to the course of action chosen, for even if the *Maria Asumpta* had been lucky enough to clear Rumps Point, she was still hard on a lee shore and exposed to the hazards of the next headland, Pentire Point (see chart). Clearing Rumps Point may have bought time, but even if successfully executed it remained a dubious escape route.

MAYDAY

A Mayday call and an abandon-ship response were options (as opposed to alternative courses of action) that would likely have preserved more lives if done sooner rather than later. Undoubtedly the delay was due to the master's fixation on sailing clear and to the lack of a bridge team to support him. Once the engines died, grave and imminent danger to life existed. If a master does not want to call for assistance on the off-chance assistance is not needed (a potential source of unwanted attention and embarrassment), then the solution is to navigate in a way that minimizes such risk. If a vessel finds itself *in extremis* for reasons beyond the master's control, then there should be no hesitation to issue a Mayday that, with luck, may prove to be unneeded.

Much about this case shows how little can be accomplished when the unexpected occurs and the master has not taken the unexpected into account. Only forethought to the possibility of engine failure coupled with an early recognition of the forces working against the ship would have caused any of the options above to crystallize in the mind of a master. Since forethought is the most critical quality a master exercises in the command of a ship, this is not considered a superhuman attribute. Engine failure may have come as a surprise that day, yet every mariner should know that engine failure is a matter of *when*, not *if*.

The Approach

Of all of the unforeseen contingencies of engine failure, tidal set, swell, and faint breeze, none was so completely in the control of the master nor so disastrous as the choice of approach. By choosing a sailing route that depended upon ideal circumstances, the captain assisted the normal uncertainties of the sea in laying hold of the *Maria Asumpta* and dashing her onto the rocks. A route that passed well to seaward of the hazards that restricted the master's options would have canceled out all the other difficulties experienced that day. Engine failure may still have occurred while the ship was entering Padstow Harbour, but navigationally this would have been defensible, for to enter any harbor a vessel must approach the hazards of the shore. Not so off Rumps Point. Although disputed by the master's defenders, the choice of approach is plainly the most inescapable mistake of all: the ship simply did not have to be where she was to get where she was going. The approach was, however, dramatic and aesthetically satisfying to those watching from shore, at least until it went wrong.

The approach was *feasible*. The water was deep enough, there were good radar targets and plenty of bearings, and the visibility was fine. Litchfield had passed that way before. There was an unmarked hazard in the form of Roscarrock, but a careful navigation plan should have been able to keep the vessel clear of that under the right conditions and with someone monitoring the radar. The real question is whether the approach was *wise*. With the wind in a more forgiving quadrant, a different state of tide, or with engines running flawlessly, the master might well have pulled it off. In doing so the crew would have admired their skipper's daring and skill, creating further confidence in his abilities. But the conditions were *not* favorable for a daring approach, and he did not pull it off. In light of this, Litchfield's approach to Padstow can now only be viewed as foolhardy.

The error chain that led to the wreck started almost four hours before the grounding when a decision was made at about 1220 to stand in toward Tintagel to view the coast and avoid the strength of the flood tide. This desire to avoid the flood tide is somewhat contradicted by the later decision to reduce sail on account of the ship being ahead of schedule. In any event, standing into the large open bay between Hartland Point to the northeast and Rumps Point to the southwest amounted to throwing away the weather gauge, or the advantage of being to windward of any point of interest. Although this decision may not have been especially risky in and of itself, it was the beginning of a dalliance with a lee shore over which the master ultimately lost control.

The second stage came with a delay in executing the planned course change once abeam Tintagel. The dogleg into Tintagel reduced some of the master's flexibility by requiring a 30-degree course change toward the wind to achieve the intended clearance at the Mouls. But by delaying the course change off Tintagel, the ship ended up to leeward of her intended track line, which, considering the windward sailing limitations of the vessel, was perhaps already overly bold. This action put the vessel hard on the wind on a lee shore for the final leg and "voluntarily embayed" her. One by one, events eroded the master's flexibility.

None of this would have mattered much if the master had appreciated that his options to improve the ship's position were slipping away, thus prompting him to action. Improving the vessel's position may have involved

clewing up the square sails and aggressively motoring back up to the original rhumb line. This is never a welcome prospect when enjoying such a
pleasant sail, but in view of the outcome, such action doesn't seem so bad.
By the time the ship passed Tintagel, the current had silently joined the fray
and was nudging the ship shoreward.

All navigators encounter unexpected currents and wind shifts near shore.
Whatever the tidal stream in more open waters, it can be expected to intensify or flag or deviate unpredictably around headlands and isolated rocks.
The Bristol Channel is renowned for its extreme tides. The slot between the
Mouls and Rumps Point would seem a particularly likely place for the tidal
current to intensify. Such variables are among the best reasons for not taking a close-hauled square-rigger that can't tack in a light breeze to within
two-tenths of a mile of a rocky lee shore that faces the open ocean. Likewise, winds are known to shift, die, and intensify in the vicinity of headlands, none of which bodes well for such an adventure even with engines.

In trying to understand how an experienced master comes to lose his
ship in fine weather and broad daylight, the *Summary Report* pointed out
that no clear, single navigational plan was being methodically implemented. This is quite typical of pleasure craft out for an afternoon jaunt,
but one would expect more of a vessel such as the *Maria Asumpta*, despite
her pleasure craft status. In addition to the absence of a sound navigational
plan, it would appear that insufficient attention was given to the dangers of
a lee shore and embayment. A lee shore is a known enemy of sailing vessels
in particular, because they do not always have the ability to drive offshore
against the wind. A variation on the same theme is *embayment*, which
occurs when a sailing ship is caught between two points of land and does
not have the windward capability to sail clear of either one. She may tack
or wear back and forth across the body of water but is gradually driven
shoreward unless she can anchor or make use of a wind shift. The Bay of
Biscay is perhaps the most notorious place for sailing ships to suffer
embayment. Even today sailing ships and yachts transiting from northern
to southern Europe depart from as far west as possible, usually Cornwall
or Ireland, even if they have engines. The case of the *Maria Asumpta*
vividly illustrates the utility of making navigation plans with the "sail-
only" capabilities of the vessel in mind.

Also weighing against the master in the hearings was that the planned
approach into Padstow, between Newland and Pentire Point, was not recognized by the Coast Pilot books. This is the least of the reasons that the
ship should not have been so far inshore. Written with merchant shipping in
mind, the Coast Pilots take very little account of the options available to a
small ship like the *Maria Asumpta*. Nevertheless, the obviously prudent

course involved passing to seaward of all hazards, including Newland. Standard rules of navigation call for an even wider margin for unmarked dangers, and, as Scott pointed out, "into this category very much falls Roscarrock." He echoed the sentiments of several sailing masters when he added, "Even with an ideal wind, I would still regard passing between Newlands and Pentire Point as something to reserve for unforeseen emergencies." The approach was feasible but risky.

The decision to continue on the starboard tack when closing with the Mouls sealed the fate of the *Maria Asumpta*. It placed the master in the position of having to make a high-stakes, all-or-nothing gamble when the engines failed. Photographs show that as the vessel reached its closest point of approach to the shore, she was passing through waters white with foam from the backwash off the cliffs. This was the point at which Litchfield thought they were "going to make it." Such hopefulness defied reality, but by that time he could trust only luck, as the full benefit of good seamanship was no longer available to him. In hindsight it may seem harsh to condemn Litchfield's fixation with sailing clear in a situation that called for radical and risky action. Would other captains really have done things differently? How would the dodge into Port Quin Bay have appeared from the deck of the *Maria Asumpta*? It seems likely that only the skipper who had carefully considered the risks and the options in advance would have had any chance of bailing out, but a skipper who gave such thorough consideration to the risks probably would have concluded that a different route had greater merit. Once the ship was *in extremis*, Litchfield's burden of decision was heavy and unenviable, but it arose from a plan of action that tempted fate in the first place.

REPERCUSSIONS

Litchfield's pursuit of certification for the *Maria Asumpta* under the Code of Practice for Small Commercial Sailing Vessels was fairly advanced by May 1995, though we do not know the extent to which outstanding issues identified by the authorities may have contributed to the casualty. If the loss of the *Marques*, having been recently certified through a flawed process, was a regulator's worst nightmare, then the *Maria Asumpta* must constitute a regulator's closest call. Had the *Maria Asumpta* attained certification and *then* been lost, the repercussions would have been quite different. As it was, official repercussions were minimal. As with the *Pride*, it could be argued that regulation had effectively separated a higher-risk vessel from the lower-risk vessels, though in this case it may not have been by much.

The stated purpose of the *Summary Report* was to contribute to safety at sea, not establish fault, blame, or liability. Yet it is perhaps telling that none of its conclusions identified a universal hazard or a general area for policy reform. Instead, the preponderance of the *Summary Report*'s conclusions pointed toward a lack of prudence and seamanlike procedure on the part of the master. In consequence, no sweeping regulatory reforms emanated from this case, despite its notoriety in the British media and the extent to which the story captured the public imagination. No doubt the compelling photographic record was instrumental in raising public awareness. One obvious repercussion was the criminal proceeding brought against the master, and this alone generated food for thought for the professional sailor. The case also highlights the ramifications of using pleasure yachts for activities that resemble sail training on traditional sailing vessels, the role of engineering in a field that historically emphasizes sailing knowledge, and the dilemma of balancing the public's desire to see tall ships under sail against the risks of carrying sail in close quarters.

Criminal Court Decision

The *Maria Asumpta* is singular among the cases in this book in that the master faced criminal charges. The prosecution was successful in its characterization of Litchfield's approach to Padstow:

> He did this to admire the coastline, let those on the cliffs admire the *Maria Asumpta* and to use up some time as they were ahead of schedule. In doing so, he put the vessel on a lee shore thereby breaking two golden rules of sailing— always maintaining a good distance from land and never getting caught on a lee shore.

Litchfield was convicted, though the decision was appealed on the grounds that in a strict legal sense the jury strayed from the judge's instructions. The judge had set a specific threshold for conviction, explaining to the jury that they could not find Litchfield guilty unless they were satisfied with the following:

1. The fuel was contaminated and the master knew it.

2. The engines failed due to contaminated fuel.

3. The master chose a route knowing that he might have to rely upon his engines.

4. The chosen approach to Padstow was inherently dangerous and constituted an obvious and serious risk of death.

Clearly, the threshold established by the judge called for some fairly positive causal connections, yet much of the evidence seemed to only partially fulfill the requirements for conviction. Nevertheless, Litchfield's appeal failed and the conviction stood.

In his summation, Judge Butterworth addressed Litchfield directly, recalling the conclusions of the jury:

> The three members of the crew who died, like the rest of the crew, showed you loyalty and devotion, and served you without reward and reposed in you their absolute trust and confidence. On the verdict of this jury you betrayed that trust by showing contempt for the very dangers they trusted you to avoid. The jury found you had a profound disregard for the lives of the crew and were reckless in your navigation and management.

The judge also addressed the fuel issue, as well as the warning from the Padstow harbormaster:

> You chose to conduct yourself as you did in the face of clear warnings of the consequences in respect of the fuel used and the course sailed. This was therefore no momentary aberration but a deliberately chosen course of conduct condemned by the jury as grossly negligent.

Despite an approach that unduly exposed the ship to bad luck and seamanship of a last-ditch order, the notion that the master intentionally undertook to lose lives does not seem reasonable. Nevertheless, the conviction stands as a fencepost in the long meandering line of maritime litigation. Seldom has that line approached traditional sail operations, but this time it did, and sailors ignore that fact at their own peril.

Pleasure Yachts and the Artful Dodge

By tradition and definition, pleasure yachts constitute an area of maritime activity that functions on a relatively laissez-faire basis. Recreational boating is minimally regulated compared with other maritime activities. Recreational boaters, unlike fare-paying passengers, are understood to be willing to accept a greater degree of risk in the exercise of their unsupervised free will. This arrangement largely suits all parties involved. The authorities charged with enforcement generally lack the resources to develop and enforce stricter regulations for such a widely divergent category of vessels and purposes. Likewise, since their activities are purely recreational, boatowners are generally unwilling to bear the additional costs and hassles that come with more rigorous standards. Unlike commercial shipping, if pleasure boating is made too costly, pleasure boaters can simply choose another outlet for their disposable income—with repercussions for the whole boating industry.

Problems with this historical arrangement become evident when a casualty involves a private pleasure yacht with a program of carrying people to sea in a traineelike capacity on the scale seen with the *Maria Asumpta*. The people aboard on the day of the casualty were not regarded as passengers or trainees in a regulatory sense because they did not pay. But it is obvious that neither they nor the twenty-four students who disembarked at Swansea were the personal guests of the owner, either. Sailing privileges were accessed through a membership arrangement that was advertised in the organization's publicity literature. Anyone could join.

The advantage of the arrangement was that it enabled a remarkable and historical vessel to stay active while providing a valuable experience to those who were interested. The open-access membership arrangement made it possible to tap into the support of those who wished to be involved without incurring the substantial expenses associated with commercially certificated sail training or passenger vessels. The downside of the situation was that, in the event of a casualty, a large number of inexperienced people would be exposed to dangers that the vessel was ill-prepared to cope with compared with certified vessels of a similar size and type. This issue could arise with any vessel, but old sailing ships have a unique, spellbinding appeal to the public. The restoration and maintenance of a vessel like the *Maria Asumpta* is sustained by the allure of ultimately taking the vessel to sea and spreading the canvas before a fair breeze. This was the tacit underpinning of participation. This unique expression of enthusiasm is not a thing to discourage, but the abiding allure highlights the lack of objectivity that can sometimes accompany beautiful old ships and their saviors.

Iron Topsail

We have already considered how a professional officer structure on the *Maria Asumpta* could have provided a level of bridge team and deck support that may have led to a different outcome. However, we have not discussed the role of engineering expertise and maintenance aboard traditional sailing vessels, of interest here because the proximate cause of the casualty was engine failure.

The designated engineer aboard the *Maria Asumpta* at the time had mere moments to discover and rectify the cause of engine failure, so it is entirely possible that the most highly trained professional marine engineer would have had no more success in the time the navigational choices allowed. Of greater interest than that individual's response is the role of engineering expertise aboard latter-day sailing ships in general. Since the 1950s, the beginning of the renaissance of traditional sail, most tall ships have had engines. Now they have increasingly complex engine rooms as compared with the mom-and-pop schooners and brigantines of the 1960s and 1970s. Many of the traditional sailing vessels coming on line in the last two decades of the twentieth century have twin propulsion units, multiple generators, bow-thrusters, watermakers, holding tanks, and various pumping systems. More elaborate plumbing and electrical systems reflect the desire for greater comfort for trainees, passengers, and guests and the need to support more sophisticated navigational suites, communications equipment, computers, and other recently invented necessities. Engine failure can occur with dire consequences on all types of vessels, but the auxiliary nature of engine systems on sailing ships imbues them with a peculiar, ugly-duckling status within the tall-ship community that can result in a lack of appreciation for their essential safety role. On many smaller vessels, including many certified sailing vessels of the *Maria Asumpta*'s size, licensing structures do not address engineering qualifications at all. Engineering duties are often carried out by a mate, the master, or a crew member who has other responsibilities on deck. This system can be successful where the plant is simple and when maintenance and operating practices allow for the inconsistency of expertise aboard. But traditional sailing vessels are not necessarily low-tech anymore, and the engineering expertise carried aboard them needs to reflect that.

The culture of traditional sail quite naturally places a special emphasis on knowledge of the rig and the sails: the sails and the rigging form the most visible and compelling aspects of traditional sail that distinguish it from other forms of seafaring. It is inevitable that those who choose a career in sail should be drawn to the skills and techniques that relate to the handling of sails and rigging, and they correctly regard this as an essential body of knowledge for mastery. Formal qualifications aside, the extent to which a sailor has mastered these skills and techniques essentially determines the speed with which a person moves up the ranks and into positions of responsibility. Once in these positions of responsibility, it is very difficult to get exposure to engine room systems in the same bottom-up manner that was experienced on deck. As a result, it is possible for the accomplished traditional sailor to be weak in the engineering skills vital to the safety of the ship. Where the manning structures provide for qualified engineers who can offset the lack of expertise in the deck department, this does not present a problem. But on smaller ships where specialization is not reflected in manning requirements, a lack of engineering knowledge among officers can be a handicap. The loss of the *Maria Asumpta* underscores the fallacy of viewing the engine as a secondary means of propulsion aboard sailing ships.

Although amateur marine engineers and volunteers with mechanical backgrounds can render invaluable service, the opinion of a licensed engineer in matters of fuel quality or general readiness for sea carries a different weight with the master and the owner. For one, the engineer's license represents a means of livelihood and a measure of legal responsibility that is independent of a given employment situation. Similarly, the recommendations of a licensed engineer carry a credibility that a master is unlikely to disregard because to do so would expose his own license in the event of an accident. In the case of the *Maria Asumpta*, had a licensed engineer insisted on disposal of the fuel or testing by a qualified professional expert, even if it did not prevent engine failure, it would have decisively eliminated the issue from debate. As it was, the master not only had to explain his navigational choices, but he had to explain what was all too easily portrayed as "an almost inconceivable neglect of duty" in the matter of the fuel. The question for the tall-ship industry is whether it will anticipate the need for qualified engineers aboard small sail training vessels, or will it wait until change is brought about by some other avenue, perhaps with unwelcome ramifications for the larger enterprise.

The Public Eye: Grandstanding Under Sail

The loss of the *Maria Asumpta* was technically no different from the loss of any other vessel that loses power and drifts ashore. But one element of this casualty broaches a question concerning the point at which satisfying the public's desire to see ships under sail can be portrayed as cavalier and irresponsible. Most skippers and crews enjoy the thrill of sailing their large, demanding ships in challenging situations of their own choosing. Whether it is beating up a channel, tacking through islands, sailing on or off a dock, or entering a harbor filled with welcoming spectators, performing these feats is part of what reinforces the knowledge and the skills necessary to operate these ships. But even if this were not the case, there is much about today's tall-ship culture that encourages showing off or "grandstanding" under sail. With cameras and spectators on the cliff above, the *Maria Asumpta* was indulging the public's fascination when trouble started. It was also an opportunity to garner publicity for herself and the larger proposition of traditional sailing. In seizing that opportunity at a particularly exposed time and place, the master's plan backfired horrifically. Nevertheless, in other situations, traditional sailing vessels are virtually required to court the public eye by carrying canvas into close quarters so the spectacle can be viewed from shore. Grandstanding is widely understood to be an effective public-relations tool, and it is not confined to large organized events, though these are the best examples. The sponsors of tallship events expect something for their money, which often takes the form of a "parade of sail." No captain who has participated in such an event has failed to marvel at the unnaturalness of attempting to make a diverse fleet of sailing ships proceed in lockstep fashion under maximum sail with the engines whining away below and the wind in exactly the wrong direction, causing all the sails to flog or go aback. On other occasions a fair wind causes faster vessels to overtake slower ones, forcing the skipper to sail along with engines in reverse or sails deliberately backed. Captains know, however, this is part of their job. Aside from any other virtues these ships may confer, sailing ships continue to exist because, unlike any old boat, they are breathtaking under sail. Publicity sailing provides immense satisfaction to those who do not get to go sailing themselves, and this, in turn, can help create a constituency for the ships and the activities they pursue during the rest of the year.

An obvious consequence of this relationship with the public is that traditional sailing vessels are called upon to carry canvas into awkward situations that would not normally occur and would not have occurred at all in the age of commercial sail. Certainly, sailing ships of old coped with far greater difficulties, but they also operated under a different standard. Despite the sound rules of good seamanship that dictate using margins of error based on "sail only," the reliance upon auxiliary power to control these parades of sail and other sorts of sailing public relations events is unavoidable. Should an engine fail, things could quickly get out of hand. This is particularly true given that many nonsailing vessels do not appreciate the maneuvering restrictions of large sailing vessels and do not always accord a safe distance. Where does this leave the modern sailing ship captain?

In a sense, concern over grandstanding under sail is taking the lessons of the *Maria Asumpta* to the extreme. After all, tall-ships events have a good record for safety. In recent years such things have become increasingly well organized as experience, both good and bad, is gained. Parades of sail are usually planned for open, well-marked harbors. Masters try to sail in a manner commensurate with the navigational circumstances, but the expectation is to put on a show. In the criminal trial of Captain Litchfield, he was specifically castigated by the prosecution for what amounted to showing off. In light of the legal outcome, masters-in-sail must consider the possibility that, in the event of an accident, grandstanding under sail may be portrayed by a lawyer as negligent and cavalier.

LOOSE ENDS

In one sense, the finding of individual negligence in this case squelched any need for a regulatory response to this casualty. Pilot error is the one contingency that can never be regulated away. Licenses, equipment, and inspections establish a certain baseline of safety, but they cannot inoculate against miscalculation, carelessness, or bad luck. But in another sense, the finding of individual fault conveniently displaces any burden to look further, and regulatory agencies do not generally seek new assignments. If there were to be a policy response, one would expect it to involve a closer look at membership arrangements that facilitate large numbers of inexperienced people going to sea in a vessel that meets standards truly intended for private pleasure boating.

The master of the *Maria Asumpta* was found to have "unnecessarily subjected his crew to a recognized risk of the vessel grounding in the event of engine failure." One of the reasons the ship was so close to shore was to "let those on the cliffs admire the *Maria Asumpta*." Carrying sail into close quarters for the benefit of spectators is a reality of modern tall-ship operations not likely to change. The professional sailor's crucial lesson from this case is, if you get into trouble—whether due to engine failure or some other cause—you jolly well better have your ship where it's supposed to be when the trouble starts. By a different token, it would be false to equate a cautious captain with a competent one. Caution is often a trademark of inexperience, and appropriately so, but ultimately command calls for a certain boldness when meeting the less-subtle challenges posed by the sea.

A tandem concern in this case is the emergence of a notion that it is somehow more negligent for a sailing ship master to rely upon his engines than for the master of a power-driven vessel to do so. Although Litchfield indisputably exposed his vessel to unnecessary danger, the idea that reliance upon engines is somehow less defensible for an auxiliary-powered sailing ship than for a power vessel is completely disconnected from everyday maritime experience. Be that as it may, in terms of vessel handling, the case reminds mariners that auxiliary power aboard a traditional sailing vessel has not eliminated the ancient perils of the lee shore and embayment.

Finally, the loss of the *Maria Asumpta* due to engine failure gives us cause to consider the role of marine engineering aboard traditionally rigged sailing vessels. The specialized knowledge in which traditional sailors are immersed may leave them less familiar with engineering systems than their counterparts aboard similar-sized power vessels. This is an acceptable situation as long as they are backed up by expertise appropriate to the vessel's complexity and activities. If not, then this situation represents a weak link in any tall ship's operations.

Watch Below

All shipmasters constantly operate between the twin demands of having every aspect of their ship in perfect readiness for a worst-case scenario, and carrying out the ship's mission in a timely fashion. Masters who go to sea routinely make judgments regarding the risk and benefits of operating under less-than-perfect circumstances because less-than-perfect circumstances characterize life at sea. Although regulations endeavor to insulate certain operational elements from the judgment of mere mortals, the dilemma remains and was very much in evidence in the *Maria Asumpta* case.

The anatomy of this casualty is largely built around negligence and liability. Every time a ship puts to sea, it enters a realm of heightened risk from which it may not return. In this case, an accident report, a qualified expert witness, and a jury all condemned the master's judgment in the execution of his duties. Litchfield had hope of clearing the rocks, but it was a hairsplitting judgment that cost three lives. Such judgments can be defended when all precautions have been taken and no other options exist. On the basis of this outcome, when precautions have not been taken and options do exist, a shipmaster—even the master of a beautiful and historic tall ship—can expect to twist in the wind.

CONCLUSION
Paying Off

IF THERE IS a common theme in these stories, it may be that for all that was done right—and in every case much was done right—the sea found the weak point. Another common element is that the vulnerabilities of these ships were understood at some level before their loss, but for various reasons that knowledge was not brought to bear. Such disconnects are with us still. A corollary observation is that official reform is seldom proactive and is usually a step or two behind a recognized need. Standards of acceptable risk change. Casualties provide the impetus. Staying ahead of that curve is preferable to being caught behind it. It is worth noting, too, that all five of these incidents sent ripple effects radiating far beyond the immediate ships, individuals, and organizations involved.

All our interactions with the sea are governed, it seems, by risks that are never entirely knowable yet never completely beyond our control. In any kind of toe-to-toe confrontation, the sea always wins because it is so strong. But what really constitutes an act of God, and what do people mean when they call something "bad luck"? Although the sea can be godlike in its fury and its fickleness, chalking these incidents up to acts of God is tantamount to surrendering our God-given capacity to be better prepared for the next encounter—a capacity that has already saved countless ships and lives that might otherwise have been lost.

If nothing else, dismissing the incidents in this book as acts of God contradicts our infatuation with technology and our persistent efforts to outfox nature at every conceivable juncture, even in tall ships. That we go to sea at all suggests an enduring confidence and a willingness to face nature on the assumption that we will succeed despite the well-known hazards. Why should that posture be abruptly abandoned when nature pulls down one of our brave experiments? The sea will continue to take ships and lives, but remedies for many of the problems that these five ships encountered are within reach. We must first, however, admit that we can do better, though such admissions are rarely easy. Addressing a problem also involves looking in more than one direction, since fatal flaws are seldom simplistic. There are many ways to look at this legacy, but for our purposes it can be broken down to the sea, the ship, and the sailor, though in reality these are interwoven.

The *Star of India* in a quartering breeze. (Corbis)

THE SEA

The sea is as inherently dangerous now as it was in the days when square-riggers were an ordinary sight. The weather, the remoteness, and the unforgiving shore all figure in these five stories. But when a vessel succumbs to these perils, it is not always a reflection on the sea alone. Rather, if a vessel has a flaw, the sea is well capable of finding it out. Flaws may be found in the ship, the gear, the crew, the leadership, and of course, the organization behind it all.

In voyaging under sail, one must accept the risk of being caught with too much sail. But behind that risk lies another: some ships are more likely than others to get knocked down and not come up. Four of the five casualties examined here were precipitated by extreme weather, and three were nearly instantaneous. The publicity surrounding the one-two punch of the *Marques* and the *Pride of Baltimore* did much to introduce the terms *microburst* and *downburst* into the lexicon of all mariners, not only tall-ship sailors. These two casualties, along with the *Albatross*, confirm the words of the *Marques* report that described a microburst as "a known phenomenon that cannot be dismissed as a freak wind." This is the only sensible interpretation of these events. However violent and destructive these weather phenomena are, to construe them over and over again as the work of the Almighty is counterproductive. Such fatalism may be primal and comforting in the wake of such an overwhelming force, but it can also be dangerous, because when the fear wears off and the facts of the incident are forgotten, we are left as exposed as we ever were. When one looks at today's fleet of traditional sailing vessels, it is clear that these incidents have not been treated as "freak winds." Standards that help sailing vessels cope with extreme experiences now exist where once they did not. Even where compliance with standards is not required, they show the way to achieve a minimum level of seaworthiness. In some instances these standards have reapplied centuries-old principles, whereas in others new research led to fresh treatment of old problems. Where useful standards already existed, they have been justified in the interest of greater safety and updated accordingly. Embracing these standards, however imperfect they may be, has proved to be one of the best ways to even the odds with the sea while advancing the ideals associated with traditional sail. The evidence suggests that the tall-ship industry has not treated violent weather as an angry god, but rather as a fact of life that needs to be anticipated.

Weather prediction continues to improve, particularly for large storm systems. Technology has enhanced the sailor's ability to access weather information at sea. Even so, the unpredictability of a late-season hurricane was amply demonstrated in 1998, when Hurricane Mitch swallowed up the four-masted schooner *Fantome* and her crew of thirty-one in the Gulf of Honduras. Hurricane Mitch was indeed an extraordinary force to reckon with, but even this incident cannot be entirely dismissed as an act of God. The low-powered *Fantome* left port in the face of a category 5 hurricane with minimal sea room to spare in a season when hurricanes are notoriously erratic. The strategy offered little margin for error and backfired when the hurricane refused to be bound by predictions that involved truly significant (and announced) margins of error.

The growth of commercial weather routing services that tailor their counsel to the capabilities of a given vessel has placed another new tool in the hands of sailors. In October of 1998, however, the *Pride of Baltimore II* encountered a hurricane off the west coast of Mexico that neither a commercial weather routing company nor government sources had detected. Only through *Pride II*'s participation in a voluntary weather reporting program was the hurricane "discovered," named, and tracked. In the case of microbursts, their highly localized and transitory character means that adequate warning remains elusive. The potential for a cold front to intensify from, say, 35 knots to 70 knots undetected also remains a fixture of offshore weather where observations are sparse. Waterspouts, extreme convection cells, and other intense wind events round out the experience.

These five cases are important not only because ships were lost but because lives were lost, as well. The survivability of survival equipment emerged as an important issue. The *Pamir* faced the age-old conundrum of how to launch lifeboats in horrific weather, when they are often most needed. The incredible speed with which several other situations deteriorated demonstrated the value of equipment that deploys automatically when a rehearsed response is impossible to execute. Whether technologically oriented, such as a life raft on a hydrostatic release, or as crude as a plywood box full of life jackets stowed on deck with a loose-fitting lid, self-deploying emergency equipment mattered to the outcome in these cases. So did its absence. Expensive suits of personal safety gear went to the bottom with the *Pride of Baltimore*, *Marques*, and *Maria Asumpta*. One member of the *Albatross* was thought to have been lost trying to free the lifeboats, though that was in days before hydrostatic release mechanisms. The presence of equipment that was commonly available but not required also mattered, as with the life rafts aboard the *Pride of Baltimore*. Whether it was the location of equipment, or the equipment itself, these stories are a powerful lens through which to look beyond what is required and to focus on what is needed.

THE SHIP

Although structural failure features prominently in the rolls of maritime disaster, it never emerged as a root cause in these incidents despite extreme weather and the advanced age of most of the vessels involved. The *Pamir* is the only possible exception. Other components of seaworthiness loomed large in the three knockdown cases, however, and to some extent with the *Pamir*: downflooding, watertight subdivision, and stability.

Clearly, preventing downflooding is essential. As long as water is kept out, a vessel will float, but once downflooding begins, the theoretical stability of the vessel goes out the window. The risk of downflooding depends in large measure on the size, position, and closure arrangement of hatches and vents. Since hatches are a necessity, information gained from past casualties is useful in designing them. Sailing along in unsettled weather with open hatches exposes a vessel to flooding in the event of a knockdown. This is a slim but real possibility that must be weighed against the comfort of those below, particularly in hot climates. A crew well acquainted with these stories will better understand the need to act decisively. It is also apparent from the *Marques* and the *Pride of Baltimore* cases that traditional cargo hatches on sailing ships that carry people in what used to be the hold can be deadly in the event of a knockdown. Too much water gets in if the hatch is not sealed, and too few people can get out if it is. That is a lose-lose situation on any seagoing vessel, regardless of certification. Such arrangements are one aspect of historical authenticity that belong in the past, and regulations for certified vessels have largely seen to this.

Watertight bulkheads are a long-recognized safety feature but were absent in the knockdown cases for various reasons. For one, they add to construction costs and are even more costly when retrofitted. Where authenticity is a priority, subdivision may present a conflict. Ironically, the authentic North Sea pilot schooner *Albatross*, built in 1921, had watertight bulkheads from the beginning because heavy weather and chance of collision were foreseen to be facts of life. Forty years later, the doors in those bulkheads were left open to the sea and she flooded. The knockdown cases demonstrate that weather can develop too quickly—as can collisions—to reestablish watertight integrity once it is compromised.

The renaissance of traditional sail has been profoundly influenced on the issue of stability through these cases, particularly the *Albatross* and the *Marques*. Uninformed modifications proved deadly, and past performance was an unworthy indicator of the future. Though the principles now enshrined in regulation were understood in the nineteenth century, "a sort of amnesia concerning previous developments" took root. Knowledge of the utmost relevance to the renaissance of traditional sail fell into disuse in many quarters until tragedy prompted its revival. One upshot is that a theoretical range of positive stability to 90 degrees has become a standard for certified sailing vessels in the United States, Britain, and many countries. Research on wind heeling moments that has emerged since the stability casualties in this book shows that a vessel with a righting arm even slightly less than 90 degrees may have an "effective stability" that is significantly less. It is worth noting that nonstatutory stability standards for high-tech ocean racing vessels now exceed 90 degrees by considerable margins. We also know that the *Albatross* was originally designed with a righting arm to 110 degrees because it seemed like a good idea to her builders and it was attainable. The 90-degree standard does not guarantee the survival of a ship any more than any single aspect of seaworthiness does. However, the creation of a robust stability criterion has been a major step forward for traditional sail in the modern era.

The pursuit of seaworthiness is not only costly, but usually results in inconvenience for those aboard. Hatches that resist downflooding typically allow less ventilation and light below because they are smaller. The higher sills impede entrance and egress. Even in 30-foot seas and winds topping 50 knots, water on deck may come nowhere near sloshing below, making high sills seem excessively conservative. Watertight bulkheads, too, are inconvenient. Yet, if all the hatches are left open and a vessel is knocked down, she may still flood and sink even if she has watertight bulkheads, so why all the fuss about them? Watertight bulkheads require going up and down companionway ladders to access other parts of the ship, inviting many slips and falls. Heavy steel watertight doors clang obnoxiously with every use and can cause injury if they get away from a crew member. Leaving the doors open at sea makes life infinitely easier, but it disables the bulkheads in their purpose. Watertight subdivision also restricts ventilation, which can contribute to rot aboard a wooden vessel, but a rotfree hull that floods in a heartbeat is a trade-off of dubious value. Obtaining a higher order of stability also drives many design features that may not be desirable from other standpoints. Higher freeboard enhances stability but may detract from aesthetics. Locating weight down low can make a vessel more stable but also stiffer, resulting in an unpleasant motion at sea. A sailing rig may be shorter or less versatile than one would like, or than would be historically accurate, resulting in slower light-air passages. Similarly, if gun-ports are designed to function as freeing ports, leaving them open at sea may result in a wetter deck; there is the additional issue of protecting the doors themselves. But the alternative, securing them shut, is like boarding up a fire escape in order to stop an annoying draft. The fact that these stratagems all entail sacrifices simply demonstrates that the quest for seaworthiness is often a matter of choosing a proven lesser evil over a proven greater evil. Features that enhance seaworthiness may present a daily inconvenience, but that is not the basis for judging their utility. They exist for what may be a once-in-a-lifetime challenge to the very existence of the vessel by an overwhelming force of nature. Habits and precautions instilled beforehand may well determine the outcome.

Watertight integrity, subdivision, and stability are only parts of the seaworthiness puzzle, but these cases make clear that a sailing vessel without them is at a grave disadvantage. If the *Marques* were still sailing as an oceangoing training ship, she would now be required to have all the features discussed above. Because she was uninspected, the *Pride of Baltimore* would still not be required to have them for the operations in which she was engaged, but the *Pride of Baltimore II* has them, anyway. The *Albatross* originally had all of these benefits, but they were compromised over time as their significance went unappreciated. Her surviving sister ship, however, met the more advanced standards and still sails.

The issue of historical authenticity is never far away in the world of traditional sail. These five incidents have not, and should not, be the justification for extinguishing an active sailing role for replicas and historic vessels. Rather, they should contribute to an awareness of limitations. This boils down to not asking more of a vessel than she can deliver, and this is not limited to historical types. An important question is how well we understand the original nature of a historical vessel type when it is suddenly brought to life again generations after it last saw regular service.

Vessels that consciously evoke history are a rich component of traditional sail and a link to the past that is integral to the entire exercise. But replica and historical vessels create a three-way tension among authenticity, intended purpose, and prevailing expectations of safety. The choices are to accept the life of a dockside attraction with no concessions to modernity other than a shore-power cord, to accept extensive aesthetic compromises in order to range the ocean, or to seek some middle way. Recent history shows that it is possible to capture the past to a satisfying degree while meeting the standards that have been crafted with modern tall-ship activities in mind.

The real danger highlighted by these cases is the risk of modifying either a ship or the purpose she was intended to serve. Mixing, changing, or expanding missions—so-called *mission creep*—is hazardous in many lines of work and of particular concern when it involves people whose safety depends upon the professional judgment of others. In several cases in this book, changes to a ship compromised its original design. This may have occurred with the *Pamir*, and it unquestionably did with the *Albatross* and the *Marques*.

And changing a ship is only part of the problem. With the *Pamir*, an important operational shift transpired when the ancient assumptions underlying cargo-under-sail were set aside for a more modern and seemingly efficient approach to transporting grain. Likewise, the migration from private yacht to film prop and sail trainer fundamentally altered the premise under which the *Albatross* and the *Marques* were operated. In these cases, the ships' nadir of seaworthiness coincided (from a stability point of view) with their entry into a service owing the greatest standard of care. In the case of the *Pride*, the ship itself was mostly altered for the better, but the scope of operations grew beyond the vision the ship was conceived to fulfill, with unforeseen consequences. The Baltimore clippers evolved at a time when the hazards and opportunities posed by enemy ships were of enormous consequence, resulting in fundamentally different priorities than those that apply to a goodwill ambassador ship. Stepping outside the original historical rubric invites misunderstandings. This is not to say that vessels or missions cannot be successfully altered. They can be. It simply means that doing so may be more involved than meets the eye. In some of the cases examined here, no useful criteria existed for assessing the risks attendant upon modifications. In other instances, criteria or partial criteria existed but were not mandatory and were not applied.

In the age of sail, nature set the schedule and ships operated accordingly: a ship arrived when it arrived, and no one except the occasional hard-driving captain or impatient shipowner expected it sooner. Bending to nature was a sort of universal safety regulation. Today we expect to impose our schedules in ways our forebears could not. The days of sailing on the tide or laying to the anchor until the breeze clocks around have long since given way to internal combustion engines and attendant expectations of arriving on time. The renaissance of traditional sail would not have been possible otherwise, and truth be told, few traditional sailors of today would choose to trade places with their counterparts of yesteryear. Decisions aboard today's tall ships are constantly made in light of the schedule without necessarily courting undue risk. Nevertheless, tall ships operate in a world that often adores them but does not always understand them. A modern mission driven exclusively by shoreside considerations can create undesirable consequences. This is why even the best of ships need solidly professional masters, mates, and crew to operate them and reconcile the realities of the ship and the sea with the yearnings and expectations of the shore.

Under admiralty law, a vessel must be reasonably fit for its intended voyage. When a casualty leads to a legal action, what constitutes "reasonably fit" is established in a court of law based on evidence. That particular test was never applied in these five cases because the formal inquiries were not courts of law. Nevertheless, a great deal emerged from the investigations that pertains to seaworthiness. None of the vessels examined here was ever considered to have violated an applicable regulation, an important fact from the perspective of liability. But it is equally important to recognize that none of these ships could have met today's safety standards for taking large numbers of people to sea. No traditional sailing vessel that has met the standards these cases helped bring about has been involved in a comparable accident. The obvious conclusion is that certified ships are safer than uncertified ones. This may seem an unremarkable conclusion, yet history shows that the renaissance of traditional sail has had to grapple with it just the same.

So, what makes a good ship? Many things, of course. A good ship embodies all that is known about design and construction in a way that minimizes risk and meets the aspirations of its operators. This involves compromise, but a ship is nothing if not a compromise. A good ship can do much to improve the odds with the sea, but it can't do everything.

THE SAILOR

At any given moment there is always some aspect of a ship's readiness for sea that is less than perfect. In the right sequence of events, even a minor imperfection may prove crucial, hence the adage: "for the want of a nail the ship was lost." But the captain who refuses to go to sea until every variable is decided in his favor and the status of every fastening, seam, seacock, or valve in the ship is known is soon without a command and finds a quieter life ashore. Beyond a certain point, assumptions must be made. The captain who enjoys a state of employment opts to get underway unless there is a compelling reason not to. In the situations we have looked at, all the captains opted to get underway. Their decisions were made in a context of precedent; thus, in going to sea, they were doing nothing that had not been done before. It is clear in hindsight that some of these ships were accidents waiting to happen. The *Albatross* and the *Marques*, in particular, had such deficient stability that their masters might well not have sailed had they known about it. But, as it turned out, they were not sufficiently equipped to question matters as they found them. It is in the acceptance of matters as they are found that good sailors can make bad decisions.

These stories teach that rationalizing a state of affairs because it has not been a problem in the past can be like accepting a lit time bomb on the merit that it has never gone off before. These stories also teach that sailors don't go to sea alone. Their fates are not always decided in tests of will and wit with Neptune. Sailors sail on the decisions of others who may not share in their fate.

With the exception of the *Maria Asumpta*, the seamanship in these casualties was not conclusively shown to have brought on disaster. Alternative actions may have mitigated events, and these alternatives warrant careful consideration by practicing mariners. Through incidents such as these, sailors are given the chance to think through in advance what they might do

Laying aloft on the U.S. Coast Guard barque *Eagle* to shake out topsails. The *Eagle* can spread 22,000 square feet of sail with five miles of rigging. (U.S. Coast Guard)

when the time comes. In most of these cases, though, there were larger problems at work. Given the good safety record that has accompanied tall-ship activities in general, one might conclude that the system by which masters and mates come to positions of responsibility has been reasonably effective, and this would appear to be more or less accurate. One might also be tempted to assert, if it ain't broke don't fix it, but this could be a mistake.

The approach to seaworthiness taken by the tall-ship industry and by regulatory authorities has focused primarily on providing a better ship. Requirements have also dealt with safety equipment, and given the speed and totality of some casualties, these measures are sensible responses. However, it is also clear that a human factor, however forgivable, contributed to these tragedies. Nowhere was this more evident than in the approach to stability. Rationalizations that were considered tenable at the time are understood not to have been, given all that has been learned. Yet little has been done to bring that learning to licensed captains and officers.

The naval architect and the certification process combine to confer an appropriate degree of stability at the outset of a ship's life or its new life. But as time goes by, the master and officers bear the burden of maintaining a desirable stability profile and taking other appropriate steps to better the ship's odds with the sea. Stability is only a part of this picture. The sailing ship master who is untutored in how the many components of seaworthiness relate to one another may expose himself or herself to risks unwittingly. For instance, a lack of familiarity with how intact stability fits with functioning freeing ports may encourage a myth that the survivability of a ship in a knockdown resides in the ship alone. This is a false impression of the worst kind. The inability of a master to interpret the ship's stability data may also result in a failure to appreciate certain limitations of a vessel as she moves from protected to more exposed situations. The master who maintains faith in the notion that the ship can recover from a 90-degree knockdown because it met that theoretical criterion once upon a time may place insufficient emphasis on the rest of the seaworthiness equation. This includes considerations relating to watertight integrity, downflooding, freeing-port function, sail area, squall tactics, heavy-weather sailing, weight changes aboard ship, crew training, and the relationship among wind velocity, wind pressure, and temperature.

Although experience remains the most important ingredient in good seamanship, the process of acquiring it can be harrowing. The growth of simulator training for merchant mariners in recent years attests to this grim fact. Yet where lies the greater duty of care? Is it with the grain-laden freighter manned by a professional crew, or the school ship with thirty or forty inexperienced trainees aboard? Other than the long road of experience, the only natural point at which to address the seaworthiness equation in the sailor is through the licensing process. Yet, in the United States, home to one of the largest commercially certified traditional fleets in the world, the Sail Addendum exam administered by the U.S. Coast Guard and required for aspiring professional sailors is disturbingly superficial. If today's sailing ships are sufficiently specialized to warrant their own regulations, then the knowledge needed to run those ships is sufficiently specialized to warrant an exam that truly addresses the seaworthiness equation for a large and complex traditional sailing ship.

As in the days of wooden ships and iron men, experience remains the best teacher, except when the acquisition of it is fatal. The training of sailing ship officers always existed in one form or another and often more formally than the swaggering jack-tars of today may realize. In the latter days of commercial sail, the mates and masters were closely examined both orally and in writing at every stage of advancement on the intricacies of sailing ship operations. These exams were administered by men who had spent decades in sail in an era when sail was all that mattered. Sea time accrued under such circumstances was pure sea time, not intermingled with twenty-first-century programming. Using the American example, how can a twenty-question multiple-choice exam administered by an agency that has historically been confounded by the renaissance of traditional sail measure up to such a process? How can the same sail exam suffice for both a 50-foot marconi-rigged sloop daysailing on sheltered waters and an eighteenth-century full-rigged ship of 500 tons making ocean voyages? Although evolving international safety requirements will continue to upgrade the general training of all mariners, specialized standards for professional sailors lag behind the efforts to improve the ships on which they sail. A licensing exam should test a person on what he or she needs to know in order to do the job he or she is licensed to do. Until the exam systems that produce modern tall-ship officers include rigorous attention to the unique elements of tall-ship operations, the world of tall ships will not reach its full potential as a profession. In the United States the number of certified traditional sailing ships has ballooned since 1995, making this a timely opportunity to reassess the Sail Addendum exam.

The importance of specialized training and exams to the future of traditional sail has already been recognized in some countries, particularly Britain. The syllabus for the Nautical Institute's square-rig exam (see next page) provides a comprehensive point of departure for what a contemporary traditional sailor needs to know. This exam is now officially recognized by British maritime authorities. The Institute's *Square Rig Sailing Handbook* by Frank Scott updates the relevant concepts for today's professional square-rig officer. A formal curriculum has been established at Southampton Nautical College to prepare candidates for careers in sail training and commercial sailing operations.

(continued page 280)

SYLLABUS

Candidates will be expected to have a detailed knowledge of the following subjects:

I SHIP CONSTRUCTION

1. General knowledge of the construction of sailing vessels:
   a Steel construction. Name of the parts. Care and maintenance.
   b Wood construction. Name of the parts. Care and maintenance. Hull fastenings.
   c Underwater integrity: Electrolytic action, marine growths, corrosion, dry and wet rot, etc.
   d Tanks, pipework and pumps on sailing ships.
   e Department of Transport Rules and Recommendations governing the construction and operation of sailing vessels including deck openings, bulkwarks, freeboard and load line rules.
   f The principles of stability and the use of cross-curves for safe conduct of sailing vessels with a clear understanding of Heeling arms (HA), righting arms (GZ), statical and dynamic stability. Inclining experiment and GM. Calculation of CE-CP under different sets of sails and different drafts. Free surface calculations. Calculation of the righting arm at various angles of heel. Damage stability.
   g Emergency repairs of hulls, masts and spars at sea.
   h Watertight doors, hatches and deck openings.
   i Design of deck eye bolts, cleats, fittings on steel, timber, and aluminium masts, wash ports.
   j Construction of steel/aluminium masts and yards.
   k Steering gears and rudders.
   l Preparing for a refit in dry dock.

II MASTING AND RIGGING

A general knowledge of steel, aluminium and wood spars of a sailing vessel and the method of calculating and setting up standing and running rigging and the day to day maintenance of the complete rig.

1. Calculating the rigging of a sailing vessel:
   a Sizing of standing rigging—wire, rigging screws and shackles.
   b Sizing of running rigging—wire, chain, rope, blocks and shackles.
   c Calculating purchases.
   d Sizing diameters of wood, steel and aluminium masts and spars.
   e Centre of pressure—Centre of effort of a vessel under full sail.

2. Make sketches of any of the following:
   a Mast partners describing how the loads are transferred to avoid distortion of the hull.
   b Timber and steel tops and crossovers, bowsprit bed and knightheads. Yards, booms, gaffs and their mast fittings.

3 Setting up a Jury rig on a dismasted vessel.

III SAILS

   a Knowledge of materials use in sail making using natural and man-made fibres.
   b Sail making:—seams, roping, cringles, clews, eyelets and protection of the sails from wear.
   c Sizing canvas, man-made materials, weight for a sail.
   d Care and maintenance of sails.

IV RIGGING SQUARE RIGGED VESSELS

   a Sending yards up and down.
   b Lowering and sending up fidded topgallant and topmasts.
   c Housing and rigging jibbooms and bowsprits.
   d Rigging a spanker.
   e Stepping lower masts and setting up the standing rigging.
   f Rigging of topmasts and topgallant masts.
   g Reeving of running rigging—leads of braces, clew garnets, downhauls, clewlines, buntines, brails, halliards, reefing gear. Bending sails.
   h Earthing timber ships against damage by lightning.

V GENERAL SEAMANSHIP

1. Ship handling:
   a Manoeuvring under sail—general.
   b In heavy weather:
      i) Ocean and coasting;
      ii) Lee shore;
      iii) In separation zones;
      iv) Use of preventers, reefing systems and storm sails.
   c Under power:
      i) Engine only;
      ii) Engine and sail;
      iii) Docking.
   d Anchor work.
      Anchoring and getting under way under sail.
   e Recovery of man overboard.
   f Knockdowns.

(Continued over)

Although there is a special emphasis on matters pertaining to square rig, this syllabus for the Nautical Institute's square-rig exam offers a comprehensive approach to essential material for the modern professional mariner-in-sail. (Courtesy Nautical Institute)

SYLLABUS—Continued

g Towage and salvage.
   i) Towage for port entry/departure, passing a towline, towage agreements;
   ii) Being towed. Accepting salvage. Salvage agreements. Responsibility of master;
   iii) Taking disabled vessel in tow—motor or sail;
   iv) Taking off crew from disabled vessel.

h Pilotage—embarking and discharging a pilot.

i Transfer of personnel to helicopter.

j Use and maintenance of roller furling gear. Hand and power operated.

k Use of bow thrusters—ballast weight and placement—calculating sail power—heeling and its effect on speed.

VI DRAWINGS AND MACHINERY

1. Drawings and Plans.
   An understanding and use of line drawings, docking plans, sail and rigging diagrams, electrical, fuel, salt water and pot water service lines. Bilge and fire pumping systems.

2. Machinery.
   A general knowledge of the machinery normally found on sailing vessels. Windlass, capstan, fisherman type anchor handling gear, halliard and brace winches, davits, fuel systems, emergency pumping systems. Steering gear, propellers and stern glands.

VII METEOROLOGY AND PASSAGE PLANNING

1. A sound knowledge of this subject with an understanding of the principles of weather forecasting.

2. Detailed knowledge of passage planning under sail—use of weather patterns—lee shores; traffic separation zones; use of anchors.

VIII SURVIVAL AT SEA

a General understanding and care of life-saving appliances.

b Methods of launching lifeboats/rafts from a sailing vessel.

c Survival in cold water, survival in high temperatures.

IX RULE OF THE ROAD

a Detailed knowledge of the International Regulations for Preventing Collisions at Sea with particular reference to sailing vessels including vessels in separation schemes.

X COMMUNICATIONS, RADIO NAVIGATION AIDS AND RADAR

a General understanding of the principles involved.

b Protection of crew from injury when transmitting by radio and from scanners when operating radar.

XI GENERAL

Familiaritywith governmental regulations Preventing pollution—the induction of novices

REFERENCES AND RECOMMENDED READING

R. M. Willoughby.   *Square Rig Seamanship,* 1989, The Nautical Institute.

F. J. M. Scott.   *A Square Rig Handbook,* 1992, The Nautical Institute.

P. M. Regan/E. H. Daniels.   *Eagle Seamanship,* 1986, Naval Institute Press.

J. Hamilton.   *Sail Training—The Message of the Tall Ships,* 1988, Patrick Stephens.

Rules for Masting & Rigging of Sailing Ships, Germanischer Lloyd.

Ocean Passages of the World, 4th Edition, 1987, HMSO.

Tracks followed by Sailing & Low Powered Steam Vessels, Chart 5309, HMSO.

The Safety of Sail Training Ships—A Code of Practice for Vessels under 24M, 1990, HMSO.

Model Stability Booklet for Sail Training Ships for Vessels Under 24M, 1990, HMSO.

REPORTS OF INTEREST

1. The Auxiliary Barque *Marques* Report of Court of Inquiry Number 8073 (1987), HMSO.

2. US National Transportation Safety Board Marine Accident Report—Capsizing and Sinking of the US Sailing Vessel *Pride of Baltimore* (1987).

2. B. Deakin (Wolfson Unit) The Development of Stability Standards for UK Sailing Vessels (Spring 1990) Royal Institution of Naval Architects.

FURTHER BOOKS AND REFERENCES ARE CONTAINED IN THE ABOVE LISTED PUBLICATIONS FOR THE SPECIALIST READER.

(continued from page 277)
   In the United States, *Auxiliary Sail Vessel Operations* by Captain G. Andy Chase presents traditional sail as a viable career choice with its own core of essential knowledge. A course by the same name is now taught at Maine Maritime Academy in Castine. These and other developments reflect a growing recognition that tall-ship sailing has continued to move beyond a nostalgic novelty into a full-fledged profession. It stands to reason that it should be possible to approach that profession as methodically as any other.

Watch Below

There are moments all sailors store in a sort of communal emotional archive bound up with the physical sensations of sailing. There is the alarm when one first feels wind fill a sail. The boat beneath comes suddenly alive with heeling and speed, as if one were astride an unpredictable beast. Even on a pond left by a retreating glacier, the ecstasy of acceleration and the fear of capsize commingle in an instant of triumph and panic. Then there is the storm, often anticipated with gusto by the neophyte and less so by the seasoned sailor. In a building sea and a rising wind the bow lifts and smashes into a curled wave, pounding downward with a violence of purpose that buckles the knee and sends torrents of green water aft and into your seaboots. If one is possessed of a constitution disinclined to feed a perfectly good dinner to the fish at such moments, the jarring exuberance suggests that this is life as it should be lived: rigorous, exhilarating, bare-knuckled.

   There is also a catalog of more sublime moments that weave rapture with achievement: sunsets followed by the green flash, plotting a passable celestial fix, quiet anchorages, crossing an ocean, island landfalls, trade-wind passages, and dolphins lunging under the bow mere inches from the surging stem, as the ship muscles through the seas with athletic vitality. And then there comes a moment, perhaps aloft beyond the sight of land, beneath the stars as night relieves twilight. Out on the footrope one feels at once solitary yet in communion with the vast splendor of sea and sky and creation, alone in thought, yet part of a community of shipmates as an organ is to a body. You pause with a fistful of canvas and glance back at the trail of phosphorescence roiled to life by the turbulence of the keel scribing its way across miles of latitude and longitude like the blade of an ice skate traversing a small, round pond. The jangled organisms far below sparkle like a marine galaxy astern. They resemble nothing so much as the trail of vapor that cools and fades behind a jet aircraft at 30,000 feet, turning lurid in the rays of a settled sun that is already shining on another time zone. The capacity

In 1915 commercial sailing ships still dominated some waterfronts, such as this pier in Melbourne, Australia. (Houlton Archives)

for the world to hold and juxtapose such marvels is startling, and forms a sort of thermocline of emotion where awe of the sea and gratitude thrive.

These ships always did transport more than cargo. Whatever ostensible purpose they served in the past, sailing ships are vehicles of human experience and dreams, and not only for sailors. This may go some way toward explaining why we cling to them through art, literature, museums, or by actually going to sea. Once upon a time sailing ships, and all the myriad trades and aesthetic implications associated with them, were objects of extraordinary familiarity that intersected every thread of society. Now they are awe-inspiring oddities, little-understood objects of mystery and wonder. Despite the fact that the world has found other ways to move goods and people, the "tall ship" of Masefield's poem is no stranger to the twenty-first century. The loss of the *Pamir* did not bring about the end of sailing ships, despite the ranting of the newspapers in 1957. Though the manner in which sailing ships are operated and their reason for being have evolved, they retain an essence that continues to rouse the blood. The sailing of traditional ships remains an idealistic endeavor that has persevered in no small part due to the sheer force of romance and enthusiasm. But in moving ahead, this renaissance has had to forego some portion of the past and squelch some of the romance in order to meet other expectations of our times. Our five stories are not solely responsible for this evolution, yet each has played a part. The repercussions of these events may contribute to a quiet parting of ways within the sailing ship community. It may be that active vessels that meet certification standards go one way and vessels that can't meet those standards go another, or that maritime historians and reenactors go one way and professional, licensed sailors go another. But hopefully the original common ground—a love of the sea and ships—will remain.

Each voyage starts with a tally of odds, a tally kept in flux by the behavior of the sea, the nature of the ship, and the choices made by those aboard and sometimes by those left ashore. Though the renaissance of traditional sail has essentially been a spectacular success, one disastrous voyage is big news, whereas a thousand successful voyages are not. That is the nature of things. There are no happy chapters in this book, except where we can say, indeed, much has been learned. The goal of this book has been to help ensure that what has been learned stays learned by those who most need to know. Like anything worth doing, sailing tall ships is not riskfree. But it is a far safer endeavor on account of these incidents. The sea will always demand respect, but this hopefully will never prevent people from venturing forth to seek what they will from it.

Appendix

STABILITY

A VESSEL stays afloat because the force of gravity pulling downward on the vessel is equally counteracted by the force of buoyancy pushing upward on the vessel. (The force of buoyancy is created by the pressure of the water that the vessel has displaced.) For the purpose of stability analysis, the force of gravity can be considered to act at one point within the vessel—the *center of gravity (G)*, the height of which is measured up from the keel *(KG)*. Similarly, the force of buoyancy can be considered to act at the *center of buoyancy (B)*, the height of which is measured up from the keel *(KB)*. The center of buoyancy is also the center of the vessel's underwater volume. In a perfectly upright vessel, B and G are in vertical alignment, providing an equal and opposite force to each other (diagram 1, next page).

Stability is the ability of a vessel to return to an upright position when inclined by an external force. The center of gravity can be calculated for any amount of cargo, fuel, passengers, crew, stores, and weights placed in a vessel. The center of gravity remains fixed as the vessel moves due to wind and waves, assuming that cargo remains fixed in place and there is no shift in position of liquids. However, every time the vessel is inclined, its underwater volume changes and the center of buoyancy shifts accordingly. As a vessel heels over, B moves to the lower side and out of alignment with G. Gravity and buoyancy are still exerting their forces, but the horizontal distance between their vectors acts as a lever, trying to right the vessel (diagram 2). The strength of this *righting lever* or *arm (GZ)* is affected by any movement in the position of G. If a load is added above the original G (such as gear aloft), the center of gravity moves up toward it, reducing the length and strength of GZ (diagram 3); conversely, if a load is added below the original G (such as more ballast), the center of gravity moves down toward it, increasing the length and strength of GZ (diagram 4). The righting arm also increases with the angle of heel, but only to the point of deck edge immersion, whereupon GZ diminishes rapidly and ultimately disappears (diagram 5).

If vertical lines were drawn up from the center of buoyancy (B) at varying small angles of heel, those lines would all intersect at a point above B

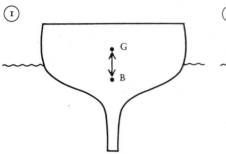

Forces of gravity and buoyancy in an upright vessel. The center of buoyancy (B) is acting directly through the center of gravity (G).

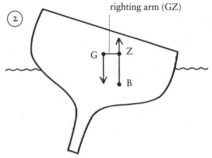

As a vessel heels, B moves outboard toward the center of the underwater portion of the vessel. This creates a righting arm (GZ).

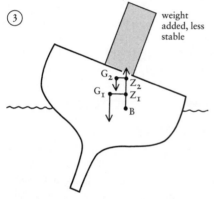

Weight added above the center of gravity moves G upward toward the new weight, G_1 to G_2. The new righting arm G_2Z_2 is shorter than the original one, reducing the ship's ability to resist external heeling forces.

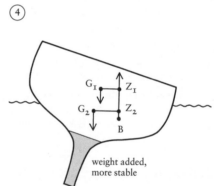

Weight added below the center of gravity has the opposite effect. The new righting arm G_2Z_2 is longer than the original one, increasing the ship's stability.

(Adapted from *An Introduction to Fishing Vessel Stability*/17th Coast Guard District, redrawn by Jim Sollers)

called the *metacenter (M)*. The distance between G and M, known as the *metacentric height (GM)*, is a convenient measure of *initial stability* (diagram 6). The greater the GM, the greater the vessel's initial stability.

Initial stability measures a vessel's GM at small angles of heel and gives a good indication of how a vessel will respond to heeling forces that are likely to be experienced under normal sailing conditions. It is useful in determining whether a vessel will have a stiff or a tender motion, which translates into the relative comfort of its occupants. It is not, however, a measure of a vessel's *ultimate stability*, which considers the response of a vessel at large angles of heel experienced under extreme conditions such as a knockdown.

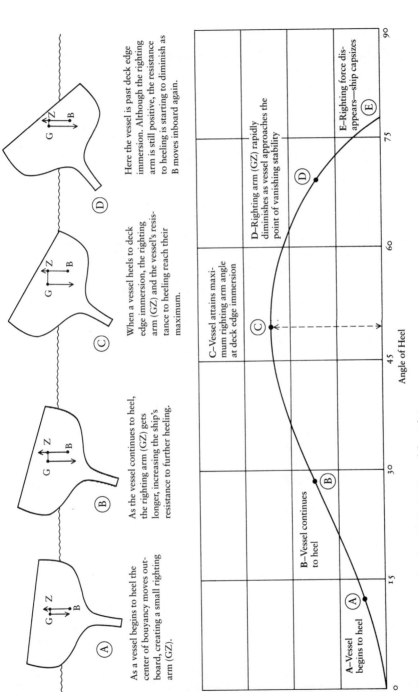

A–Vessel begins to heel

As a vessel begins to heel the center of bouyancy moves outboard, creating a small righting arm (GZ).

B–Vessel continues to heel

As the vessel continues to heel, the righting arm (GZ) gets longer, increasing the ship's resistance to further heeling.

C–Vessel attains maximum righting arm angle at deck edge immersion

When a vessel heels to deck edge immersion, the righting arm (GZ) and the vessel's resistance to heeling reach their maximum.

D–Righting arm (GZ) diminishes as vessel approaches the point of vanishing stability

Here the vessel is past deck edge immersion. Although the righting arm is still positive, the resistance to heeling is starting to diminish as B moves inboard again.

E–Righting force disappears—ship capsizes

Righting Arm (GZ)

Angle of Heel

5 Righting arm curve showing the diminishing of the righting arm upon deck edge immersion.

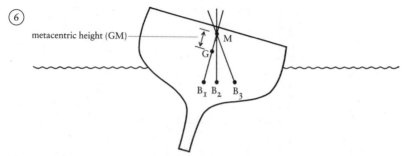

⑥

metacentric height (GM)

Metacentric height (GM) is particularly useful for measuring stability at small angles of heel.

A vessel's ultimate stability is the angle at which it will cease to resist heeling forces and will capsize. This is the lesser of the angle at which GZ becomes zero, or the angle at which water can flood into the vessel through ports, hatches or ventilation openings.

Additional factors affecting stability:

The shape of a vessel's hull influences its stability characteristics. *Freeboard* (the vertical distance from the lowest point in the deck to the waterline) can affect how quickly the point of deck edge immersion is reached. A higher freeboard allows a vessel to heel farther before its deck edge meets the water. Furthermore, beamier vessels have more initial stability than their narrower counterparts because, as a wider vessel heels, its underwater volume increases dramatically, resulting in a greater outboard shift in the center of buoyancy, and therefore a larger righting arm.

The amount of sail area exposed to the wind is another stability factor. The geometric center of a sail plan is its *center of effort*, the point at which the pressure of the wind can be assumed to act. The higher the center of effort, the greater the heeling force that the vessel has to resist. Reducing sail, especially the higher sails, will lower both the center of effort and the amount of sail area exposed to the wind, thereby decreasing the heeling force and the inherent stresses on the vessel. *Sail trim* also impacts the effect of the heeling force in that sheeting in sails tightly will generate the greatest heeling moment, whereas easing the sheets will spill the wind and reduce the heeling effect.

Free-surface effect can occur in various ways to compromise the stability of a vessel. For instance, the liquid (or loose ballast that flows like liquid) in any partially filled tank will slosh from one side of the tank to the other as the vessel rolls. Typically the liquid will flow to the low side as the vessel heels, thereby exaggerating the vessel's roll. Water trapped on deck and unable to run off through freeing ports will also create a free-surface effect as it floods the leeward scuppers and increases the heeling angle. Additionally, the added weight of the water on deck will usually raise the vessel's center of gravity, resulting in a diminished righting arm.

BEAUFORT WIND SCALE
WITH CORRESPONDING SEA STATE CODES

Beaufort number or force	Wind speed				World Meteorological Organization (1964)	Effects observed far from land	Estimating wind speed — Effects observed near coast	Effects observed on land	Sea State — Term and height of waves, in meters	Code
	knots	mph	meters per second	km per hour						
0	under 1	under 1	0.0–0.2	under 1	Calm	Sea like mirror.	Calm.	Calm; smoke rises vertically.	Calm, glassy, 0	0
1	1–3	1–3	0.3–1.5	1–5	Light air	Ripples with appearance of scales; no foam crests.	Fishing smack just has steerage way.	Smoke drift indicates wind direction; vanes do not move.	Calm, rippled, 0–0.1	1
2	4–6	4–7	1.6–3.3	6–11	Light breeze	Small wavelets; crests of glassy appearance, not breaking.	Wind fills the sails of smacks which then travel at about 1–2 miles per hour.	Wind felt on face; leaves rustle; vanes begin to move.	Smooth, wavelets, 0.1–0.5	2
3	7–10	8–12	3.4–5.4	12–19	Gentle breeze	Large wavelets; crests begin to break; scattered whitecaps.	Smacks begin to careen and travel about 3–4 miles per hour.	Leaves, small twigs in constant motion; light flags extended.	Slight, 0.5–1.25	3
4	11–16	13–18	5.5–7.9	20–28	Moderate breeze	Small waves, becoming longer; numerous whitecaps.	Good working breeze, smacks carry all canvas with good list.	Dust, leaves, and loose paper raised up; small branches move.	Moderate, 1.25–2.5	4
5	17–21	19–24	8.0–10.7	29–38	Fresh breeze	Moderate waves, taking longer form; many whitecaps; some spray.	Smacks shorten sail.	Small trees in leaf begin to sway.	Rough, 2.5–4	5
6	22–27	25–31	10.8–13.8	39–49	Strong breeze	Larger waves forming; whitecaps everywhere; more spray.	Smacks have doubled reef in mainsail; care required when fishing.	Larger branches of trees in motion; whistling heard in wires.	Very rough, 4–6	6
7	28–33	32–38	13.9–17.1	50–61	Near gale	Sea heaps up; white foam from breaking waves begins to be blown in streaks.	Smacks remain in harbor and those at sea lie-to.	Whole trees in motion; resistance felt in walking against wind.		
8	34–40	39–46	17.2–20.7	62–74	Gale	Moderately high waves of greater length; edges of crests begin to break into spindrift; foam is blown in well-marked streaks.	All smacks make for harbor, if near.	Twigs and small branches broken off trees; progress generally impeded.	High, 6–9	7
9	41–47	47–54	20.8–24.4	75–88	Strong gale	High waves; sea begins to roll; dense streaks of foam; spray may reduce visibility.		Slight structural damage occurs; slate blown from roofs.		
10	48–55	55–63	24.5–28.4	89–102	Storm	Very high waves with overhanging crests; sea takes white appearance as foam is blown in very dense streaks; rolling is heavy and visibility reduced.		Seldom experienced on land; trees broken or uprooted; considerable structural damage occurs.	Very high, 9–14	8
11	56–63	64–72	28.5–32.6	103–117	Violent storm	Exceptionally high waves; sea covered with white foam patches; visibility still more reduced.		Very rarely experienced on land; usually accompanied by widespread damage.		
12	64 and over	73 and over	32.7 and over	118 and over	Hurricane	Air filled with foam; sea completely white with driving spray; visibility greatly reduced.			Phenomenal, over 14	9

Note: Since January 1, 1955, weather map symbols have been based upon wind speed in knots, at five-knot intervals, rather than upon Beaufort number.

(Reproduced from Bowditch, *American Practical Navigator,* 1977 edition, volume I [Defense Mapping Agency Hydrographic Center], appendix 5, 1,267.)

Modern Materials on Traditional Ships

FROM TIME TO TIME it has been postulated among sailors that the use of modern materials aboard traditional vessels may have contributed to the weather-related casualties in this book. The general argument is that in the old days when rigging and sails were made from weaker, organic materials they would fail under extreme conditions, thus acting as a safety-release valve for heeling forces under extreme conditions such as those experienced by these five ships. Canvas sails stitched with cotton twine would shred or blow out under pressure, and manila lines would part. Wooden spars would fail, and hemp shrouds tensioned with deadeyes and lanyards would either part or be deliberately cut away if the ship were in danger of capsizing. The windage and weight of the masts and rigging going overboard would relieve the ship, and she would come upright. Modern materials such as wire shrouds and stays, steel masts, synthetic line and sailcloth are far stronger than their earlier counterparts and, in the case of the standing rigging, cannot readily be dispatched in time of need. The notion of sails and rigging saving the day by self-destructing undoubtedly had some real-world basis, and there is no question that deliberate dismasting was a well-known form of seamanship that is not so well appreciated in today's sailing fleets. But there is no convincing evidence that any of the casualties in this book were caused by nonperiod or nonorganic materials that either wouldn't or couldn't be jettisoned under extreme conditions.

The *Pamir*, for instance, was rigged much as she always had been with wire rigging, turnbuckles, and steel spars connected to a steel hull. Wire rigging had been in use since the late nineteenth century and was traditional aboard the Cape Horners from that time onward. Based on reports the *Pamir*'s sails did, in fact, blow out, and she may have been partially dismasted, yet that did not prevent her internal stability from plummeting.

Both the *Marques* and *Albatross* had at least some synthetic sails and incorporated wire and rigging screws into their rigs, as well. Given the periods of their construction (1917 and 1921, respectively) wire rigging was likely what they had always sailed with, though initially it supported much smaller rigs. The topgallant on the *Albatross* was supposedly so old and worn that a new one had already been made, yet the old one held up in the squall. Though it can be said that by not failing in a squall the rigs and sails contributed to these two capsizings, it has been clearly demonstrated that deficient stability and the *size* of the rigs doomed these ships. More conservative rigs of the same materials quite likely would have led to the survival of both. As noted in a journal for naval architects, in connection with the *Pride of Baltimore*, "there is no evidence that weak standing rigging which would let the top-hamper unpredictably fall to the deck was ever considered a safety feature."

Though the *Pride of Baltimore* also had wire standing rigging and synthetic running rigging, she was rigged with deadeyes and lanyards. The lanyards were polyester and therefore stronger than natural fiber of an equivalent diameter. All her spars were grown timber and of slender proportions. Nearly all her sails were canvas, although the two newest ones were synthetic (Duradon). The reefed mainsail set at the time of the squall was canvas and not new. The forestaysail was new and built from Duradon. None of this carried away. Theoretically the crew could have cut away the rig at the lanyards, just as those aboard the *Albatross* and *Marques* theoretically could have cut the halyards and sheets to spill the wind. But it appears there was simply no time for that.

Although natural materials may have periodically given out in times of extreme need, it seems likely that such failure was happenstance rather than intentional. After all, new suits of sails and freshly rove running rigging in the age of commercial sail were intended to stand up through the worst of weather, and usually did. Historical capsizing events can testify to this. That nothing carried away on any of the ships in this book may say as much about wind strength as about the strength of the materials. The theory that modern materials in a traditional application contributed to these casualties is not well supported by what we know.

Other observers have faulted the use of wire standing rigging tuned with turnbuckles on an older wooden hull, suggesting that the superior mechanical advantage of turnbuckles, or rigging screws, over the older deadeye-and-lanyard method make it possible to induce significantly greater stresses on the hull, which may disturb the planking under extreme conditions. Among the cases in this book, however, only the *Marques* used wire rigging tensioned by turnbuckles on a wooden hull, though the method has been widely used elsewhere. But structural failure was rejected as a possible cause of the *Marques*'s rapid sinking. Although it may be conceptually attractive to think that modern materials played a role in compromising the hull, in this casualty such a premise does not find support in the record.

In Memoriam
The Names of the Lost

Pamir, 1957

Sönke Andresen, able-bodied third class
Volkert Arfsten, able-bodied first class
Karl-Otto Beck, able-bodied third class
Hans-Dieter Bollmann, able-bodied third class
Hans-Gerd Born, ship's boy
Johannes Buscher, 2nd officer (chief lieutenant at sea)
Gunther Buschmann, 2nd officer (mate)
Alois Daiser, 1st steward
Rolf Dellit, able-bodied first class
Johannes Diebitsch, captain
Artfried Dierbach, able-bodied third class
Gerhard Dorow, ship's boy
Klaus Driebold, able-bodied third class
Werner Eggerstedt, ship's cook
Raimund Ellinghaus, ship's boy
Peter Fischer, able-bodied third class
Jürgen Fleischmann, able-bodied third class
Werner Fluck, able-bodied third class
Klaus Förster, ship's boy
Peter Frederich, able-bodied third class
Hermann Geller, able-bodied second class
Manfred Gerstenberg, ship's boy
Klaus Grunewald, able-bodied third class
Hartmut Gundermann, able-bodied first class
Erich Halbig, 2nd engineer
Ingo Hamburger, cook's mate
Holger Hartmann, ship's boy
Uwe Hasselmann, ship's boy
Manfred Hastedt, able-bodied third class
Gert Hein, able-bodied second class
Peter Hensel, able-bodied third class
Albrecht Hepe, ship's boy
Manfred Holst, ship's boy
Gerd Holzapfel, sailmaker, able-bodied
Franz Hutschenreuter, able-bodied third class
Axel Jensen, ship's boy
Wilfried Kehr, carpenter's apprentice
Rolf-Dieter Köhler, 1st officer (mate)
Dieter Koopmann, able-bodied first class
Jan-Peter Kröger, able-bodied third class
Günther Krohn, assistant engineer
Manfred Krumm, ship's boy
Richard Kühl, 1st bosun
Bernhard Küper, able-bodied third class
Wolfram Leppert, able-bodied second class
Olaf Lind, able-bodied third class
Rolf Lühring, able-bodied first class
Helmuth Lütje, 2nd bosun
Klaus Meier, able-bodied third class
Jürgen Meine, ship's boy
Kurt Richter, chief engineer
Christiano Riemann, able-bodied third class
Heiner Rosenbrock, ship's boy
Dr. Heinz Ruppert, ship's doctor
Hans-Peter Scheer, mess steward
Peter Scheider, ship's boy
Günter Schinnagel, assistant engineer
Helmut Schlüter, able-bodied second class

Alfred Schmidt, 1st officer (mate)
Heiner Schmidt-Brinkmann, able-
  bodied third class
Jürgen Schmitz, able-bodied second
  class
Jochen Schnalke, ship's boy
Winfried Schüler, able-bodied third class
Wilhelm Siemers, radio officer and
  purser
Hans-Jürgen Stampe, ship's boy
Erwin Stangl, ship's boy
Uwe Stever, able-bodied third class
Julius Stober, sailmaker
Peter Stöcks, able-bodied third class
Dieter Streeck, ship's boy
Eberhard Strigler, able-bodied third
  class
Gerd Thies, ship's boy
Klaus-Diedrich Thorborg, able-bodied
  third class
Friedrich von Bechtold, able-bodied
  third class
Rüdiger von Mindern, able-bodied third
  class
Hermann Walter, ship's carpenter
Helmut Westerkamp, able-bodied third
  class
Bertel Wippermann, able-bodied third
  class
Peter Wittrock, ship's boy
Dietrich Woite, able-bodied third class

Albatross, 1961

Christopher Corstine, student (17)
John Goodlet, student (17)
Rick Marsellus, student (16)
George Ptacnik, cook
Dr. Natalie Alice Sheldon, ship's
  physician
Robert Wetherill, student (17)

Marques, 1984

Ian Brims, trainee
Benjamin Rufus Bryant, deckhand (19)
Aloma H. Finlay, wife (31)
Christopher Finlay, child (1)
Stuart A. Finlay, captain (42)
Janice Gravelejs, trainee
Jack Heath, trainee
Thelma Heath, trainee
Rodney Hector, trainee
Susan Peterson Howell, instructor
Thomas Lebel, trainee
Andrea Lee, trainee
Carl Mason, trainee
James F. McAleer, trainee
Peter Messer-Bennetts, 2nd mate (20)
Augustine Nathaniel, deckhand
Clyde Raybowen, trainee
Stanley Seon, trainee
Gillian Shaughnessy, cook (24)

Pride of Baltimore, 1986

Barry F. Duckworth, carpenter (29)
Armin E. Elsaesser III, captain (42)
Vincent C. Lazzaro, engineer (27)
Jeannette F. (Nina) Schack, deckhand
  (23)

Maria Asumpta, 1995

Emily MacFarlane, crew (19)
John Shannon, assistant engineer (24)
Anne Taylor, cook (50)

NOTES

Introduction: Signing On

1 **last known position.** Heinrich von Brentano, Foreign Minister, Federal Republic of Germany, letter to U.S. Secretary of State J. F. Dulles, 7 October 1957, State Department Press Release 563, Department of State Bulletin.

1 **the North Atlantic.** "Sixth Survivor of Sailing Vessel Found by U.S. Cutter Off Azores," *New York Times*, 25 September 1957.

1 **for this epoch."** "West Germans Consider Suggestions that the Use of Such Ships Be Ended," *New York Times*, 25 September 1957.

2 **commerce and profit.** See Stability, in the appendix.

7 **traditions and visions."** Captain David V. V. Wood, former master of the USCG barque *Eagle*, personal interview, 8 February 1996.

7 **walks of life."** Quoted in David V. V. Wood, "Sail Training: The Next Century," *Sea History* 70 (summer 1994).

11 **dawn breaking.** John Masefield, "Sea Fever" in *Salt-Water Poems and Ballads* (New York: Macmillan, 1916).

Pamir (1905–1957)

15 Vessel details from Jack Churchouse, *The* Pamir *Under the New Zealand Ensign* (Wellington, N.Z.: Millwood Press, 1978). Details regarding tonnage varied slightly among sources; however, Churchouse's information is to date the most complete of any English-language publication on the *Pamir*.

16 *fast* **passages."** "Instructions to My Captains" aboard the *Preussen* in 1903, quoted in Alan Villiers, *The Way of a Ship*, 2nd ed. (New York: Scribner, 1970), 398.

16 **to their seamanship.** Churchouse, *The* Pamir *Under the New Zealand Ensign*, preface, xi.

17 **it remained.** Twelve books in English and German (published as recently as 1991) specifically concern the *Pamir*. *Pamir* also receives attention in numerous reference volumes of maritime history.

17 **Rio de Janeiro.** Jean Randier, *Men and Ships Around Cape Horn, 1616–1939*, trans. M. W. B. Sanderson (New York: David McKay, 1969), 338.

17 **built in 1839.** Villiers, *Way of a Ship*, 31.

17 **the letter *P*.** Ibid., 35. The origins of the naming tradition are unconfirmed, but Villiers suggests that it started in 1856 with an "especially favored barque" named the *Pudel*, which was a nickname of Mrs. Carl Laeisz.

17 *Padua* **was launched.** It has been said that these last P-Liners would not have sailed without government subsidies. Although there may have been subsidies

in one form or another, a great many shipping lines both then and now would not sail without subsidies, either, so it makes little difference. A. D. Bordes of France, Laiesz's chief competitor, was utterly reliant on mileage subsidies that discouraged efficient passagemaking. When the French subsidies were discontinued, virtually the entire Bordes fleet was tied up and scrapped. The point is, through the House of Laeisz there was an abiding interest in sail that actually amounted to something in Germany.

18 produced the *Pamir*. Villiers, *Way of a Ship*, 1–68.

18 critical watershed. Niels W. Jannasch, telephone interview, 15 March 1998. Jannasch served in the four-masted barques *Viking* and *Passat*. He sailed in *Passat* under the Finnish flag in the Australian run in 1948–49 and again under the German flag in 1952. Being among the few to be involved in both stages, he witnessed firsthand changes in operational methods. He later directed the Maritime Museum of the Atlantic in Halifax, Nova Scotia.

18 not in winter." Captain R. Miethe, quoted in Alan Villiers, *The War with Cape Horn* (New York: Scribner, 1971), 272.

18 exploit the opportunities. Villiers, *Way of a Ship*, 23–45.

18 not prone to shifting. Villiers, *War with Cape Horn*, 267.

19 continued investment. Villiers, *Way of a Ship*, 34.

19 by sailing ship. It is a measure of the quality of construction of the P-Liners, and of the skill with which they were handled, that several have survived to populate maritime museums around the world: *Peking* (South Street Seaport, New York), *Passat* (Travemünde, Germany), and *Pommern* (Mariehamn, Åland Islands, Finland). The *Padua*, renamed *Kruzenstern*, was seized by the Soviets after World War II and continues to operate as a sail training ship for the Russian navy.

19 from the period. Harold A. Underhill, *Sailing Ship Rigs and Rigging* (Glasgow: Brown, Son & Ferguson, 1938), 21.

19 came into vogue. Ibid., 21.

21 countless voyages. The dismasting of the P-Liner *Pinnas* off the Horn 6 April 1929 was caused by that other nemesis of a sailing ship: a sudden rolling calm after prolonged high winds have built a fully developed seaway.

21 capital-intensive steamers. Villiers, *Way of a Ship*, 44. *Lightering* is a common means of loading large ships in ports that had little in the way of dockside infrastructure for loading. Lighters transport the cargo between the shore and the ship laying at anchor, where it is stowed into the hold. In some ports lightering could be more economical for a sailing ship where dockside facilities were available only at a premium or not at all.

21 the same route, *Windjammer* (London: Mariners International), no. 4 (1995): 2. In Cornwall, near the mouth of the English Channel, the Lizard represented a convenient point of departure and arrival for ships trading with northern Europe.

21 to the Lizard. Churchouse, *The* Pamir *Under the New Zealand Ensign*, 228.

21 light conditions. Villiers, *War with Cape Horn*, 264.

21 to that design. Jannasch, correspondence with the author, 8 October 2001.

22 **would be sailing.** Villiers, *War with Cape Horn*, 262, 288.

22 **drive her hard."** Ingemar Palmer, president of the Mariehamn chapter of the Cape Horners Society; also former third officer of the four-masted barque *Viking* in the Australian grain trade 1947–48, interview, Mariehamn, 3 September 1997.

23 **for four years.** Roger Morris, *Pacific Sail: Four Centuries of Western Ships in the Pacific* (Camden, Maine: International Marine, 1987), 176.

23 **four-masted barques.** Villiers, *War with Cape Horn*, 249.

24 **forty cadets.** Jannasch, interview.

24 **value for them.** Randier, *Men and Ships Around Cape Horn*, 348.

24 **1920s and 1930s.** Palmer, interview, Mariehamn, 3 September 1997.

25 **sailing ship voyage.** This type of trainee was sometimes referred to as a *passenger*, but unless they paid for a passenger berth, they functioned as entry-level crew in terms of duties.

25 *Pamir* **under Laeisz.** Heinrich Hauser, *Die letzten Segelschiffe: Schiff, Mannschaft, Meer und Horizont* (The last sailing ships: ship, crew, sea, and horizon) (Berlin: Fischer, 1930). Not published in English translation.

25 **and** *Windjammer.* Eric Newby, *The Last Grain Race* (London: Hart-Davis, 1968); Eric Newby, *Windjammer: Pictures of Life Before the Mast in the Last Grain Race* (New York: Dutton, 1968).

26 **hull insurance.** Palmer, interview, 3 September 1997.

26 **including the trainees.** Jannasch, correspondence with the author.

27 **port of discharge.** Of the Erikson ships, only the *Viking* is known to have carried a wireless set in the late 1930s. The two Laeisz ships were fitted with wireless, as well as the *Abraham Rydberg* (formerly *Hawaiian Isles*), the *Kommodore Johnsen* (formerly *Magdalene Vinnen*), and perhaps a few others.

27 *Herzogin Cecilie.* *Herzogin Cecilie* beat out the *C. B. Pedersen* and *Beatrice*, all four-masted barques.

27 **war broke out.** Newby's title, *The Last Grain Race*, refers to the fleet's return voyage of 1939. In point of fact, the trade resumed after the war but with very few sailing vessels participating.

28 **two nations.** Churchouse, *The* Pamir *Under the New Zealand Ensign*, 7.

28 **her topsides.** Ibid., 11.

28 **sailors and officers.** Morris, *Pacific Sail*, 176.

28 **their midteens.** Churchouse, *The* Pamir *Under the New Zealand Ensign*, 213.

28 **North America.** Horst Willner, *Pamir, ihr Untergang und die Irrtümer des Seeamtes* (*Pamir*, her loss, and the errors of the maritime court) (Herford: Mittler & Son, 1991), 141. Not published in English translation.

28 **sink the** *Pamir.* Jannasch, personal correspondence. This account is from his own interview with the former New Zealand master of the *Pamir* at that time, Captain Champion, conducted 24 November 1989 at Christchurch, New Zealand.

28 **training experience;** Unfortunately, such a charitable outlook did not always carry the day: the captured barques *Killoran* and *Penang* were sunk by the Germans. A third vessel, the four-masted barque *Olivebank*, struck a mine in the North Sea in 1939.

28 **mission to tell us.** Willner, *Pamir*, 141.
29 **what they saw.** Alex A. Hurst, *Square-Riggers: The Final Epoch, 1921–1958* (Brighton: Teredo Books, 1972), 480.
29 **criticism as support.** Churchouse, *The* Pamir *Under the New Zealand Ensign*, 246.
29 **in November 1948.** Ibid., 215.
29 **for either vessel.** Basil Greenhill, *The Ship: The Life and Death of the Merchant Sailing Ship, 1815–1965* (London: Her Majesty's Stationary Office, 1980), 53.
30 **the shipping world.** Churchouse, *The* Pamir *Under the New Zealand Ensign*, 267.
30 **the necessary funds?** Quoted in Villiers, *Way of a Ship*, 355.
30 **or *Segelschulschiff.** Segelschulschiff* translates as "sailing school ship." Ironically, this new role also marks the end of *Pamir*'s life as a pure sailing vessel, because the modifications made in preparation for sail training included the installation of a diesel auxiliary engine.
30 **laying at Mariehamn.** Hurst, *Square-Riggers*, 491–92.
30 **and January 1952.** Jannasch, personal notes, 10 May 1998.
30 **on each ship.** Ibid.
30 **with *Pamir*'s loss.** Two ships in which I sailed, the British brigantine *Eye of the Wind* and the Australian topsail schooner *Solway Lass*, were originally riveted hulls but had been restored with welded plates to no apparent detriment. These were, however, much smaller hulls than any of the four-masted barques.
31 **moving at sea.** Morris, *Pacific Sail*, 177.
31 **also installed.** The installation of auxiliary power was harshly criticized by many who had served in pure sailing ships who were of the opinion that it "spoiled" a vessel. Certainly the sense of competition and professional pride that accompanied swift passage-making was severely undermined by auxiliary power. Figures for point-to-point passages became diluted and virtually meaningless if they were achieved in any part by the use of engines, as it was no longer a case of ship against ship, captain against captain, and all hands against nature.
31 **Germanischer Lloyd."** Churchouse, *The* Pamir *Under the New Zealand Ensign*, 268.
31 **for sea trials.** Ibid., 268.
31 **on freight rates.** Villiers, *Way of a Ship*, 356.
31 **the two barques.** Morris, *Pacific Sail*, 177.
31 **bulk grain homeward.** Jannasch, telephone interview.
31 **had been built.** Churchouse, *The* Pamir *Under the New Zealand Ensign*, 268, 269.
32 **the principle was."** Villiers, *Way of a Ship*, 356. Alan Villiers (1903–1982) was born in Australia and became a preeminent square-riggerman and tireless advocate for both commercial sail and sail training. In the course of his long career at sea, Villiers sailed in a wide variety of traditional sailing vessels, including many ocean voyages carrying cargo. He was a part owner of, and bosun in, the four-masted barque *Parma*, a former P-Liner. He ran her profitably in the Australian grain trade during the 1930s under the command of the

famous Åland captain, Ruben de Cloux. Later (1937) Villiers bought and skippered the full-rigger *Joseph Conrad* for an around-the-world sail training voyage that was one of the most ambitious of its type at the time, and was a forerunner of modern sail training. He used his skills as a journalist, photographer, and author of almost thirty books to document all aspects of the traditional seafaring life. Villiers had an uncommon passion for the sea that manifested itself in all his undertakings.

32 **carried in bags."** Jannasch, telephone interview, 10 May 1998. Jannasch served aboard the four-masted barque *Viking* and then aboard the *Passat* for her final commercial voyage to and from Australia in 1948–49. He returned to *Passat* after her conversion in 1952 for a voyage from Germany to Brazil and Argentina. Jannasch later directed the Maritime Museum of the Atlantic at Halifax, Nova Scotia, for approximately twenty-five years.

32 **metacentric height."** Churchouse, *The* Pamir *Under the New Zealand Ensign*, 270. Metacentric height is a fundamental indicator of stability. See Stability, in the appendix.

33 **a good thing."** Hurst, *Square-Riggers*, 493.

33 **across the deck."** Hans Georg Wirth with Lawrence Lader, "Last Voyage of the *Pamir*," *Reader's Digest* (June 1958), 25, 26.

33 **distress calls.** Morris, *Pacific Sail*, 177.

33 **and last calls.** Ibid., 177.

34 **the storm struck."** *Newsweek* 50 (7 October 1957): 49. A virtually identical account appears in Churchouse's book.

34 **barque broken."** "Big German Bark in Danger at Sea," *New York Times*, 22 September 1957.

35 **slowly diving.** Quoted in Churchouse, *The* Pamir *Under the New Zealand Ensign*, 270.

35 **the pot overturned."** Wirth with Lader, "Last Voyage of the *Pamir*," 26.

36 **vessel capsized.** Quoted in Churchouse, *The* Pamir *Under the New Zealand Ensign*, 270.

36 **West German government.** "*Pamir* Hunt Fruitless" and "*Pamir* Survivor Hunt Goes On," *New York Times*, 27 and 28 September 1957.

37 **only meager results.** "*Pamir* Hunt Fruitless."

37 **cut and dried."** Hurst, *Square-Riggers*, 495.

37 **of the inquiry.** "*Pamir* Survivors Questioned," *New York Times*, 29 September 1957; Jannasch, interview, 12 May 1998.

38 **"highest classification."** Churchhouse, *The* Pamir *Under the New Zealand Ensign*, 268.

38 **ship in 1950.** Villiers, *Way of a Ship*, 357.

39 **by age alone.** At least two sailing vessels built by Blohm and Voss in that period have continued to voyage. *Annie von Hamburg* under German flag was sighted by the author in 1991 in the Canary Islands, making a routine autumn voyage from Europe to the Caribbean; *Eye of the Wind*, built in 1911 and restored under British registry, was voyaging extensively worldwide as late as 2001, and made a Cape Horn passage (west to east) in 1991. Both vessels are around 150 tons and are substantially original.

39 **spray all night.** William Frederick Stark, "The Last of the Windjammers" (1950), Special Collections, Dartmouth College Library, 8–9.

40 **maritime court).** See full citation at note for page 28.

40 **as they went.** Ibid., 78.

40 **structural failure.** Ibid., 79.

40 **still intact.** Ibid.

41 **No. 2 hatch."** Captain James S. Learmont, untitled selection from *Master in Sail* (London: Percival Marshall, 1954) in *The Last of the Cape Horners: First-hand Accounts from the Final Days of the Commercial Tall Ships*, ed. Spencer Apollonio (Washington, D.C.: Brassey's, 2000), 129.

42 **wave height,** Wirth with Lader, "Last Voyage of the *Pamir*": "Now 40 foot high waves were smashing across the deck." Hasselbach, quoted in *Newsweek* 50: "Eighty-foot waves tossed us about like a shuttlecock."

42 **to *use* storms."** Villiers, *War with Cape Horn*, 326.

42 **(*Mid-Pacific, 1945*)** Ibid.

42 **(*Near the Cape Verdes, 1947*)** Ibid., 228.

42 **(*Southern Ocean, 1949*)** Churchouse, *The* Pamir *Under the New Zealand Ensign*, 258.

42 **completely immersed.** Stark, "The Last of the Windjammers," 9–10.

43 **oddly behaved.** Villiers, *War with Cape Horn*, 326.

44 **trips earlier.** Churchouse, *The* Pamir *Under the New Zealand Ensign*, 269.

44 **sailing vessels.** Morris, *Pacific Sail*, 178.

45 **what occurred.** Hurst, *Square-Riggers*, 499.

45 **things have gone.** Villiers, *Way of a Ship*, 357.

45 **he could find.** Villiers, *War with Cape Horn*, 326.

46 **was omitted.** Jannasch, correspondence with the author, May 1998.

46 **receive a reply.** Ibid., 16 January 1997.

46 **been broken."** Ibid.

47 **past the ship.** A hurricane is a massive low-pressure system of tropical origins. In the Northern Hemisphere, winds in a low-pressure system revolve counter-clockwise around the center, or eye, of the storm. In the Southern Hemisphere the winds revolve clockwise around the eye.

49 **professional management."** Villiers, *War with Cape Horn*, 327.

50 **to 60 degrees.** Captain Grubbe, Letter to the Inquiry, 6 February 1958, quoted in Willner, *Pamir*, 128.

50 **slipped to port,** Ibid.

50 **not sailed since.** *Passat* lies at Travemünde, Germany, and is maintained as a museum ship and youth hostel.

50 **fear of capsize."** Hurst, *Square-Riggers*, 495.

51 **for Laeisz.** Ibid.

51 **as well.** Correspondence from Piening, quoted in Hurst, *Square-Riggers*, 499.

51 **loose stuff.** Jannasch, telephone interview, 10 May 1998.

51 **big hollow."** Correspondence from Piening, quoted in Hurst, *Square-Riggers*, 499.

51 **vessel's stability.** Henry E. Rossell and Lawrence B. Chapman, *Principles of Naval Architecture*, vol. 1, *Statics of Naval Architecture* (New York: Society of Naval Architects and Marine Engineers, 1939), 126.

52 **full-rigger** *Royalshire.* Though Lubbock refers to his ship as the *Royalshire,* other sources call this ship the *Ross-shire.*

52 **was under water.** A. Basil Lubbock, *Round the Horn Before the Mast,* reprinted by Brown, Son & Ferguson, Glasgow, 1986, first printed 1902, p. 219–21.

53 **the disaster.** Hurst, *Square-Riggers,* 493.

53 **bulk did it!"** Ibid., 498.

53 **grain in sacks."** Palmer, interview, 3 September 1997.

53 **befallen the** *Pamir.* Hurst, *Square-Riggers,* 498.

54 **members intersected.** Ibid., 499.

55 **international practice.** Ibid., 496.

55 **in Germany."** Ibid.

55 **classification society.** Correspondence from Piening, quoted in Hurst, *Square-Riggers,* 498.

55 **less objectionable.** Morris, *Pacific Sail,* 178.

55 **but a scam."** Quoted in Jannasch, correspondence with the author, 16 January 1997.

55 **unbearable.** Hurst, *Square-Riggers,* 498.

56 **an even keel."** "Lifeboats Found in Hunt for Ship," *New York Times,* 23 September 1957, 49.

56 **for this epoch."** "Sixth Survivor of Sailing Vessel Found by U. S. Cutter off Azores," *New York Times,* 25 September 1957.

56 **waste-paper basket."** Hurst, *Square-Riggers,* 498.

58 **needy communities.** Daniel Moreland, *Picton Castle* Project Summary and Update of Business Plan, March 2001, and various communications to shareholders, December 2001.

58 **sail training voyage.** The barque *Picton Castle* was built in England in 1928 as a power-driven fishing vessel. She was renovated and rigged by Captain Daniel Moreland in Nova Scotia and in New England between 1992 and 1997. Her purpose is to make "long voyages with expense sharing crew under the direction of experienced professionals" (ASTA *Directory,* 1995). The *Picton Castle* is registered in the Cook Islands.

58 **cargo investment.** Moreland, *Picton Castle* Project Summary.

60 **for differing reasons."** Hurst, *Square-Riggers,* 493.

60 **"a scam."** Quoted in Jannasch, correspondence with the author, 16 January 1997.

60 *Derbyshire* **in 1980.** Frank J. Scott, "Stability," chapt. 14 in *A Square Rig Sailing Handbook* (London: Nautical Institute, 1992, rev. 2001).

61 **carried in sacks.** Hurst, *Square-Riggers,* 493.

Albatross (1921–1961)

65 Vessel details from Ernest K. Gann, *Welcome Aboard the Brigantine Albatros* (unpublished), 1958, 5. Owner and master Gann prepared this booklet not long before he sold the *Albatross* to Sheldon. Having purchased the vessel in Europe, near her origins, Gann gained some insight into her early activities. He

wrote, "by talking with members of her original crew, and such records as did survive, at least a fairly accurate history has been obtained." Captain Christopher Sheldon kindly lent me a copy of this booklet.

66 **the relevant details.** The U.S. Coast Guard at Tampa interviewed Sheldon, John Perry (the math teacher), and Phillip LeBoutillier (a student). The interview lasted approximately half an hour and resulted in a two-page report and a follow-up memo. These are the only official documents dealing with the incident.

66 **deemed appropriate."** C. W. Quinby, Commander 7th Coast Guard District, letter to the Commandant (MVI), 26 May 1961.

67 **based on the** *Albatross.* The film *White Squall* was directed by Ridley Scott and starred Jeff Bridges. It was based on a book by one of the surviving students, Charles Gieg, and Felix Sutton (*The Last Voyage of the Albatross*, New York: Duell, Sloan & Pearce, 1962).

67 **close to the** *Albatross."* Chuck Gieg, *White Squall*—Conference 2 (e-mail), April 1996.

67 **ship for the job."** Christopher Sheldon, personal interview, Norwalk, Connecticut, 13 March 1996. The *Eye of the Wind* was not a pilot schooner, but she was built in Germany of riveted iron in 1911. Although she was larger than the *Albatross* and built for deep-sea trading, in certain respects they were constructed similarly, particularly in the curve of the stern and rise of the bow.

67 **the early 1920s.** John Lieby, consulting naval architect for the Tabor Academy's *Tabor Boy* (formerly *Bestebaer*), the first of this class built in 1914, personal interview, 24 March 1996.

67 **back to port."** Captain and Mrs. Irving Johnson, *Westward Bound in the Schooner Yankee* (New York: Norton, 1936), 10. The comment refers to Johnson's first *Yankee*, which predated the *Albatross* but was also a North Sea pilot schooner.

67 **the same reason.** Gann, *Welcome Aboard*, 1.

68 **bronze chocks remain.** Ibid., 1.

68 **dubious reliability.** Ibid., 1–2.

68 **renamed the** *Alk.* Ibid., 2.

68 **World War I.** Von Luckner was a German nobleman of a military family who acquired a reputation for his daring yet genteel approach to warfare on the high seas. He and his crew had a remarkable, if brief, career raiding Allied commerce in the Atlantic and Pacific Oceans for the German Imperial Navy during World War I. Masquerading as a hapless Norwegian sailing ship carrying lumber, his preferred method was to lay the *Seeadler* alongside some flash packet steamer under the pretext of needing to correct his chronometer or some such artifice. With passengers staring on, mouths agape, the *Seeadler*'s guns would pop out and the steamer was typically captured without a fight.

68 **depth charges!"** Sheldon, interview, Norwalk, Connecticut, 13 March 1996.

68 **U-boat navigators."** Gann, *Welcome Aboard*, 2.

69 **in Massachusetts.** As of 2002 the *Tabor Boy* continued to engage in sail training year-round along the U.S. East Coast and the Caribbean.

69 **with trainees."** Gann, *Welcome Aboard*, 2.

69 **a sailing ship.** Ibid., 3.

69 **transpacific air travel.** Ian Birnie (former mate aboard the *Albatross* under Gann in Hawaii), correspondence with the author, 1996.

70 **the Panama Canal.** Gann, *Welcome Aboard,* 3.

70 **autobiographical vignettes.** Ernest K. Gann, *Song of the Sirens* (New York: Simon & Schuster, 1968).

70 *Twilight for the Gods.* Gann, *Welcome Aboard,* 3.

70 **hermaphrodite brig.** The correct usage of traditional rigging terminology is fairly well-established yet sometimes still leads to debate. By one definition the *Albatross*'s final rig complies with the characteristics of a *hermaphrodite brig.* This clumsy term refers to a vessel that is fully square-rigged on the foremast, and fore-and-aft rigged on the main, as the *Albatross* was. *Half brig* is also sometimes used to describe this configuration. However, the *Albatross* and many similarly rigged vessels are widely referred to as *brigantines.* By an older definition, a true brigantine is square-rigged on the foremast as well as the mainmast, but the course yard on the main is significantly higher than the course yard on the foremast. This allows a "true brigantine" to carry a full gaff mainsail, with the length of the luff approximating that found on the mainsail of a schooner. Above it are a square topsail and topgallant. Sometimes a course sail is also rigged. This is distinct from a *brig,* which also carries square sails on

Standard terminology for sailing rigs. (Jim Sollers, after artwork of the Peabody Museum)

1. Ship: square-rigged on all (three or more) masts

2. Barque (bark): a vessel with three or more masts, square-rigged on all but the mizzen (last) which carries a schooner (fore-and-aft) rig

3. Barkentine: vessel of three or more masts, with square sails on its foremast (the first mast), but schooner (fore-and-aft) rigging on its main and mizzenmasts

4. Brig: a two-masted vessel with square sails on both masts

5. Brigantine: a two-masted sailing vessel with square sails on its foremast and square-rigged topsails and a gaff-rigged mainsail on its mainmast

6. Hermaphrodite brig: a two-masted vessel with square sails on its foremast and schooner (fore-and-aft) rig on its mainmast (also known as a "half brig")

7. Topsail schooner: fore-and-aft rigged, two-masted vessel with square sails set on the foretopmast

8. Three-masted schooner: fore-and-aft rigged on all masts

the main, but has a course yard of approximately the same height as the course on the foremast. On a brig this results in the short-luffed mainsail frequently termed a *spanker* rather than a *mainsail*. Records available for the *Albatross* after the conversion in California invariably refer to her as a *brigantine;* therefore, correct or not, that is the term applied to her post-California rig in this work.

70 **above the deck.** Christopher J. Sheldon, "Remarks of Capt. Christopher J. Sheldon," in *Proceedings of the ASTA/ISTA International Safety Forum: Microbursts and the Mariner* (Newport: U.S. Naval War College, 1997), 4.

70 **fourteen days.** Sheldon, "Remarks," 4.

72 **W. P. Hincks.** Roger Long of Woodin and Marean, "Boothbay Harbor, Maine" memo to the Sailing School Vessels Council and Other Interested Parties, 19 September 1984.

72 **center of gravity).** Roger Long of Woodin and Marean, "Capsizing of Brigantine *Albatross*" memo to the Sailing School Vessels Council and Other Interested Parties, 19 September 1984, 5. In the professional papers of Roger Long. See Stability, in the appendix, for detail on metacentric height and center of gravity.

72 **all sail set."** Gann, *Welcome Aboard,* 4.

72 **accurate prediction."** Ibid., 4.

73 **as a liner's."** Gann, *Song of the Sirens,* 235.

73 friends and acquaintances. Gann, *Welcome Aboard*, 4.
73 the Big Island." Birnie, correspondence with the author.
73 that he be captain. Ibid.
73 hired as mate. Ibid.
73 reef points. Gann, *Welcome Aboard*, 5.
73 Christopher B. Sheldon. "Intent to Sell the Ship upon Completion of Film," *San Francisco Examiner*, 2 December 1957, section I.
73 with Johnson. Johnson's second *Yankee* (the steel one) is widely described as a *brigantine*, but pictures show her to be a topsail schooner with staysails between the masts.
74 accepted his word. Sheldon, "Remarks," 4.
74 but as crew." Sheldon quoted in "Tragedy in the Gulf," *Newsweek*, 15 May 1961.
75 private schools. The Ocean Academy, postcard advertisement, 1959; former student Phillip LeBoutillier.
75 the same reasons. Robert Johnson, interview, 19 January 2002.
77 about 3,500 pounds." Sheldon, interview, 20 January 2002.
77 well-equipped to do so. John Lieby, interview, 13 January 2002.
77 marginally smaller. William H. Bunting, interview, 12 September 2001. Bunting sailed in both ships. Robert Johnson, interview, 19 January 2002. The son of Irving Johnson, Robert sailed frequently aboard *Yankee* between 1948 and 1958. He visited aboard the *Albatross* on more than one occasion. He was concerned enough about the lack of freeboard to question Captain Sheldon about it and heard the explanation about the removal of the old main engine and the need to reballast.
78 two weeks earlier. A Hollywood-invented scene in the movie *White Squall* depicted Cuban military officials boarding the ship and smashing the compass. In fact, there had been no contact with Cuba whatsoever, though the ship was boarded by armed Mexican authorities at one point.
78 time of year. Sheldon, interview, 13 March 1996.
78 dwindling fuel supply." William H. Bunting, as told to Jack Ryan, "My Miraculous Escape from the *Albatross*," *Family Weekly* (2 July 1961).
78 have been motoring." Sheldon, interview, 13 March 1996.
78 during the watch. Richard Langford, *The Death of a School Ship* (typescript), 1. In the collection of the G. W. Blunt White Library, Mystic Seaport, Mystic, Connecticut.
78 bring some wind." Ibid.
78 tropical squall." Bunting, correspondence with the author, 19 September 2001.
78 ordered sharply. Gieg and Sutton, *Last Voyage of the Albatross*, 6–7.
78 not black—sky. Bunting, correspondence with the author, 22 January 2002.
78 in this lightning." Bunting, as told to Ryan, "My Miraculous Escape," 5.
79 our main staysail. Sheldon, "Remarks," 1.
79 let the sheet out. Ibid., 2. Sheldon puts the arrival of the squall at "0900 or 0930," whereas Gieg puts it at 0830. In my experience, captains tend to be more attuned to the sequence and timing of events because they control the decision-making process that leads to orders for the crew to follow.
79 to reduce sail. Sheldon, interview, 20 January 2002.

80 **the way it felt.** Sheldon, "Remarks," 2.

80 **terrifying suddenness.** Gieg and Sutton, *Last Voyage of the Albatross*, 7–8.

80 **within 60 seconds.** Sheldon, "Remarks," 2.

80 **poured in on me."** Richard E. Langford, "I Went Down with the *Albatross*," *Reader's Digest* (October 1961): 64.

81 **sheer strength."** Ibid., 65.

81 **an eerie green.** Bunting, as told to Ryan, "My Miraculous Escape," 6; Bunting, correspondence with the author, August 2002.

81 **foot of airspace.** Ibid.

81 **a pile driver."** Ibid.

81 **charthouse doors.** Gieg, *White Squall*—Conference 2 (e-mail).

81 **sinking too fast.** Ibid.

81 **his way out.** Langford, "I Went Down with the *Albatross*," 65.

81 **forty feet down.** Richard E. Langford, *White Squall: The Last Voyage of the Albatross*, ed. Jerry Renninger (Enola, Penna.: Bristol Fashion, 2001), 106.

82 **the United States."** U.S. Coast Guard Report, From Officer in Charge (William T. Corfield), Marine Inspection, Tampa to Commander, 7th Coast Guard District (Miami), regarding capsizing of Brigantine *Albatross*, 22 May 1961, 2. Hereafter USCG Report (Corfield).

82 **we climbed up."** Gieg, *White Squall*—Conference 1 (e-mail).

83 **step or steps."** United States Coast Guard Memorandum from Commander, 7th Coast Guard District (C. W. Quinby) to the Commandant (MVI) regarding capsizing of the Brigantine *Albatross*, 26 May 1961, 1.

84 **movement below.** Christopher Sheldon, interview, 20 January 2002.

84 **through every hatch."** Langford, *Death of a School Ship*, 6.

85 **capsized by northers.** *Boston Journal*, 8 December 1877.

86 **surface of the sea.** Philip McFarland, *Sea Dangers, the Affair of the Somers* (New York: Schocken, 1985), 250.

86 **produces a microburst.** In discussing squalls, there is a tendency, even among sailors, to refer to rain showers as squalls. Technically, a squall is a wind event, that may or may not be accompanied by precipitation. The approach of showers is not synonymous with a wind increase, and in fact, often the opposite occurs.

87 **range much higher.** T. Theodore Fujita, *The Downburst: Microburst and Macroburst: Report of Projects NIMROD and JAWS* ([Chicago]: Satellite and Mesometeorology Research Project, Dept. of the Geophysical Sciences, University of Chicago, 1985), 63.

87 **activity in the area.** Winds over 100 knots were recorded on the Isles of Shoals, New Hampshire, on 10 August 2001. Summer weather warnings on the Great Lakes and Chesapeake Bay routinely include winds in excess of 50 knots with thunderstorms, which are essentially convection cells.

88 **to replace it."** Gieg, *White Squall*—Conference 1 (e-mail).

88 **own recollection.** Quoted in Langford, "I Went Down with the *Albatross*," 67.

88 **before and afterward."** Sheldon, interview, 13 March 1996.

88 **in the appendix).** USCG Report (Corfield), 2.

88 **to the ground.** Fujita, *Downburst*, 6.

88 **about six knots.** *Industrial Journal*, 27 July 1888. In the papers of William H. Bunting.

88 **"in complete calm."** Fessenden S. Blanchard and William T. Stone, *A Cruising Guide to the Chesapeake: Including the Passages from Long Island Sound Along the New Jersey Coast and Inland Waterway*, rev. ed. (New York: Dodd, Mead, 1962), 15.

89 **running under water.** Lemuel Norton, *Autobiography of Lemuel Norton* (n.p.: Concord, Hadley & Co., 1864), 71–72. In the papers of William H. Bunting.

89 **ship-killing conditions.** Sheldon, interview, 20 January 2002.

90 **could take effect.** Frank J. Scott, "Stability," chapt. 14 in *A Square Rig Sailing Handbook* (London: Nautical Institute, 1992, rev. 2001).

90 **They'll sink us!"** Langford, *Death of a School Ship*.

90 **situation called for.** Sheldon, interview, 13 March 1996.

90 **affected the outcome.** Ibid.; Bunting, interview, 12 September 2001.

91 **of similar size.** The brigantine *Eye of the Wind* carries approximately 6,800 square feet of canvas for 262 tons displacement versus 5,000 square feet for the *Albatross*, for about a third more gross tonnage. Brigantine *Zebu* carries 4,800 square feet for about 25 percent more gross tonnage.

92 **cancelled the order."** Gieg, *White Squall*—Conference 1 (e-mail).

92 **capsizing had begun.** Sheldon, interview, 20 January 2002.

93 **been to sea.** Alice Sheldon had been part of the same eighteen-month circumnavigation that Christopher Sheldon had made aboard the *Yankee*, plus the long voyage from Lisbon to the United States. George Ptacnik, the cook, had been aboard for three years. John Perry, a former paratrooper, and Richard Langford had prior experience, but how much is not known.

93 **even desirable.** Sheldon, interview, 13 March 1996.

93 **build a sailor.** Ibid.

93 **they were equal.** Ibid.

93 **seemed to work.** The participants aboard the *Yankee* on her worldwide cruises were generally older, ranging from their late teens to midtwenties. Also, a first mate was engaged who was quite senior in experience to the other student-crew.

94 **a "crack sailor."** Gieg, *White Squall*—Conference 2 (e-mail).

94 **the schooner *Verona*.** Sheldon, interview, 13 March 1996.

94 **to get photographs.** Bunting, interview, 12 September 2001.

96 **hoisted for launching.** William H. Bunting, correspondence with the author, 22 January 2002.

97 **fairly constant.** Long, "Capsizing of Brigantine *Albatross*" memo, 6.

98 **stability characteristics.** Ibid., 1.

99 **57.0 degrees** Ibid., 9, 13.

99 **began to change.** The classic technical study, "On the Stability of Sailing Vessels" by J. G. Beebe-Center and R. B. Brooks (paper presented to the Chesapeake Section of the Society of Naval Architects and Marine Engineers, Washington, D.C., 2 March 1966), which proposed many of today's methods for sailing vessel stability analysis, did not appear until almost ten years after Hincks's analysis of the *Albatross*.

100 **still occur.**" Beebe-Center and Brooks, "On the Stability of Sailing Vessels," 2.
100 **design under sail.** Ibid., 2.
100 **regard to stability.** Ibid., 3, 7.
100 **general design tool.**" Ibid., 2.
101 **any such vessel.** Ibid., 3.
101 **calculating GM.** Ibid., 7.
101 **oceangoing yachts.**" Ibid.
101 **stability criteria.** Parker E. Marean III and Roger W. Long, "Survey of Sailing Vessel Stability Leading to Modified Regulations" (typescript), paper presented to the New England Section of The Society of Naval Architects and Marine Engineers, 1986, 4. In the professional papers of Roger Long.
101 **"successful" vessels.** Parker E. Marean III and Roger W. Long of Woodin and Marean, "Expansion of a Sailing Vessel Data Base Used for Development of Dynamic Stability Criteria," 19 March 1986, 1–2. In the professional papers of Roger Long.
101 **stability characteristics.** Ibid., 2.
101 **what did not.**" Ibid.
102 **Beebe-Center and Brooks.** Marean and Long, "Survey of Sailing Vessel Stability," 3–4.
102 **intended to prevent.**" Long, "Capsizing of Brigantine *Albatross*" memo, 1.
102 **known stability casualties.** Marean and Long, "Survey of Sailing Vessel Stability," 4.
102 **academic interest.** Long, "Capsizing of Brigantine *Albatross*" memo, 1.
103 **schooners in general.** Marean and Long, "Survey of Sailing Vessel Stability," 13.
103 **it was lost.** Long, "Capsizing of Brigantine *Albatross*" memo, 5.
103 **most decisively.**" Ibid., 6.
104 **and safety.**" Bunting, as told to Ryan, "My Miraculous Escape," 4.
105 **she was beautiful.**" Langford, "I Went Down with the *Albatross*," 62.
105 **in her stride.**" Gieg and Sutton, *Last Voyage of the Albatross*, 8.
105 **flooding or capsize.**" Roger Long, draft of "Simplified Assessment of Sailing Vessel Stability for Masters and Operators," Portland, Maine, 1986, 1. In the professional papers of Roger Long.
105 **have saved her.**" Long, "Capsizing of Brigantine *Albatross*" memo, 5.
107 **another vessel.** Bunting, correspondence with the author, January 2002.
107 **a 90-degree knockdown.** Sheldon, interview, 13 March 1996.

Marques (1917–1984)

109 Vessel details from Richard Stone, E. G. Venables, and B. N. Baxter, *The Report of the Formal Investigation into the Loss of the Auxiliary Barque* Marques *Under the Merchant Shipping Acts of 1894 and 1970, Report of Court No. 8073* (London: Her Majesty's Stationery Office, 1987), appendix 2:79. The Wreck Commission Report had difficulty establishing the dimensions of

the *Marques* when attempting to recreate her stability characteristics: "There were no original plans for the *Marques*, and accurate particulars were sparse." A discrepancy existed between the measurements recorded in 1974 at the time the *Marques* was registered in Britain, and measurements taken in Spain in 1966. In the end the investigation settled on a compromise that favored the Spanish figures based on the methods and the quality of the work. Often, however, the investigation proceeded with figures that were based on a variety of sources and some educated guesswork, rather than certainty.

111 **people always suffer."** *Traditional Ship News,* Anglian Yacht Services, 28 Spital Road, Maldon, Essex, U.K., no. 9 (1984): 1.

112 **and elsewhere.** Basil Greenhill, *The Ship: The Life and Death of the Merchant Sailing Vessel, 1815–1965* (London: National Maritime Museum, Her Majesty's Stationery Office, 1980), 55.

112 **were prohibitive.** Ibid., 57.

112 **a sailing ship."** *Report of the Formal Investigation,* 7.

113 **extinct by 1960.** Greenhill, *Ship,* 57.

113 **with his family."** Except where noted, all information in this History section that is given as fact was derived from the *Report of the Formal Investigation.* *Report of the Formal Investigation,* 7.

113 **liquid contents.** *Report of the Formal Investigation,* 8.

113 **Mediterranean origins.** *Polacca* refers to a pole style mast rather than a sectioned mast typically found in western Europe. The *Marques*'s foremast was reportedly donated by the Forestry Commission in Britain (Henry H. Anderson, "Sail Training Loss," file 9, *Marques* Collection, G. W. Blunt White Library, Mystic Seaport, Mystic, Connecticut).

114 **BBC Design Department.** *Report of the Formal Investigation,* 9.

114 **to carry sail.** Ibid., 10.

114 **stability characteristics."** Ibid.

115 **"sound and stable."** Ibid.

115 **aft deckhouse.** Donald Treworgy, interview, Mystic, Connecticut, 19 September 2001.

115 **"reception conditions,"** Ibid., 11.

116 **coastal waters.** The Merchant Shipping Act (Load Line Act) of 1967 was enabling legislation passed in Britain pursuant to the International Maritime Organization Load Line Convention of 1966. The IMO, a department of the United Nations, oversees maritime conventions. The Merchant Shipping (Load Line) Rules 1968 (S.I. 1968) No. 1053 gave statutory effect to the act and established the first stability criteria in Britain. The criteria established under the rules were designed for power-driven merchant ships and required a range of positive stability of 40 degrees and a maximum righting lever occurring at not less than 30 degrees. All vessels to which the rules applied were required to have either a Load Line Certificate or a Load Line Exemption Certificate, both of which involved an extensive structural survey and full stability data. The rules exempted pleasure yachts, leaving open to interpretation the status of the *Marques*, depending on her activity. By 1983 the Department of Transport had "taken the firm view that for . . . sail training beyond U.K. coastal waters the

[Marques] fell within the Act." The rules also allowed sailing vessels of less than 80 net register tons, *not carrying cargo*, to operate within U.K. coastal waters without a Load Line Certificate or a Load Line Exemption Certificate. The Merchant Shipping (Safety Convention) Act of 1949 required masters be provided with stability data, but set forth no criteria. As early as 1973, Instructions for the Guidance of Surveyors included a list of necessary stability information for British sail training vessels; however, there were no legal criteria.

117 and "filmmaking." *Report of the Formal Investigation*, 11, 12.

117 were added. Ibid.

118 Exemption Certificate. Ibid.

118 years of service." Ibid., 14.

119 *Ciudad de Inca.* Ibid., 56.

119 out my belief." Ibid., 14.

119 inclining weights. Ibid., 57.

120 inclining experiment." Ibid., 56, 57.

120 Clipper Challenge." Ibid., 16.

120 for such work. Ibid.

120 firefighting equipment. Ibid. There was no question that the ships could not have met requirements for passenger vessels.

120 Load Line Act. The inadequacy of the Load Line Act Rules for sail training is further seen in the fact that even if the *Marques* had been required to come under the rules at this point, there was no stability criterion appropriate to sailing vessels, as the existing criteria established by the IMO was designed for motor-driven merchant ships. See note for page 116.

121 financially viable. *Report of the Formal Investigation*, 116.

121 under surveillance." Ibid., 17.

122 be no solution. Ibid.

122 Department Surveyor." Ibid., 18.

122 was concerned." Ibid., 15.

123 unusual venture." Ibid., 18.

123 act with caution." Ibid.

123 sailing was limited." Ibid., 19.

123 next two years. Ibid., 20.

124 Perryman's survey. Ibid.

124 Declaration," he wrote. Ibid., 21.

125 to sailing vessels. Ibid., 19.

125 conventional survey. Ibid., 17.

127 wrangling with Litchfield. Ibid., 22.

127 "no undue concern." Ibid., 23.

127 further damage. Ibid.

127 routine and discipline. Ibid., 27.

128 educational experience. Ibid., 27.

128 maintenance of the vessels. The investigation does not comment as to how the terms of the Load Line Exemption applied to passenger daysailing in Antigua.

129 tall-ships race. *Report of the Formal Investigation*, 24.

129 seemed well run. McAleer and Lebel v. Smith, including the American Sail

Training Association, C. A. No. 88-0544L, U.S. District Court for Rhode Island, 1994, 29. Plaintiffs were Edward McAleer, Administrator of the Estate of James F. McAleer, Hardy Lebel and Joan Lebel, Administrators of the Estate of Thomas Lebel. Defendants were Traver C. Smith Jr., Administrator of the Estate of Stuart A. Finlay, Mark Shirley Portal Litchfield, and Robin Patrick Cecil-Wright, dba The China Clipper Society, Berry Brothers and Rudd Ltd. dba Cutty Sark, American Sail Training Association, and Lloyds of London. Hereafter McAleer and Lebel v. Smith et al.

129 training sextant. Treworgy, telephone interview, 13 February 2002.

130 for a trainee. Connie Baehm, telephone interview, 10 March 2002.

130 main hatch amidships. Treworgy, interview, Mystic, Connecticut, 20 September 2001.

130 allow ventilation. McAleer and Lebel v. Smith et al., 30.

130 regarding the hatches. Treworgy, interview, 20 September 2001.

130 was overrigged. Stuart Gillespie, telephone interview, 8 February 2002.

130 closed at sea.” *Report of the Formal Investigation*, 28.

132 severe disturbance. McAleer and Lebel v. Smith et al., 36.

133 was out there.” “Storm that Sank *Marques* Forecast Before Race Began,” *Royal Gazette*, 28 July 1984.

133 start the race.” Ibid.

136 crew of seven. The *Report of the Formal Investigation* states that there was “a permanent crew of nine under the command of Mr. Stuart Finlay” (1). Using the figure of nine, along with the rest of the crew breakdown provided by the investigation, the total number of people on board comes to thirty, yet the report states that the nineteen were lost out of a ship’s complement of twenty-eight. The arithmetic suggests that, if all other figures are correct as they appear to be, then the regular crew numbered seven, not nine, which corresponds with the crew list departing Antigua. The most likely explanation for the discrepancy is that two of the Antiguan trainees were double counted as trainees and as crew when they were promoted to deckhands.

137 occasional showers. Ibid., 32.

138 cold front.” Ibid.

138 the suggestion.” Ibid., 33.

138 using that night. Ibid.

138 making a flyby. Gillespie, telephone interview, 8 February 2002.

138 bulwark rail.” *Report of the Formal Investigation*, 34.

139 bath of milk.” Ibid.

139 batten was used. Ibid., 35.

139 two minutes.” Ibid., 34.

140 standard to apply.” Ibid., 64.

140 thousands of pounds.” Quoted in Mick Brown, “Doomed *Marques*: Refit Budget Was Cheeseparing,” *Marques* Collection, G. W. Blunt White Library, Mystic Seaport, Mystic, Connecticut.

141 to Halifax.” *Report of the Formal Investigation*, 51.

141 vessel sank. Ibid., 35.

142 deck level. Ibid., 81.

142 replacing it. Ibid., 49, 71.

143 to discuss it. William Peterson, telephone interview, 16 April 2002.

143 at the dock." Treworgy, interview, 19 September 2001. Treworgy related this exchange from a meeting with Hughill at the Mystic Seaport Music Festival in June 1984.

143 sailing ships. Treworgy, interview, 19 September 2001.

143 not seamanship." *Report of the Formal Investigation*, 49.

143 the doors open. Herald of Free Enterprise, Report of the Court no. 8074. Formal investigation, London.

144 downflooding began. Roger Long, "Sailing Vessel Stability Criteria Based on Analysis of Sample Population with Static Methods—A Draft," Portland, Maine: Roger Long Marine Architecture Inc. (March 1987): 6.

144 to 15 minutes. *Report of the Formal Investigation*, 50.

145 was foreseeable. To access the main living space, the *Pride of Baltimore* also used a cargo hatch, which was also kept partially open for ventilation under certain conditions. Despite this parallel flaw, the *Pride of Baltimore*'s hatch was fully battened at the time of her loss and was not believed to have been a point of ingress when flooding occurred.

148 get slammed." Evan McLeod Wylie, "Race to Terror," *Yankee* (May 1985): 104, 105.

148 or Force 12." *Report of the Formal Investigation*, 43.

148 destructive type." Ibid.

149 tall-ship races. Ibid., 77.

150 other competitors." Ibid., 76.

151 North of Bermuda." Ibid., 45.

151 would materialise." Ibid., 49.

152 the forecourse." Ibid.

152 those aboard." Treworgy, interview, 19 September 2001.

154 greater safety." *Report of the Formal Investigation*, 47.

154 Cuttyhunk, Massachusetts." Ibid., 24.

155 of the loss." Ibid., 47.

155 selection process. Ibid., 45, 20.

159 *by the master.* Ibid., 66.

159 knowledge of the vessel." Ibid., 19, 66.

159 chartered engineer." Ibid., 64.

159 Naval Architect. Ibid., 66.

160 it was issued. Ibid., 46.

160 regulatory requirement." Ibid., 15.

160 necessary action. Ibid., 65–66.

161 57 degrees Given the dynamic environment of a ship at sea, and inherent uncertainties in the data, these figures are regarded as reasonable approximations, rather than absolutes.

161 stability is essential. *Report of the Formal Investigation*, 71–72.

162 should be obtained. Ibid., 65.

162 non-coastal waters. Ibid., preface.

163 converted vessels. Ibid., 68.

163　**for naval vessels.** Ibid., 52.

163　**Royal Navy designs.** Ibid.; Frank J. Scott, "Stability," chapt. 14 in *A Square Rig Sailing Handbook* (London: Nautical Institute, 1992, rev. 2001).

163　**through 1894.** W. H. White, *A Manual of Naval Architecture* (London: John Murray, 1882).

164　**subject of stability.** Edward J. Reed, *A Treatise on the Stability of Ships* (London: Griffin, 1885).

164　**the nineteenth century.** Scott, "Stability." The *Eurydice* was returning from the Caribbean when she was caught in a squall off the Isle of Wight. Her gunports were open, which effectively lowered her freeboard, and she flooded. She was said to be a "well-proven" vessel.

164　**late nineteenth century.** Parker E. Marean III and Roger W. Long, "Survey of Sailing Vessel Stability Leading to Modified Regulations" (typescript), paper presented to the New England Section of The Society of Naval Architects and Marine Engineers, 1986, 2–3. In the professional papers of Roger Long.

164　**around the world.** N. T. Tsai and E. C. Haciski, "Stability of Large Sailing Vessels: A Case Study," *Marine Technology* 23, no. 1 (January 1986): 2. *Horst Wessel*, now the *Eagle* of the United States; *Gorch Fock*, now the *Tovaristsch* of Russia; *Albert Leo Schlageter*, now the *Sagres II* of Portugal.

164　**future development."** Scott, "Stability."

164　**to the *Marques*.** Roger Long of Woodin and Marean, "Capsizing of the Brigantine *Albatross*" memo to the Sailing School Vessels Council and Other Interested Parties, 19 September 1984, 1. In the professional papers of Roger Long.

164　**vessel's stability.** *Report of the Formal Investigation*, 64–65.

165　**90 degrees.** Ibid., 68.

165　**Kingdom in 1983."** Ibid., 66.

166　*any persons on board.* Ibid., 68, 69–70.

166　**stability information.** Ibid., 69.

167　**the United Kingdom."** Ibid., 66–67.

167　**interest and research."** Scott, "Stability."

168　**training ships."** *Report of the Formal Investigation*, 71.

168　**alone is sufficient.** Ibid., 71.

168　**training ship."** Ibid., 73.

168　**wherever possible.** Ibid.

168　**cabin is dependent.** Ibid., 74.

168　**and unobstructed.** Ibid.

169　**type of ship.** Department of Transport (U.K.) Merchant Shipping Notice, "The Stability of Sail Training Ships: Notice to Shipowners, Masters, Builders, Designers and other persons engaged in the operation of sail training ships," May 1997, 1.

169　**United States).** Ibid., 2.

169　**larger vessels.** Ibid., 5.

169　**rather than athwartships.** Ibid., 3.

169　**openings be closed."** Ibid.

169　**Department for approval.** Ibid., 4. The author was an officer in the British brigantine *Eye of the Wind* at the time the notice was issued. The investigation found that the stability characteristics of the *Marques* and the *Eye of the Wind* compared closely, and the vessel was detained from a scheduled six-month voyage into the Pacific until her stability was assessed. She was found to be deficient, and the next several months were spent reballasting and bringing her stability characteristics up to the new criteria.

169 informed discussion." *Report of the Formal Investigation*, 73.

169 in existence." B. Deakin, "The Development of Stability Standards for UK Sailing Vessels," paper presented in London at a meeting of the Royal Institute of Naval Architects, 23 April 1990, 1.

170 apparent direction. Ibid., 7, 2.

170 a given vessel. Ibid., 10.

170 weather conditions." Deakin, "Development of Stability Standards," discussion comment by R. Holstead, Marine Directorate, Department of Transport, 12.

170 design and stability. Ibid.

170 their activities. In 1990 the Marine Directorate of the Department of Transport published *The Safety of Sail Training Ships—A Code of Practice* (London: Her Majesty's Stationery Office, 1990). These regulations covered a full range of operational standards including construction, machinery, equipment, stability, manning, operation, and inspection of sail training vessels. In 1993 it was subsumed into *The Safety of Small Commercial Sailing Vessels—A Code of Practice* (London: Her Majesty's Stationery Office, 1993), which applied to vessels of up to 24 meters in commercial use and that do not carry cargo or more than twelve passengers. Finally, in 1997, sail training vessels larger than 24 meters were addressed under *The Code of Practice for Safety of Large Commercial Sailing and Motor Vessels* (London: Stationery Office, 1997).

171 never be guaranteed." Surveyor General's Organization, *Safety of Small Commercial Vessels*, 2–3.

171 (STCW 95) protocols. Standards of Training, Certification and Watchkeeping for Seafarers. The 1995 IMO convention came into force on 1 February 2002. It was the most ambitious attempt up to that point to establish uniformity in training and knowledge in the international community of commercial mariners. The emphasis of the convention was on safety and communications.

171 the exemption." Mark Kemmis-Betty, correspondence with the author, 3 March 2002.

172 loss of the *Marques*." Ibid., 10 March 2002.

172 stability criteria." N. T. Tsai and E. C. Haciski, "Stability of Large Sailing Vessels: A Case Study," *Marine Technology* 23, no. 1 (January 1986): 2.

172 eventually bore fruit. Graeme Smith, Ocean Youth Club, personal interview, Newport, Rhode Island, 7 March 1998.

173 *Marques* was lost. Capt. David V. V. Wood, "Opening Remarks," *Proceedings*, ASTA/ISTA International Safety Forum, Toronto, 1993 (Newport, Rhode Island: American Sail Training Association, November 1993).

173 to do with it." Ibid.

175 part of that." Ibid.

Pride of Baltimore (1977–1986)

178 prior experience. Information relating to the *Sophia* comes from surviving crew member Christopher Janini. Other interesting details include the fact that EPIRB was stowed below and went down with the ship, as on so many other vessels at the time. The life rafts had been lashed without hydrostatic releases but nevertheless became free. The survivors drifted for approximately five days, often within sight of land, seeing numerous vessels and aircraft daily and using their entire supply of flares before being picked up by a Soviet freighter that nearly ran over them.

179 nautical archaeology. Thomas C. Gillmer is one of the most accomplished American naval architects of the twentieth century, having been a professor of naval architecture and naval engineering at the United States Naval Academy for many years and author of the U.S. Navy's standard textbooks on ship design. He has created many successful designs for recreational and cruising sailing craft, some of which, notably *Blue Moon* and the *Seawind* 30s and 32s, have been built many times over all around the world. With respect to large historic replica vessels, Gillmer designed the *Pride of Baltimore*, *Pride of Baltimore II* (both Baltimore clippers), *Lady Maryland* (Chesapeake Bay pungy schooner), and *Kalmar Nyckel* (seventeenth-century full rigger of Dutch origins that brought Swedish settlers to Delaware).

180 Norway, and Sweden. Crew exchanges were arranged in 1985 with the three-masted sail training schooner *Sir Winston Churchill* (Britain); the full-rigged ship *Sørlandet* of Kristiansand (Norway); and the Swedish navy sail training schooner *Falken*.

180 dockside exhibits. Due to safety regulations and practical considerations, very few of the traditional sailing vessels operating today could qualify to be described as exact replicas. The word *replica* as applied to today's traditional sailing fleet carries with it an understanding that authenticity has been compromised in varying degrees, but that the ships retain enough of their original essence to convey a useful and valuable idea of how their predecessors once operated.

181 Baltimore Clipper privateers. The term *Baltimore clipper* is not universally accepted by historians. The terms *sharp-built*, *Baltimore-built*, *Baltimore schooner*, *Virginia pilot schooner*, or just plain *pilot schooner* are sometimes used to describe the hull form that corresponds closely with what is here called a *Baltimore clipper*. In his well-researched book, *Tidewater Triumph* (Centreville, Maryland: Tidewater Publishers, 1998), Geoffrey M. Footner takes issue with the term *Baltimore clipper* and offers alternative views on the evolution of the relevant terminology. However, since the world knows the *Pride of Baltimore* and the *Pride of Baltimore II* as Baltimore clippers, this term is retained here for simplicity's sake.

181 degree of excellence." Howard Irving Chapelle, *The Baltimore Clipper: Its Origin and Development* (Valdosta, Georgia: Edward Sweetman, 1968), 66.

181 great deadrise, *Deadrise* is the transverse angle that a hull's shape rises above horizontal when going from the keel to a vertical orientation.

181 **total sparred length.** *Headrig* refers to the spars and rigging that extend forward from the bow of a sailing vessel, and includes the bowsprit and jibboom.

182 **a fast vessel.** Chapelle, *Baltimore Clipper*, 105.

182 **feet of sail."** National Transportation Safety Board (NTSB), *Marine Accident Report on the Capsizing and Sinking of the U.S. Sailing Vessel Pride of Baltimore in the Atlantic Ocean on May 14th, 1986* (Washington, D.C.: Government Printing Office, 1987), 31. Hereafter NTSB *Report*.

182 **possessed in total.** Chapelle, *Baltimore Clipper*, 66.

184 **a lesser priority.** Thomas C. Gillmer, *Pride of Baltimore: The Story of the Baltimore Clippers, 1800–1990* (Camden, Maine: International Marine, 1992), 60.

184 **shipbuilding and design."** Ibid., ix.

184 **more thinly.** Ibid., xii.

184 **unable to afford."** Ibid., 48.

184 **two-year conflict.** R. J. Holt, 1983, in the collection of Chesapeake Bay Maritime Museum, St. Michaels, Maryland.

184 **to intervene.** Gillmer, *Pride of Baltimore*, 34–36.

185 **British prizes.** Ibid., 29.

185 **years later.** The connection to this historical episode was perpetuated aboard the *Pride of Baltimore II*, whose longboat was named *Chasseur*.

185 **rigorous blockade."** Boyle's Proclamation, copy on board the *Pride of Baltimore II*.

185 **laying the keel.** Gillmer, *Pride of Baltimore*, 71.

185 **cargo schooners.** Footner, *Tidewater Triumph*, 158.

185 **long lives."** Ibid., xiii.

185 **would have expected.** Chapelle, *Baltimore Clipper*, 104.

186 **of the period.** Reprinted in Gillmer, *Pride of Baltimore*, 117.

186 **twentieth century.** Chapelle, *Baltimore Clipper*, 3.

186 **sensible statement.** Gillmer, *Pride of Baltimore*, 133.

187 **size limitation."** Ibid., 122.

187 **lignum vitae.** Ibid., 123.

187 **City of Baltimore."** NTSB *Report*, 28.

187 **space available."** Gillmer, *Pride of Baltimore*, 134.

187 **only two sails.** Andy Davis, interview with Peter Boudreau, "A New Pride for Baltimore," *WoodenBoat* 96 (September–October 1990): 59. Boudreau was raised aboard schooners sailing with his family throughout the North Atlantic. He has captained several schooners of note and was master shipwright for the construction of the *Pride of Baltimore II* and *Lady Maryland*. He directed the reconstruction of the Portuguese fishing barquentine *Gazela* of Philadelphia and the full-rigger *Constellation*. Boudreau has done design work for several new traditional sailing vessels.

189 **original vision.** NTSB *Report*, 28.

189 **was not pursued.** Ibid., 28–29.

189 **developed accordingly.** The *Pride of Baltimore* was documented with a "white certificate." This entitled the USCG to inspect the vessel at its discretion during haulouts or, theoretically, any time it had a specific concern. This privilege reflected a standing desire on the part of the coast guard to maintain at least

minimal oversight over noncommercial U.S. vessels of some significance. The coast guard exercised that right with the *Pride* at routine haulouts on a number of occasions, but there is no record of these visits being related to a specific concern regarding the condition of the hull.

189 **its revenue stream.** Underway activities requiring USCG certification amount to less than 10 percent of annual revenue generated by *Pride of Baltimore II* over the years. This figure does not include overnight passenger carrying, which, being limited to six, does not require coast guard certification.

191 **in July 1986.** Gillmer, *Pride of Baltimore*, 139.

191 **in seventeen days.** Entries by Armin Elsaesser, Scott Jeffrey, and John "Sugar" Flanagan in *Pride of Baltimore, Final Log* newsletter (Baltimore: Pride of Baltimore Inc., 1986), 7.

191 **the Virgin Islands.** Elsaesser and Jeffrey entries in *Pride of Baltimore, Final Log*, 7–9.

191 **last leg home.** Robert Foster (*Pride* crew member at time of sinking), interview, 6 August 2002.

191 **in from the east.** Flanagan, "Statement of First Mate," in *Pride of Baltimore, Final Log*, 10. Except where indicated otherwise, all details in this Final Voyage section are taken from Flanagan, "Statement of First Mate," released 21 May 1986 in *Pride of Baltimore, Final Log*.

191 **starboard tack.** United States Coast Guard (USCG), United States Department of Transportation, report of the *Sailing Vessel* Pride of Baltimore—*Investigation into the Capsizing and Sinking with Multiple Loss of Life on 14 May 1986*, Baltimore, Maryland, 22 October 1986, 10. Hereafter USCG report.

192 **aft cabin hatch.** NTSB *Report*, 5.

192 **gaff and all.** Ibid., 6.

192 **amount of sail up."** Flanagan, "Statement of First Mate," 10.

192 **the earlier course.** USCG report, 10.

192 **over on its side.** Flanagan, "Statement of First Mate," 10.

194 **of my eyes.** NTSB *Report*, 7.

194 **abandon ship.** Flanagan, "Statement of First Mate," 10.

194 **to five minutes.** NTSB *Report*, 7.

195 **to impossible.** Flanagan, "Statement of First Mate," 10.

195 **force 7–8 conditions.** NTSB *Report*, 11.

195 **about four hours."** USCG report, 12.

195 **nights were hell."** "Statement of First Mate," 10.

195 **allowed to sink.** NTSB *Report*, 12.

198 **the "hinge."** Captain G. Peter Boudreau, interview, 22 March 1998.

198 **mast partners.** Ibid.

198 **heel was against."** Andy Davis, "Thomas Gillmer and the Prides," *WoodenBoat* 96 (September–October 1990): 59.

198 **area of the hull.** Boudreau, interview, 22 March 1998.

201 **may have recovered."** NTSB *Report*, 44.

201 **Penobscot Bay in 1779.** Thomas C. Gillmer, "An American Topsail Schooner," *The Mariner's Mirror* (Society for Nautical Research, National Maritime Museum, London) 66, no. 3 (August 1980): 252.

201 **lunch preparation.** McGeady, interview, 1 September 2002; Foster, interview, 3 September 2002.

202 **all of them."** B. Deakin, "The Development of Stability Standards for UK Sailing Vessels," paper presented in London at a meeting of the Royal Institute of Naval Architects, 23 April 1990, discussion comment by P. G. Winch, 16.

202 **flooding and loss."** Quoted in Richard "Jud" Henderson, *Chesapeake Sails: A History of Yachting on the Bay* (Centreville, Maryland: Tidewater, 1999), 94.

203 **modest loads."** Andy Davis, "A New Pride for Baltimore," *WoodenBoat* 96 (September–October 1990): 56.

204 **the rudder action."** NTSB *Report*, 44, 36.

204 **to the outcome.** Henderson, *Chesapeake Sails*, 92–94.

205 **answer her helm.** The USCG report shows a wind approximately 30 degrees abaft the beam (11). It has been written that the presence of a relieving tackle on the tiller offered no other option but to fall off, but this is not so. When rigged in its normal fashion, the relieving tackle on the *Pride of Baltimore* in no way restricted the helmsman's ability to round up or fall off. Its chief purpose was to counteract weather helm and it was never made fast. Not only did the running gear render easily, but the tackle connected by an open S-hook with no keeper; thus, it could be unhooked from the tiller with the flick of a wrist.

206 **would have survived.** Henderson, *Chesapeake Sails*, 93.

206 **similar situation.** The USCG report indicates that striking the foresail had been preceded by an order to reef it. This order was belayed and the sail taken to the deck. The master's reasons for aborting this plan are not known; however, loose-footed brailing foresails such as those used by Baltimore clippers are notoriously clumsy to reef compared to boomed sails. As with other features of a fighting ship, they are labor-intensive and carry over from a time when crews were many times larger.

206 **twenty minutes.** USCG report, 3, 5. The mechanics of microbursts are discussed in the *Albatross* chapter under Weather.

206 **to 30 minutes."** NTSB *Report*, 26.

207 **thunderstorms elsewhere."** Ibid., 59.

207 **vicinity of thunderstorms."** Ibid., 47.

208 **to 100 gross tons.** USCG report, 18.

208 **show off a boat."** Ibid.

209 **was out there.** Joseph K. McGeady Jr. (second mate aboard the *Pride of Baltimore* at the time of the sinking), interview, March 2002.

209 **experience among them.** Ibid.

209 **emergency equipment."** NTSB *Report*, 45.

210 **saved several lives."** Ibid., 44.

210 **them on duty.** On the advice of the treatment staff, sheath knives were forbidden aboard the three-masted topsail schooner SSV *Tole Mour* in Hawaii when the Marimed Foundation started its youth program in early 1996. This policy was reversed while the author was master aboard in 1996–97.

210 **of its misuse.** At this writing there have been no reported incidents of trainees using sailors' knives against them, or vice versa, on U.S. sail training ships.

211 **were picked up.** Sheldon, interview, 13 March 1996.

211 of a knockdown." NTSB *Report*, 45.

211 commercial vessel. The IMO SOLAS convention binds signatory nations to certain international standards and is a chief mechanism for introducing new standards to the maritime community. Due to her construction, the *Pride of Baltimore* could not have achieved SOLAS certification, though any vessel can purchase the equipment.

212 oceangoing yachts. NTSB *Report*, 40.

212 type that occurred. Ibid., 33.

212 this was done. National Transportation Safety Board (NTSB), "Recommendation Report, Log Number M-0357, Recommendation #M-87-001," Washington, D.C., 14 March 1998, 4.

212 rescue forces. NTSB *Report*, 39.

213 in the mid-1980s. The *Harvey Gamage* (Maine), *Spirit of Massachusetts* (Mass.), *Rachael and Ebenezer* (New York), and *Voyager* (Conn.) are examples of passenger and sail training schooners that routinely voyaged to Bermuda and to the Caribbean from New England waters and did not maintain daily call-in schedules in the early and mid-1980s. Although call-ins were periodically made in the course of a voyage, it was not a daily protocol. Other vessels, notably the Sea Education Association's schooner *Westward*, are thought to have adopted the practice earlier than others.

213 upon arrival. NTSB, "Recommendation Report," Recommendation #M-87-008, 6.

214 knocked it down." USCG report, 25.

214 would be required. NTSB *Report*, 29.

214 low in the water. Davis, "Thomas Gillmer and the Prides," 58.

215 gravity overall. Ibid., 37.

215 and removed weight This list is based on interviews conducted in January 1998 with Captain Christopher Rowsom (chief mate on *Pride* in 1984 and 1985) and Captains G. Peter Boudreau and Jan C. Miles. All three participated in directing this process of weight removal, but none recalled any single significant removal of weight at any level.

216 deck level. Formula: displacement × KG = moment. A change between two moments divided by the change in two measures of displacement equals the height of the change to KG.

Displacement   KG   Moment

$$\frac{\begin{array}{c}120.1 \times 9.75 = 1{,}170.975 \\ -\ 112.55 \times 9.42 = 1{,}060.22\end{array}}{7.55 \times\ ?\ \ =\ 110.755} = \frac{110.755}{7.55} = \begin{array}{l}14.7 \text{ feet above the}\\ \text{baseline}\end{array}$$

The baseline is usually measured from the rabbet at amidships.

216 to 5.55 feet." NTSB *Report*, 50.

216 August 1984 inclining. Thomas C. Gillmer, "An American Topsail Schooner: A Proposal in Experimental Archaelogy," *The Mariner's Mirror* (Society for Nautical Research) 66:3 (August 1980): 252.

216 from Europe." USCG report, 20.

216 the final leg. Foster, interview, 10 September 2002.

216 about the stability. NTSB *Report*, 37.
217 **Modified Regulations."** Parker E. Marean III and Roger Long, "Survey of Sailing Vessel Stability Leading to Modified Regulations," SNAME, New England Section. Vessels in the study were not always identified by name, but Roger Long confirmed that the 90-foot topsail schooner in the study was the *Pride of Baltimore*. References in Gillmer's book, *Pride of Baltimore* (154), confirm this, though Gillmer rejected the data.
217 **vessels considered.** Gillmer, *Pride of Baltimore*, 154.
217 **interested parties.** Notes from an interview between Donald Treworgy and naval architect William Peterson (USNR), 30 May 1986, G. W. Blunt White Library, Mystic Seaport, Mystic, Connecticut. Corroborated in interviews with William Peterson and Roger Long in April 2002.
217 ***Pride* investigation.** Gillmer, *Pride of Baltimore*, 154.
217 **inexplicable reasons."** Ibid.
218 **at 87.7 degrees.** USCG report, 20.
219 **in Portland, Maine.** USCG report, 21.
219 **sailing vessels."** Ibid., 25.
219 **than the *Pride*.** The Wolfson Unit in England has continued to do groundbreaking stability research on the *Pride* case. The methodology and results of that research differ from those applied above and may offer a direction for further research.
222 **or liferafts."** NTSB *Report*, 38.
222 **to be upgraded.** Ibid., 38.
222 **operate offshore."** Ibid., 45.
222 **signals, and liferafts."** Ibid., 46.
222 **operating offshore.** Ibid.
222 **House of Representatives.** NTSB, "Recommendation Report," Log Number M-0325, Recommendation #M-87-003, 2.
223 **other means.** NTSB, "Recommendation Report," Recommendation #M-87-001 and 003, 1–2.
223 **different types.** NTSB, "Recommendation Report," Recommendation #M-87-004, 3.
223 **in this book.** Michael Brown, NTSB, personal interview by telephone, 10 March 1998. The policy impact to which the *Pride* is linked involved the cumulative impact of many casualties, most of which involved fishing vessels. Brown estimated that upwards of thirty casualty cases, many involving fishing vessels, have been factors in the reform of regulations for uninspected vessels on ocean waters.
223 **on communications."** Captain Bert Rogers, executive director, Harvey Gamage Foundation in Cornwall, New York (now the Ocean Classrooms Foundation), interview, 19 May 1998.
224 **associated recommendations."** NTSB *Report*, 46.
224 **Unacceptable Action."** NTSB, "Recommendation Report," Log Number M-0325, Recommendation #M-87-006, 5.
224 **of these events.** SPSSM briefly had a sister organization known as ORAGSSM: Organization of Recently Aground Sailing Ship Masters. At the time of writing there had been no recent meetings. Courtesy Captain Richard Bailey.

225 **Baltimore Clipper.**" Gillmer, *Pride of Baltimore,* 161.
225 **sailing vessels.** NTSB *Report,* 47.
226 **more canvas.** Davis, "A New Pride for Baltimore," 54.
227 **United States alone.** Steven J. Callahan, "Microbursts and the Mariner," *Proceedings,* ASTA/ISTA International Safety Forum, Newport, 1997 (Newport, Rhode Island: American Sail Training Association, 1997), 1.
228 **sustain such ships.** Gillmer, *Pride of Baltimore,* 159.
229 **through the night.**" This oft-repeated phrase appears in Andy Davis, "A New Pride for Baltimore" (55).

Maria Asumpta (1858–1995)

231 Vessel details are from Friends of the *Maria Asumpta, The Brig Maria Asumpta* promotional brochure for the *Maria Asumpta* (101 High St., Lenham, Kent ME17 2LA, Britain: Friends of the *Maria Asumpta,* circa 1991), 3–4.
232 **like cardboard.**" Louise Jury and Greg Swift, "A Voyage to Disaster," (London) *Daily Mail,* 31 May 1995.
232 **before my eyes.**" Quoted in "People Watched from Cliff as Doomed Ship Splintered on Rocks," on-line newspaper posting, *Electronic Telegraph, UK News,* no. 805, July 1997.
232 **to apportion blame.** Marine Accident Investigation Branch, *Summary Report of an Investigation into the Grounding and Foundering of* Maria Asumpta *off Padstow on 30 May 1995 with the Loss of Three Lives,* January 1996, preface. Hereafter MAIB *Summary Report.*
233 **regularly sails.**" FMA, *Brig Maria Asumpta,* 2.
233 **a salt vessel.**" Ben Fenton, "Three Lost as Ship Sinks Off Cornwall," *Electronic Telegraph, UK News,* 31 May 1995, front page.
233 **complete with funnel.** FMA, *Brig Maria Asumpta,* 2.
233 **of the engines.** Ibid.
233 **masts and spars.** Ibid.
234 **a winter storm.** David Connett and Simon Trump, "Second Sinking of the *Maria Asumpta,*" *Today* (1 June 1995), p. 16. In the collection of News International Library.
234 **trapped her in Canada:** Ibid.
234 **in the *Marques.*** Ibid.
234 **photographic appearances.** FMA, *Brig Maria Asumpta,* 2. In 1991 the author was aboard the *Maria Asumpta* on three occasions and learned about the vessel's activities from the crew.
234 **acting as lookouts.**" Quoted in Connett and Trump, "Second Sinking of the *Maria Asumpta,*" p. 16.
234 **a tree surgeon.** "Sailor Tells of Fight for Life as Ship Hits Rocks," Schooner-Man—Schooner and Tall Ships, www.schoonerman.com/amsink.htm. Reprinted from *Guardian* (London), interview with helmsman John Howells, 3 June 1995.
234 **much larger casualty.** Knight, Gorman, Kennedy, "Three Drown as Sailing Ship Is Wrecked," *Times,* 31 May 1995, p. 1.

235 foregone conclusion." Quoted in Connett and Trump, "Second Sinking of the *Maria Asumpta*," p. 16.

235 training operations. Friends of the *Maria Asumpta*, *To Whom It May Concern from Friends of the Maria Asumpta*, statement prepared by the Friends of the *Maria Asumpta* in defense of Captain Litchfield after his conviction (101 High St., Lenham, Kent, ME17 2LA, Britain: Friends of the *Maria Asumpta*, 1998), 4.

235 valves, and filters. Ibid., 5.

236 was disposed of. Ibid.

236 taken aboard. Ibid., 9.

236 Litchfield's command. MAIB, *Summary Report*. The details presented as fact in this Final Voyage section were established by the fifteen-page *Summary Report* and are generally referenced only where quoted directly.

236 more closely." Ibid., 3.

236 to look at it." Quoted in "People Watched from Cliff."

236 under sail only. MAIB, *Summary Report*, 3.

239 ten minutes apart. Ibid., 4.

239 and Rumps Point. Quoted in "People Watched from Cliff."

239 obviously pursuing. Sean O'Neill, "Tall Ship Skipper Jailed Over Deaths," *Electronic Telegraph, UK News*, no. 805 (8 August 1997), p. 2.

239 bad seamanship." Quoted in Connett and Trump, "Second Sinking of the *Maria Asumpta*."

239 doing there." Quoted in Glenda Cooper, "Rocky End for the *Maria Asumpta*," *Independent*, 1 June 1995, home section, p. 6.

239 fast to leeward. Quoted in MAIB, *Summary Report*, 4.

239 could be serious." Quoted in "Sailor Tells of Fight for Life."

240 maintopgallant spanker. Cooper, "Rocky End for the *Maria Asumpta*," photo sequence, p. 6.

240 "slightly discoloured." Quoted in MAIB, *Summary Report*, 5.

240 vertical at times. Quoted in "Sailor Tells of Fight for Life."

240 far in the bay." Knight, Gorman, Kennedy, "Three Drown," p. 1.

242 by the rocks." Quoted in "People Watched from Cliff."

242 failure and grounding. Tim Jones, " 'Charismatic' Skipper Denies Manslaughter," *Times* (London), 2 July 1997, edition 511, p. 3.

242 You bastard." Quoted in "People Watched from Cliff."

242 tremendous thud. Quoted in Knight, Gorman, Kennedy, "Three Drown."

244 exacerbated the situation. Frank J. M. Scott (expert witness called by the prosecution), "Frank Scott's Working Notes of MA Case (Basis of Statement to Police)," England, 1997. In the personal papers of Frank J. M. Scott.

244 hold that box." Quoted in "Sailor Tells of Fight for Life."

244 churning sea." Quoted in "People Watched from Cliff."

244 fishing vessel. MAIB, *Summary Report*, 6.

245 master's negligence. O'Neill, "Tall Ship Skipper Jailed Over Deaths."

245 after his conviction. All the signatories had either been directly involved with Litchfield's sailing enterprises or had considerable experience with other traditional sailing ships. Many of them had extensive experience with yachts and other maritime operations.

245 that occurred. MAIB, *Summary Report*, 11.

247 hold-on solenoids." Ibid.

247 actuated manually." Ibid.

248 practice aboard ship. Scott, "Frank Scott's Working Notes," 8.

248 certified vessels. Decca is a land-based electronic position-fixing system prevalent in Europe. It is somewhat similar to loran in the United States.

251 of all others. Captain A. J. Swift, *Bridge Team Management* (London: Nautical Institute, 1993), 11.

251 the 'error chain.' " Scott, "Frank Scott's Working Notes," 6.

253 much more quickly. Ibid.

255 "voluntarily embayed" her. Ibid., 8.

256 methodically implemented. From the *Summary Report*: "The Skipper was prepared to pass on either side of Roscarrock. However, in view of the already small margin for error allowed in planning to pass between Newland and Pentire Point, it would have been prudent for him to have decided upon a single intended track to seaward of Roscarrock, and to have plotted that track on the large scale chart (BA 1168). The Skipper made no attempt to monitor the position of the vessel between fixes other than by visual assessment. In this regard it would have been prudent to use radar parallel indexing techniques in order to have been able to immediately detect any deviation from the intended track."

256 and embayment. According to the MAIB *Summary Report* (11), specific advice aimed at avoiding the dangers of lee shore and embayment is found in *Navigation* (Royal Yachting Association) and in F. J. M. Scott, ed., *A Square Rig Sailing Handbook: Operations, Safety, Training, Equipment* (London: Nautical Institute, 1992, rev. 2001).

257 unforeseen emergencies." Scott, "Frank Scott's Working Notes," 4, 1.

258 on a lee shore. Jones, " 'Charismatic' Skipper Denies Manslaughter."

259 navigation and management. Quoted in O'Neill, "Tall Ship Skipper Jailed Over Deaths," 2.

259 grossly negligent. Quoted in ibid.

262 matter of the fuel. Scott, "Frank Scott's Working Notes," 6.

264 pleasure boating. For these purposes, "large numbers" is considered to be greater than twelve, which is the threshold at which international requirements established under the Safety Of Life At Sea conventions (SOLAS) take effect.

264 engine failure." MAIB, *Summary Report*, 10.

264 the *Maria Asumpta*." Jones, " 'Charismatic' Skipper Denies Manslaughter."

Conclusion: Paying Off

269 margins of error. Hurricane Mitch was a large and powerful Atlantic storm system in the fall of 1998, at one stage reaching category 5, in excess of 156 knots on the Saffir-Simpson scale. Mitch was the fourth fiercest storm in Atlantic history, with recorded gusts exceeding 200 knots. At one point in its development, the cloud print encompassed the area from the Florida Keys to the Pacific Ocean. The master of the *Fantome* left Belize City to try to skirt south around

the storm center and shelter in the lee of Roatán Island, but the relatively confined waters between the storm center and the mainland left little room to maneuver. The enormity of the system and the close proximity of the ship to the center meant that relatively small changes in the track of the hurricane all but erased the margin of error for avoiding it. The eye repeatedly changed direction for short periods of time and eventually stalled very close to the ship's last known position. Contact with the ship was lost on 27 October 1998. Minimal flotsam was found by search-and-rescue efforts, and there were no survivors. Although some 11,000 people were killed ashore in Central America, primarily in mudslides caused by heavy rains, *Fantome* was the only ship known to have been sunk by Mitch in that area. The *Fantome* was registered in Equatorial Guinea.

269 **named, and tracked.** Many commercial vessels participate in voluntary weather reporting systems worldwide to help supply data for weather prediction. In the United States the National Oceanographic and Atmospheric Administration (NOAA) is the government agency that collects and disseminates weather data.

270 **took root.** C. A. Marchaj, *Seaworthiness: The Forgotten Factor* (London: Adlard Coles, 1986), vii.

274 **people to sea.** Under international law, vessels may carry up to twelve passengers for hire with minimal regulation. This applies to U.S. vessels but, under U.S. law, vessels under 100 tons may carry only up to six people for hire with minimal regulation.

277 **on which they sail.** The STCW 95 (Standards of Training, Certification and Watchkeeping) is an International Maritime Organization convention designed to upgrade and bring uniformity to training standards worldwide. Topics include firefighting, medical, radar, bridge team management, and communications training. These standards became mandatory worldwide for all seafarers on international voyages on 1 February 2002.

280 **core of essential knowledge.** G. Andy Chase, *Auxiliary Sail Vessel Operations: For the Aspiring Professional Sailor* (Centreville, Maryland: Cornell Maritime Press, 1997).

Modern Materials on Traditional Ships

288 **their rigs, as well.** The *Marques* had Duradon sails (*Report of the Formal Investigation*, 80); the *Albatross* had Dacron sails (Sheldon, interview, 13 March 1996).

288 **up in the squall.** Chuck Gieg, *White Squall*—Conference 2 (e-mail), April 1996.

289 **considered a safety feature."** Howard A. Chatterton Jr. and John C. Maxham, "Sailing Vessel Stability with Particular Reference to the *Pride of Baltimore* Casualty," *Marine Technology* 26, no. 2 (April 1989): 99.

Acknowledgments

I HAD TO write something in order to graduate. One of my professors in the Marine Affairs Department at the University of Rhode Island suggested I write about dredging. Dredging is, of course, a very important issue and perhaps a more sensible suggestion than what I ended up doing, but I knew that I would never finish the job unless I wrote about something that I found personally compelling. I had been sailing professionally for sixteen years at the time and if experience taught me anything it was that you never know it all. This is true of many things, but especially the sea. But I needed to find a professor who would let me write about these incidents so that I could learn what was important to know as a captain, yet still graduate. I thank Dennis Nixon for being that professor and allowing me to pursue an unconventional topic in the name of Marine Affairs. I also thank Dennis for pointing out upon my graduation that I had written a book, so I might as well get it published.

Primary sources have played an important role in this book. The contemporary nature of these events is a double-edged sword in this respect, for there is always another view to weigh and more information to add to the mix. The traumatic nature of these cases also means that the discussion of events with survivors or relatives of those lost is always charged with emotion. As with anything of a retrospective nature, accounts may be dimmed by time, shaded by prejudice or recolored more brightly than things actually were. Be that as it may, if history is to be written at all, we must proceed with what is there, and the writer must make choices. This book has benefited enormously from the generous input of individuals personally involved with these events, and this cannot have been easy for any of them. Therefore I wish to acknowledge and thank the contributors of all such insights, large and small.

No book of this type comes into being without the help of others or without a certain amount of encouragement from the sidelines. With that in mind it is necessary to acknowledge the following people: Captain David V. V. Wood, USCG (Retired), who from the earliest stages patiently listened to my incipient ideas, commented on drafts while I gained purchase on the subject matter, supplied resources and steered me toward yet other sources, all of which proved invaluable; Lieutenant Commander Mark W. Kemmis-Betty, RN (Retd.), who from the outset brought a lifetime of experience in sail training internationally, and who replied without fail to a relentless stream of queries concerning the two British cases in this book and regulatory developments in the United Kingdom; Niels Jannasch, formerly of the *Passat*, the *Viking*, and the Maritime Museum of the Atlantic (Halifax, Nova Scotia) for translation, for reading multiple drafts of the *Pamir* chapter, for being a taskmaster, and for constant support delivered in uproarious tones over the telephone—it is my particular regret that he passed away before the project was complete and before I could meet him; Ingmar Palmer and Jocelyn Palmer of Mariehamn for hospitality, discussion relating to Cape Horners under Erikson, and a unique tour of the Cape Horners Room at the Ålands Sjöfartsmuseum; Karen Rosenflanz, Ph.D., for conscientious translation of segments of the *Pamir* inquiry; Captain Christopher Sheldon for meeting with me to share the difficult story of the *Albatross* and, more importantly, for sharing it with us all at the International Sail Training Safety Forum of 1997 at Newport, Rhode Island; Captain William H. Bunting for perspective on the *Albatross*, for material that enriched the larger work, and for the example of a true writer; Roger W. Long for sharing the important stability work he did in connection with the Sailing School Vessels regulations, and for his perspective on all three stability casualties that appear in this book; Donald Treworgy, planetarium supervisor at Mystic Seaport Inc. for material relating to the *Marques*, for his time, and for his dedication to the memory of Susan Peterson Howell, who was lost aboard the *Marques*; the G. W. Blunt White Library, Mystic Seaport Museum, for resources and assistance; Captain George W. Crowninshield, USN (Retired), former Executive Director of ASTA, for his review of the *Marques* chapter; Howard A. Chatterton Jr., naval architect, for close technical readings of all three stability casualties, for sharing his experiences with the *Pride of Baltimore* investigation and with book-writing, and above all, for his steadfast encouragement; Joe McGeady and Robert Foster for candor regarding their experiences aboard the *Pride of Baltimore* at the time of her loss; Gary "LeRoy" Surosky for responding to queries regarding his experiences with the *Pride*; Pride of Baltimore Inc. for the extraordinary opportunity to work aboard the *Pride of Baltimore* and *Pride of Baltimore II*; Captain Jan C. Miles of the *Pride of Baltimore II* and previously of the *Pride of Baltimore* for history and insight into both vessels; and Lieutenant Commander Frank J. M. Scott, MA, MNI, RN, for material relating to stability casualties and his involvement with the *Maria Asumpta* case; Mervyn Scarfe of Caerphilly, South Wales, for tracking down material relating to the *Maria Asumpta* otherwise beyond my reach; Jon Wilson, founder of *WoodenBoat* and *Hope* magazines, for an early read and pressing me to publish; Captain G. Andy Chase of Maine Maritime Academy for an early read and insisting that I publish; Jim Sollers for his artwork; International

Marine for hard work and professionalism, with special thanks to Deborah Oliver for steel-trap editing, Molly Mulhern and Janet Robbins for artistic design, and Jonathan Eaton for sparking the project and gathering my thoughts; my parents, A. Leonard and Cynara Sullivan Parrott, for unqualified support, including my sailing career; my wife, Kimberly Hannon Parrott, for early confirmation that I had indeed written a book whether I went through the ordeal of publishing it or not, for editing, organizing the text, gathering artwork, indefatigable support, and countless hours given and lost.

INDEX